Interviewing

Interviewing

Situations and Contexts

Larry Powell

University of Alabama—Birmingham

Jonathan Amsbary

University of Alabama—Birmingham

Boston   New York   San Francisco
Mexico City   Montreal   Toronto   London   Madrid   Munich   Paris
Hong Kong   Singapore   Tokyo   Cape Town   Sydney

Executive Editor: *Karon Bowers*
Series Editor: *Brian Wheel*
Series Editorial Assistant: *Heather Hawkins*
Senior Marketing Manager: *Mandee Eckersley*
Composition and Prepress Buyer: *Linda Cox*
Manufacturing Buyer: *JoAnne Sweeney*
Cover Administrator: *Joel Gendron*
Editorial-Production Coordinator: *Beth Houston*
Editorial-Production Service: *Modern Graphics, Inc.*
Electronic Composition: *Modern Graphics, Inc.*

For related titles and support materials, visit our online catalog at *www.ablongman.com*

Copyright © 2006 Pearson Education, Inc.

Between the time Website information is gathered and then published, it is not unusual for some sites to have closed. Also the transcription of URLs can result in unintended typographical errors. The publisher would appreciate notification where these errors occur so that they may be corrected in subsequent editions.

ISBN 0-205-40195-3
Library of Congress Cataloging-in-Publication Data
Powell, Larry, 1948–
  Interviewing : situations and contexts / by Larry Powell and Jonathan H. Amsbary.
   p. cm.
  Includes bibliographical references and index.
  ISBN 0–205–40195–3
   1. Employment interviewing. I. Amsbary, Jonathan H. (Jonathan Howard), 1956- II. Title.

HF5549.5.I6P685 2005
650.14´4—dc22

2005040995

Printed in the United States of America
10 9 8 7 6 5 4 3 2 1   09 08 07 06 05

Contents

Preface

The idea for this book grew out of our realization that most interviewing books (1) focus on a limited number of interviewing situations, (2) often focus heavily on employment interviews, and (3) do not equip the student to handle interviews in different situations. We first realized the need for a new type of interviewing text after we were called to testify in a few court situations. The interview techniques that we had been teaching as part of our organizational communication classes were totally inadequate for the courtroom environment.

To correct those problems, we have written a book that begins with an introductory overview of interviewing and interview techniques. Following the introductory chapters, each part of the book is devoted to a major interview context. The chapters in each part focus on the unique interview factors related to a specific situation. By providing the reader with an understanding of how interviewing techniques differ by situation and context, we hope to provide a more complete understanding of how interviewing is used in a variety of settings.

The text is divided into six parts that reflect the various interview contexts. These parts are: (1) Introduction, (2) Interviewing in the Organizational Setting, (3) Interviewing in the Media, (4) Research Interviews, (5) Interviews in the Legal Setting, and (6) Interviews in the Healing Community.

Introduction

The first part of the text consists of two chapters. The first chapter, **The Basics of Interviewing**, examines the fundamentals of the interviewing process: the basic types of interviews, the phases of the interview process, interviewing techniques, interview relationships, and nonverbal issues.

Chapter 2, **Informal Interviewing: Interviewing in Daily Life**, expands on the fundamentals presented in Chapter 1 and provides a more thorough discussion of the communication variables at play in the interviewing context. The chapter also examines interviews that take place in more informal settings. Specifically, the chapter examines interpersonal communication, relationship development, group communication, educational communication, interviewing and listening, and interviewing in the public arena.

Interviewing in the Organizational Setting

Part 2 includes four chapters on organizational interviewing. Chapter 3, **The Employment Interview: The Employer's Perspective**, investigates the role of interviewing in the hiring process and examines modern interviewing techniques. In addition, the legal aspects of employment interviews are discussed.

Chapter 4, **The Employment Interview: The Job Applicant's Perspective**, examines the employment interview from the applicant's perspective. This chapter examines job searches and various strategies used by job seekers. Resumes, cover letters, interview preparation, and interview performance are all covered in this chapter.

Chapter 5, **The Persuasive Interview**, examines an often-overlooked aspect of professional interviewing. This chapter delves into the role of interviewing in the process of persuasion, specifically those situations involving sales interviews and negotiations.

Chapter 6, **Performance Appraisal and Exit Interviews**, examines the role of interviewing in upward and downward organizational communication. It demonstrates the importance of interviewing in supplying feedback to both supervisors and subordinates.

Interviewing in the Media

Part 3 consists of three chapters on media interviews. Chapter 7, **Interviews on Radio and Television**, deals with perhaps the most visible interviewing context. This chapter explores the use of interviews by broadcast media, focusing on how interviewing shapes the reporting process.

Chapter 8, **Newspaper Interviews**, deals with interviewing in print media. It explores how reporters use interviews to create stories and how interview subjects use the media to get their point of view across to the public.

Chapter 9, **Interviews in the Political Arena**, deals with the political process and how politicians use the media in general and interviews specifically as public relations tools.

Research Interviews

Part 4 consists of three chapters. Chapter 10, **Qualitative Research Interviews**, demonstrates the importance of interviews to qualitative researchers. The chapter examines in-depth interviews, focus groups, participant-observation research, and data analysis.

Chapter 11, **The Quantitative Research Interview**, demonstrates the use of interviewing by quantitative researchers. This chapter examines public opinion surveys, questionnaire development, sampling, intercept interviewing, and pseudo-polling.

Chapter 12, **Oral History Interviews**, demonstrates how oral historians and storytellers use interviewing as a research tool and as a method to communicate their work. This chapter explores how oral interviews are used and how they are conducted.

Interviews in the Legal Setting

Part 5, which focuses on interviews in the legal setting, is divided into two chapters. Chapter 13, **Police Interviews**, shows how interviewing is a critical tool in criminal investigations and prosecutions. This chapter examines how the police use interviews to gather evidence and secure confessions.

Chapter 14, **Interviews for Lawyers**, explores how lawyers use interviewing in working with clients and preparing their cases.

Interviews in the Healing Community

Part 6 is divided into two chapters. Chapter 15, **Interviews in the Medical Setting**, examines how health-care providers use interviewing in the practice of medicine.

Chapter 16, **Counseling Interviews**, examines the importance of interviewing as both a diagnostic tool and as a therapeutic tool. Various contexts and therapy styles are discussed that demonstrate the importance of interviewing to therapists and their patients.

Acknowledgments

From Both Authors: Both authors wish to thank Professor Mark Hickson (University of Alabama at Birmingham) for his guidance and inspiration on this project—from the initial concept through completion. His encouragement was helpful to both of us.

We also would especially like to thank everyone who graciously agreed to be interviewed for this book. We know many of you were nervous, but this book could not have achieved its distinctive perspective without your contributions.

Further, we would like to thank Jennifer Trebby and Heather Hawkins—the editorial assistants who herded this project to the finish line—and their reviewers, whose observations and criticism were insightful and presented in a helpful way.

Our thanks also to the reviewers of the manuscript, Kimberly S. McDonald, Indiana-Purdue University; Jerry Thomas, Lindsey University; and Esin C. Turk, Mississippi Valley State University.

From Larry Powell: I wish to express my appreciation to several people who had direct and indirect contributions to the completion of this book. The first recognition goes to my wife, Clarine Powell, who had the patience and love to tolerate the hours that her husband spent with a computer while working on this project.

The second acknowledgment goes to my co-author Jonathan Amsbary, who had the idea for writing an interviewing book from a different perspective. It has been a pleasure to work with him on this project.

The third acknowledgment goes to Hank Flick, professor of communication studies at Mississippi State University. Hank is probably the best interviewing teacher that I've ever known. Many of the concepts that he taught me have been incorporated into this book.

The fourth acknowledgment goes to the late Lin Wright, another former colleague from Mississippi State University. Lin served as an unofficial tutor and mentor for many of the topics discussed in this work.

Finally, I wish to express special thanks to Professor Douglas G. Bock of Eastern Illinois University—the person who first stirred my interest in communication studies and who also served as director of both my master's thesis and my doctoral dissertation.

Again, to each of you, my sincere thanks.

From Jonathan Amsbary: First of all I would like to thank my co-author, Larry Powell. This has been an enjoyable and informative collaboration. He has been an excellent writing partner.

I also would like to thank a number of professors who have helped shape my thinking on the topics covered in this text: John Wittig (University of Alabama at Birmingham),

C. T. Hanson (University of Minnesota, Moorhead), Robert Littlefield (North Dakota State University), Dirk Gibson (University of New Mexico), Daniel DeStephen (Wright State University) and my former advisor Patricia Andrews (Emeritus, Indiana University).

Finally, I would like to thank my family: Kate Amsbary and Daniel Amsbary. You have always supported and inspired me.

Everyone mentioned (and many who are not) has made what is good in this book much better. I will take credit for anything that is lacking.

Interviewing

1

The Basics of Interviewing

John sits nervously in the outer office of a major corporation. Within a few minutes, he will have a job interview that, if successful, could get him a position with the company of his dreams.

June works for a telephone research center. Each night, she places calls to people she has never met with the intent of asking them a series of questions about a new product that will soon be on the market.

Carlos is a reporter for a major newspaper. His job involves gathering information from news makers, asking them questions about what is happening that is of importance to the public.

Juanita is a nurse. Part of her job is talking with patients, getting a brief summary of their symptoms and problems, so that the physician can diagnosis their condition.

Each of these people is engaged in the process of interviewing. Indeed, in modern society, the role of interviewing has been increasing, with more and more jobs requiring some element of interviewing skills. For the purposes of this book, interviewing is defined as "a process of purposeful interaction involving two parties and that involves the asking and answering of questions." Consider this definition in terms of its component parts.

First, an interview is a purposeful interaction. Each person enters the interview with a goal in mind, and each person participates with the intent of increasing his or her chances of achieving that goal. John will enter his employment interview with the intent of impressing the interviewer enough that he will be hired by the company. Across the desk, his interviewer will be working toward a different goal; he will be seeking to assess the strengths and weaknesses of each applicant for the purpose of hiring the best new employee for the company. As a reporter, Carlos will be seeking information that can be used in the writing of an informative news story. Some of the people he interviews, though, may try to hide information that would be useful to his story. The purposes of the participants may vary, but an interview must have a purpose.

Second, an interview involves two parties. The operative word here is parties, not people. In some instances, the interviewee may be more than one person, for example, as when a group of people are brought together and interviewed at the same time. Such interviews are known as panel interviews (Hamilton & Parker, 1990; Dipboye, Gaugler, Hayes, & Parker, 2001). They are frequently used in research studies in the form of panel studies or focus groups. In other instances, the number of interviewers might outnumber the number of interviewees. Such instances create what is known as a board interview. For example, a Congressional subcommittee may call for testimony from an expert on terrorism. The expert would then appear before the entire committee, and each committee member would be allowed to ask questions of the expert.

Third, an interview involves the asking and answering of questions. However, interviews are not merely an exchange of questions and answers. Sometimes the interviewer simply makes a statement and waits to see how the interviewee responds. Sometimes the interviewer simply remains silent, encouraging the interviewer to provide more information. Still, the asking and answering of questions is the backbone around which the rest of the interaction is organized. The purpose of most interviews involves some element of information exchange or sharing, and the questions-and-answer process is crucial to its success.

Interviewing is often, but not always, a zero-history interaction. The parties in an interview sometimes will have a history of interaction with each other. Counseling, performance interviews, health-care interviews, and exit interviews all encompass situations in which the interviewer and the interviewee have had some previous interaction. In many other situations, however, there is likely to have been no previous interaction. Market research interviewers randomly call people they've never met before. College graduates seeking their first job may have never met the people who will be deciding whether to hire them. News reporters may write stories on individuals they've never met before. Indeed, one of the purposes of many interviews is for the parties to meet and learn something about each other. Because of this, interactions in interviews tend to be more formal than in other contexts.

The purpose of this book will be to help the reader understand the various elements of the definition of interviewing. As a starting point, it is important to understand the basic factors that influence the structure and effectiveness of an interview. These factors are (1) the different types of interviews, (2) the different stages of the interview process, (3) the various techniques that might be used in interviews, and (4) an understanding of how the structure of interviews can vary. This chapter will look at these four elements from a basic perspective. Each of the following chapters will explore them in more detail, showing how they pertain to interviews in differing types of situations.

Types of Interviews

Interviews can be classified into several categories, based on the purpose and/or location in which they occur. These include (1) workplace interviews, (2) informational interviews, (3) interrogations, and (4) health interviews.

Workplace Interviews

Workplace interviews include employment, performance review, grievance, exit, and persuasive interviews.

Employment interviews are the poster child of interviewing techniques. Most books that talk about interviews focus on this area. Although it is not the only type of interview, it is easily the most visible and the one that most people will experience at some time during their career. Employment interviews are a screening technique by which organizations make initial evaluations regarding hiring decisions. They involve multiple aspects and functions, including information gathering and assessment.

The performance review interview is an interview that is used to assess the work of an individual or group. Devito (2000) calls it an "appraisal" interview (p. 224). Many organizations use annual performance review interviews. Such interviews enable employers to identify those workers who are performing at an exceptional level, identify potential weak spots in performances before they become troublesome, create a clear understanding between the employer and employee regarding the employer's level of satisfaction with the employee's work. In addition, it allows both parties to focus on future performance.

Hamilton and Parker (1990) define the grievance interview as "any type of one-to-one encounter involving conflict and resolution" (p. 200). Some organizations have a formal grievance procedure whereby any employee with a complaint against the company can file for and request a grievance interview. For others, the grievance interview is an informal process whereby a dissatisfied worker simply makes a request to his or her immediate supervisor regarding a complaint. In either instance, though, the grievance interview is a combination of information exchange and persuasive effort.

A persuasive interview takes place anytime someone attempts to use the interviewing context to change the beliefs, attitudes, or behavior of another. Many interviews are, in fact, persuasive interviews. The short interviews that take place at job fairs, college campuses, or professional conferences are usually attempts to recruit candidates and promote the company. Ironically, these interviews are often called screening interviews when they are actually recruiting interviews. Most companies refer to their screeners as "recruiters." The final workplace interview is an exit interview. Serving an almost exclusively informative purpose, exit interviews take place when an employee leaves an organization and provides the useful feedback regarding the employee's tenure with the organization.

Some people switch jobs, moving to one that offers better pay, better benefits, or a better work environment. Some people simply burnout from working too long and too hard at one single position. Some people just decide to retire. Organizations, though, may never know why any one person leaves a job with the company unless they ask. That's why many organizations schedule exit interviews with all personnel who decide to quit or retire. Such interviews give the employer a chance to assess what mistakes the company may be making that would drive people away from their jobs. They give the departing worker one last chance to contribute to the success of the company.

Informational Interviews

Informational interviews include information-seeking (or research interviews), information-giving, and information-sharing interviews. A telephone survey represents a type of information-seeking interview; the interviewer asks specific questions designed to provide the researcher with specific information. A telemarketing sales call would be an example of an information-giving interview; the sales person hopes to speak with the interviewee long enough to give them some information about the product. Three people on a panel, responding to a moderator's questions, would be an example of an information-sharing interview. The questions would spark different responses so that multiple views on the same topic may be obtained.

Informational interviews may vary in terms of (1) the level of information needed and (2) the expertise required to conduct the interview. For example, a doctor who interviews a patient for the purpose of diagnosing the patient's condition may need more information than that gathered by some other types of informational interviews. Similarly, the expertise required for such a medical interview would be higher than the skills needed for a telemarketing interview.

Interrogation

Interrogation interviews are used primarily to gather information from a reluctant source. Hamilton and Parker (1990) noted that some type of offense or misdeed is nearly always associated with an interrogation interview (p. 202). Not surprisingly, the most frequent use of interrogation interviews is by law enforcement officials or by attorneys.

Health Interviews

Health interviews include information-gathering (history) and therapeutic (treatment) interviews. History-taking is an integral part of the health-care process. No effective diagnosis can take place without a clear understanding of the patient's complaint. Patient-centered interviews have been found to be a highly effective technique in both understanding and treating patients (Marvel et al, 1999).

The primary purpose of a therapeutic interview is to establish a supportive relationship that will help an individual identify and work through personal issues, concerns, and problems. Benjamin (1981) called such interviews "helping interviews." Others (e.g., Hamilton & Parker, 1990) label them as "counseling interviews." Regardless of the name, therapeutic or counseling interviews may be used in a number of situations. They are common tools for social workers, nurses, doctors, chaplains, and psychologists.

Phases in the Interview Process

Most interviews can be divided into four distinct stages: (1) preparation, (2) opening, (3) Q&A, and (4) closing.

Preparation

Successful interviews start with anticipating and planning. Anticipating the situation allows both the interviewer and the interviewee to evaluate and assess their own strengths and weaknesses as it relates to the approaching interview. Planning helps identify the goal of the interview. Identifying the goal of the interview is critical. To make the interview more effective and efficient, Edwards and Brilhart (1982) recommend that interviewers use their preparation time to identify the goal of the interview and then be prepared to reveal it to the other person quickly.

Opening

The opening, or first contact, of the interview is often crucial to its success or failure. The initial interaction sets the tone and mood for the interactions that follow, creating a climate for the rest of the interview (Klinzing & Klinzing, 1985). The first few moments of any health-care interview are important, but they are absolutely critical in therapeutic situations. In those instances, the interviewer's first goal must be to establish a climate that will foster trust and understanding (Northouse & Northouse, 1985). For that reason, the interviewer cannot rush into some topics. Instead, many interviewers use this time at the beginning of the interaction to introduce themselves, to learn the name of the interviewee, and to ask a few questions about the interests of the interviewee in an effort to find common ground that can help in establishing rapport (Banyard & Fernald, 2002).

For information-oriented interviews, the opening stages of the interview should be used to clarify the purpose of the interview and to establish mutual goals with the interviewee. A common understanding of these goals is a key factor here. If the interviewer and interviewee dance around issues for the remainder of the interview, little will be accomplished. This may seem like a simple concept, but it is easily ignored—particularly if the interviewer rushes through this stage too quickly. False agreement can easily be achieved by speaking in vague terms about the purpose and goal of the interview, and the interviewer may move on to the next stage under the mistaken belief that the interviewee is ready to follow and participate freely in the discussion.

Q&A

Q&A is the exploration, or working, phase of the interview. It is during this phase of the discussion that the interviewer offers questions and seeks responses from the interviewee. The interviewer must constantly monitor feedback from the interviewee for any indication that necessary information is being held back. The interviewer must also carefully monitor his or her own communication behavior so that he or she can maintain an effective relationship with the other person, and thus continue the interview in a productive manner.

One factor affecting the behavior within the interview is the expectation level of each participant. Burgoon's (1993) expectancy violation theory posits that preconceived expectations influence observers' reactions to behaviors and the actors who perform them. Nonconformity to expected norms will either be condoned or condemned. Violators who are seen as threatening will be condemned for their violations while no threatening violators will be allowed to stray from expected norms. Valence, or the combined positive and negative assessment, is important. A highly credible medical professional is allowed to deviate more from social norms before his or her behavior is perceived as a violation. In contrast, female personnel and those in positions of low credibility have less freedom in message selection, because, for them, aggressive strategies would be a negative violation of expectations that would inhibit attitude change (Burgoon & Miller, 1985).

Closing

Interviews should not be abruptly ended just because the interviewer has all of the information he or she needs. Instead, a successful interview will include an identifiable closing stage in which both participants realize that it is time to close the interview (Sundeen et al., 1981). Unfortunately, that doesn't always happen. Ideally, the closing of the interview should (1) summarize the key points of the interview and (2) ensure that the interviewee has had an opportunity to say the things that he or she believes should be said. At the very least, the interviewer should ask if the interviewee has any final questions.

Interview Techniques

An understanding of how questions are sequenced and phrased is one specific technique within the broader context.

Question Sequence

Stewart and Cash (1982) identified three different question sequences that are used in interviews: (1) the funnel sequence, (2) the inverted funnel, and (3) the tunnel sequence. In the funnel sequence, the interviewer begins by asking broad questions and then proceeds to more specific questions. This approach gradually focuses the discussion to a specific topic.

The inverted funnel, as its name implies, reverses the above process. In this approach, the interviewer begins by asking a series of specific questions and gradually broadens the approach to obtain an overall view of the topic being discussed. The inverted funnel is particularly useful in stimulating responses from reticent or nontalkative interviewees. If a person is reluctant to talk, he or she will tend to fend off broad, open-ended questions—particularly at the beginning of the interview. If the interviewee will respond to short, specific questions, these can be used as icebreakers to get the person to talk more freely.

The tunnel sequence is an interview technique that uses a series of similar questions of the same format. The tunnel sequence is effective when the interviewer needs to cover a number of different topics but in-depth information on those topics is not necessary.

Verbal Tools

The interviewer's ultimate tool is his or her personal set of verbal skills. The ability to use language that the interviewee can understand and that will also elicit the desired information is essential to the success of the interview. The adept interviewer will learn a variety of techniques that can be used to elicit information from interviewees. Those tools include, but are not limited to, questions and the use of silence.

Types of Questions. The adept interviewer has several different types of questions that can be used to elicit valuable information. These options include open-ended questions, closed-ended questions, probes, third-person questions, and projective questions. Open-ended questions are phrased in such a manner as to encourage the interviewee to respond using his or her own words (e.g., "Tell me about yourself"). This open-ended approach allows the interviewee to discuss the topic from his or her own perspective, with less chance that the interviewer will guide the discussion along a predetermined path. The broadest form of an open-ended question is simply the process of addressing a topic (e.g., "Tell me about the early years of your career"), whereas other forms may direct the interviewee along a slightly more narrow path (e.g., "How did your early career influence the success you have today?").

Closed-ended questions offer only limited options for response; such questions would include those that have only a yes-no answer (e.g., "Have you ever worked in the fast food industry before?") or limited response options (e.g., "How would you evaluate your math skills—good, bad, or about average?"). Closed-ended questions are used when the interviewer is seeking clarification or needs to know a specific piece of information. Some interviews will start with a broad, open-ended question and become more closed ended as the interview progresses. Thus, a section of an interview that starts with, "Tell me about your early career," may end with specific, closed-ended questions such as "What year was that?" and "How old were you at the time?"

Follow-up questions are probes that seek more information from an initial response. Sometimes a probe is a simple imperative request (e.g., "Tell me more about that"). Other forms of probes include the simple use of question words and phrases such as "Why?" or "What happened next?" Another form of probe is the connective question; that is, a question created by taking one element of the interviewee's response and building on it (e.g., "You just said you were only 17 when you first worked professionally, how did you get started at such a young age?"). Two nonverbal behaviors—silence and head nods—also can be used as probes. Both of these techniques can be used to encourage a person to continue talking about a subject for a little longer.

Third-person questions are an indirect technique that can be used if the question is one that covers a sensitive topic; in such instances it is usually easier to get the person to talk about a topic in an indirect manner. For example, if a manager is interviewing a subordinate about a job, the manager is likely to get little information if he or she asks, "What do you think about the job I'm doing?" In such an instance, an indirect question would work better (e.g., "What do most of the other workers think about the job I'm doing?").

Although not appropriate for all interviews, projective questions are sometimes used in some interview formats—particularly in therapeutic and market research interviews. The typical projective question asks the interviewee about an unrelated concept (e.g., "If you were a car, what would you be?" "If this product were a car, what would it be?"). The responses to such questions can provide insight into an individual's self-esteem ("A Cadillac" versus "A used car with 150,000 miles") or the individual's image of a product ("One that needs to go to the repair shop"). Further, projective questions frequently trigger responses that can be followed up with other questions that probe for more details.

Phrasing of Questions

How questions are phrased is, of course, critical to the success of any interview. Questions must be phrased so that the interviewee can respond both intellectually and emotionally in an open and honest fashion. Since health interviews are especially emotionally charged, they provide an excellent example of how phrasing of questions affect the interview process. At a basic level, the interviewer has the option of phrasing questions from an open-ended approach (e.g., "Tell me about your problem") that allows for a wide range of responses or using closed-ended questions (e.g, "Does your jaw hurt?") that have a limited number of possible answers. Interviewers using the funnel sequence, for example, typically start with open-ended questions and then switch to closed-ended ones as the interview progresses. Use of the inverted funnel sequence could result in the reversal of that process, with the interviewer starting with closed-ended questions and waiting until he or she feels that the reticent patient is comfortable enough to answer open-ended questions. Open-ended questions encourage a wider range of responses from the interviewee, whereas close-ended questions enable the interviewer to focus more on the specific information needed to make a judgment.

Another important factor is the word choices used in phrasing the question. The skillful medical interviewer learns to ask question without using professional jargon. Questions should be phrased so that the interviewee can respond to them in his or her own terms. Care also must be taken not to use words or phrases that will place the interviewee in a psychologically defensive position.

Improper Questions

What is proper and improper to ask during an interview will vary with every situation. Given the range of what is legally and ethically accepted in each situation, the notion of improper questions will be handled in more detail in each individual chapter. Generally, though, bad questions fall into one of five categories: loaded questions, leading questions, vague questions, double-barreled questions, and cross-purpose questions.

Loaded questions are those that have no correct answer. Suppose, for example, that a teacher asks a student, "Do you still cheat on exams?" Notice that either answer—yes or no—hurts the student. "Yes" admits current guilt, whereas "no" is an admission of past guilt. The most effective response to a loaded question is to identify it as such and not limit one's answers to the options posed by the interviewer.

Leading questions are biased questions that direct the interviewee toward the response sought by the interviewer. In some instances, such questions are considered both ethical and legal. A lawyer interviewing a hostile witness in court, for example, is often allowed to ask leading questions so that the jury can have a more complete picture of the crime under discussion. In the employment setting, interviewers often will betray what they feel to be the correct answer. For example, an interviewer might ask, "Don't you agree that it's important to stay late and get the work done?" By asking the question in this way, the interviewer tips off the interviewee. All interviewees will typically answer with the "correct" answer rather than the truthful one. This leaves the interviewer with no ability to make an informed choice.

Vague questions are those questions that provide few semantic anchors—so few that the interviewee doesn't understand the purpose of the question or the type of information sought by the interviewer. In some highly unstructured interviews, these questions might have some utility purely as conversation starters. In most situations, though, they are ineffective and disruptive to the interview process. When the interviewee doesn't understand the question, he or she may answer inappropriately. Or, the interviewee may become confused and unsure of how to continue. That uncertainty disrupts the flow of the conversation.

Double-barreled questions occur when the interviewer asks two or more questions in the format of a single question. For example, the interviewer might ask: "Do you support abstinence and safe sex as a means of combating AIDS?" That question is really two different questions: "Do you support abstinence as a means of combating AIDS?" and "Do you support safe sex as a means of combating AIDS?" A person could conceivably answer "yes" to one part and "no" to the other. Double-barreled questions are likely to trigger limited and perhaps inaccurate responses.

Cross-purpose questions are those questions in which the nature of the question is counter to the interviewer's goal. One of the most common forms of the cross-purpose question is the asking of a closed question when the interviewer is seeking an open-ended response. This is frequently done as an inappropriate means of identifying a topic while pointing the interviewee toward a desired response. The reader has probably seen dozens of examples. An example of a cross-purpose question would be the reporter who wants a specific sound bite and asks someone whose home has been destroyed by fire, "Were you upset to learn that your home had been destroyed?" The obvious answer ("yes") is the proper response to such a closed question, but what the reporter was probably seeking was an open-ended response ("How did you feel when you learned your home had been destroyed?").

Monitoring

Klinzing and Klinzing (1985) argue that the cornerstone of effective interviews is the ability of the interviewer to employ empathic listening skills to monitor what the other person is saying. Patients become frustrated if they think the interviewer is not listening to them. Listening is effective, though, only if the interviewer has an accurate assessment of what the person is trying to say. To ensure that his or her perception is accurate, the interviewer must occasionally employ one of several techniques to assess the accuracy of the information. The most common techniques for doing this are (1) paraphrasing, (2) requesting clarification, and (3) checking perceptions.

Paraphrasing is simply the restatement of the interviewee's response using the interviewer's words. A variation of the paraphrase is the reflective comment (i.e., a statement that provides a verbal mirror for the person's statement). Thus, an interviewer may use a reflective statement to summarize his or her general impression or summary of several of the interviewee's comments (e.g., "You seem to be saying that you think you'd enjoy working here").

A less frequently used technique is the request for clarification, which is when the interviewer asks for further explanation of what the interviewee means. Clarification requests seek more detail about who, where, and when. A common variation of this approach is to ask the interviewee for an example of what he or she means. Asking for the example allows the interviewer to get a clearer view of the response and also encourages the interviewee to look at his or her answer from a different perspective.

Perception checking is a technique whereby the interviewer gives the interviewee a chance to correct any of his or her previous statements. In this approach, the interviewer interrupts the interview for a moment to ask the interviewee about the accuracy of interviewer's impression.

Feedback

Most of the techniques just presented not only increase the listening skills of the interviewer, but also provide feedback to the interviewee. Feedback is essential in letting the interviewee know that the interviewer understands what he or she is saying. Three feedback techniques that can be used to enhance that perception even further are (1) reflection, (2) interpretation, and (3) confirmation.

Unlike paraphrasing, which is a restatement of what the person has said, reflection focuses on how something was expressed (e.g., "This whole problem seems to be beating you down."). Such statements can increase the interviewee's perception that the interviewer understands his or her views.

Interpretation is similar to perception checking, but its purpose is different. In this instance, the interviewer offers an explanation to the person and solicits his or her reaction. Brammer (1973) noted that the goal of this form of feedback is to encourage a person to provide his or her own interpretation of the situation.

Finally, confirmation remarks (e.g., "I see what you mean") can be used to acknowledge understanding while encouraging the person to continue talking.

Interview Structure

DeVito (2000) noted that interviews generally fall into one of four different interview structures: the open interview (unstructured), the topic interview (moderately structured), the guided interview (highly structured), and the quantitative interview (standardized). These four options reflect a continuum that reflects the research goals of the interview [i.e., whether the interview is part of a qualitative (unstructured) or quantitative (highly structured, standardized) research project]. Thus, the structure of the interview is related to the goals of the interviewer. To the extent that the interviewer wants quantitative explanations of "why," the interview will lean toward the unstructured side of the continuum and also rely heavily on open-ended questions. The unstructured format allows for exploration of areas that were not anticipated by the interviewer—something that's not always possible with a highly structured interview.

Conversely, when the interviewer wants quantitative information (i.e., numbers that describe or represent a larger audience), the interview structure moves toward the more highly structured end of the continuum.

The open interview has the least amount of structure and is used in those situations in which the goal is to encourage the interviewee to talk as much as possible about a topic relevant to him or herself. This structure is often used in participant–observation research. When done well, the interviewee will often forget that he or she is being interviewed and respond as if he or she is participating in a conversation rather than an interview. The interviewer engages the interviewee in a conversation, raises the topic on which he or she is seeking information, and encourages the interviewee to take that topic along the paths that best reflect that person's feelings on the subject.

Another form of unstructured interview is the informal interview, in which the interview takes place in an informal situation. The discussion also will be informal, sometime broaching the topic at hand and sometimes branching off into unrelated areas. Informal interviews often are used after the first round of employment interviews. Assuming that the potential employee has made the first cut, he or she may be invited to have dinner or lunch with a current employee. The encounter will provide the interviewer the chance to interact with the applicant on an informal basis, thus allowing the interviewer to learn more about the applicant. In the business world, such informal interviews are a common occurrence and may take place anywhere from the golf course to the board room.

The topic-sequence interview is a moderately structured interview that represents the type of interview that most people think about when interviews are mentioned. The interviewer typically uses a lot of open-ended questions and does as much as possible to encourage the interviewee to talk. Still, there are several points that the interviewer considers critical to the success of the interview, and these are inserted into the exchange at some point. Oral history interviews and employment interviews often fall within this structure. An oral historian will encourage the interviewee to speak as freely as possible, but also will occasionally bring the discussion back to some key events such as births, marriages, careers, and deaths in the family. Similarly, many employment interviews are dominated by open-ended questions that allow the interviewer to obtain a better understanding of the interviewee as a person; at the same time, however, the interviewer will occasionally refocus the discussion on such topics as the applicant's employment history and educational background.

The guided interview is one in which the interviewer directs the interviewee to address a predetermined topic. Journalistic and television interviews often follow such a format. An actor who appears on a talk show to promote a new movie, for example, will likely meet with the interviewer or his or her representative in advance so that the interviewee will know what questions or topics will be discussed. Journalists often do the same thing when seeking information on a story, particularly from experts. They will call the expert, give them a description of the story they're working on, and then tell them the type of information that they're seeking. Such preliminary discussions serve as a guide for the rest of the interview. Another form of a guided interview is the focus group discussion. This group interview employs a trained interviewer who gets the interviewees to discuss a series of specific topics. The questions are open-ended—often no more than an introduction to a topic—but the interviewer works from a discussion guide that identifies all of the topics that will be discussed within the session.

The most structured form of interviewing is the standardized quantitative interview. The purpose of such interviews is to gather quantitative data from a large sample of people. The data must be gathered in such a manner that it can be assimilated and condensed mathematically to provide some means of summarizing the information. Such interviews are commonly used in survey research. They require the heavy use of closed-ended questions that limit the interviewees' responses.

The Interviewer–Interviewee Relationship

As stated earlier, interviews often reflect information-gathering sessions in which the two participants have had little or no previous interaction with each other. Still, the nature of the relationship can vary tremendously. At least three different scenarios are possible: high individual interest, comparative individual interest, and low individual interest.

High levels of individual interest reflect those situations in which the interviewer directs his or her entire focus on the person who is being interviewed. Such a situation exists in relatively unstructured interviews, such as counseling interviews. In the counseling interview, the interviewer's job is to concentrate solely on the interviewee and his or her responses; the goal of the session, after all, is to help that person overcome some personal crisis. Similarly, a lawyer who is cross-examining a witness in the courtroom will also focus entirely on the individual being questioned; the goal here is to ensure that the witness' testimony has been thoroughly examined for any weaknesses or indications of deception.

Conversely, some interviews, such as public opinion surveys using quantitative interview techniques, have little or no interest in the interviewee as an individual. The interviewee's responses are important, but only to the extent that they reflect or represent the opinions of the group or target audience that is the focus of the survey. Such interviews typically do not even bother to ask the interviewee for his or her name, because it could mistakenly lead the interviewee to believe that he or she is being approached on an individual basis rather than being randomly selected for sample representation.

In the middle is the level of comparative individual interest. In these scenarios, the interviewer is indeed interested in the individual as a person, but also needs to compare that individual with others. Employment interviews are the prototype for this type of scenario. Several individuals may be interviewed for a position for which only one person will be hired. The interviewer may be impressed with several of the applicants, but will only be able to hire one of them. In those instances, the interviewer must gather information that can be used to form a comparative evaluation.

Nonverbal Issues in the Interview

Interviewing is sometimes viewed as only a verbal communication skill, but nonverbal behaviors also play an important role. One authority has suggested that as much as 65 percent of the total meaning of a message is based on nonverbal behavior (Birdwhistle, 1970). Regardless, an interviewee's nonverbal behavior contributes to the total image that he or she presents to the interviewer. Sometimes, in fact, a person's nonverbal behavior can override his or her verbal messages, particularly if the nonverbal behavior is viewed as subconscious "leakage" that conveys the person's true feelings (Hybels & Weaver, 2001). Suppose, for example, that an interviewee greeted the interviewer and said that she was happy to be invited to the interview. However, if she expressed those words in a sarcastic tone of voice while frowning, the interviewer is likely to believe just the opposite. Verbal messages convey what you want the other person to know, but nonverbal messages can show your feelings and emotions (Malandro & Barker, 1983).

Touching

Many employment interviews begin with a handshake between the two participants. That initial contact can have a significant impact on the interviewer's impression of the interviewee. The handshake becomes a nonverbal way for the two individuals to acknowledge the presence of the other person while conveying an initial message. Was the handshake the proverbial limp fish, so soft that the person seems to lack self-confidence? Was it too strong, as if the person were trying to assert the power of his personality through the vise-like strength of his hand? Or was it firm and steady—confident without being cocky? The impression created by that first physical touch can endure for much of the interview.

Touching behavior also may be used appropriately and effectively in therapeutic interviews. Such interviews often touch on sensitive issues that can trigger emotional responses from the interviewee. If the response is strong, and the interviewee starts to cry, words may not always be adequate. However, a simple touch on the shoulder may tell the interviewee that the interviewer understands and is there to help.

Silence

One underused interview technique is simply to say nothing. Sometimes, by remaining silent, the interviewer can encourage the interviewee to provide more information. It doesn't always work, though. Baker (1955) noted that there was a difference between positive silence and negative silence in an interview. Negative silence makes the participant feel uncomfortable, particularly when tension is high, whereas positive silence indicates acceptance and satisfied contentment. Silence can be effectively used, particularly during the exploration stage, to encourage the interviewee to continue talking. It is highly ineffective, though, in both the initiation and termination stages. In the initiation stage, silence creates an awkwardness and sense of uncertainty that can make the interviewee feel uncomfortable. In the termination stage, it can indicate that the interviewer doesn't know how to close the conversation.

Eye Contact

Individuals who are really good at interviewing also are good at maintaining eye contact with the interviewee. Eye contact serves two major purposes for the interviewer: (1) It non-verbally demonstrates to the interviewee that the interviewer is interested in what he or she is saying, and (2) it allows the interviewer to monitor the interviewee's nonverbal behavior. For example, the interviewee may occasionally let his or her eyes stray from direct contact with the interviewee. But, when the interviewee is finishing a statement and getting ready for the interviewer to talk again, the interviewee will often reestablish eye contact with the interviewer. Ekman and Friesen (1969) describe this behavior as a regulation function; the alert interviewer picks up this move and knows that the interviewee has given a turn-taking cue.

The amount of eye contact will vary based on the level of interest in the person or topic. Maintaining the proper amount of eye contact can sometimes be difficult. Too little eye contact may convey a lack of attention; too much may make the other person uncomfortable and leave him or her with the feeling of being stared at. Generally, the person who is in the listening role at any point in the conversation is expected to maintain more eye contact than the speaker. One technique for doing this, without making the person feeling stared at, is for the interviewer to focus concentration on the interviewee's nose or a spot between the eyes.

Smiling

Never underestimate the power of a good smile. The advice is obvious, but in the pressure of an interview, that advice can be forgotten. Like eye contact, smiling is considered an overt indication of information processing (McCall, 1972; Sroufe & Waters, 1976; Zelazo, 1971, 1972; Zelazo & Komer, 1971) and of interest while also sending a positive affect signal to the interviewer. An interviewee who is almost constantly smiling is indicating high interest in the job, the topic, and the interviewer. The interviewee who rarely smiles is telling the interviewer that he or she is not really interested in the job or the topic at hand. In all likelihood, the interviewer won't be interested in the interviewee either.

Body Movements

Two nonverbal body movements can impact the nature of an interview: the head nod and body positioning. The head nod is a form of nonverbal feedback that encourages the interviewee to continue talking. Interviewers frequently use the head nod—combined with silence—to indicate that he or she wants the other person to expand on what he or she just said. As such, the head nod is essentially a turn-refusal cue. That is, one person comes to an end of a thought, completes his or her statement, and offers the other person a turn to speak. The other person, however, wants to hear more; rather than speaking, he or she simply nods to the other person. The nod acknowledges recognition of the turn-taking signal sent from the first person, but politely declines the offer and asks that the other person continue speaking. It is a simple but effective means for encouraging an interviewee to expand on the topic under discussion.

The head nod also can be used by the interviewee to provide positive feedback to the interviewer. When the interviewer says something that the interviewer likes and wants to address, nodding by the interviewee sends a signal of agreement to the interviewer and also indicates a willingness to address the issue further. Thus, the interviewer might say, "We want our employees to be self-starters, people who can develop their own ideas for improving the company." The interviewee might start nodding when the interviewer says "starters," indicating agreement with the premise of the statement and a willingness to address the issue (e.g., "I know what you mean. At my last job, I developed a plan that lowered our overhead while increasing our sales volume.").

Body positioning is another important nonverbal element in the employment interview. Body positioning refers to the general physical orientation of an individual's body in relation to another person. Measurement of body position is usually done along two bipolar dimensions: closed-open and away-forward. You are probably familiar with the closed position: an individual sits with his or her arms and legs crossed, erecting physical barriers. If an interviewer says something that bothers the interviewee, the interviewee may cross his or her arms in a subconscious expression of disagreement. In the open position, the individual's arms and legs are not crossed; the individual is indicating that he or she trusts other people and has self-confidence.

The second dimension of body position—away-forward—also sends signals related to openness and willingness to communicate. The "away" body position is one in which the individual leans his or her body away from the other person. This is most often done while sitting down, with the person letting the upper part of his or her body shift backward. Such a position can convey an attitude of arrogance or remoteness—either of which can send a negative signal to an interviewer. The forward position, by contrast, can indicate a willingness to communicate. The individual who sits on the edge of his or her seat, leaning forward while maintaining eye contact, is telling the other person, "What you have to say is important to me."

Artifacts

Nonverbal artifacts are those objects associated with an individual that have communicative value. They include such things as clothing, jewelry, smoking paraphernalia, or any other objects that a person might use to draw assumptions about another person.

In an interview, "defining the self socially" involves dressing appropriately. In some interview situations, the dress code is prescribed to the point that the clothing is really a uniform (Joseph, 1986). In most business interviews, though, the range of acceptable dress may vary, and the interviewee must hit the proper level. Underdressing can convey a sense of disrespect for the position. Overdressing may tell the interviewer that the interviewee doesn't have a good understanding of the norms of the group. The ideal mark is for the interviewee to be dressed at the same level or slightly higher than that of the interviewer.

Jewelry may convey a person's sense of taste or give another person an indication of one's hobbies. Generally, jewelry that represents a specific religious or political affiliation should be avoided, because either could offend the interviewer or his or her associates (Molloy, 1996). Smoking is also an interview taboo, unless the interviewer indicates it is acceptable. Even then, it may be inappropriate and reduce the credibility of the interviewer.

Territory and Space

One factor that can have an indirect but critical impact on the interview is the place in which the interview occurs. This can occur along three dimensions: (1) the impact of the location itself, (2) the information that can be learned from artifacts at the location, and (3) the resulting placement of the interviewer and the interviewee. Interviewers usually prefer to conduct the interview on their home territory (i.e., a place in which the interviewer feels comfortable); the interviewee must quickly adjust to this environment.

Interviewees can adjust by looking around the room for any artifacts that may tell them something about the interviewer. Are there any family photos? A trophy for a company softball team? Professional journals reporting the latest developments in the field? Books that identify a major topic of interest? Such information can be helpful in the initial conversations of the interview.

What is the resulting placement of the interviewee in relation to the interviewer? Does the interviewer sit behind a desk, asking questions of the interviewee across the desk? Or, does the interviewer move from behind the desk, so that the conversation can occur with no barrier between the parties? Such placements can have an indirect impact on the resulting exchange of information. Indeed, individuals sitting across a desk from each other are more likely to be argumentative (Powell, Vickers, Smith, Amsbary, and Hickson, 2002), whereas an open seating arrangement is more conducive to a friendly discussion.

Most interviews occur within a spatial environment that Hall (1959, 1969) called social distance. Social distance is the distance of 4 to 12 feet in which people feel comfortable conducting social interactions. Communication in social space is slightly more formal than that that takes place in personal space (used for informal, one-on-one conversations). Occasionally, group interviews may occur in a space range known as public distance (12 feet or more). That range is more accommodating for a situation in which the interviewee is asked to respond to questions from multiple interviewers. Communication in a public-distance climate is even more formal than that that occurs in a social-distance one.

Vocalics

Vocalics refers to the way in which individuals use their voice. One classic consultant in the art of impression management has argued that an interviewee's voice represents his or her "passport to success" because it represents 15 percent of the person's "personality appeal" (Cheney, 1968, p. 29). Mehrabian (1981) goes further, estimating that 39 percent of the meaning associated with a message is based on vocal cues.

Because success in the workplace is as much a product of how a person is perceived in terms of work ethic and motivation as it is of skills and training, one's voice can play an important role in establishing that attitude. This concept is supported by research that indicates that most people can accurately identify the emotions that an individual is feeling based on that person's voice expressions (Malandro & Barker, 1983). However, it is also a form of nonverbal communication that is difficult to self-monitor. People often don't realize how they sound to others. This can be partially corrected by listening to recordings of one's own voice and evaluating it in terms of the impression it might be making on others.

It also is important for the interviewee to control his or her tone of voice during an interview. The interviewee should avoid being loud, monotonous, or whining. For example, if the interviewee is asked why he or she has had bad luck in previous jobs, the interviewee should tell the interviewer, but not in a whining voice that begs for sympathy.

Time

Hybels and Weaver (2001) have noted that time can be used for "psychological effect" and is often connected with status (p. 151). The interviewee should remember that and adhere to one major, time-based rule: Don't be late. Tardiness sends an overt message to the interviewer—that the interviewee doesn't consider the interview to be important. Tardiness shows a lack of respect for the interviewer, the organization, and the job under consideration. Unfortunately, the rule regarding tardiness only applies to the interviewee. The interviewer, because he or she is in a stronger status position, can be excused for being a few minutes late. But the interviewee lacks such latitude. An interviewee who shows up late for a job interview will have little chance of getting the job. Punctuality should be a concern for all interviewers and interviewees, being late for an appointment will undermine anyone's professionalism.

Summary

Interviewing is a purposeful interaction involving two parties that involves the asking and answering of questions. The asking and answering of questions is the framework in which information is exchanged within the interaction.

Interviews vary by type and purpose. Employment interviews are a screening technique by which organizations make initial evaluations of potential employees. Informational interviews are those that place an emphasis on content. Informational interviews may be information-seeking, information-giving, or information-sharing interviews. Interrogation interviews are primarily used to gather information from a reluctant source and are frequently used by law enforcement officials and attorneys. The primary purpose of a therapeutic, or counseling, interview is to establish a supportive relationship that will help individuals identify and work through personal issues, concerns, and problems. The performance review interview is used to assess the work of an individual or group. The grievance interview is one involving conflict and resolution. The exit interview is commonly used by organizations to assess employees' reasons for leaving the organization.

Most interviews can be divided into four distinct stages: (1) preparation, (2) opening, (3) Q&A, and (4) closing.

Effective interviewers often use question-sequence techniques. Three different question sequences are commonly used—the funnel sequence, the inverted funnel, and the tunnel sequence. The adept interviewer will develop question-related skills and use silence effectively. The different types of questions that can be used during an interview include open-ended questions, closed-ended questions, probes, and third-person questions. Interviewers also must be aware of improper questions—loaded questions, leading questions, and illegal questions. Sometimes, by remaining silent, the interviewer can encourage the interviewee to provide more information.

Nonverbal skills also are important within the interview context. It is important to arrive early, make a good impression with one's clothing and body presence, and speak in a confident voice. The interviewee should use other nonverbal cues, such as eye contact, smiling, and nodding, to indicate that he or she is paying attention to what the interviewer says. The interviewee should also monitor the nonverbal behavior of the interviewer to pick up cues for turn-taking (i.e., when they are expected to speak).

FOR FURTHER DISCUSSION

1. Review your interactions with other people over the past week. How many involved situations in which you were being interviewed? How many were interactions in which you were asking questions of someone else? What kind of interactions were these?

2. Think of the last time that you were interviewed by someone else. Were you satisfied with how you handled that interview? What did you like or dislike about what you did during that interview? What did you like or dislike about the questions asked by the other person?

3. Observe a television interview. What interview techniques were used by the interviewer? By the interviewee? Were these techniques effective or ineffective?

2 Informal Interviewing: Interviewing in Daily Life

Sue goes to her office in the morning and finds a sales representative from a new supplier waiting for her. Instead of pressuring Sue with a generic sales pitch, the representative merely asks Sue a few questions about her position and her expectations from vendors and then leaves her office. During a quick trip to the local mall during lunch, Sue is approached by a young man with a clipboard who asks her a few questions about a local clothing store. That night, during dinner, she receives a phone call from the local newspaper, asking for whom she will vote in the upcoming election.

Like most people, Sue never gave much thought to interviews or interviewing techniques. If asked, she would probably say that she never solicits interviews nor has ever been interviewed. The truth, however, is that she often is interviewed, and interviews affect her life in ways in which she is unaware. Interviewing may be a narrow context of communication, but it is used widely in everyday life.

One advantage of studying interview techniques is that the skills obtained through interview training have many applications to other communication situations. After all, at its basic level, interviewing is a process of gathering information about a topic or another person that can be useful in a variety of professions (O'Hair & Friedrich, 1992; Wilcox & Nolte, 1997, p. 15). Overall, interview training makes one more adept at asking questions, and that, in turn, leads to improvement in one's listening skills (O'Hair & Friedrich, 1992).

People with good interviewing skills also will be successful in a wide range of professions that are enhanced by the ability to examine a problem from multiple perspectives. Chapter 1 showed how interviewing techniques can enhance job performance for those who work in an organizational environment, law enforcement, the legal community, or the medical community. Not surprisingly, many people find that interview training helps them in their everyday life. Specifically, many of the skills used in interviewing also are useful as a form of *informal interviewing* in (1) daily interpersonal interactions, (2) relationship development, (3) group communication, (4) conflict resolution, (5) education, and (6) the public arena.

Interpersonal Communication

Initiating Conversations

Have you ever met someone new at a party, but did not know what to say? That is because you are taking the wrong approach. The most effective way to start a conversation with strangers is not to talk about yourself, but to ask questions about them, that is, to interview them.

The advantage of asking questions to initiate conversation is that it encourages the other person to talk about him or herself, an approach that Fisher (1984, 1987, 1989) called the *narrative paradigm*. Cragan and Shields (1998) describe narration as a force that contributes to value justification for human action. According to Fisher, five assumptions underlie the narrative paradigm theory: "(1) Humans are essentially storytellers, (2) human communication is achieved fundamentally through stories, (3) through discourse humans use 'good reasons' for believing or action, (4) humans have an inherent narrative logic that guides their assessments of communication, and (5) the world as we know it is a set of stories that allows each of us to construct and adapt our realities" (Fisher, 1987). Interview techniques can be particularly helpful at eliciting such stories and getting people to talk about themselves.

Reducing Uncertainty

Berger and Calabrese (1975) suggest that the primary motive behind much communication activity is the reduction of uncertainty in one's life. This theory is based on an assumption about human nature; specifically, that humans have an inherent dislike of uncertainty and ambiguity. As a result, any potential communication event can create a sense of uncertainty that triggers questions that one wants to be resolved. For example, if invited to a party next weekend, one's initial response would probably be "I need more information. What time will it start? How will most people dress? Who else will be there?" Answers to such questions reduce uncertainty and make the person feel better about the approaching event. Obviously, the primary technique for reducing uncertainty is informal interviewing, that is, asking questions.

Seeking Feedback

Asking questions is the most important means of getting feedback from others. Feedback is crucial to successful communication. Effective feedback increases decision-making effectiveness and helps make life's tasks easier (Graetz et al., 1998). It is a remarkably easy and effective technique, and one often employed by communication consultants. Ken Blanchard (*The One-Minute Manager*) reported that he was hired as a consultant to help with an "uncooperative" corporate vice president. He met with the corporation's president and asked him to name the things he wished the vice president would do. Blanchard wrote out a list of the president's wishes and then went to the vice president, gave him the list, and said, in effect, "Try this and see what happens." A few weeks later, the president called Blanchard to thank him for the vice president's "miracle" transformation.

The value of seeking feedback through informal interviewing also is important in family communication. Laura Stepp (2000), in her guidelines for raising children, emphasized the importance of seeking feedback from children—particularly 10- to 15-year-olds—by asking their opinions on important family issues and showing respect for their answers.

Relationship Development

Initiating Contact

"What's your sign?" This informal interviewing question represents the stereotypical and banal "line" for a guy to introduce himself to an attractive girl he would like to meet. Trite as it may be, this form of flirting often engages many of the same techniques that are effective in initiating any conversation—with a few extra items added.

Developing Relationships

People tend to be attracted to those who have communication skills comparable to their own (Burleson & Samter, 1996), and informal interviewing is included among those skills. If the relationship continues to the level of marriage, these same communication skills continue to be a factor that is associated with happy marriages (Burleson & Denton, 1997). Further, relationship satisfaction also is related to how a couple resolves problems and makes decisions. When one's decision-making style is other-oriented—an attitude inherent in interview training—the level of relationship satisfaction and overall communication satisfaction is higher (Ramirez, 2002).

One factor that can inhibit a relationship is topic avoidance. Topic avoidance is an acceptable communication technique for minor issues (Samp 2002), but it should not be applied to major issues (Sargent, 2002). Informal interviewing skills can be an effective means of initiating discussions on such issues. Sometimes topic avoidance reaches an extreme level and the topic becomes a *taboo topic*. Taboo topics arise when people experience conflicts that are so strong that the topic is removed from future discussion (Roloff & Johnson, 2001). If that topic remains taboo for too long, it can fester under the surface of a relationship. How can such topics be reintroduced? Roloff and Johnson (2001) suggest that the topic can be reintroduced through a planned interaction. Informal interviewing offers one means of doing this.

Providing Emotional Support

"What can I do to help?" may be a simple question, but it implies more than a simple request for information. It also indicates a willingness to be available as a means of emotional support. Generally, offers of emotional support are more effective when they come from a close friend rather than a casual acquaintance (Clark et al., 1998). Females, in particular, are highly receptive to such comforting messages (Hale, Tighe, & Mongeau, 1997).

Generally, five different approaches are used to comfort a relational partner: suggesting a diversion, expressing optimism, providing an external account, offering assistance, and explaining the perspective of the offender. Still, many people do not know what to say in difficult emotional situations. This can be addressed by asking a simple question rather than making an awkward statement.

Communication in the Family

The skills obtained from interview training can also pay off in better communication within one's family. The family is a complicated panorama of communication situations that involve parent-to-parent, parent-to-child, and sibling communication situations. Parents often have to learn parenting skills as they go, and children have different communication needs at different ages as the form and explore their own identities.

Noller (1995) concluded that effective communication within the family is based on five factors: (1) continuing renegotiation of roles and rules, (2) providing a comfortable climate for identity exploration, (3) enhancing the self-esteem of the other family members, (4) providing appropriate models for problem solving, and (5) involving adolescents in important decisions. Those individuals with interview training should be better prepared to do each of these. Furthermore, when the process is a positive one, children model their own communication behaviors from those of their parents, thus providing the potential for positive communication skills to be continued for another generation.

Relationship Maintenance and Reconciliation

When relationships hit trouble points, interviewing skills also can play a positive role in maintaining or reconciling the relationship. Even after the dissolution of a relationship, reconciliation is still a possibility for both participants (Wineberg, 1994). Increased interpersonal contact, however, is essential for such reconciliation (Lannutti & Cameron, 2003). Further, those partners who are serious about maintaining the relationship must be able to understand the disagreement from their counterpart's perspective (a key interviewing skill) while seeking information about that perspective (Bevan, Cameron, & Dillow, 2003). Failure to do either could seriously hamper chances at reconciliation. The key point, though, is that someone who has honed his interviewing skills will understand this basic concept.

Educational Development

Interview training can improve classroom performance through two techniques: asking questions in class and getting better feedback from instructors.

Asking Questions in Class.   While a student in graduate school, one of the authors was in an advanced class outside of his major and sometimes found it difficult to keep up with the doctoral students who had studied the topic for years. The author was, after all, one of only two nonmajors in the class. One day, when a particularly complex topic was being presented by the professor, he waited for someone in the class to ask a question that would clarify the concept. When no one did, he finally raised his hand and asked the question himself—feeling that he was probably demonstrating his ignorance by doing so. You can imagine the surprise when, after class, the other students stopped to thank him for asking the question. "We had no idea what he was talking about either," one said.

This anecdote illustrates the value of students asking questions in class. The ability and opportunity to ask questions in class is a key component of a successful educational process (Hassenplug & Harnish, 1998). The ability to ask questions has even been found to be critical to student satisfaction with distance-learning techniques (Efendioglu & Murray, 2000). The learning process is enhanced even more if the student learns to ask the right questions. That skill can benefit the student as well as the rest of the class.

Audience Interviews

Individuals who give public speeches often find themselves answering questions from the audience afterwards. Interview training can provide the speaker with the tools to handle such questions. Here are a few tips that have been suggested by some communication scholars.

1. The speaker should anticipate likely questions in advance and be prepared to address controversial questions.
2. The speaker should repeat the question. Some members of the audience will not be able to hear the question. The speaker should repeat it for everyone's benefit before providing an answer.
3. The speaker should treat the person who is asking the question with respect. The speaker should not try to build him or herself up by putting the other person down. Ideally, the speaker should be able to say something positive about the person and/or their question.
4. The speaker should look for a point of agreement. If the speaker disagrees with the premise of the question, he or she should identify that before starting to answer.

The toughest part of audience interviews is handling questions for which the speaker has no answer. O'Hair and Friedrich (1992) offer four alternatives for this situation: (1) rephrase the question into one that can be answered, (2) narrow the focus of the question to one within the speaker's area of expertise, (3) redirect the question to the questioner (i.e., "What would you do?"), and (4) the speaker can admit that he or she does not know the answer. If the last option is used, it usually is combined with a promise to provide the answer at a later date (e.g., "I don't know that offhand, but I can check and get back to you").

Source: O'Hair, D., & Friedrich, G. W. (1992). *Strategic communication in business and the professions*. Boston: Houghton Mifflin.

Getting Feedback from Professors.   The ability to ask the right questions can also be important in obtaining individual feedback from instructors. Too many students are reluctant to approach their instructors when they are having problems in class. Not so, for interviewing students. They know the importance of initiating such conversations, and they know how. Further, they know those important probes—follow-up questions—that can give them the specific information that they need to improve their class performance.

Interviewing and Listening

This book examines a wide range of interviewing situations. In some, interviewing is viewed as a medium of information exchange—with both participants learning more about each other. Some situations, such as media interviews, are focused on obtaining information. Other situations, such as legal interviews and sales interviews, often have a persuasive intent. And still others have therapeutic purposes. The different goals and situations of these various types of interviews have led to the development of different interview tools and techniques. However, one skill is critical regardless of the situation—listening. A good interviewer is also a good listener.

Barriers to Effective Listening

Listening is the key to successful interactions in both the business environment and in interpersonal situations. So this begs the question: If it is such a potent tool, why don't people do it very well? The answer is that listening is difficult and a lot of things get in the way.

Lack of Training.   Despite its importance to communication, relatively few people have any real training in listening. Other forms of communication are major parts of the educational process. Students are taught the essential elements of written communication early and continuously through elementary and secondary schools. Special courses are often devoted to public speaking and other forms of oral communication. But few high schools or universities devote much effort to teaching students how to listen. The one major exception is those who are trained in active interviewing skills.

Listening is an integral part of the interview process. Effective interviewers quickly learn the importance of listening to what the interviewee says, framing follow-up questions and probes to elicit more information. This training is one reason that Nelson (1997) argues that lawyers are often so effective in dealing with everyday problems. "Good listening is what distinguishes an ordinary trial lawyer from a great trial lawyer," she writes (p. 190). The statement could just as accurately be applied to any form of interviewing. Good interviewers learn to overcome the barriers that interfere with hearing what the other person is saying.

Physiology.   Another barrier to listening is that people talk at the wrong speed. Many think that people talk too fast, but the truth is that people speak too slowly. With a little practice, individuals can learn to listen and comprehend what someone says even if the person speaks at 250 words per minute (wpm) or faster. College debaters routinely speak at these rates or even faster to get more arguments out in the strictly enforced time limits they have. Initially, novice debaters are overwhelmed, but they quickly learn to keep up and understand what is said. They take notes and formulate rebuttals to their fast-talking opponents.

Most Americans speak at 125 to 150 wpm (it is even slower in the American South— 100 to 120 wpm). Some may think that it is good that they can listen faster than people speak, but the truth is that they get bored. They spend their time wishing a speaker would hurry up and finish what they were saying. They think, "Okay, I get it, move on." They become distracted and start thinking about other things. They plan their responses. They think about other things they have to or want to do. They stop paying attention.

The Speaker.   Speakers do all sorts of things to distract and annoy listeners. They may talk with funny accents. They may use words differently than the listener does, they may dress funny, and they may have odd nonverbal behaviors. In short, speakers do all kinds of things to distract and annoy listeners. This causes many listeners to prejudge their meanings.

At a workshop given by one of the authors, a participant told of a time when he had to hire a computer expert for his company. One of the candidates for the job showed up in jeans and a T-shirt and muttered a lot. In most cases, this would have been grounds for not hiring the person, and the interviewer did not really pay much attention to anything the candidate said. The problem was that the candidate was brilliant. He certainly was not someone they wanted out front dealing with the public, but he was exactly who they wanted digging around in their computer network. The others on the hiring committee picked up on this and the candidate was eventually hired for the position. Still, they almost missed an excellent employee because they had prejudged this person. To be sure, it would be nice if everyone were articulate, clear, and said things in comfortable ways. However, the trouble is, people hardly ever do. Good listening requires a great deal of empathy and a willingness to set judgments aside. Good interviewers learn to do this, and they carry that skill over into their everyday life.

Psychology.   The stuff going on in people's heads often gets in the way of effective listening. Everyone is busy. Everyone is easily distracted. Interviewers start thinking about their next questions while they should be listening to the interviewee. It is a good idea for interviewers to set interviews in places with minimal distractions. Although everyone likes taking interviewees out to lunch on an interview, restaurants are generally terrible places to conduct an interview. Restaurants are noisy, the interview will be interrupted by servers, and the interviewer will probably pay more attention to the menu than to the interviewee.

A good interviewer goes into an interview with a commitment to set personal distractions aside and a willingness to pay close attention to the interviewee's words and meanings. To paraphrase an old Southern saying: "You were given two ears and only one mouth, use them in that proportion." Interviewers do exactly that.

Types of Listening

People use several different types of listening. Some interactions do not require the intense concentration and thought that others do. Sometimes listeners let the speaker's words wash over them, and sometimes they pay very close attention to every detail of the words and the nuances of how they were spoken. To understand the listening process, it is necessary to first understand the types of listening and the levels at which listening takes place.

Hearing.   Hearing and listening are not the same things. *Hearing* is the physiological process of sensing vibration in the air in a particular range of frequency that, in turn, transmits electrochemical signals to the brain. The psychological process of ascribing meaning to those signals is called *listening*.

People have very little control over what they hear. Most people have experienced annoying sounds, especially in the dead of night, that make them wish they could somehow turn their hearing off. If something vibrates at the proper frequencies, a person will hear it. This does not mean, however, that that person is listening to it. If something is loud or if there is an absence of distracting noises, people will listen. But to say that a person has heard something does not mean that he or she has listened to it.

Pseudo-listening.   Pseudo-listening is merely listening to certain vocal cues, such as tone and inflection, so that the listener can display the appropriate nonverbal reactions to what the speaker is saying. Though a person may give the appearance that he or she is listening, that person is not actually hearing the words that are being spoken. Students learn to sit at their desks and pretend to listen while daydreaming. This usually involves smiling and nodding, often with their chins squarely planted on their fists. Students learn at an early age that if they don't "look" like they are listening, they will likely get called on. The student may check in every once in a while, but he or she will actually miss a lot. This is deadly for an interviewer. A student may be able to fool his or her professor when sitting in a classroom full of other students, but this is not the case in one-on-one situations. In these situations, the speaker likely will pick up on the fact that the other person is not really listening and will lose interest in providing the listener with information.

Some scholars do not consider pseudo-listening to be listening at all, because pseudo-listeners do not actually remember much, if anything, that they hear. But pseudo-listeners do, in fact, listen. They listen to nonverbal cues and respond accordingly. Pseudo-listening would not work if a person just plastered a silly grin on his or her face and nodded at random moments. To fool the speaker, the pseudo-listener must respond at the appropriate times. This is an important distinction, because it is easy to pseudo-listen and fool a speaker. If a pseudo-listener's attention wanders, the listener will not likely be betrayed by his or her nonverbal reactions. This can be a fatal mistake in almost every interviewing situation, because the pseudo-listener will have missed everything that the speaker said. Even if an interviewer tape records an interaction, he or she will miss a plethora of contextual information and will not be able to ask effective follow-up questions. Good interviewers have learned to avoid pseudo-listening, and instead approach listening as an active process.

Enjoyment.   When people listen for enjoyment, they are truly listening, just not very actively. When people listen to enjoy, they are "in the moment." People listen, comprehend, interact, and respond. However, the listener just will not remember much of what was said. When listening for enjoyment, the listener holds the speaker's words just long enough to enjoy them. Then the words float away as if they never existed.

People spend a great deal of time listening for enjoyment. When people listen to the radio, watch television, or idly chat with friends, they are most likely listening to enjoy. Most people can spend hours on the phone with an old friend, but few can remember much of what was said within minutes after hanging up.

Unfortunately, people often listen at this level when they should be trying to remember what was said. Most students have had teachers who were very amusing or told really funny jokes. Such teachers piqued students' interest and held their attention. The students often looked forward to going to class, but they just did not remember much of what was said. They were in the moment, they responded, they laughed at the right times, but they just did not put any energy into trying to remember what was said.

Many people who conduct employment interviews have had the experience of talking with a candidate and having an enjoyable time, but when asked to report to the other members of the organization, the interviewer really cannot remember much of what was said, just his or her impression. Such interviews lapsed into enjoyment listening.

Remembering.   Remembering is where the true work begins. Listening with the goal of remembering takes concentration and hard work. It also is tiring, but unfortunately it does not burn a lot of calories. An hour or two of dedicated listening to remember will likely exhaust anyone. This is why students do not remember everything their teachers say; it is too much work. To listen to remember, the listener must dedicate considerable mental energy in filing and categorizing the speaker's words, and effective interviewers do this well.

When asked, most people report that they are very good at remembering what others say. Typically, most people rate their listening skills at 90 percent or better. The truth is, however, that people are very poor listeners, and their abilities test out at 30 percent or less. This causes many problems, because people over-rely on their ability to remember and wind up forgetting more than they want and more than they know.

The other problem, especially for interviewers, is that people often confuse remembering with understanding. Just because a person remembers what was said does not mean that he or she truly comprehends what was said. To determine the meaning of words, the listener must also pay attention to nonverbal cues to gauge the speaker's honesty and veracity. The listener must pay attention to context and consider the communicative history he or she has with the speaker. Ideally, the listener must imagine him or herself in the speaker's story and try to assess the meaning of the ideas behind the words. All of these things require that the listener actively engage in making inferences about what he or she is listening to. Listening to remember, although tiring, does not require the listener to make any inferences. Students are often very good about remembering definitions, but then find that they cannot apply the information they learned in any way. They remember what the teacher said, but they did not really understand it.

Comprehension. Interviewing is a serious endeavor. For this reason, the interviewer should listen for the deeper, subtle meaning of the interviewee's words. The same words can mean different things to different people. Consider the phrase, "I love you." It means one thing coming from one's mother and an entirely different thing coming from a boyfriend or girlfriend. It is important to consider who is saying the words, how they have said things in the past, what relationship the speaker has with the listener, what the speaker really means, and more importantly, what the speaker wants.

Employment interviewers must attempt to gauge when an interviewee is telling a solid truth, engaging in puffery, or out-and-out lying. Counselors must pay close attention to their clients' demeanor. Reporters must often dig for the story behind the interviewee's words. The interviewers must ask intelligent follow-up questions. They must learn to dig where there is likely to be interesting and important information. All of this takes a tremendous amount of mental effort.

A second, more subtle reason for listening at this level is that it helps build a bond between the interviewer and the interviewee. One of the best ways to demonstrate interest and liking in another human being is to truly listen to them. An interviewee is more likely to trust an interviewer if the interviewer remembers what an interviewee has said and responds in ways that demonstrate that he or she has not only remembered what the interviewee has said, but is also making an honest effort to comprehend the interviewee's meanings. Good interviewers—those people whose very profession requires interviewing as part of their daily jobs—do this well.

Summary

The skills obtained through interview training can be applied to many other communication situations as well as to everyday life. Interview training improves one's interpersonal skills and provides tools for negotiating with other parties, initiating conversations, reducing uncertainty, and developing a mindset for seeking feedback. Interviewing is important in developing relationships, from the initial stages of getting to know another person to the advanced stages of providing emotional support. Interviewing plays a significant role in group communication in the process of learning the rules of the group, gathering information to make decisions, and in diffusing conflict that may arise. Students with good interviewing skills are more likely to do better in the classroom, because they understand how to ask relevant questions and the need for seeking feedback from their professors. Good interviewers also are good listeners. Listening is an important communication skill that can be used in a wide range of situations.

FOR FURTHER DISCUSSION

1. Keep a log of your communication activities for one week. How many of those activities were interview situations? How many used interviewing skills?

2. Consider the skills that you have developed from this course. Has the study of interviewing caused you to be more sensitive to the feedback that you get from other people? Are you more adept at monitoring nonverbal behavior? Are you better at controlling your own behavior to ensure that your verbal and nonverbal communications are consistent with your intended message?

3. Go to a local mall and conduct a participant–observation study in (1) one of the anchor stores, (2) one of the other retail establishments, and (3) the food court. How are interviewing skills used by both customers and the retailers in each of these situations?

3

The Employment Interview: The Employer's Perspective

Jill, an account executive at a large advertising firm, needs to hire an assistant. She has received over a hundred résumés and has taken the time to narrow the field to two candidates. She brings in the top two for interviews and now must choose which one to hire. The first candidate has a lot of experience and presents himself as confident and controlled. He demonstrates a superior command of the concepts and techniques of the field, but seems a little set in his ways.

The second candidate is fresh out of school and has no real experience in the field of advertising. He seems very nervous during the interview and trips over his words a few times. He has received recommendations from his professors and seems eager and able to learn.

Jill is faced with the same problem that all employers face. She has to predict which candidate is the most qualified. She also has to decide which one will fit into her company's way of doing things, which one will more readily subject himself to her authority, and which one will best fit the workplace. She also may have to consider which one she can afford, which one fits the hiring and recruiting parameters of her organization, and which one will stay with the company for the longest period of time.

Many employers can remember times when they were faced with two different candidates, one of whom seemed so much better in an interview. One candidate may have been magnificent during a two-day round of interviews, impressing the committee and the other members of the organization. After he was hired, though, he failed to demonstrate the skills needed to perform the job or the temperament to work with other people in the organization on a daily basis. Within a couple of years, he departed for another position.

Were the interviews misleading? Are all interviews misleading? Can we learn anything by interviewing candidates? At first blush, one may come to the erroneous conclusion that interviews are a waste of time, that one might as well take the top candidates and draw their names randomly out of a hat. But a closer analysis supports the notion that it is not the interviewing process that is to blame, but rather poorly trained interviewers. A glib candidate who may not be able to do the job may easily fool an interviewer with little or no training. Interviewers may miss the proverbial diamond in the rough.

These two examples illustrate the problems associated with the employment interview. Despite the heavy reliance on such interviews, organizations still find that the interview is not a perfect mechanism for making employment decisions. Still, the interview remains the most frequently used element in job-hiring decisions. Although its utility may be questioned, its widespread use demands that workforce participants be familiar with it and, hopefully, skillful in the use of its techniques.

The Purpose of Job Interviews

Employment interviews can be divided into two separate categories: job interviews and screening interviews. *Job interviews* are the ones that come to mind first and most frequently. These are formal sit-downs between a job applicant and a representative of an organization. Yate (1994) describes the job interview as a "measured and ritualistic mating dance . . . that . . . should have all the appearances of a relaxed conversation and produce as much information as an F.B.I. dossier" (p. 16). One misconception about the job interview is that its primary purpose is to assess a candidate's qualifications for a job. Actually, this is rarely the case. In most instances, the purpose of an interview is to assess (1) the candidate's willingness to do the job and (2) the candidate's ability to fit in and work within the organization. If the candidate does not have the qualifications, he or she will probably never reach the job-interview stage.

Screening interviews are often held at job fairs, conventions, or college campuses by company recruiters. Although they often have the feel of formal job interviews, they are, in fact, very different. First, screening interviews tend to be very short. Formal interviews may literally take days, whereas screening interviews usually last about 20 minutes to an hour. Second, formal interviews take place after the employer carefully sifts through the applicants' résumés and applications, whereas screening interviews typically take place before formal applications are made. Most large employers use recruiters to screen applicants, but they view this as a method of recruiting promising applicants, not choosing whom they will ultimately hire. It is important for applicants to go on screening interviews, but they should understand that such interviews are an opportunity to make an initial contact with someone in the company and should be used as a fact-finding tool. Applicants should not expect to be offered a job after a screening interview; it rarely happens.

The Interviewer's Preparations

Preparations for conducting an employment interview begin well before the interview actually occurs. Generally, the interviewer must assess the organization's needs, advertise for applicants, and filter the applicants.

Assess the Organization's Needs

This is not a solitary assignment, but rather one done through discussion with other members of the organization. What type of personality is needed for the position, particularly in terms of integrity, ambition, motivation, and communication skills? What professional skills and behavioral patterns are necessary? Should the organization hire someone who works well under direct management, or does the position call for a self-starter who will take on added responsibilities? What type of performance will be expected from the applicant? Will applicants be judged primarily on the basis of the profits they may generate, their efficiency in the position, and the process and procedures that they follow? Such parameters need to be established before any formal interviews are started.

This preparation is so important to a successful interview that Cohen (2001) recommends that interviewers adopt a "behavioral interviewing" technique, in which the focus of the interview is to find employees whose talents and values, rather than their résumé, match the job description. In other words, the focus of the interview should be on the talents and values of the applicant, in terms of how those features match the job description. Employers should not rely on an applicant's résumé as a means of making that decision.

Advertise the Position

In some cases, advertising a position may be as simple as putting a help wanted sign in a shop window or taking out an ad in the local paper. In some cases, however, it will be a time- and money-consuming endeavor that will have wide-ranging consequences. It is important to know where the potential employees are. If a company is hiring for a highly specialized position, travel to conferences and conventions that cater to the professionals in question may be required. Many conferences have employment services that are an excellent venue for recruiting candidates and conducting screening interviews. Most universities provide similar services for company recruiters who are interested in hiring recent college graduates.

Word-of-mouth advertising can be invaluable to employers. It is not uncommon for employers to contact friends and colleagues in their profession to find if they can help them identify potential candidates for a position.

Online databases and Web-based services also can be useful, especially if the company is filling a position in the information technology field. One danger with such tools is that they tend to have a "one size fits all" approach, and employers may become frustrated with the candidates produced by such searches.

Professional employment consultants also are becoming popular. The cost of these services can be prohibitively high, often costing $100,000 or more. However, some organizations have found that hiring (headhunter) firms provide excellent candidates for their consideration when hiring high-level or other critical employees.

Filtering the Applicants

Desirable positions generate often more applicants than the organization can effectively interview. Some means must be developed to filter out some of the applicants and develop a short list of finalists. A couple of techniques can be used to accomplish this, with the most common being the *résumé review*. A review of applicants' résumés will reveal that many of them lack the educational background or experience to qualify for the position. Another option might be to conduct a preliminary interview with the applicant—either at a job fair or over the telephone—to get a basic assessment of whether they have the skills and knowledge required for the job. At this point, the questions largely should be limited to those that will expand upon the applicant's résumé, such as asking about the applicant's past experiences, attitudes toward his or her present job, and areas in which he or she has been most successful. Yate (1994) recommends asking a few "knock out" questions at this stage, questions that will eliminate applicants from consideration if they cannot answer them. His examples of knock-out questions include:

"What are the broad responsibilities of your position?"
"What are the major qualities that this job demands?"
"How does your job relate to the overall goals of your department or company?"

Such questions provide an assessment of how involved the applicant is in his or her current job and provide a barometer of potential ambition in the new position.

Conducting the Interview

As with all interviews, the interviewer should open the session with questions that will make the applicant feel at ease. Early questions should focus on the past, such as the applicant's previous jobs and educational background. Such questions are less threatening to the applicant and will help the applicant feel comfortable while the interviewer obtains some basic information about the person's skills.

The specific questions for the interview will vary with the position, but some guidelines can be established. First, the goal of the interview should be to make an assessment of the applicant in terms of three basic categories: capability, work ethic, and interpersonal maturity.

Assessing the Applicant's Capability

Capability refers to the applicant's ability to do the job, and it is the area that should be investigated first. The interview might begin with a review of the applicant's responsibilities with the previous company or the applicant's educational experiences (for new graduates). Other questions that can often show up in this assessment stage are:

"Why did you apply for this job?"
"What have you learned from your previous jobs?"
"Have you ever had to make unpopular decisions?"

Assessing the Applicant's Work Ethic

Organizations prefer applicants who demonstrate a willingness to work—both alone and with others. What they do not want are "clock watchers," people who work just enough to keep their jobs. Identifying such laggards in advance can be difficult, because "clock watchers" are usually competent people. They will score well on most measures of capability, but they lack the ambition and motivation to put their capability to effective use. Questions that might be used for assessing work ethic include:

"Do you set goals for yourself?"
"Did you do much work on your own, or do you usually work better with others?"
"How do you plan and organize major projects?"

Assessing the Applicant's Interpersonal Maturity

The workplace can be a fragile personal environment. A collection of people is forced into the same environment on a daily basis for an extended period of time. Personality differences will lead to irritation and conflict. The ideal applicant is someone who can handle such situations with maturity and not add to the volatile mixture of personalities already on the job. To make these assessments, the interviewer might seek to identify applicants with inflated egos by asking "What have you done that you're proud of?" or "How would you rate your progress in your previous job (or at school)?" Ability to work with others might be ascertained by asking for opinions of their current boss and co-workers; a negative response on either point could indicate trouble getting along with others. Or the interviewer may ask, "When was the last time you got really angry?"

The Behavioral Interview

As mentioned earlier, one means of assessing interpersonal maturity is a technique known as the *behavioral interview*. The focus of the behavioral interview is to evaluate the talents and values of the applicant in terms of how those features match the job description. Pincus (1999) describes such an interview as one in which "The interviewer puts the focus on personal conduct, your *modus operandi*" (p. 48). Fry (2000) notes that the form of the questions "stay in the realm of the known" (p. 37), in that they focus almost exclusively on past experiences.

In such interviews, applicants are asked to describe how they have handled a variety of work situations in the past. If leadership skills are needed, the interviewer may ask the applicant to describe a time in which he or she had to compel others to complete a major project. It is not enough for an applicant to say that he or she is a team player; the applicant must give an example. Thus, the interviewer may ask such questions as: "What happened the last time you had a conflict with a co-worker?" or "How do you respond when a colleague gossips about you?" The focus is always on seeking responses that supply specific information, with the interviewer using the information as a basis for making extrapolations about behavior in future job situations.

Multiple Interview Situations

When seeking an applicant for a long-term position, a single interview may not suffice. Multiple interviews may be needed (1) to get behind any facades that may be developed and held during a short interview and (2) to assess the extent to which the candidate will work well with other members of the organization. In such instances, three or more interviews may be employed, with the follow-ups focusing on such areas as judgment, emotional maturity, and manageability. Subsequent interviews—usually in an informal social setting—may be necessary to requestion the applicant on sensitive areas.

Structuring the Interview by Employment Purpose

One factor that influences the format and structure of the employment interview is the type of position the organization is seeking to fill and the candidate being considered. Different positions require different skills and types of people, and interviewers will have different questions for each type of position. An interviewer would not ask someone entering the field the same questions he or she would ask of an applicant with years of experience. The

An Interview with Brenda Pickelsimer

Brenda Pickelsimer is owner and operator of BJ Designs based in Austin, Texas. She is a design architect and oversees the interior design work for office complexes. She provides support for commercial interior design firms and manages installation crews. She hires a variety of skilled and unskilled workers in her position.

Q. Can you describe your hiring process a little—the steps you go through before getting to the interview?

A. We have done an analysis on the total cost of a new employee, pay, benefits, necessary space for them to work versus the need for getting a job done faster. We work project to project, so we adjust our hiring based on a minimum amount of work each month and hire additional persons when a larger project comes along or when one is under a time constraint. We generally get most of the applicants through referrals from co-workers. We post job openings in areas like college job boards, citywide facilities management networking groups, and sometimes in the newspaper under General Contracting.

Q. What kind of things do you want to know about an applicant that can't be found on the résumé or application?

A. I want to know more of their personality. Are they whiners, do they have agendas that might interfere with their getting along with their co-workers? Are they polite, how do they dress? I want to know in their words why they left the other jobs, where they want to be in a year. In other words, will they be gone in three months after I've trained them, to a competitor?

Q. Do you have preplanned questions?

A. I have an outline of what I want. I might vary from that. If they tend to try and lead me to what they want to talk about, well that tells me something else. It sends up red flags if I have to ask the same question more than two ways. I might give them some installation plans and ask them to see if they spot problems.

Q. So how do you tell if someone is a winner, etc.?

A. I try to double-check their references before they show up for the interview. I like to see their reaction when I tell them I have done this. Someone's a winner who seems genuinely interested in the work, who sees a project as a whole, not just their specific part. They appear to be able to independently think, without being so ambitious as to think they are going to be crew chief in two months.

Q. Do you ever get surprised by an interviewee? I mean you think someone is going to be great and they're a dud or vise versa?

A. All the time! Words on paper don't convey the real person, and you have to be aware that what you see in the interview is not really how they will be in a general day, during eight or more hours. They are pushing the most positive image they can. Whether it's going to be real on 4 PM on a Friday afternoon is another story. One of the hardest things to decide is whether the natural nervousness is just the stress of the interview or from something else going on that I don't know about.

(continued)

Continued

A. An enthusiastic attitude and a "can-do" problem-solving skill have masked other problems with the employees that I've missed. Yes, I get in trouble for hiring those, too. In small firms, you do everything, the hiring, the firing, the paperwork. If anything, the biggest mistake I make is hiring people who end up skipping the quality along the way for the end result. That leads to nasty things like desks falling over onto people, so now I am more leery of that.

Q. What's the biggest deal killer in your mind? Is there something that will turn you off to a candidate immediately?

A. Anything that smacks of substance abuse. Wandering conversations, seeming to not care, seeming to care too much, glazed eyes, alcohol breath.

Q. What advice would you give to a brand new manager who's now responsible for hiring people?

A. Remember your bottom line. Remember the goal you want to accomplish with this new person. Don't just look at personality or experience, but look to see what this person will be capable of (even if it's after you have to train them) giving toward your business. For sure, don't hire to be able to add another person managed to your own résumé.

---

specific requirements of each position will necessitate some task-specific questions that would not be necessary for some other positions. Exploring every potential variation, based on task, is beyond the scope of this book, but a few examples can be provided.

The College Graduate

Employment interviews for applicants just out of college will differ from those in which the applicants have more experience. New graduates typically have a broad range of educational skills that qualify them for several different entry-level positions within the organization. The goal of the interviewer is to decide if each applicant (1) will fit well within one of the slots, (2) will fit well within the organization, and (3) has long-range potential with the organization. Yate (1994) recommends using three specific questions in this type of interview:

1. "What kind of work interests you, and why?" This question allows for probing of areas of interest that may be mutually beneficial to both the applicant and the organization.
2. "How did you spend your vacations during school?" Some students have summertime experiences that demonstrate their ambitions, interests, and work ethic.
3. "Do you plan further education?" On the positive side, an applicant who wants additional education demonstrates a desire to further his or her career, and that could be good for the organization. On the negative side, if the applicant is planning to be a full-time student at the graduate level, that person's tenure with the organization may be short.

Sales Positions

Yate (1994) argues that the interviewer must be particularly careful in interviewing applicants for sales positions because the interviewer may be more easily deceived by sales applicants than others. After all, if the applicant is a good salesperson, he or she will view the interview as a sales opportunity. The interviewer is not interviewing as much as the applicant is trying to sell him or herself. As a result this may seem to be one of the easiest employment interviews to conduct, but the interviewer should be especially vigilant. Probe questions should focus on such assets as persistence, persuasiveness, ability to handle stress, resilience, and sales maturity.

Management Positions

Employers seeking to fill a management position face a unique situation. In essence, the interviewer has to determine how the applicant would conduct such an interview if their roles were reversed. Why the role reversal? The management position is dependent on the skills of the applicant at working with the personnel from a variety of positions within the organization; superiors, subordinates, and peer managers. If the applicant were in management, what would his or her hiring practices be? What would be the applicant's attitude toward employee turnover? What is the applicant's attitude toward discipline and the role of authority? What factors would be required in the orientation of new employees? How would the applicant communicate with and motivate the organizational staff? And what is the applicant's record on fiscal responsibility? The goal of such questions is to identify the management philosophy of the applicant, and thus be able to assess whether the applicant's approach would fit with the general approach of the organization.

The Résumé Probe

On paper, everyone is potentially a great employee. One part of the interviewer's preparation is to review the résumés of those who have been selected for interviews, looking for gaps that must be probed during the interview. A résumé can tell the potential employer what an applicant has done in the past, but it is a relatively poor device for telling the interviewer what that person can actually do. Thus, the first job of the interviewer is not to be misled by the résumé, because there is no necessary connection between the quality of the résumé and the quality of the job candidate. As Yate (1994) noted, résumés ". . . are like mirrors in a fun house: They offer a distorted image of reality whose main function is to deceive the eye" (p. 49). Indeed, individuals who have good writing and presentation skills, but not much else, will present some of the best résumés. Some of the worst résumés, including some that get eliminated in the early filtering process, belong to people who would have made excellent employees.

The interviewer has to look beyond the résumé and try to identify those qualities that reflect the usefulness of the applicant to the organization. If a decision is made to interview the applicant, one goal of the interview should be to see behind the résumé, filling in gaps of information that have been omitted. Part of the interviewer's job is to identify those

Hiring Mistakes

With all of the focus on job seekers, the common mistakes made by employers are often ignored. Hiring mistakes can be costly to an organization in terms of time, lost productivity, and financial and legal damage from lawsuits. The following is a list of common hiring mistakes.

- **Rushing the process.** Companies often rush the process, resulting in critical errors (Lousig-Nont, 2003).
- **Being overly emotional.** Companies are often fooled by glib or overly social employees who are likeable but cannot really perform in the long run (Lousig-Nont, 2003).
- **Relying on employer recommendations.** Past employers have many reasons for recommending someone. In some cases, it is a quick and easy way of getting rid of a problem employee. Interviewers should not be overly swayed by a glowing recommendation from a past employer (Lousig-Nont, 2003).
- **No background check.** One of the best ways to get a positive outcome from an employment interview is to check references and confirm the applicant's employment history (Simbasku, 2002).
- **No clear job description.** This may be the worst mistake. If the company is not clear as to what it wants, there is no way it is going to make a successful hire (Vessenes, 2001).

gaps and be prepared to ask questions about them. Are they any gaps in the work history or educational history that needed to be explained? Why is the applicant seeking to leave his or her present job? Why leave a position when the applicant has risen in the ranks so quickly? Are there any gaps in productivity in previous jobs that might indicate a potential for burnout at some stage? What elements are missing from the applicant's educational background that would be desirable for the company? Such questions will allow the interviewer to obtain a more complete picture of the applicant and his or her skills as they relate to the organization.

Puzzle-Based Interviews

A popular trend in many organizations today is *puzzle-based interviews*. These interviews subject applicants to high stress, basically unanswerable questions to see how well they "think on their feet." For example, the interviewer might ask, "Imagine I have a revolver with one loaded chamber, before I fire it at you, do you want me to spin the chamber?" The interviewer is not attempting to gauge the interviewee's understanding of probability, but rather how well they cope with bizarre questions.

Poundstone (2003) argues that this type of interview may reveal some important personality characteristics and may be useful with some younger applicants who enjoy this type of approach. He goes on to say, however, that employers run a very big risk of antagonizing older, more experienced applicants and that employers would do better by sticking to more traditional questions about experience and abilities.

The Legal Side of Employment Interviews

Personnel who conduct employment interviews must do so under a strict list of rules that limit the types of questions they can ask. They must gather information necessary for hiring decisions without asking some specific questions. A number of different legal acts apply to what can and cannot be asked with regard to a number of topics (DeLuca, 1997). Several areas are of special concern.

Race and National Origin

The Civil Rights Act forbids any action that discriminates against a person on the basis of his or her race or national origin. To ensure that they meet that requirement, employers generally follow several guidelines. Specifically, the interviewer cannot ask questions that deal with:

- An applicant's skin color or complexion
- The skin color or complexion of the applicant's family
- The applicant's nationality, ancestry, parentage, or next of kin
- The applicant's birthplace

Sometimes a thin line separates a legal question from an illegal question. For example, it is illegal to ask a candidate how he or she learned to speak a second language, but it is perfectly acceptable to ask the applicant how many languages he or she speaks. The difference between the two questions is that the second question deals solely with a skill that could be useful on the job, whereas the first has the potential to require the applicant to reveal something about his or her ethnic or racial background. Any question that hints at the second aspect is taboo.

Political Beliefs

The interviewer should not ask the applicant any questions related to his or her political beliefs or political affiliation. The interviewer should not ask the applicant to identify his or her voting preference in any past election or upcoming election. Further, the interviewer cannot ask about partisanship or political ideology. Thus "Are you a Democrat or a Republican?" and "Do you consider yourself a liberal or a conservative?" are both taboo within the context of the interview.

Religious Beliefs

The interviewer should not ask any question that requires the applicant to reveal his or her religious beliefs or affiliations. Taboo questions include any that ask about the applicant's religious denomination, religious organization, religious activities, or observance of religious holidays. If the nature of the job requires that they be available to work on Saturdays or Sundays, the interviewer can usually ask the applicant about his or her willingness and availability to work on those days; otherwise, those questions should be avoided, too.

Gender

Hypothetically, gender discrimination could be directed toward either men or women. Realistically, though, most of the gender discrimination in the modern workplace is directed toward women (Yate, 1994). As a result, most professional employment interviewers take special precautions when interviewing a woman applicant. The following topics should generally be avoided:

- Whether the applicant's name is her maiden name or married name
- Whether the applicant's preferred form of address is Miss, Mrs., or Ms.
- The applicant's marital status, including the name of the applicant's spouse
- Whether the applicant has children, particularly questions about the number of children and their ages
- The applicant's birth control practices

Age

The Age Discrimination Act prohibits discrimination against candidates between 40 and 70 years of age. Similarly, résumés cannot require that the applicant include a date of birth. The only age-related question that an interviewer is allowed is related to minimum age requirements. For most positions, then, the only legal age question is whether the applicant is at least 18 years old.

Disabilities

The Americans with Disabilities Act prohibits any discrimination on the basis of an applicant's disability or physical handicap. Generally, most interviewers judiciously avoid questions that might be construed to apply to this area. Still, some problems still exist. As consultants Wendleton and Dauten (2000) note, ". . . that doesn't make doubts go away: Interviewers hate uncertainty. They hire the person with the fewest question marks. Only the interviewee can inoculate against those doubts" (p. 2G).

Military Background

Employment interviewers are allowed to ask if the applicant has had military experience, but they cannot ask questions about which branch of service the applicant served in or the type of discharge that the applicant received.

Exceptions to the Rules

The legality of a question is gauged not only by its subject, but also by its context. Employers may ask questions that are germane to the job for which they are hiring. By sticking to bona fide occupational qualifications, an employer can usually keep out of trouble. For instance, a church committee has every right to question potential ministers about their religious beliefs or knowledge, but it should not ask a custodian the same questions. Firefighters must conform to physical requirements that clearly favor men, but applicants cannot be asked about their choice of child care (or whether they have children at all).

Summary

The employment interview is the gate through which new employees join an organization. The person conducting the interview serves as the gatekeeper. The interviewer's goal is to identify applicants who will best fit in with and be productive for the organization. Preparation for conducting such interviews includes identifying the needs of the organization and filtering the résumés for qualified applicants. The goal of the interview itself should be to gather information that will assist the organization in assessing the capability, work ethic, and interpersonal maturity of the applicant. All of this must be done within strict legal guidelines that protect the rights of the applicant.

FOR FURTHER DISCUSSION

1. As a group, decide what characteristics are generally possessed by good employees (e.g., hard working, good listener, etc.) Devise a list of questions that an interviewer could ask a potential employee to learn these things.

2. Have you ever been asked questions on an interview that you thought were unfair or illegal? What were they? Why were they unfair or illegal? Are there ways to avoid answering such questions that will not anger a potential employer?

3. How do you think employment interviewers are fooled by applicants? What can interviewers do to prevent this from happening?

4. Determine whether each of the following questions is legal or illegal.
   a. Are you a citizen of the United States?
   b. What church do you attend?
   c. Who will watch your children when you work on the weekends?
   d. What school do your children go to?
   e. Where do you live?
   f. What type of boss do you like?
   g. Are you available for night work?
   h. Can you travel out of town with little or no advance notice?
   i. Who did you vote for in the last election?
   j. What are your hobbies?
   k. How will you get to work?
   l. Jamal? Is that an Islamic name?
   m. Are there any special accommodations you will need to get around on the job?

4

The Employment Interview: The Job Applicant's Perspective

Joe shifted in his seat, waiting anxiously until the receptionist called his name. In a few minutes, he would be interviewing with a personnel officer with a major company. If things went well, he could seal his first job out of college and establish himself in a career with a top national firm. It all depended on the interview. Would he get the job or not?

Joe's anxiety illustrates the importance of the job interview in modern society. Crucial hiring decisions are made on the basis of the interview, sometimes unfairly so. Some highly qualified people simply do not interview well; if given the chance, they would do a good job. Many do not get the chance, however, because of a poor or mediocre performance in the interview.

Others seem to excel at the job interview. When brought into the interview environment, they turn on performance skills that impress and dazzle the interviewer. Those skills, though, may not always be relevant to the skills needed for the job. Regardless, the job interview is the major means that companies use to assess job applicants. According to Gottesman and Mauro (1999), "In a very limited amount of time—probably longer than two minutes, but shorter than an hour—an interviewer needs to find out who you are so she can assess how you'll perform in the future" (p. xiv). And, they add, "It is undeniably true that the job can be won or lost in the time you spend sitting opposite the decision maker" (p. 2). Yeager and Hough (1998) stress the importance of training and preparation, noting "that you had better be better at selling yourself than the competition or you will not win the job" (p. xi). Similarly, although Fry (2000) notes that employers are looking for "self-managing" workers who can get the job done, "you can't get started proving yourself without making it through the interview process" (p. 5).

Starting the Process

Joe, a graduating senior who has majored in business, is offered an interview with a large company. He excitedly goes to one of his professors and asks for some tips on what he should talk about during the presentation that the company wants him to make.

Some Do's and Don'ts for Employment Interviews

Do's

- Pronounce your interviewer's name properly. Learn it in advance, if possible.
- Answer questions with specifics. Give examples of how you have dealt with similar situations.
- Dress properly, at an equal level or slightly better than the interviewer.

Don'ts

- Don't say bad things about your former or current employer.
- Don't slouch.
- Don't say "no" when asked if you have any questions.
- Don't call the interviewer by his or her first name, unless invited to do so.
- Don't ask a top manager "What do you do here?"
- Don't bring up the subject of money; that will come when an offer is tendered.

His professor tells him, "I don't have a clue, but I bet the person you talked to on the phone does. Why don't you call him back and ask about their target clientele, what products they are developing, generally what they are looking for in an employee?"

Joe looks at his professor in astonishment, "I can do that?"

"Of course you can," the professor replies.

Joe takes the advice and calls his contact person back. He asks the personnel officer a number of questions and generally discusses the job for about a half an hour. Joe gets a really good idea about what he should and should not talk about during his presentation and goes into the interview with a great deal of confidence.

The Informational Interview

Joe has conducted an informational interview. An informational interview is a technique used by applicants to gather information about a potential position. An aggressive job applicant may hold informational interviews with people in the company or within the industry. As Yeager and Hough (1998) note, "Current employees are the best source of information about the inner workings of a company" (p. 25). Such interviews do not directly contribute to a company's hiring decision, but they provide a number of advantages to the job applicant.

Networking. By interviewing people within the company and industry, one gradually will develop a network of contacts. In essence, if a person conducts enough informational interviews, he or she will become an insider with an edge over outsiders being considered for positions. In addition, informational interviews can serve as a source for identifying those at higher levels within an organization—another networking function that can be of value later in the hiring process. Informational interviews can be helpful at any level within the organization. When used to gain a job interview, though, they typically need to be conducted with an individual at least two levels above the position to be filled.

Informational interviews can lead to other networking opportunities. By conducting informational interviews, a person may learn about organizations and associations that most of the employees at the organization join and the conferences and conventions they attend. Such networking opportunities allow a person to identify job opportunities of which others may not be aware. Andrea Bradford (2003), a vice president at Rights Management Consultants, estimates that 75 percent of all jobs are not advertised. Most, in fact, are filled through informal networking.

Research.   Informational interviews are an effective technique for researching individuals and companies. The authors remember one student who had a job interview for a marketing position with a retail company who prepared for the interview with a series of informational interviews in advance. She visited the retail portion of the company prior to the interview, talking with sales associates and observing their dress, behavior, and demeanor. She used that information to select attire for the interview and used information from these visits in her responses to some of the interview questions. Such research also can be supplemented with online research about the company and its policies. Such advance information can be invaluable for discussing topics raised during the employment interview.

Experience.   Informational interviews are an effective way of gaining interview experience that will be helpful during an actual job interview. An applicant will become more comfortable with the process from the sheer repetition of doing it, and also will supply potential responses that are appropriate or inappropriate. Increased knowledge of the company will lead to more appropriate responses, presented in a more confident manner. Further, the applicant will be more comfortable during the actual interview, having contacted so many people who are already a part of the organization.

Résumés

Interview skills are relatively unimportant to the job applicant who cannot get an interview. This is why the résumé is so important. It is the "foot-in-the-door" that determines whether a potential employer is willing to look further at an applicant and his or her credentials. Although there is no single best way to construct a résumé, the following general guidelines are important.

What to Include

The résumé should provide enough information so that the reviewer résumé can develop some idea of whether the applicant's skills are appropriate for the organization. The following should be included in a résumé.

Formatting Résumés for Online Databases

Online databases are becoming more and more popular with employers and job seekers alike, but the new technologies require some adaptation on the part of job hunter.

- Emphasize *nouns*. Keywords are replacing action verbs as the important element in résumés. A résumé often will be screened by a computer that is programmed to search for job-related nouns.
- Format the résumé in plain text. The database's software may not recognize special characters and formatting (i.e., bold faced or italic characters).
- Use the space bar, not the tab key, to align text.
- If the résumé is right-justified, set the right margin at 72 characters or fewer.
- Replace bullets with hyphens.
- Test the résumé with an online service to see what should be reformatted.
- Don't send the résumé as an e-mail attachment. Instead, cut and paste the résumé into the text of the e-mail. Fear of virus attacks have made most companies leery of opening e-mail attachments.
- Remember that getting hired is *still* about getting noticed. Try to establish direct interpersonal contact with potential employers.
- Avoid being too generic. There is no such thing as a one-size-fits all résumé. Employers are looking for résumés that target their needs.
- Be professional. Professionalism is still a key factor in the hiring process. Avoid typical e-mail shorthand and emoticon characters (i.e., LOL or :+>) and create a professional e-mail address. Cute e-mail addresses (e.g., sexylegs442@hotmail.com or archeryking@yahoo .com) may get you noticed by your friends, but they will not impress a potential employer.

Source: LaVine, J. M. (2000). How to land a job using the Web. *R&D Magazine, 42(4)*, 25–26.

Contact Information.   A résumé should include the applicant's name, address, telephone number, and (for many positions) an e-mail address. Personnel workers may review dozens, maybe even hundreds, of résumés. They will not want to spend excessive time tracking down a person if insufficient contact information is provided. If they run into a snag when trying to contact a particular applicant, they will frequently move on to another applicant.

Employment History.   The résumé should identify positions the applicant has held in the past and work skills from those experiences. Even relatively minor positions can have implications for future employment.

Educational Background.   Some jobs require the completion of specific degrees. Others are more likely to be filled by people with specific types of training.

Résumé Format

Résumés can be formatted in a variety of ways. No one specific style is preferred by employers, but most demand that the résumé be neat, free from errors, easy to read, and concise. Although some professions may allow a résumé that is two pages or longer, the overwhelming preference is for a one-page résumé (Blackburn-Brockman & Belanger, 2001). Most software packages provide *résumé templates*. Such templates can automatically format entered information in a variety of ways. Experiment and choose a style that best fits your needs.

Résumé Don'ts

Personnel officers often use their first view of résumés for filtering purposes. They eliminate as many of the résumés as possible before taking a closer look at those they will consider interviewing. They look for negative elements, frequently things that have nothing to do with the position itself. One employer, for example, once told the authors that he had more than 100 applications for a single position. His first filtering element was to discard résumés sent with a hand-addressed envelope, an approach that cut the pile by about half. Thus, the goal is to create a résumé that will not be quickly discarded. The following are a number of common mistakes that should be avoided.

Lack of Professionalism.   Handwritten envelopes are just one example that falls into the category of "unprofessional." A résumé is a person's first contact with a potential employer, and it must demonstrate a professional mentality. That's not always easy, particularly for new college graduates who have spent four or more years developing highly casual behavioral patterns. The résumé should not identify the applicant as an amateur in the profession.

Too Cute.   One common mistake often made by new college graduates is to make their résumé "too cute." The use of computer graphics to "jazz up" a résumé is tempting, but usually these are interpreted by personnel management for what they are—attempts to cover up a weak résumé with an interesting design. Common mistakes in this area include the addition of unusual graphics and the use of eye-catching paper colors.

Résumania.   A few typos in a résumé or cover letter will attract a personnel officer's attention. Such carelessness will quickly eliminate an applicant from consideration. Robert Hall (2004) coined the term "résumania" to describe careless résumé mistakes. Classic examples of résumania include a cover letter with the closing sentence: "Hope to hear from you shorty," or the person who listed his or her skills as "Excellent memory, strong math aptitude, excellent memory."

Written Arrogance.   Some people are too proud of their résumés. They record all of their achievements with grand flourishes, sometimes scaring off a potential employer. Such people often assume they lost a position because they were overqualified. Sometimes that is the case, but often the reason is that the personnel officer could not imagine having to work with such a person on a daily basis. Self-promotion is good, but arrogance can be a detriment.

Misrepresentation.   Perhaps the worst mistake an applicant can commit is to submit a résumé containing errors or one that overexaggerates achievements. In some states, such misdeeds are considered felony crimes. At the very least, though, they represent a fatal mistake that ultimately ruins a person's chances of being hired. Educational background seems to be a common area in which this occurs, with candidates listing unearned degrees. The authors have seen the following educational misrepresentations: (1) a person taking a post-graduate night course implies that she will soon have a master's degree; (2) a person obtains a mail-order degree and implies that it came from a legitimate university; (3) a person misrepresents grades in some key courses. Past work experiences sometimes offer chances for exaggeration; the authors remember one résumé for a management position that claimed experience in maintaining a cost-efficient and balanced budget for three departments. A little research revealed that two of those three budgets consistently had operated at a financial loss during the person's tenure. The final advice here is simple: Do not lie or exaggerate on a résumé.

Cover Letters

An applicant should include a cover letter tailored to the specific job and company. A person may apply simultaneously to several positions with different job descriptions. For example, a student just graduating with a broadcasting degree might apply for a sales position with one station, a production assistant position at another, and an assignment desk position at a third. The student may be qualified to handle all three, but the cover letter to each organization should be tailored to fit the specific position.

Many people starting their first job search ask, "Do I have to include a cover letter?" The answer to this question is a resounding "*yes*!" A cover letter should be sent with every application, regardless of whether the employer asked for one. The cover letter is a persuasive document that helps to highlight and emphasize things that the employer will find on the applicant's résumé. With so many people applying for jobs online, a "good cover letter can set a candidate apart from the rest of the pack" (Franzinger, 2001, p. 164).

One of the major complaints of employers is poor cover letters. The writing of a cover letter is not a perfunctory task created to waste time, but rather an invaluable opportunity for the applicant to make a strong case as to why he or she is the best person for the job. The cover letter is a business letter and should be written as such. Unlike the résumé, which should only be one page in length, the cover letter should be as long as it needs to be, though typically they are one to two pages in length. At a minimum, the cover letter should include the following paragraphs.

■ *The First Paragraph: The Introduction.* In the first paragraph, the applicant should introduce him or herself to the employer and identify the desired position. Many applicants make the mistake of being too general, making statements such as, "I am applying for the position you have open" or "I am writing because I am interested in working for your company." A company may be hiring for multiple positions; the employer should not have to guess the one for which the applicant is applying. If the reader is not sure what to do with the application, he or she will likely just throw it away. The applicant should also state where he or she learned of the job. This provides marketing feedback for the employer (which they like) and shows that the applicant is plugged into the network, especially if the announcement was in a trade publication or other "insider" venue. The first paragraph should end with a strong thesis statement regarding the applicant's "fit" for the job.

■ *The Second Paragraph: Blowing Your Horn.* While a résumé is a fact sheet, a cover letter is a narrative document that allows the applicant to discuss his or her greatest strengths for the position.

■ *The Third Paragraph: Why Them?* An often overlooked, but potentially powerful element, of the cover letter is some discussion of why the applicant wants to work for the company. Remember that most companies want to develop relationships with their employees and find people who seek more than just a paycheck. If there is something special about a particular company, the applicant should say so. If the applicant sees the position as an opportunity to grow and develop professionally, now is the time to discuss this. In short, the applicant should discuss why he or she wants to work for the company and what the applicant hopes to accomplish in the position.

■ *The Fourth Paragraph: Availability.* The cover letter should end with information on where and when the employer can contact the applicant. The applicant should note availability at a home phone number, whether voice mail is an option, or if e-mail is the best contact method. Most employers will not spend a lot of time trying to track down a person. If they try once or twice and cannot get in touch with an applicant, then they will likely give up and move to the next person on their list.

The applicant should write a new cover letter for each position. The applicant's strengths as a candidate may change from position to position. If, for instance, a person is applying for advertising positions, he or she may apply both to large, established firms and to more trendy "hot shops" (small firms that do more cutting-edge work). Cover letters to established firms should emphasize a person's stability, attention to detail, and ability to be a team player. Letters to "hot shops" should emphasize the applicant's knowledge of cutting-edge campaigns, risk-taking, and aggressiveness. A person's résumé probably will not change, but cover letters will guide the reader to important information for the position in question.

Preparing for the Interview

Preparation is the key to successful interviewing.

Research

The first thing a person should do when invited for an interview is conduct as much research about the company as possible. Of course, the applicant will have done some research when preparing the résumé and cover letter, but now is the time to really dig. The more the applicant can talk about specific things that the company does and how he or she can help, the better the interview will go.

Web Sites. An invaluable source of information is the company's Web site, which often contains information on where the company has offices, the company's plans for future growth, and its mission statement. Such information can provide insight into the company's culture and help the applicant figure out how he or she can fit (e.g., "I noticed that you have a branch office in Atlanta, I grew up in Central Georgia and I know the area very well").

Newspaper Stories. Newspapers are another potential source of information about a company. Again, this can provide the applicant with insight into historical issues and help the applicant understand how the company has grown and evolved and possibly where it wants to grow.

Stock Prospectuses. If the company is publicly held, the company's investor prospectus is another source of information. This is an especially good document for finding out a company's plans for future development.

A Baker's Dozen Tough Questions

Most employment interviews will include some questions that may be difficult to handle. The wise applicant anticipates these questions and has an answer prepared. Some tough questions include:

1. "What are your greatest strengths?"
2. "What is your greatest weakness?"
3. "What is an example of a time you failed?"
4. "Where do you see yourself in five years?"
5. "Why do you want to leave your current job?"
6. "Why are you applying for this position?"
7. "What would you do differently if you were to start college again?"
8. "What do you believe it takes to be a professional?"
9. "What are the most important rewards you expect from a job?"
10. "Do you believe grade-point-average is a predictor of how successful you would be in this job?"
11. "How did you determine your career choice?"
12. "How would you be described by a close friend?"
13. "What kind of on-the-job problems have you faced?"

Sources: Fry, R. (2000). *101 great answers to the toughest interview questions* (4th Ed.). Franklin Lakes, NJ: Career Press; Gill, A. M., & Lewis, S. M. (1996). *Help wanted*. Prospects Heights, IL: Waveland; Yeager, N., & Hough, L. (1998). *Power interviews: Job-winning tactics from Fortune 500 recruiters*. New York: John Wiley and Sons.

Set Goals

Often the most important things an interviewee can do is compile a specific list of goals that he or she wishes to accomplish during the interview. This does not mean saying, "I want to get hired" or "Look like the best candidate." Rather, the interviewee should make a personal inventory and figure out what strengths need to be emphasized during an interview and what weaknesses need to be addressed.

Strengths.   The applicant should identify the assets that he or she will bring to the particular company. During the interview, the applicant should point out any specific experiences or talents that make him or her especially qualified for the job. The applicant should plan in advance how to communicate these strengths.

Weaknesses.   As unpleasant as it may be, every person must confront his or her liabilities as a potential employee. Coming out of college, most students do not have a lot experience (if any). Also, the applicant's educational background may differ from the company's usual hires.

Weaknesses are difficult to hide. The employer will be fully aware of them and will probably want to discuss them at length. Interviewees can use a few strategies to help compensate for weakness and even turn them into strengths.

First, *be realistic*. No one is perfect. Everyone has some liabilities. Good employers know this. What concerns them is how maturely applicants cope with their weaknesses. Even candidates with years of experience have liabilities.

Second, the interviewee should *counter a weakness with a strength*. For example, someone coming out of college may not have experience in their chosen profession. The inexperienced candidate needs to show assets that outweigh his or her lack of experience. Up-to-date knowledge of the field, flexibility of schedule, willingness to learn, ability to learn, and the ability to work long hours are attributes that younger, less experienced candidates can convey to make up for their lack of specific job experience. If done correctly, this can even turn a weakness into a strength. The authors know one candidate who, when confronted with his lack of job experience said, "You bet I don't have any experience. Now you can start training me right away, you don't have to spend six months untraining me."

Third, the applicant should show how he or she intends to *overcome the weaknesses*. An applicant who details a specific plan for overcoming his or her weakness shows a great deal of professionalism and maturity. This shows that although an applicant may not be a seasoned professional, he or she has a plan to become one. No one really expects recent college graduates to have a long list of professional accomplishments, but they hope that they have a plan.

Dress Appropriately

How you dress for an interview is important. As Pincus (1999) notes, "Although not everyone is good-looking, everyone can look good. And proper business attire and good grooming helps everyone project a positive image" (p. 33). That means that the expansion of casual dress codes to the modern office applies only to workers who have already been hired. Applicants need to dress better than that. After all, the applicant has only a few seconds at the beginning of the interview to convince the interviewer that he or she will fit into the company's work environment (Nicholson, 1999); an applicant's clothes should not detract from that message. As Nicholson (1999) notes, a person who looks like he or she will fit in often has an edge on getting the job.

Although the level of casualness will vary, depending on the type of job under consideration, some basic guidelines should be followed. First, the applicant's level of dress should be equal to or slightly above the general dress of the office; "dressing down" sends a negative signal. Second, flashy clothes are not acceptable; the job interview is no time to experiment with new colors or Hawaiian shirts. It is better to be too conservative than too flashy. Applicants with extensive body piercings, for example, are less likely to be hired by corporate interviewers (Seiter & Sandry, 2003). Third, the applicant's clothes should be well-fitting, pressed, and make the applicant "look like someone who could work for the company" (Gottesman & Mauro, 1999, p. 46).

Interview Performance

Advance preparation is only the first step. There is still the interview itself. Several guidelines can help the prospective employee improve performance during an interview.

Don't Be Late

First impressions are important. Showing up late for the interview can essentially eliminate a candidate from consideration. Employers expect their employees to be on time; if the candidate cannot be on time for the interview, the person is probably not that interested in the position. One *Fortune 500* executive noted that it was "inexcusable" to be late for an interview, but "by the same token, never show up more than five minutes early" (Pincus, 1999, p. 81). Such behavior demonstrates an understanding of how professional organizations value time.

Getting Off on the Right Foot

Gill and Lewis (1996) compare the employment interview with a blind date in which both parties have to prove their worth to the other. The candidate's first impression should be a positive one. The candidate should not, for example, complain about how difficult it was to find the office, find a parking space, or find time to keep the appointment. Instead, the interviewee should look for an easy icebreaker to get the conversation off to a good start: perhaps commenting on an award or photograph in the interviewer's office, or (if the interview is outside the office) an interesting piece of jewelry that the interviewer is wearing.

In addition, candidates should always carry an extra copy of their résumé; it shows that the candidate is prepared and can serve as a reference copy should the interviewer make a comment about the résumé or its content.

An Interview with Jeremy Foshee

Jeremy Foshee is a Human Resources Generalist (Personnel Representative) for Schlumberger Oilfield Services, Houston, Texas. His company is responsible for the production of safety valves and other internal components that are used in oil rigs around the world. Mr. Foshee is a former Sergeant in the U.S. Army and has almost 10 years' experience in human relations and related fields. He is currently responsible for recruiting, benefits administration, and assisting upper-management in staying in compliance with affirmative-action issues.

Q. When screening applicants, what kinds of things do you look for?

A. I usually look for the most common errors first; the easy-to-find errors. These would include misspelled words, irregular patterns of employment, education credentials, etc. By looking at these errors, I am able to disregard 70 percent of the résumés. With the remaining 30 percent, I evaluate the content in conjunction to the required skills needed to fill that particular position. What kind of work has the candidate done in the past? Is it similar and creditable to the open position?

Q. So the first thing you do is try to find a reason not to hire an applicant?

A. Yes, that's about it.

Q. How important is experience?

A. Because most of our plant workers need only a high school diploma to qualify for the assembler/machinist positions, experience is vital. All of the parts made here are made to fit a certain environmental and safety standard; if one thing is miscalculated, the whole unit is worthless, which could lead to major catastrophes if not detected. Trial and error, and pure experience, is the main way to reduce these risks. In our professional positions, which include personnel, accounting, engineering, etc., experience is important, but not as vital.

Q. How important is education?

A. Education is very important for most of our positions. If an applicant has some type of education, whether it be high school, trade school, or college it shows me (the gate-keeper) that they are not only dedicated enough to put forth the interest in bettering themselves, but also that they are willing to enhance their career with optional training necessary to achieve the level of success needed to stay proficient in the future.

Q. How important are the application materials: the cover letter, résumé, etc.?

A. The cover letter is very important. Some companies have strayed from traditional cover letters, making them optional and not required, but what these companies don't admit is that an applicant who insists on providing a cover letter when it is not required holds an edge on the competition. This just showed the company that this person is willing to go beyond the standard in order to achieve success. Big brownie points!

Q. When interviewing a candidate what kinds of things draw your attention to the person in a good way?

A. Poise, self-confidence, and credentials win me over. I want someone who can look me in the eyes and convince me that he will be an asset to this company. What most applicants fail to realize is that the person interviewing him/her has no clue what to look for.

Continued

I have no idea what a machinist does, and how the equipment works. I want to be asked honest and intelligent questions. When I want questions answered, I expect honest intelligent feedback.

Q. What will immediately turn you off to a candidate?

A. A candidate who seems unfocused is a major turnoff. I like eye contact and strong concentration. I don't want someone who's easily distracted or seems uninterested.

Q. What do you know now, that you didn't when you were looking for a job? What inside info can you give job seekers?

A. The biggest element that I know now that I did not know when looking for a job is just how political the corporate world can be. In other words, who you know and whom you contact with is every bit as important as the values you possess. Employers like to see applicants who believe in themselves, and who stay focused and persistent while job searching. Employers want applicants who can make a positive statement.

Q. How aggressive should an applicant be? Can they be too aggressive?

A. An applicant can be too aggressive. There is a fine line in the job market between aggressive and desperate. It is vital that applicants come across as confident and qualified, but playing hard to get at the same time. "Don't throw yourself at the employer."

Maintaining Composure

One of the key elements that will influence the hiring decision is the way the candidate communicates during the interview. In fact, research indicates that the communication impression conveyed during the interview is the single-most important factor influencing hiring decisions (Powell et al., 1975). This impression is influenced by both verbal and nonverbal behavior. On the verbal level, some applicants seem not to pay attention to the interviewer's questions; they often provide information they consider relevant instead of the information asked for by the interviewer. On the nonverbal level, nervous applicants often fidget with their clothing or hair during the interview, something that makes them look both nervous and inattentive. This impression also can be created in nontraditional settings. Companies frequently invite candidates for lunch, where they have a chance to meet and see how they handle themselves. In these situations, the candidate's image can be influenced by a variety of factors, including table manners, treatment of servers, and selection of entrees (nothing extravagant) and drinks (no alcohol) (Collins, 2001).

When responding to questions, interviewees should follow two guidelines: (1) be brief and (2) answer the question. Brevity is important; interviewees should say what they mean in clear and concise sentences and take care to answer the question that was asked. The interviewee should not waffle on difficult questions; each should be addressed directly and quickly. Generally, interviewees should avoid the temptation to use a question as a transition to another topic. Most interviewers will find this to be irritating, because they likely asked the question for a specific reason.

Several researchers argue that impression management is a key variable in the interview process (Delrey & Kacmar, 1998). Impression management considers the applicant's ability to use the interview to address image elements related to one's self (self-focused) and to the interviewer's (other-focused) image (Kacmar, Delrey, & Ferris, 1992). Several researchers have noted that self-focused messages are used more frequently, perhaps because other-focused messages can be problematic if viewed as attempts at ingratiation (Gilmore & Ferris, 1989; Stevens & Kristof, 1995).

Seven types of verbal impression management tactics can influence the interviewer's evaluation of the applicant (Gardner & Martinko, 1988; Stevens & Kristof, 1995). These include (1) self-enhancement—describing positive or admirable attributes; (2) exemplification—acting as a role model; (3) entitlements—taking responsibility for positive events in one's background; (5) self-promotion—describing the knowledge, skills, and abilities one possesses; (6) other enhancements—making favorable evaluations of the interviewer's attributes; and (7) opinion conformity—expressions of agreement with the interviewer's comments. Conversely, those verbal behaviors most likely to create a negative impression include self-defensive tactics, such as providing excuses, claims of innocence, or attempts at justifying past mistakes (Gardner & Martinko, 1988). Researchers have also identified several factors that influence the use of such messages (Lamude, Scudder, & Simmons, 2003). Males tend to use self-enhancement more frequently, whereas females are more likely to use self-promotion. Latinos are more likely to use entitlements and less likely to use self-promotion. African Americans are more likely to use exemplification and are less likely to use entitlements, whereas Euro-Americans more frequently use self-promotion.

Handling the Tough Questions

Most interviewers will start with a series of basic questions. If they are serious about hiring a candidate, though, they eventually will move to a series of tough questions they expect the applicant to handle well (DeLuca, 1997; Fry, 2000). DeLuca argues that answering tough questions is "the most important aspect of the job search" (p. 1). If the candidate is not sure about a tough question, he or she should ask for clarification before answering. This will help the candidate to understand the question and provide more time to consider an answer.

The nature of the questions will vary by discipline, but some seem to be asked of nearly every applicant. The following are five questions frequently asked by interviewers:

1. *"What are your greatest strengths?"* The candidate should respond with specific traits relevant to the position. The interviewee should be as specific as possible, giving examples and avoiding generic responses such as "I'm a hard worker" or "I'm a people person," unless specific examples are provided (e.g., "Last month we had an unexpected deadline change, and I volunteered to work over the weekend to get the report completed"). Nearly every applicant will give generic responses; the interviewer will remember specific ones.

2. *"What is your greatest weakness?"* The temptation here will be to list an attribute that can be displayed as an asset, not as a weakness. Many people, for example, might say something like "I'm too easy to get along with, and I end up doing too much work that should be done by others." That sounds nice, but it does not give the interviewer much useful information. A better approach is for the candidate to be honest about a past weakness, telling the interviewer how the problem was overcome and finishing with a strength (e.g., "I used to be bad at record keeping, but I took a course at night to improve those skills. Last year, I received a letter of commendation from my supervisor for my improvement in that area").

3. *"Where do you see yourself in five years?"* This question, or some similar variation, seems to show up in nearly every job interview. The best response is to mention a realistic position within the organization, usually a title that is two or three steps ahead of the position being sought. This not only answers the question but also demonstrates that the candidate has an understanding of the organization. However, whatever goal is mentioned should be a realistic one; the candidate should not say something that implies shifting to another organization (which indicates a lack of loyalty), and it should never be the position of the person who is conducting the interview.

4. *"Why do you want to leave your current job?"* This is a tough, double-bind question. The candidate must want to leave the current job, or he or she would not be applying for this one. Ultimately, the candidate must answer this question in a positive way. An overly negative response about previous employment is viewed as unprofessional behavior that will make the candidate less desirable to a potential new employer.

5. *"Why are you applying for this position?"* This is usually a means of identifying the candidate's long-term goals (Gill & Lewis, 1996). Candidates should prepare their answers from that perspective.

Salary Negotiations

The general rule is that the applicant should not ask about salary during the first interview. If salary is negotiable, the position likely is one that will require multiple interviews before it is filled. Thus, there is nothing to be gained by bringing up the topic early, and the only potential impact such an early question might have is to inhibit the candidate's chances of being hired.

If the question of money is brought up by the interviewer, that usually is a positive sign, because it indicates that the candidate is still being considered. Typically the interviewer has two ways of bringing up the topic; the interviewer may ask "What salary are you looking for?" or "How much are you making now?" Both questions should generally be answered in the same manner: The candidate should give the interviewer an understanding of his or her current salary and how it compares with what he or she is seeking. A crucial element here is honesty; the candidate should not exaggerate. If the candidate's current salary is relatively high, it provides the interviewer with a sense of that person's market value. If the candidate is looking for an increase, he or she should say so and explain why.

Asking the Right Questions

One common misconception about employment interviews is that the potential employer (or their agent) should be asking all the questions. Actually, the person interviewing for the job should be asking questions, too. Marshall (2000) notes that asking questions is one of the most effective tools for opening up a healthy relationship with another person. In fact, the person conducting the interview for the company is likely to ask—as one of their final questions—if the candidate has any questions. The candidate should be ready to respond by asking questions that (1) demonstrate that the candidate understands the job and the company, (2) elicit information about the desirability of the job, and (3) express interest in the company.

Business writer Michael Kinsman (2001) recalls the time he first learned the value of asking good questions of the interviewer. As his interview progressed, he asked his interviewer such questions as: "Where is this company headed?" "Why do you do things this way?" "Why is this important to you?" "What makes you feel I can help?" As his questions came out, he recalls, "The chief executive moved to the front of his chair and articulately answered each question that was being thrown his way. When he wasn't sure how to answer, he would lean back in his chair and reflect for a few moments before answering. What I had accomplished . . . was how to engage someone in a discussion that was both stimulating to him and illuminating to me" (p. 1G).

Yeager and Hough (1998) suggest that questions from the interviewee can potentially focus on four different areas: (1) the future of the organization, (2) the future of the position, (3) expectations, and (4) attitudes about change, growth, and organizational development. The first area might include questions such as "What opportunities and threats do you see facing this company?" or "What is the company's strongest asset?" Questions about the position might include why it was created and how it contributes to the company. Questions about expectations should ask about typical work days and criteria for a raise or promotion. Attitudes about the company can be addressed by asking about the chief competition and the factors that will determine the company's future growth.

Mock Interviews

Some professionals recommend that job applicants enlist their friends or a university placement center to help them prepare by undergoing mock interviews in which they practice the techniques needed for an effective job interview. Yeager and Hough (1998) note that practicing in front of a mirror or with a friend is essential, because "it is unreasonable to think that you can just do it, and perform well on command" (p. 13). This concept is perhaps articulated best by Gottesman and Mauro (1999), who compare the job interview to that of an actor auditioning for a role as a cast member of a theatrical production. They recommend that the applicant begin by "visualizing yourself in the job" (p. 33), creating a mental picture of how they would perform the job. This can then be followed by a practice session with a friend posing as the interviewer. Pincus (1999) recommends videotaping mock interview sessions so that the interviewee can review it and evaluate his or her performance. Gottesman and Mauro (1999) recommend that each practice session should at least be audiotaped.

Understanding the Company

Demonstrating an in-depth knowledge of the company is an excellent way of making a potential employer sit up and take notice of you. This is how you make the research and preparation discussed earlier in this chapter pay off. The author remembers one applicant who was interviewed by two members of the department. When his time for questions came, he asked one question immediately: "Where's the third person?"

"What do you mean?" one of the interviewers replied.

"There are three people in your division," the applicant replied. "Why am I being interviewed by only two of them?"

"The third one's in Japan," the interviewers said, "He couldn't be here."

Not surprisingly, that applicant got the job. Although many factors, including his résumé, contributed to that decision, both interviewers recounted that story in making their recommendation for hiring. Such a question indicated that the applicant understood the company and its personnel. It also showed a level of initiative that was not demonstrated by other applicants. No wonder he got the job. A job seeker's questions may not be quite as precise as that one, but candidates should go prepared to ask at least two questions that are company-focused and show that they have prepared for the interview.

Such preparation does not necessarily require a great deal of advance work. In fact, too much research on a company may make a person appear to be an arrogant "know it all." Gill and Lewis (1996) recommend that the applicant adopt the mentality of a "ten-minute researcher" and learn enough about the company to demonstrate interest. Candidates should spend a few minutes talking with people who know about the organization. The candidate should use this information to plan some questions in advance. Relatively "safe" questions that can be used for most interviews include such standards as (Gill & Lewis, 1996):

- What resources are available to get my job done?
- What are the opportunities for growth in this position?
- How long has this position been open?
- What makes this position attractive to a candidate?
- What did the previous person do well and what were some areas of improvement?
- What is the major reason that the company needs this position?
- What is the managing style of my supervisor?

Job Desirability

People who are job hunting are often so interested in obtaining a job—any job—that they focus on getting the job instead of evaluating its desirability. Some jobs are better than others, and bad jobs can have a long-term negative impact on a person's career. In essence, it is better to pass on a really bad job, because it may haunt one for the rest of a career. So, how can job seekers identify bad jobs in advance? Yeager and Hough (1998) recommend using informational interviews for this purpose, noting that "Nobody knows better what working in a place is like than someone who works there" (p. 25). Still, the job interview itself offers the applicant a chance to gather some additional information. There's no sure-fire technique, but some indication of the desirability of a job can be gleaned from the interviewer. Although the specific types of questions will vary, depending on the job, Kennedy (1980) recommends four questions that apply to most jobs:

1. *"What kind of performance-appraisal system does the organization use?"*
2. *"What has the turnover been in the department and the position?"*

3. *"Why is the job vacant and what happened to the person who held the job previously?"*
4. *"Will I have a chance to meet the people with whom I may work?"*

Expressing an Interest in the Company

The informational goal of the interviewee's questions should be to learn more about the company and the desirability of the job, but the questions the applicant asks can also leave an impression with the interviewer that may influence the hiring decision. The general rule here is that while it helps to demonstrate knowledge about the company, it is even better to express interest. Candidates should not try to impress the interviewer with how much they know, but rather show an interest in what the company will be doing in the future.

Closing the Interview

The request on the part of the interviewer for questions from the applicant is usually a signal that the interview is approaching its conclusion. The applicant's questions will play a significant role in his or her final impression, but other factors also are important. The most important factor is politeness; the applicant should be sure to thank the interviewer before departing. A nonverbal indicator (such as a parting handshake) can also provide positive closure to the meeting. The candidate should not just get up and leave. Something must be said or done to leave the interviewer with a final positive impression.

Post-Interview Behavior

Yeager and Hough (1998) note that "The people who get the important interviews, and the important jobs, are the ones who understand the importance of follow-up" (p. 12). Once the interview is over, the applicant should write and mail a thank-you note "within 24 hours of your interview" (Pincus, 1999, p. 110). Depending upon the organization, the thank-you note can be typed, handwritten, or sent by e-mail. Regardless, it should come across as if it was individually written for that specific person. Indeed, if more than one thank-you letter is needed, each person should be given a customized response.

Dealing with Rejection

Unfortunately, not all interviews end on a positive note. Even if an applicant does an excellent job during the interview, he or she still might not get hired. A number of other factors—including budgets, internal conflicts, and the competition—will ultimately play a factor in influencing the hiring decision.

One common scenario is for a person to have a great interview and leave expecting to get an offer, but the hiring manager still has other interviews to conduct, and one of those also goes well. Further, the new candidate may bring up different issues and attributes—things the interviewer forgot to mention. The applicant may call back to see how things are going and will typically be told that the organization is still interviewing. However, unless the company gives more specifics than the "still interviewing" answer, the candidate is already out of the loop. The company will likely hire somebody else. What happens is that as the company interviews a number of different applicants, it learns something about the potential skills of all the applicants. As a result, toward the end of those rounds of interviews, the image of the ideal candidate has shifted. The candidate may have met that image early on, but is unlikely to do so later in the process. This is another reason why the first person interviewed has the least chance of getting the job, and why the last person interviewed has the best chance. For an early interviewee to have a good chance at such a job, he or she typically has to do some type of follow-up work to remain competitive. Such follow-up may include a telephone call in which the candidate has an in-depth conversation with the hiring manager or a letter that provides the manager with additional information to consider.

Candidates should not take rejection personally. As Yeager and Hough (1998) note, "Keep in mind that the interview process is a flawed one and that often the reasons for your rejection have nothing to do with you or your performance" (p. 29). Further, the interview can still be valuable if the candidate learns something from the experience. The interviewee should review the interview, thinking about "what went well and what didn't" (Gottesman & Mauro, 1999, p. 104). Interviewees should ask themselves: "What would you do differently the next time?" "What worked well?" Pincus (1999) recommends keeping a notebook to record these key points immediately. The goal should be to make each interview a learning experience.

Summary

Employee interviews—employment interviews from the perspective of the job seeker—are the job applicant's means of entry into the employment world. They represent a particularly important form of interview for college students who are approaching graduation and seeking their first major job in their profession. Those applicants who are prepared and perform well in these interviews enhance their chances of getting job offers.

FOR FURTHER DISCUSSION

1. As a student who is preparing to enter a new phase of your life, what qualities do you possess that make you valuable to employers in the field that you wish to enter? Given the list of tough questions, how might you communicate these qualities to an interviewer?

2. What weakness do you have as a potential employee? How might you discuss these weaknesses with an interviewer? What can you do to compensate or overcome these weaknesses in the short term/long term?

3. Beyond the specific job, what types of working environments do you find most satisfying? How would you determine if a potential employer has these characteristics?

5

The Persuasive Interview

Since the ancient Greeks, communication scholars have agreed that communication is either primarily persuasive or informative. While it may be tempting to believe that interviewing is first and foremost an informative activity (almost by definition), there is a strong persuasive component in almost all interviewing contexts. Job applicants, particularly new graduates, typically want to appear more professional and capable than is the case. Similarly, the potential employer often wants to persuade the applicant that a "good job" is being offered. Similarly, a reporter wants to tell a story and may manipulate an interviewee to give more information than he or she may have intended; the interviewee also wants to tell a story and may attempt to persuade the reporter to print that story. Lawyers and law enforcement agents try to build cases. Even some survey interviews are used to persuade groups of people, rather than measure them. It is therefore incumbent on the interviewing scholar to understand the nature of persuasion within the interview context. This chapter will explore some basic, definitional information about persuasion, present a number of seminal theories of persuasion and then explore the persuasive interview, which is clearly the most persuasive context of interviewing.

Theories of Persuasion

In some ways, it is difficult to discuss communication without discussing persuasion. Indeed, most theorists would argue that communication is a tool that humans use to manipulate their world. Whether simply conveying information or implicitly attempting to manipulate someone else, all communication is arguably persuasive in nature. However, a distinction is often made between overly persuasive communication and other forms of communication. For the purpose of this chapter, the discussion of persuasion will be limited to communication that is intentionally aimed at changing another's beliefs, attitudes, or behavior.

At its most fundamental level, persuasion is used to manipulate other's beliefs. A *belief* is something that people hold regarding the truth of an issue. Your professors spend much of their lives arguing with each other about the nature of theories, supporting the ones they believe in and arguing against others. In doing so, they are engaged in arguments of belief. One might weigh the pros and cons of whether to buy a house or rent an apartment. Politicians argue about various social and economic theories in order to decide which laws to pass. Although certainly there are policy implications to these beliefs, the communicative focus is on whether a belief is true or false.

Sometimes people argue about costs and benefits. Persuasion may focus on the value of an object. When it does, persuasion is an attempt to change a person's *attitude* about something. Parents constantly try to persuade their children to value their education more. Preachers do the same with religion. A car salesman may try to persuade a buyer that fuel efficiency is more important (valuable) than he or she initially thought (although a salesperson may try and persuade the opposite depending on the models he is currently trying to sell). As stated earlier, most job applicants try to persuade potential employers about their value as an employee.

In most cases, the end result of persuasion is to change someone's *behavior*. People use communication to get others to do something that they ordinarily might not do, or to do something differently. Retailers try to encourage consumers to buy their products or services. Politicians try to influence voters' attitudes and beliefs, but ultimately they are really interested in the voters' behavior—if and how they will vote.

Most classical theories of persuasion have focused on public forums of communication and mostly ignored the interpersonal contexts that encompass interviewing (Infante et al., 1997). Aristotle's *Rhetoric* and most of the discussion that followed helped teach the reader how to move audiences, rather than persuade someone in a one-on-one dynamic. For this reason, most modern theorists discuss contemporary theories when attempting to explain persuasion in the interpersonal dynamic in general, and in the interviewing context specifically.

One of the major differences between public and interpersonal contexts is that the interpersonal context is much more dynamic. When addressing a large audience a speaker must prepare his or her words and devise a plan of attack. Listeners, in contrast, do not operate in such a linear fashion and tend to wander in and out of the discussion. Their ideas flow in a "stream of consciousness." The public speaker must cope with this and attempt to control the audience's attention. The interviewer can exploit these tendencies and use a much more fluid, less linear approach to persuasion (Roloff, 1980). The following is a brief discussion of three theories of persuasion that have a high degree of applicability in the interpersonal and interviewing contexts.

Social Judgment Theory

Sherif, Sherif, and Nebergall (1965) focus on a receiver's psychological state of mind, specifically, the consumer's prior attitudes and their level of ego-involvement, i.e., the extent to which they are involved with the issue. The social judgment theory attempts to explain how people are moved, through persuasion, from one attitude to another. The social judgment theorist views attitudes as being bipolar; the subject's attitude can be placed along a positive-to-negative continuum.

Preparing to Buy

An understanding of the consumer's role in the sales interview puts the consumer on an even footing with the salesperson. The informed consumer is better prepared to make informed buying decisions, and less susceptible to being victimized by consumer fraud. Alsever (2004) offers eight tips for car buying that are applicable for anyone setting out to make a large purchase:

1. *Look online.* Whether buying a car, a computer, or any other large purchase, the Internet may have vendors who offer the best deal and also provide sites to do research to help you decide what features or brands you really want and what you can expect to pay for them.
2. *Buy on a full stomach.* Purchasing a car or other high-priced items may take all day. You should not let hunger drive you to make a bad deal.
3. *Buy on weekdays.* Weekends are busy times full of buyers. On a weekday, you will more likely get the salesperson's full attention. The salesperson also will be more motivated to make a deal on a "slow day."
4. *Get pre-approved financing.* Many salespeople distract you with what you can spend in a given month, rather than what you want to spend on the final deal. Many consumers wind up spending hundreds or thousands of dollars more than they intended by not paying attention to the final price.
5. *Don't negotiate until you are ready.* Be sure you want the object before you begin talking money. Many dealers hook a consumer with questions like, "Do you want to buy today?" to pressure a consumer to make a deal. You should begin to negotiate only when you are convinced that you want the item.
6. *Try and control the situation.* The salesperson will get up and leave throughout the negotiation. You should do the same. Take a lot of breaks; focus on issues that you want to talk about when you want to talk about them.
7. *Take a friend to help you control the situation.* Often it is easier for a friend to say, "What a rotten deal!" or "Let's go eat, I'm hungry, let's come back tomorrow." This may help you control the situation.
8. *Nothing is final until it is in writing.* The salesperson may tell you that he or she can do this or that or get you this or that; but it isn't true until it's in the contract.

Initial placement of the subject's attitude is determined by previous experience. Therefore, someone who is attempting to engage in persuasion must know the target's initial placement, so as to know how to move the subject to the new, desired position. Specifically, an interviewer may determine the subject's initial position through a series of questions.

Initial placement is not the only variable that the interviewer must understand. The subject's ego-involvement must also be determined. Ego-involvement is the degree to which the subject finds similar, yet differing, views to be reasonable. Highly ego-involved subjects have few positions, beyond their own, that they find to be reasonable. Low ego-involved subjects have many positions they consider to be reasonable. Sherif, Sherif, and Nebergall (1965) predict that persuasion likely will be successful when the interviewer tries to move a subject to positions already found to be reasonable. These positions reside in the subject's *latitude of acceptance*. Positions that the subject finds unreasonable fall into the *latitude of noncommitment* or *latitude of rejection*. Therefore, the persuader should learn how ego-involved the subject is, as well as the subject's initial belief.

The implications of this for persuasive interviewing are two-fold. First, a persuasive interviewer must learn the interviewee's initial positions and ego-involvement. This gives the persuasive interviewer a tremendous advantage over the public communicator. Whereas the public communicator is limited to engaging in research and ultimately guessing the subjects' positions, the interviewer may go further and directly ask subjects what their positions are.

The second implication is that persuasion is a long-term, continuous process, not a short-term, one-shot affair. The social judgment theory holds that people's attitudes are constantly in flux, and that they change slowly over time. The public speaker will likely have only one attempt, whereas an interviewer may have repeated exposures to a subject, gradually pulling the subject in the desired direction.

Cognitive Dissonance Theory

A second theory, which takes a larger view of related issues, is *cognitive dissonance theory*. The foundation of dissonance theories is that people are uncomfortable with inconsistencies and often attempt to resolve them (Festinger, 1957). If, for instance, one person is a Democrat, but discovers that a best friend has volunteered to work for a Republican candidate, this will cause the person to be in a state of dissonance. According to the theory, the person either will like the friend less or develop a positive opinion of the Republican candidate.

The persuasive interviewer can use this theory to identify what the interviewee already likes (or dislikes) to bolster his or her case. For instance, an interviewer hiring for a position may detect that the interviewee, although qualified, is reluctant about certain aspects of the job. If the interviewer can identify significant people in the interviewee's life who work in similar situations, then the interviewer can help the interviewee become more comfortable in accepting the position. Army recruiters, for instance, often ask potential recruits if they have friends or family (especially fathers) in the service. If they do, then the recruiter often uses this to help the recruits take on the hardships of military life ("Your best friend survived basic training just fine, didn't he?").

Elaboration Likelihood Theory

A third approach to persuasion, and one that incorporates elements of the others, is O'Keefe's (1990) *elaboration likelihood theory* (ELM). Like the social judgment theorist, the ELM theorist understands that people hold attitudes of various strengths and, like the dissonance theorist, understands that other factors influence people's decisions. According to ELM, some attitudes are central to a person's self-image, whereas others are not. When an attitude is important to a person, that person is likely to carefully weigh the strengths and weakness of the attitude, examine the evidence, and expose him or herself to messages regarding the attitude. For instance, college professors often read *Discover* or other popular science magazines, not to learn about their own field of study, but to keep up on the general world of science and research. They expose themselves to this because learning is important to them.

When an attitude is important to a subject, the interviewer must take a *direct route*. The subject is likely to be highly informed about the issue, and the persuader must take time to elaborate a well-documented and logical case. However, many people also hold attitudes that are not important to them. In this case, ELM suggests that the interviewer take an *indirect route*. This may include talking about how friends of the subject agree with the persuader's position. Celebrity endorsements are essentially an indirect route of persuasion. Obviously, the indirect route is easier than the direct route. Therefore, the persuader must learn how important the attitude in question is to the subject. In the interviewing context, the interviewer has the opportunity to ask the subject questions to gauge the subject's depth of knowledge on the issue and its importance to them.

Although there are many other theories of persuasion, and no single theory will encompass all aspects of the persuasive process, the three discussed here provide a good foundation for understanding the sales interview and other types of persuasive interviews.

The Sales Interview

Robert entered the dealer's showroom with mixed emotions. He wanted and needed to purchase a car, but he had questions about the process. Would the salesman treat him fairly? Would he get stuck with a "lemon" that would only cause him problems? Could he afford the type of car he wanted?

In Robert's case, his fears were unjustified. The car salesman answered his questions and provided him with important information. Robert left this sales interview with the car he wanted, at a price he could afford. Such positive encounters are the theoretical goal of any sales interview. When the customer is satisfied, both the customer and the salesperson will benefit.

Unfortunately, not all sales interviews end on such a positive note. Most people can cite examples in which an unethical salesperson took advantage of a customer who had insufficient knowledge about the product, resulting in the sale of a product that the customer did not need or the purchase of one that was more expensive than necessary.

Students of the communication process should not be surprised by the range of positive and negative encounters during the sales interview. The sales interview is, after all, a complex communication interaction that is affected by a variety of conflicting forces—some positive and some negative—that can influence the outcome. Consider the following examples.

1. *The sales interview is precisely that—an interview—but one in which the salesperson has a persuasive goal.* The sales interview may be the most frequent interview in which people participate. It is so frequent, and occurs in so many situations (a waiter taking an order for lunch, a student purchasing school supplies, etc.), that many people forget that it is an interview, and that both parties should be active participants. The customer frequently forgets this, but the successful salesperson rarely does.

2. *Most salespeople are better trained and better prepared for the sales interview than customers.* The sales position is, after all, the salesperson's career and means of earning a living. A salesperson's professional success depends on his or her expertise and skill. Good salespeople think about and use the techniques that make them successful every day, continually honing and sharpening their skills. The customer, conversely, may make purchases every day, but spend little time or effort on becoming better at the sales interview. This situation creates the potential for a major training gap between the two parties.

3. *In most sales situations, the customer makes the first approach to the salesperson, which places the customer in a position of need and gives the salesperson a potential advantage.* The person with the biggest need is generally at the biggest disadvantage in any bargaining situation. This is why telemarketing sales are so difficult; it is also why showroom sales are relatively easy. The woman who visits a furniture store probably needs furniture and wants to buy some. The salesperson that recognizes this need is in a position to make a sale.

4. *The salesperson is usually more knowledgeable about the product than the customer.* The salesperson is, after all, a professional who often has years of experience in dealing with the product in question. That knowledge is, in some ways, an advantage for the consumer in that the salesperson can use that knowledge to assist the consumer in making a wise purchase decision. Unfortunately, the salesperson may also use that knowledge gap to gain an unfair advantage in negotiations that may occur during the transaction.

Given such situations, the need for the average person to have a better understanding of the sales process in understandable. Most individuals will be involved in thousands of sales interviews during their lifetime—either as customers or as sales personnel. An understanding of the sales interview will provide an individual the tools to be more successful at either role.

Stages of the Sales Interview

Heller (1999) divides the sales interview into a five-stage process: (1) identification of the customer's objectives and needs, (2) development of a sales plan based on those objectives, (3) presentation of a proposal based on the customer's objectives, (4) negotiation for terms that meet both parties' goals, and (5) culmination of the deal.

The first stage is crucial for a successful sales interview. As Heller notes, the secret to successful sales is to "Ask customers what they want and give it to them again and again" (p. 9). The importance of this stage is such that the salesperson needs to "find out what the customer really wants as early as possible" (p. 7). Poor salespeople often make inaccurate assumptions about the needs and wants of their customers, resulting in the formulation of a sales plan that is doomed to failure. Even if the salesperson can accurately identify those needs, he or she may have trouble identifying the top priority for each customer. The easiest way for a salesperson to overcome this obstacle is simply to ask the customer what they need, a process that Rugg (1971–1972) describes as the "salesman as interviewer" (p. 625). The salesperson should use open-ended questions to elicit as much information as possible from the customer. The salesperson should talk with the customer and learn his or her wants and needs before making a sales pitch.

Assessing Your Sales Skills

Sales guru Robert Heller recommends that salespeople should regularly reevaluate their sales techniques using a multi-item self-assessment scale. Some of these self-assessment items are listed below. Each item is rated on a four-step scale: (1) never, (2) occasionally, (3) frequently, and (4) always. The items are as follows:

1. I make a sales plan before approaching customers.
2. I develop sales strategies and check activities against a master plan.
3. I make a point of learning new sales skills and techniques.
4. I use information technology to help organize myself and aid my selling.
5. I keep a record of how I spend my time in order to improve its use.
6. I identify the customer's needs so that I can vary my approach accordingly.
7. I prepare myself carefully before going into a sales meeting or interview.
8. I approach companies knowing exactly who to contact.
9. I use research to build my knowledge of the industry and its customers.
10. I keep meetings with customers friendly, brisk, and focused.
11. I take great care with my letter-writing and develop letter-writing skills to aid selling.
12. I put myself in the customer's shoes when preparing for negotiations.
13. I end sales presentations on a positive note, inviting a definite action.
14. I adapt my selling approach to match the way the customer reacts to me.
15. I tell the truth, even if the truth is not what I want the customer to hear.
16. I search for the key sales point that will persuade the customers to buy.
17. I endeavor to get the other party to name their price objectives first.
18. I stress value for money in negotiations, rather than price alone.
19. When I complete a sale, both sides are satisfied with the deal.
20. I try to anticipate any objections the customer may present to me.
21. I respond quickly to inquiries or complaints from any customer.
22. I get feedback to ensure that my customers are very satisfied with the purchase.

Source: Heller, Robert (1999). *Selling successfully*. New York: DK Publishing.

In the second step, the salesperson develops a plan. For major sales presentations, the salesperson will have time to develop a sales plan based on information obtained from the initial interview with the customer. In many retail situations, though, the sales person may have to skip step two and move directly into the third step: presentation of the sales proposal. This requires the salesperson to assess the needs of the customer and to match those needs with a product offered by the company.

A variety of outlines for making sales presentations have been proposed. Most are similar, because, as Toler (1994) has noted, there has been little change in basic sales techniques over the years. Heller's (1999) AIDCA model is typical of such a sales model. The AIDCA model divides the sales interview into fives steps: Attention, Interest, Desire, Conviction, and Action. Students of communication studies will recognize that these five steps are similar to the traditional motivated sequence (Attention, Need, Satisfaction, Visualization, Action) that is taught in basic courses on persuasive speaking.

In both cases, the concept is the same. To be successful, the salesperson must get the attention of the consumer ("May I help you?"), recognize the customer's need ("So you need a car that's fuel efficient"), offer a product that can handle that need ("Our Model X gets 38 miles to the gallon"), convince the customer that the product will sufficiently meet that need ("That makes it one of the most fuel-efficient cars on the market, and it costs less than its competitors"), and then close the deal with an action step ("We can set up a payment plan within your budget").

Salespeople use a number of methods to get customers' attention. Pollock (2003) recommends that salespeople should not use the traditional technique of introducing themselves to get a customer's attention. Asking a question is an effective method—as long as the question is not trite or banal ("How do you plan to use this car?")—because it immediately gets the customer involved in the conversation. Another approach—the startling statement—is effective as long as the statement is relevant to the product and situation. Another approach—giving a gift—is used widely by sales personnel, who frequently provide their potential clients with pens, calendars, letter openers, and a variety of other handy, but inexpensive, items.

The second step is called the interest stage. The goal here is for the salesperson to recognize the customer's need, thus gaining their willingness to listen to the rest of the sales presentation. The key is addressing the issue in terms of what the customer needs, not what the salesperson wants to sell.

The third step is the desire stage. At this point, the salesperson explains how the product or service can fulfill the need identified previously. The sale can be won or lost at this stage; if the customer does not believe that the product does what they need it to do, he will reject the proposal.

In today's society, the conviction stage often means offering assurances about post-sales service. Brechbüühl (2004) notes that the modern, time-conscious consumer is turning to retailers that offer complete solutions to their needs (i.e., the product, its installation, and service). It also involves reducing the inherent uncertainty with which the customer approaches the sales interview (Eriksson & Sharma, 2003). Again, though, the ability to assess the customer's level of uncertainty will depend on the information gathered in the first stage of the interview.

The action step may be quick ("I can ring that up for you now") or time consuming ("Let's work out a financing plan"). In the latter case, some form of negotiation may be necessary. Success at this stage often depends on the attitude of the seller. Mentally, it means approaching customers as "allies rather than opponents" (Heller, 1999, p. 16). If that approach is taken, though, the sales interview can become a true "win-win" situation that "consists of creating a satisfied customer [and] earning satisfactory profits for the company" (Heller, 1999, p. 6).

Situational Sales Interviews

Most sales interviews occur in retail situations, with a consumer entering a store with the intention to shop. The cost of the item to be purchased may vary, and the sales interview becomes considerably more complex as the price of the product increases. Still, many of the basic concepts of interviewing apply regardless of the price of the item. After all, all consumers expect the salesperson to provide information that will help them with their decision.

However, in some sales situations, the nature of the salesperson–consumer relationship is remarkably different. The two most noticeable variations are those of (1) the traveling salesperson and (2) the telemarketer.

Traveling Salespeople

Some readers may be familiar with *The First Traveling Saleslady*, a 1956 film starring Ginger Rogers as an early twentieth-century corset saleswoman who wants to sell barbed wire out West after all the men who had held the job had been either lynched or run out of town. The comedy poked fun at some of the stereotypes associated with traveling salespeople. The negative aspects of that image were apparent in another classic film, *Paper Moon* (1973), which featured Ryan O'Neal as a door-to-door, con-artist, Bible salesman.

In modern society, though, traveling salespeople have evolved into "road warriors" who carry their wares in briefcases that can fit neatly into the overhead compartments of commercial airplanes or who carry sophisticated laptop computers as they drive from city to town to update the inventories of their retail customers. Still, one stereotype from those old movies seems correct: The successful traveling salesperson has to be a self-motivated individual who can successfully work away from the office environment.

Borg and Kristensen (1999) note that traveling salespeople have an unusual working environment. They often spend long periods of time away from their firm, may have a low level of social contact with their colleagues, and often face high work demands that may create conflicts with normal family life. Several factors can make the job harder, creating stress that can lead to mental health problems. Those factors, as identified by Borg and Kristensen, include the number of working hours per week, the number of customers per week, night work, and a high level of perceived job demands.

Conversely, the sales interview itself has a positive impact on the salesperson's mental outlook. Specifically, the number of hours spent with customers per week has been positively associated with mental health. Further, some other factors—time away from the office, nights away from home, and a lack of support from colleagues and superiors—had no impact on the salesperson's mental outlook. Thus, according to Borg and Kristensen, the major sources of stress for a traveling salesperson are long hours, too many customers, working on weekends, and high job demands, whereas the sales interview itself is a positive experience for the salesperson.

Schweingruber and Berns (2003), in a case study of a door-to-door sales company, note the importance of incentives by the company for impression management i.e., maintaining a positive image for the salesperson as a representative of the company. The component was crucial, because self-confidence and a positive self-image play a central role in the door-to-door sales interview. Further, the success of salespeople in this environment is often related to (1) the relationship between the salesperson and his or her manager and (2) how the salesperson uses "time between doors" to make sense of the situation and thus motivate themselves to continue.

The salesperson–customer relationship—is an important factor in achieving a successful sale. Hawes and Baker (1993) note that exchange relationships that benefit both the salesperson and the customer are an essential element of the sales interaction, but that there is often a gap between the perceptions of the buyer and seller regarding the nature of that relationship. This gap can be bridged, however, if the seller integrates their selling practices with a solid program of customer service (Alessandra & Wexler, 1985).

Telemarketing Interviews

Perhaps the sales interview that carries the strongest negative image is that of the telemarketer. Many people view them as a nuisance, with their incessant calls interrupting dinner or family TV time. Even worse, the format has been abused by unscrupulous individuals who have used the telemarketing format to defraud people—particularly the elderly—of millions of dollars (Reiboldt & Vogel, 2001). These two negative features have led to the implementation of a national "Do Not Call" list, enactment of the Telephone Consumer Protection Act (Miller & Biggerstaff, 2000), and the development of the National Telemarketing Victim Call Center (NTVCC) to combat telemarketing fraud (Aziz & Bolick, 2000).

Despite such efforts, telemarketing fraud is still a problem, although not as widespread as often believed. Reiboldt and Vogel (2001), for example, studied a gated, middle-class community that had been reported as a highly targeted area by telemarketing scammers, but found only 25 victims. Although the researchers were surprised by the relatively small number of victims (less than 7 percent of their sample), those numbers were still higher than the minimum level (5 percent) that Bly (1997) argues makes a telemarketing campaign financially successful. Further, it represents a relatively large number of fraud victims and a high profit margin for the criminals behind the scams. Victims are typically senior citizens, perhaps because they more frequently answer their phones. But, other than that, Reibolt and Vogel were unable to establish a consistent profile of the victims. Only one variable—telephone persuadability. (i.e., believing what a salesperson tells you over the phone is true)—was found to be related to victimization. Horvitz and Pratkanis (2002) examined one technique often used by unscrupulous telemarketers—the one-in-five prize tactic. In this approach, the telemarketer calls and tells the respondent that they have won one of five possible prizes in a random drawing, but they need to pay a processing fee to claim the prize. Four of the five prizes will be high-value items, while the fifth will have relatively little value. If the person agrees to pay the fee, he is sent the low-value item. Horvitz and Pratkanis (2002) found that the tactic was effective in misleading many people because it effectively used phantom fixation and other psychological technique as an underlying basis for the tactic.

Despite the negative image associated with telemarketing, the technique, when used appropriately, still has an important and viable role in the sales interview. Telemarketing has been a major growth industry since the 1980s (Cobbin, Kozar, & Michaele, 1989). The rise in its use has corresponded with an appreciation for telemarketing as a cost-effective and time-saving alternative over most other forms of sales and marketing (Bendremer, 2003). Bly (1997) calls telemarketing ". . . a sales tool that combines the economy of mass promotion and the personalized approach of one-on-one, face-to-face selling" (p. 4). Even if it is not the primary sales medium, Heller (1999) notes that the telephone should be viewed as a valuable medium for any career in sales, particularly in setting up appointments for a full sales interview. Jolson (1986) agrees, arguing that the telephone is an effective application of "the foot-in-the-door technique" (p. 39). The more traditional approach—direct selling over the telephone with payment via credit cards—is a direct result of the explosion in modern information and communication technologies (Cobbin, Kozar, & Michaele, 1989). As the use of telemarketing has grown, businesses that rely on telemarketing have become more sophisticated in their training techniques, often employing modern theories of psychology (such as social learning theory) as a means of motivating their workers (Kalechstein & Nowicki, 1994), implementing sales contests to maintain motivation (Worman, 1992), and analyzing worker productivity in terms of motivational factors (Fellows & Mawhinney, 1997).

Because of the negative image often associated with telemarketing, Bly (1997) argues that telemarketers should make a conscious effort to avoid high-pressure sales. Thus, he wrote, "The secret to successful telephone selling: Do not try to push junk on people who don't want it or need it. Instead call the right people with the right offer—something that solves a problem they have, fills a need, or delivers a result or benefit they want" (p. 6).

Cold Calling.   The most infamous form of telemarketing is *cold calling*; that is, those instances in which the telemarketer makes a call to a random telephone number with no advance information regarding the likelihood that the consumer is a potential customer (Greene, 1999; Schiffman, 2003). Greene (1999) compares cold calling with a root canal. The negative image associated with the task is so strong that it has engendered its own research topic—*call reluctance*—which is the tendency to resist making a sales contact with a potential customer. Some authorities believe that call reluctance is tied to a psychological fear of self-promotion, which is a byproduct of individual modesty (Dudley, Goodson, & Weissenburger, 1993).

However, cold-calling interviews do have their place in the sales world. Goldner (1995) considers cold calling to be an essential means of prospecting for potential clients. Although it has dubious value when used alone, cold calling can be an efficient and effective means of trimming a large list of potential sales leads into a small list of potential customers.

Negotiation

Once the buyer and seller have identified a product to be purchased, many sales situations move into a stage in which the parties strive to reach a settlement regarding the price and terms of the agreement. The interactions involved in developing this settlement are called *negotiation*. Cohen (1980) defines *negotiation* as "the use of information and power to affect behavior within a 'web of tension' " (p. 16). Hindle (1998) defines it as "an attempt by two people to achieve a mutually acceptable solution," adding that the process is "based on attempting to reconcile what constitutes a good result for you with what constitutes a good result for the other party" (p. 6). Under either definition, negotiation is an integral part of modern society, but one that is often overlooked or ignored. The latter seems to be the more common choice, because many people simply do not like to negotiate. "Haggling," as some people call it, has a negative connotation to many people—to so many, in fact, that many retail businesses now advertise "no haggle" prices.

Why the negative outlook on such an important communication process? One reason is that negotiation is often presented from a win-lose perspective that is full of hidden traps for the unwary (Fuller, 1991). To engage in negotiation is to attempt to get the better of another person. Even if the negotiator is successful, his or her gain has come at the expense of somebody else. As a result, winning a negotiation session can be as painful for the winner as for the loser, inducing guilt that the winner would rather not experience. Others view negotiation as a series of compromises in which nobody wins. One person makes an offer, the other person counteroffers. This process is repeated until some mid-level figure or compromise is reached—one that is acceptable to both, but ideal for neither. Both parties lose a little.

However, not everyone has such a negative opinion of negotiation. Some thrive on it, motivated by its competitive nature. Such people are valuable assets to most organizations; they can negotiate bargains and deals that are beneficial to both themselves and their company. Hindle (1998) believes a positive attitude is essential to successful negotiations and advises students to "Start by visualizing possible gains, not losses" (p. 7). No wonder, then, that companies and corporations often hunt for people who are "natural" negotiators.

They never find them. Negotiation is a skill, not a talent. Further, success in negotiation is more often a by-product of preparation than of verbal jousting ability. In other words, anyone willing to work at the art of negotiation can be successful at it.

Planning for Negotiation

Athletic coaches have an adage to emphasize the value of practice: "Failing to prepare is preparing for failure." The same axiom applies to negotiation. Successful negotiators do not wait for the face-to-face encounter to begin working. More often than not, success can be linked to the advanced preparation of the participants. Those who are better prepared have the edge.

Researching the Issue.   Cohen (1980) identified three crucial variables to negotiation: information, time, and power. A participant is at a negotiation disadvantage if the other person (1) knows more about the participants and the issue (information), (2) the other side isn't under the same deadline (time), and/or (3) the other side has more authority (power). All three of these factors can be analyzed in advance of the negotiation, but the starting point is *information*. Successful negotiation requires information. When purchasing a car, for example, the salesperson has more information. The salesperson is more likely to know the wholesale price of the car, the finance options available, and the lowest price at which the dealer can make a reasonable profit. The potential buyer armed with similar information in advance, gathered through prenegotiation research, is in a better position to negotiate for a bargain. In other words, successful negotiation requires that both parties do their homework. In a financial transaction, this means knowing an item's fair market value and how much bargaining room the other person has. In other forms of negotiation, the same rule applies—one should learn as much as possible about the issue and the other party's position on it.

Analyzing the Situation.   Three attributes—power, time, and precedents—are the situational components of negotiation. An understanding of these factors provides the person

The 12 Commandments of Negotiation

Preparations for a negotiation ultimately culminates in a face-to-face exchange. Once that exchange begins, negotiation skills depend largely on the individual's ability to use the material he or she has prepared ahead of time and to make adjustments in the presentation based on what the other person says. With this in mind, the following tips can be useful in negotiations.

1. *Don't get down to business immediately.* The development of the relationship is critical, so do not immediately move into the issues at hand. Spend some time in casual talk with the other person, preferably getting them to talk about themselves. This should be relatively easy to do if the other person is someone within your organization; it takes a little more preparation for an outsider. Either way, such a casual start can provide a natural segue into a discussion of what you are trying to achieve.

2. *Resist making the first offer.* Let the other person make the first move. The first offer is new information, and new information always benefits the recipient. When making a counteroffer, Acuff (1997) recommends the tried-and-true method of asking for more than you want, but always keep it reasonable. Your counteroffer shapes the other side's perceptions, defining the latitude of the negotiation for them. Therefore, the counteroffer should be reasonable; if it is not, negotiations will break down.

3. *If money is involved, don't make opening offers in round numbers.* As McCormack (1988) notes, "Round numbers beg to be negotiated. Odd numbers sound firmer."

4. *Build allies.* As Cohen (1980) notes, "No individual is an isolated entity. Everyone that you deal with is being reinforced by those around them" (p. 178). If you can gain the commitment of those around the party, it provides incentive for them to collaborate with you.

5. *Listen more than you talk.* Listening may be the toughest part of negotiation, but successful negotiation is based less on your arguments than on your response to the other person's arguments. That requires careful monitoring of what the other party says. Encourage them to talk about their position by asking questions about their view of the issue. The more you learn about their viewpoint, the easier it will be to approach the negotiation from their perspective. This will make it easier to seek a solution that is mutually beneficial. If you understand their problem, you can craft a creative solution. At the very least, you can say, "I understand your problem. I don't know what to do, but let me think about it."

6. *Don't give away unnecessary information.* A general rule is to seek more information than you give, and this is particularly true in consumer negotiations. Still, novice negotiators often reveal more than is necessary, putting themselves at a disadvantage. Saying something positive about the product, for example, gives a salesman a slight edge in the exchange.

7. *Piggyback on their ideas.* If you listen carefully, well enough to understand the other party's position, you will find that you share key ideas. Identify those and show how your idea can be used in conjunction with theirs.

8. *Don't feel pressured to speak.* Silence is often interpreted as dissatisfaction with the offer. By hesitating or voicing a need to consult with others, you put more pressure on the other person to offer more. Even in consumer negotiations, silence accompanied by a small flinch can gener-

Continued

ate a better offer. Other times, merely the willingness to walk away from the negotiation is sufficient to spark another offer.

9. *Be willing to take moderate risks.* Cohen (1980) notes that "You must be willing to take
risks while negotiating . . . If you don't take calculated chances, the other side will manipulate
you" (p. 60). That axiom applies more to consumer negotiations than to organizational exchanges,
but it still has some applicability.

10. *Don't bluff.* Don't take any risks that require you to run a bluff. Professional negotiations
are not poker games in which the pot goes to the winner. Attempts to induce compliance by making implied threats, particularly if you have no intention of carrying out the threat, are ineffective
and damage your credibility. Before you make any threats or arguments, be sure you are willing
to actually go through with them if the negotiation breaks down. If you do not, your credibility in
future negotiations is ruined.

11. *Don't retaliate.* At least not immediately. Fisher and Ury (1983) call this technique "negotiation jujitsu" (pp. 108–109). If the other person attacks you, do not react with a counterattack.
Instead, look behind the problem to identify the reason for the attack. You can often find a need
that you can satisfy, getting some concessions on your own behalf in return. The "don't retaliate"
rule is not a hard and fast one, particularly if the other participant insists on confrontation tactics.
When confrontation does occur, a "tit-for-tat" response can be a show of strength that the other
person will respect, but it must be followed by an offer that will let him return to productive negotiations without losing face.

12. *Let them save face.* And that brings us to the last major point. Always give the other party
the opportunity to save face. Cohen (1980) says that "Even when you are right, shun all opportunities to humiliate people—at least in public" (p. 193). A person's *face* is their public image—how
they want others to see them—and any attacks on that can create problems. Included in this admo-
nition is the advice never to ask for too much. If the disparity between the two positions is too
great, offer a "bonus" item to the other person. By sweetening the deal, the other party can com-
ply with your request without losing face. If you can do something to positively affect other
party's public face, that is even better. Martin Luther King, Jr. for example, used to emphasize the
need to offer opponents a face-saving way to join the Civil Rights Movement.

---

involved in a negotiation with an understanding of the advantages and disadvantages he or
she faces. Sometimes, realization of a weakness provides the cue for overcoming it.

Power discrepancies are critical. The person with the most power has an edge in any
negotiation. Within an organization, the most common source of power is legitimate
power—perceived authority that is not questioned. Low- or mid-level employees are at a
disadvantage when dealing with a supervisor. The high-power person is in a position to
block negotiation efforts, sometimes with little justification. The low-power person can do
little to alter an outcome once a decision is made. However, power discrepancies can be
dealt with by lining up allies in advance of negotiation. Numerical support can compensate for differences in power, particularly if one of the allies is of equal or higher rank than
the other party. Power even comes into play in consumer negotiations; for example,

people can use their "clout" to get a discount if they know someone who works at the retail establishment.

Time constraints also affect negotiations. The party under the shortest deadline is at a disadvantage. The person who is under no time constraints can extend the negotiations over a longer time period, putting more pressure on the party facing a deadline to concede on some points of the issue. The effect of time constraints is apparent even in consumer negotiations; customers often get better deals near the end of the month if a salesperson is approaching a deadline for his or her monthly quota. In terms of advance preparation, the parties should each try to extend their deadlines; the party with the later deadline is in a better negotiating position. As Hindle (1998) notes, "If you agree in haste, you may repent at leisure" (p. 11).

Precedents are also a factor. Within the organization, some situations typically are not open to negotiations. Others offer only limited options. And some have normative behaviors that limit the strategies that can be used. Understanding these organizational precedents is critical, because violation of any one of them can doom the success of the negotiations.

Analyzing the Opposition.   "Successful negotiation lies in finding out what the other side really wants and showing them a way to get it, while you get what you want" (Cohen, p. 161). Seeking such common interests requires that advance preparation include finding out as much as possible about the other party. Successful negotiations require rapport and trust with the other party. This requires an understanding of the other party's needs and concerns.

Typically, differences of opinion on an issue stem from one of three areas: (1) differences in information, (2) differences in experiences, or (3) differences in roles. The first component, information, can be handled with adequate research. Without adequate research, each participant will enter the negotiation with a different base of information. Advanced research can close that information gap, and having the same information as the other party enables one to better understand their counterpart's position. Differences in experiences are harder to decipher, particularly if the parties do not know each other well, but such factors can play a vital role. Experiences color a person's outlook on their own position and that of others, and each participant sees the negotiation through that biased view. Rather than seeing the issue objectively, each party views it from his or her own experience. A person who has had a negative experience with a previous plan is less likely to accept a similar plan again, even if it is the logical choice.

Within organizations, divergent views revolve around differences in organizational roles. An administrator, whose primary role is to obtain resources for her department, is likely to always be in a constant state of negotiation with a supervisor who is concerned with controlling costs. An understanding of these role discrepancies can make negotiations easier. One way to counter this problem is through role playing. Having a co-worker act out the role of the other participant can lead to an increased understanding of the other party's position and how he or she came to hold that position. Sometimes the role-playing process gets beyond the organizational role, perhaps providing insight into the reasons for the opposition from the other party.

The Game Plan

After completing the preparation stage, the person engaging in negotiation should have enough information to develop an overall game plan. The game plan should include (1) arguments supported by information, (2) trade-offs to be offered, and (3) trust-building tactics.

A party's arguments will be based on the research gathered, with some of the supporting information prepared for use in the negotiation and some withheld for strategic purposes. Arguments should be established based on the needs of the other person. This may sound like a simple idea, but it is rarely followed. Most novice negotiators develop their arguments from their own perspective and needs. It is more effective for the negotiator to explain how compliance benefits the other party.

Information often is more useful if it is in some tangible format—a chart, list, graph, or other format. Some people are more impressed by information that can be seen. For example, even if a supervisor agrees with an employee's negotiation requests, that person may lack the power to implement the action. A tangible piece of information provides the supervisor with supporting material so that information and arguments can be passed up the chain of the organization.

As mentioned earlier, a party in a negotiation should withhold some information. Such information may include trade-offs that one would be willing to offer to the other side. Before entering into a negotiation, one should identify goals and divide them into three areas: (1) essential, (2) desired, and (3) trade-offs. Essential goals are those that must be obtained from the negotiation. If these are not met, the negotiation has not been useful, and nothing is gained by reaching an agreement with the other party. Essential goals are the last line of defense, the point at which the person will not retreat or concede on any other issue. Desired goals are those that have a high priority, but are not essential. A party would like to meet those goals, but could conclude the negotiation without meeting them. Desired goals are the second wall of defense; these goals are held as long as possible. They are sacrificed only if they contribute to the attainment of all essential goals. Trade-offs are items that would be nice to win, but have a low priority. These are the first wall of defense, the first things that can be given up and offered to the other party in exchange for obtaining essential and desired items. Trade-offs should be withheld until the negotiation reaches a critical juncture; surrendering something too soon lessens one's power in the negotiations.

It is important for the person to build trust with the other party in the negotiation. The stereotypical image of a negotiator is someone who tries to take advantage of the other party, getting as much as possible for themselves at the expense of the other person. However, such results-oriented negotiation can occur only when the negotiation is a one-time event, and those are relatively rare occurrences. Most negotiations, particularly those within an organization, involve ongoing relationships. A victory occurs when both sides are satisfied with the results. Each party should seek to build trust, taking only what he or she needs without making the other party look bad.

Cohen (1980) calls this attitude the "lubricant demeanor" (p. 155) and notes that it can be engendered by trying to see the problem from the other's perspective. It also helps to trust the other person. Hindle (1998) recommends that the participant maintain a flexible attitude by remembering that flexibility during negotiations "is a sign of strength, not weakness" (Hindle, 1998, p. 11). Generally, the more trust a person places in the other party, the more the other party will justify that trust. The goal is a trusting relationship in which each party has a firm belief in the honesty and reliability of the other. Trusting relationships can quickly be transformed into collaborative relationships.

An Interview with Maria Smith

Maria Smith was a telemarketing account representative with BellSouth for fours years. During that time she won many sales awards, including Top Telemarketing Sales Representative and the President's Club Award, and was consistently rated as one of the top BellSouth salespeople. She worked mostly with small business clients.

Q. How important is interviewing to the sales process?

A. Extremely important. The entire sales process begins with understanding your client and their needs, you can't sell anything if you don't know who your buyer is.

Q. What kinds of things do you hope to learn when you interview a prospective client?

A. What his needs are now, and where he hopes to be in one to ten years. You have to know their growth potential. You really have to know what their budget is, you have to know what they can afford to spend. You can't bankrupt your client.

Q. How do you go about learning that?

A. I ask him to tell me about his business. If the information I need to put a proposal together is not offered, I'll then ask specifically.

Q. So you basically ask the client how to write your business proposal?

A. Right, people will buy from you if they feel you are meeting their needs. Only they can tell you what those are.

Q. How much of the initial interview is planned in advance?

A. Only those first three questions, the rest I play by ear depending on what he's told me. You have to listen carefully; too much preplanning will turn your client off.

Q. I know I hate it when some salesperson is reading from a script.

A. Right, people hate it when they feel you are just reading from a preplanned spiel. The client wants to know you are listening to them.

Q. What do you need to know about a client before the first meeting?

A. I take incoming calls so I usually don't know anything before the first meeting. That's why the initial interview/conversation is so critical. I may only get that one chance.

Q. How important is the first impression that you make?

A. Very important. It's like what they tell you about a job interview, the first few minutes are critical.

Q. In what way?

A. If the customer doesn't think I know my products and services and that I'm going to be there to take care of future needs and/or problems, I'm dead in the water.

Continued

Q. How much of sales is feeling and how much is facts?

A. About fifty-fifty. You've got to know your stuff, but also have a feel for what they're really telling you.

Q. Is the salesperson selling the product or themselves?

A. A little of both, I'd never sell a product I don't believe in.

Q. How do you sell yourself?

A. By presenting a professional image, by being courteous, by being helpful.

Q. What advice would you give someone fresh out of school who wanted to go into sales?

A. Know what you're willing to do to make a sale. If you want to be able to sleep at night, you have to know that you'll only sell what the customer needs (with a little of what they want on top of it) and can afford. You don't want to put him out of business with his purchase!

Q. Is there anything else you'd like to add?

A. Be true to yourself, know your customer, have fun with it!

Summary

Many interviews fall within the classification of persuasive interview, with various forms of the sales interview being the most prevalent.

The sales approach in the persuasive interview usually is based on one or more theories of persuasion, such as the social judgment theory, the cognitive dissonance theory, or the elaboration likelihood theory. Social judgment theory focuses on the receiver's previously held attitudes and ego-involvement with the issue. Cognitive dissonance theory is based on the assumption that individuals feel uncomfortable when confronted with attitudinal inconsistencies and often attempt to resolve that feeling of dissonance through attitude or behavioral change. Elaboration likelihood theory is based on the extent to which attitudes are central to an individual's self image.

Sales interviews are one-on-one interactions that intentionally are aimed at changing another's beliefs, attitudes, or behavior. The salesperson often has an advantage in such interviews, because they usually are more knowledgeable about the product or service than the customer, and they usually have more experience in these types of interactions. The sales interview usually encompasses a five-stage process: (1) identification of the customer's objectives and needs, (2) development of a sales plan based on those objectives, (3) presentation of a proposal, (4) negotiation for terms, and (5) culmination of the deal.

Most sales interviews occur in retail situations, with a consumer entering a store with the intention to shop. However, in some sales situations, the nature of the salesperson–consumer relationship is remarkably different. The two most noticeable variations are those of (1) the traveling salesman and (2) the telemarketer.

Negotiation skills are becoming increasingly important in today's organizational world. The effective negotiator is the person who plans for negotiation by (1) gathering information and (2) considering the needs and desires of the other person. Ideally the goal of most negotiation sessions should be a collaborative solution, one that meets the needs and desires of both parties.

FOR FURTHER DISCUSSION

1. Consider the three theories of persuasion discussed at the beginning of this chapter. What features of these three theories are similar to each other? How can each of these relate to a specific retail sales situation?

2. John is planning to buy a new car. Jill is a salesperson for a local car dealer. What information should Jill seek from John before suggesting an automobile for him to consider?

3. What ethical elements should be considered when discussing persuasive interviews and negotiation? To what extent should such interactions be collaborative efforts or competitive games?

CHAPTER

6

Performance Appraisal and Exit Interviews

Carol had just completed her first year at a new job. By most standards, it had been a positive first year. Her productivity had been high, her colleagues liked her, and she had won a major industry award (an unusual achievement for a new employee). Then she received a notice that it was time for her annual performance review. She was to meet with her supervisor and his assistant to discuss her performance for the year and her goals for the following year. She found the idea of having to defend her work in front of more experienced and higher-ranked employees to be somewhat intimidating. As the interview approached, she expressed her fears to fellow employees, but that did little to relieve her anxiety. Eventually, she entered the room, sat down before the two reviewers, and the interview began. Thirty minutes later, she left smiling, happy to learn that both reviewers were elated with her work during the year. It was, she later noted, "Not as bad as I was expecting."

Maybe. But she did not talk about it as a positive experience either. Further, employees with a less admirable work record may leave a similar meeting with a list of criticisms that may be a major blow to their egos. Such possibilities reflect growing concerns among employees with the role of performance appraisal interviews. Still, during a time when an increasing number of organizations are requiring individual assessments and documentation of employment decisions, such interviews are likely to remain a staple in organizational procedures. Consequently, most employees likely will find themselves involved in numerous appraisal interviews—far more, in fact, than the number of employment interviews in which they are likely to engage. Once hired, they will have relatively few additional employment interviews. Performance appraisal interviews, however, may occur as frequently as once a year. Understanding the purpose and functions of such interviews is thus a necessary skill for advancement within many organizations.

Purposes of Appraisal Interviews

Performance appraisals serve many purposes in modern organizations (Arvey & Murphy, 1998). Most often, performance appraisals serve as an attempt to integrate human resource activities into organizational policies (Fletcher, 2001). From that perspective, the performance appraisal is perhaps the single most important factor in helping an organization reach its goals. Goals that are formulated at the top of an organization often are lost in translation as they get filtered down to line personnel. Most employees of large organizations have seen more than one change in upper management that has had little or no effect on their day-to-day organizational lives, in spite of broad statements of change made by upper management. If upper management truly wants to initiate change within an organization, it must clearly communicate those changes and, more importantly, evaluate its employees according to organizational goals. At the heart of the superior–subordinate relationship is the performance appraisal. Almost every decision that a manager makes regarding his or her subordinates should be grounded in a reliable and valid performance appraisal.

Promotions.   Promotion decisions should be rooted in a complete performance appraisal. The manager in charge of promotions must not only understand who the outstanding performers are and who is worthy of promotion, but also who is best suited for the new position. Just because someone performs well in one job does not necessarily mean he or she will do well in the next one. An effective manager understands each employee's strengths and weaknesses, not just the employee's productivity.

Separations.   Firings and layoff are important issues in most organizations. Not only is turnover an economically and emotionally costly event, it now carries legal and social ramifications for organizations. Lawsuits, and the threat of lawsuits, are terrifying prospects for most organizations, and terminations must be handled delicately and correctly.

Pay.   Most salary decisions should be based on some form of performance evaluation. Pay decisions include raises and bonuses. Some organizations use a *merit model* and make each decision on a case-by-case evaluation. In these organizations, careful records and clear communication is necessary for the managers who make these decisions. Other organizations use an *equity model* to make these decisions. In these organizations, individual performance is not as much an issue as unit productivity (Bain, 2001). In such organizations, specific units are designated for a given raise or bonus, often expressed in terms of a percentage of salary.

Feedback.   On a day-to-day basis, employees need to understand how they are viewed by their employers. Mistakes need to be pointed out, and exemplary behavior needs to be recognized in a timely fashion. These assessments often are done by unit managers and supervisors and are usually informal in nature. How that feedback is handled can have a major impact on the organization and its employees. Positive feedback can motivate employees to accomplish more or may make them too self-satisfied with past accomplishments. Negative feedback may motivate them to try harder or may trigger a violent outburst, causing them to physically harm other workers (Geddes & Baron, 1997). Such potential consequences of feedback from appraisal interviews demonstrate how important it is to handle these encounters with thoughtful preparation.

Organizational Development.   Training and development are critical issues in organizations. With rapidly changing technologies and business environments, it is critical for organizations to provide ongoing, up-to-date training for employees. Assessments are a first critical step in providing this training, enabling organizations to identify where resources are best used.

Coping with an Unfair Appraisal

Knippin and Green (1995) offer the following tips for coping with a performance appraisal that you feel was unfair, inaccurate, or biased:

1. **Take some time**. Don't respond immediately; wait a few days. This allows time to prepare a case and present it in a calm manner. You are more likely to be listened to by approaching a superior in a calm, nonconfrontational manner.
2. **Make a list of how you feel you should have been appraised in writing**. Don't just barge in claiming that you are unhappy. Making a list shows that you have a case; it also helps keep the conversation focused on issues of assessment and not on the personalities involved. Having a written list makes you look more serious and will help you remember what you want to talk about.
3. **Make an appointment with your boss**. Don't just barge in on your boss. A surprise visit will likely make your supervisor defensive and unwilling to listen to you. Setting a time aside will give you the time and psychological space needed to fully discuss the issues.
4. **Focus on the future as much as possible**. While you do want to talk about what you have done, it is important to keep in mind what you will do in the future. Remember that a fair appraisal makes you a better employee. Reminding your boss that you are mostly concerned with making sure your performance is meeting, and possibly exceeding, expectations makes you look like a serious person who deserves to be listened to. Whining about past injustices will likely get you nowhere.
5. **Phrase your concerns in terms of the boss's concerns**. It is obvious why you would like a better evaluation, but you need to show how giving you a better assessment will help your boss achieve his or her goals.
6. **Summarize everything; paraphrase everything**. Make sure there is explicit understanding on both sides. Review your key terms so that both participants agree on the specifics of what has been said.
7. **Thank your boss for listening to you**. Reminding your supervisor that you appreciate being listened to can do nothing but help your case.
8. **Follow up**. Keep a record of any agreements made between you and your boss. Let your boss know when you have kept up your end of the bargain.

Levels of Assessment

Performance is not always an easy thing to assess. The decisions made from these assessments are therefore very difficult. Sometimes individual performance is a minor factor in making certain decisions. Organizations often divide evaluations into various levels (Szilagyi and Wallace, 1990):

- *Organizational outcomes* are evaluated to determine the overall health of the organization. Layoff and bonus decisions are often made at this level.

■ *Divisional outcomes* are evaluated to determine the efficiency of specific units. Beyond productivity, safety, morale, and turnover are measured. Organizational development decisions often are made at this level.

■ *Individual outcomes* are important measures for managers. Although individual productivity is not the only measure of importance to organizations, it is still the primary unit of analysis when it comes to making decisions about a given employee.

■ *Individual behaviors* often are evaluated by organizations to compare employees against a given ideal. Often called *human engineering*, organizations keep track of a variety of behavioral measures (steps taken, hours per task, etc.) and evaluate employees not so much on output, but on day-to-day or task-to-task behaviors. The most popular method of behavioral assessment is the *Behaviorally Anchored Ratings Scales (BARS)*, which will be discussed later in this chapter.

■ *Individual traits* are evaluated by managers in the assessment process. Many organizations are shying away from such evaluations (at least on the formal level), because they are viewed as being subjective on the part of managers and not very instructive to employees. A manager may feel that a given employee's attitude is substandard, but it often is difficult for the employee to know what to do when confronted with the phrase "You have a bad attitude." Most organizations prefer a behavior assessment that shows how the bad attitude is manifested. For example, "You never stay late when we have a deadline to meet" (Dunnette, 1966; Dalton and Standholtz, 1990).

Legal Issues

As with hiring, the manager who engages in performance appraisals and assessments must be acutely aware of the day-to-day legal concerns that govern most workplaces. Some managers may feel that once an employee is hired that the legal restrictions may weaken, but this is not the case. It is arguable, in fact, that there are more legal concerns once someone is hired. Two issues need to be firmly in a manager's mind at all times: discrimination and harassment (Hickson and Stacks, 1998).

Discrimination

Discrimination is not just a hiring issue. Antidiscrimination laws are aimed at a wide variety of employment issues. These include firing, promotion, compensation, working conditions, and all other terms of employment. Because most of these decisions are, to some extent, based on performance appraisal and review, it is incumbent on the manager to be systematic and thorough when engaging in these reviews. The manager *must* be able to demonstrate that an assessment is work related and not based on the employee's race, gender, national origin, physical handicap, or age.

Harassment

In contrast, harassment is a verbal or physical act that creates an uncomfortable environment for an employee based on sexual, racial, or other equal-opportunity issues. On its

What Is Discrimination?

Many people think that discrimination is limited to issues of race or gender, but a wide variety of issues are covered under Title VII and other antidiscrimination laws. According to the U.S. Equal Opportunity Commission (2003), it is illegal to discriminate in any aspect of employment, including:

1. Hiring and firing
2. Compensation, assignment, or classification of employees
3. Transfers, promotions, layoffs, or recalls
4. Job advertisements
5. Recruiting
6. Testing
7. Use of company facilities
8. Training and apprenticeship programs
9. Fringe benefits
10. Pay, retirement plans, and disability leave
11. Other terms and conditions of employment.

Discriminatory practices under these laws also include:

1. Harassment on the basis of race, color, religion, sex, national origin, disability, or age
2. Retaliation against an individual for filing a charge of discrimination, participating in an investigation, or opposing discriminatory practices
3. Employment decisions based on stereotypes or assumptions about the abilities, traits, or performance of individuals of a certain sex, race, age, religion, or ethnic group, or individuals with disabilities
4. Denying employment opportunities to a person because of marriage to, or association with, an individual of a particular race, religion, national origin, or an individual with a disability.

Title VII also prohibits discrimination because of participation in schools or places of worship associated with a particular racial, ethnic, or religious group.

face, this guideline may appear to be common sense and easy to follow. Few reasonable people would defend the use of racial epithets or sexually suggestive behavior in the modern American workplace. However, an evaluating supervisor must be aware of a number of issues to ensure that he or she is in compliance with the law.

First of all, the issue of harassment is in the mind of the recipient. It does not matter if the supervisor did not intend to harass the employee. Harassment occurs if the employee feels that he or she has been harassed. Supervisors must refrain from actions that may be seen as harassing, especially during a performance interview. A manager who uses diminutive terms such as "sweetie," "missy," or "darling" when interviewing a female subordinate certainly is asking for trouble, even if the manager feels these terms demonstrate familiarity and friendliness.

Second, it is important for managers to recognize that they have an affirmative responsibility to deal with harassment issues, even when they are not the harasser. The courts have been very clear on this issue; even when the offending behavior comes from other employees, an organization that allows such behaviors to continue will be held accountable (*Meritor Bank v. Vinston*, 1986). For example, if during an interview an African American employee says, "Everything is great with you, but Hal keeps making racial jokes in my presence and it bothers me," the interviewing manager is obligated to follow through on the employee's complaint. At the very least, the manager must advise the employee about what procedural actions can be taken to stop the offending behavior. Advising the employee to "toughen up" or "roll with the punches," or telling him, "Hal bugs everyone!" is not enough. Most organizations have formal grievance procedures especially designed for such situations (Peterson et al., 1994).

Common Problems with Performance Reviews

As with survey interviews, the two major problems managers face while conducting performance reviews are issues of *reliability* and *validity*. The reliability of a measure basically refers to its consistency; its validity is its relation to what the manager is actually interested in knowing. A supervisor may give unreliable evaluations if outside noise or other distractions do not allow for a thoughtful review. If the supervisor is drawn to irrelevant issues, then the performance review would be invalid. If all you discuss is the fact that you have a disorganized desk, the resulting evaluation may have nothing to do with your overall job performance.

Problems with Reliability

Any issue that affects a supervisor's consistency in obtaining results on performance appraisals impacts the supervisor's intrarater reliability. *Intrarater reliability* refers to the consistency with which a supervisor assesses similar situations in dissimilar ways. A big factor in this is the manager's state of mind. If the manager is in a good mood, then he or she might be more favorable than if in a bad mood. Time of day, whether the evaluation was before or after a meal, the time of week, or the time of year, can all affect intrarater reliability.

Interrater reliability also pertains to how consistent different managers are in assessing the same subject. Managers get reputations for being soft or hard, biased or fair, lax or strict. Ultimately, it should not matter who is conducting the evaluation; the evaluation should be similar no matter who is conducting it.

Problems with Validity

Szilagyi and Wallace (1990) have identified four common problems with performance review validity. One of the more pernicious problems is *stereotyping*. Years of legislative and judicial effort have been focused on racial, ethnic, and sexual stereotyping. Although there has been widespread and continuing debate on how to overcome discrimination based on stereotypes, there is broad consensus that stereotyping is detrimental to the evaluation process. In short, everyone agrees that one should focus on the performance of the employee and avoid stereotyping.

Researchers Feltovich and Papageogiou (2004) have shown in an experimental setting that a manager's preconceived ideas have a profound impact on his or her distribution of rewards. They find that the more strongly held a stereotype is, the harder it is for a manager to overcome it. They suggest, however, that repeated exposure to people who do not fit the manager's stereotypes does have some mitigating effect.

However, it is important to note that not all stereotypes are racial, ethnic, or sexual. For instance, many professors prejudge student athletes, assuming they are below average students. Blonde women often face the same prejudices as other women with the added "dumb blonde" stereotype (Foege, 2004). Whatever their source or target, stereotypes are a serious problem for managers wishing to conduct valid performance evaluations.

Similar to stereotyping, *halo effects* also create validity problems (Thorndike, 1920). Halo effects are opinions that a person makes early on in a relationship with another person. Like stereotypes, managers often let these early opinions color their view of employee performance. If a manager has a good initial impression of an employee, that employee will have a good halo. If that employee makes a mistake, the manager will be more likely to forgive the mistake and claim, "Well everyone messes up from time to time." If the manager's initial impression is bad, that employee will have a bad halo. The manager will be less likely to forgive similar mistakes and claim, "I knew they were trouble, right from the start." Similarly, managers are more likely to overrate the accomplishments of employees they personally like and underrate the accomplishments of those they do not like (Lefkowitz, 2000). The employee's halo effect may also be affected if the manager is influenced by organizational politics, such as whether the employee is a political ally or supportive of an internal organizational opponent (Tziner, 1999).

The initial halo need not have anything to do with the issues at hand. Ross et al. (1977) found that test subjects made evaluations based on initial halos, even when the halos were based on inherently unfair, biased, or other situational factors. The subjects completely ignored the inherent biases and let the halos affect their ultimate evaluations. The researchers argue that this tendency is so basic to human thinking that they call it the *fundamental attribution error* (Ross et al., 1977) and claim that it is at the heart of most of evaluation errors.

The third validity error is *contrast errors* (Becker & Miller, 2002). Unlike halo and stereotyping errors, contrast errors occur when a manager allows the evaluation of one employee to affect the evaluation of another. These contrasts can take a number of forms. For instance, a manager may find that a number of her employees have committed the same error. Early in the day, she may write the errors off, but after a time, she becomes frustrated that she sees the same thing over and over again. By the end of the day, she may give an unduly harsh evaluation just because she is tired of seeing the same thing.

Most employees know that it is a bad idea to be evaluated shortly after someone who gets an excellent evaluation. Employees in this situation often find themselves being unfairly contrasted with the company's "shining star." Most would prefer to be evaluated after the company's main buffoon. In each situation, previous evaluations create unfair and invalid evaluations of the current employee. Research has shown that any number of factors can contribute to the contrast effect, including the sequence of interviews and any significant delay between the interview and the assignment of the ratings (Becker & Miller, 2002).

The fourth validity error is the *similar-to-me* error. In this case, the manager focuses on traits and behaviors that are similar (or dissimilar) to him or herself to make the evaluation. This is a very natural and human characteristic. People often compare themselves with their subordinates. The comment "You remind me of myself when I was your age" is considered high praise. In fact, some similarities may be a good thing, but this is not always the case. It is important for managers to understand that the same task can be accomplished in a number of different ways. Systems theorists call this concept *equifinality* (Katz & Kahn, 1966) and claim that it is important to respect people's difference as well as their similarities. It has been demonstrated that diversity, not similarity, leads to creativity and, ultimately, more profitability (Hickson & Stacks, 1998).

McCrosky et al. (1975) discuss the similar-to-me error in terms of the communication concept of *homophily*, arguing that people are attracted to those who are similar in three distinct areas: demographics, background, and attitudes. Subsequent research has shown that such perceptions of similarity may have a direct impact on performance appraisals (Strauss, Barrick, & Connerley, 2001).

Demographic homophily is based on the basic categories people use to assess others. Southerners tend to like other southerners and dislike northerners. Often a source for racial and other stereotyping, most people are generally more comfortable with those of their own race, religious background, region, ethnicity, and age. Some physical characteristics, such as eye color, body type, or height, can be considered demographic homophily traits.

Background homophily is based on similarity of experience. Sailors like other sailors and hate Marines. People like those who attended the same schools they did, who belonged to the same fraternity, or who share the same hobbies. Some view this as a root cause of sexual discrimination, because female managers and male managers often come from vastly different backgrounds and engage in different activities. Some consultants have begun special classes to teach young women basic golf skills, because golf is such a common game in the business world.

Attitudinal homophily is perhaps the deepest and most meaningful dimension of homophily (Strauss, Barrick, & Connerley, 2001). People naturally are drawn to those who share the same seminal attitudes. A person's work ethic, morals, or attitudes toward religion may affect attitudinal homophily. Note that most people consider their attitudes to be deeply personal, and they tend not to reveal them until they know someone well. For example, most people have heard that they should not discuss religion or politics with people they do not know very well. For this reason, it is often difficult to learn a person's attitudes about something. Oftentimes, people make incorrect assumptions about others based on the little they know about them. For example, just because someone is a Southern Baptist does not mean that they are politically conservative. Similarly, just because someone is a college professor does not mean that they are politically liberal. Such assumptions often are wrong.

Performance Review Methods

Organizations often develop their own rating system for performance reviews. Generally, most approaches fall within one of three categories: (1) management by objectives, (2) behavioral evaluations, and (3) forced rankings. The ultimate goal of each approach is to improve the validity and reliability of the organization's performance appraisal interviews.

Management by Objectives

One of the most popular forms of assessment is *management by objectives (MBO)*. This method encourages the manager and employee to work together to systematically establish a set of objectives that the employee should meet over the upcoming performance period. An early proponent of MBO, Peter Drucker (1954) claims that it addresses four critical factors of an employee's job: (1) people work better when they have clear objectives and know how those objectives impact the larger organization; (2) people want to have input into their objectives; (3) people need clear feedback regarding their work; and (4) rewards need to be specifically linked to achievement of objectives.

The MBO process is divided into the following eight steps (Szilagyi & Wallace, 1990):

1. *Diagnosis.* Overall, what current employment issues does the organization face (e.g., employee shortages, technology improvements, etc.)?
2. *Planning.* What is the organizational commitment (resources) available to the training and development process?
3. *Defining the employee's job.* In this step, the manager and employ strive to learn what activities and contributions the employee makes to the organization as a whole. This may be done in light of the employee's job description, but it may also evolve during the tenure of the employee.
4. *Goal setting.* The employee develops and submits a list of goals to be accomplished during the next evaluation period.
5. *Superior review.* The supervisor reviews the goals submitted by the employee.
6. *Joint agreement.* Steps 4 and 5 are repeated until consensus is reached between the supervisor and the employee.
7. *Interim review.* The superior and employee meet during the evaluation period to review progress toward the goals.
8. *Final review.* At the end of the review period, the supervisor and employee meet to formally review the results. The process begins again.

The first distinguishing feature of MBO is that emphasis is placed on the outcomes (goals) of the employee's work. The process does not focus on specific employee behaviors. Behaviors are only discussed in light of goals that were or were not met. Many organizations that use flextime favor this approach. They focus on what the employee has accomplished, not how often the employee was physically present.

The second distinguishing feature of MBO is a focus on the future. Most of the process looks forward and does not dwell on past performance.

The third distinguishing feature is that MBO is an evolving process. With its focus on organizational goals and job descriptions, MBO may appear bureaucratic in nature, but the final step acknowledges that the organization and its needs are constantly changing and that the employee is constantly evolving. The employee's role within the organization, therefore, also needs to be renegotiated on a frequent basis.

Stanley (2004) argues that because employees are intimately involved in negotiating their own goals and objectives, they will look more favorably on organizational change. They will have more practical goals (often higher than management would have set on its own). They will feel greater loyalty to management and the organization because they have a say in its operation. Finally, MBO offers an important feedback tool to the organization to assess its own need to grow and change.

Behavioral Evaluations

Another school of thought argues that managers should examine the specific behaviors exhibited by their employees and provide evaluation and feedback about their behaviors. Two early examples of behavioral evaluations were the *critical incident* and the *forced choice* methods. With both methods, supervisors rate their employees on an objective behavioral scale. Managers and organizations like these types of reviews because they feel that they are more easily defended if a legal challenge is launched against the organization (Jacobs et al., 1980).

Taking a page from the MBO employee–supervisor negotiated steps, William Kearney (1979) presented a step-by-step process that incorporates employee input into a behavioral evaluation now called the *Behaviorally Anchored Rating Scale (BARS)*. This process consists of a series of small steps and typically takes place over a short evaluation period.

1. *Orientation*. The supervisor discusses the terminology and process with the employee.
2. *Job review*. The supervisor meets with the employee and other job incumbents to identify relevant dimensions of performance.
3. *Develop anchors*. The supervisor develops a worksheet that identifies critical behaviors and expectations regarding those behaviors. These become the behavioral anchors.
4. *Reach consensus*. The supervisor must negotiate acceptance of the scale among all the job incumbents.
5. *Weight*. The users decide which of the scales (anchors) best represent critical job performance factors and weigh them accordingly.
6. *Publication*. The scales are distributed to all concerned parties.

It is important to note that the anchors are *behavioral*, not *attitudinal*. By focusing on behavior, BARS has a much greater developmental value than if it focused on attitudinal questions. For example, managers are encouraged to avoid phrases such as "Employee show's enthusiasm" or "Employee has good attitude" and focus on behavioral concerns such as "Employee greets customers with a smile." For this reason, BARS has been found to be an excellent training tool (Daley, 1992). However, critics complain that as an appraisal tool it can lead to inflated evaluations and is less reliable than other methods (Solomon & Hoffman, 1991).

Forced Ranking

A method popularized by John Welch, former CEO of General Electric, to make upper management leaner and more efficient is *forced ranking*. Simply put, forced ranking involves using a standardized measure and identifying the top 20 percent of managers and putting them on the fast track, leaving the middle 70 percent alone, and then firing the bottom 10 percent. In Welch's (2000) own words, "Not removing that bottom 10 percent early in their careers is not only a management failure, but false kindness as well—a form of cruelty—because inevitably a new leader will come into a business and take out that bottom 10 percent right away, leaving them—sometimes midway through a career—stranded and having to start over somewhere else" (p. 1).

Forced ranking is seen as a way to make companies more competitive. In spite of widespread criticism (Sears & McDermott, 2003), this method of performance appraisal is growing in popularity. It is now estimated that 20 percent of all *Fortune 500* companies use some form of forced ranking (Johnson, 2004). Note, however, that forced ranking should be clearly and fairly implemented, that it should be limited to top managers, that it is best used with other performance review techniques, and that it will likely work only for about three years (Rodgers, 2002).

Improving Performance Appraisals

The problems associated with rating errors, reliability and validity, and negative feedback all point to the potential weaknesses of performance appraisal interviews. These problems are big enough to cause some authorities to question the value of even using such interviews in the organizational setting (Juncaj, 2002), particularly for the stated purpose of making decisions about merit pay (Gray, 2002). Rasch (2004) notes that such interviews can be counterproductive, creating divisiveness within the organization, and recommends that organizations instead focus on professional growth that encourages employee success and leadership development for supervisors.

The Rasch approach, though, like the others, has its own strengths and weaknesses. Many organizations consequently use a variety of methods or blends of various techniques to overcome the problems associated with performance appraisal interviews. Regardless of which method is used or the gender of the raters, the individuals who participate in the process must believe in its validity for it to be effective (Tziner et al., 1998; Tziner & Murphy, 1999).

Such interviews are more effective when the interviewer is more attentive, takes notes, and is held accountable for the evaluations (Mero, Motowidlo, & Alexandra, 2003).

Success also is enhanced if the interviewer seeks objective information from a variety of sources before making the final evaluation (Shore & Tashchian, 2002; Raymark, Balzer, & Delatorre, 1999). Seeking additional information and opinion becomes more important if there are differences of opinion regarding the evaluation process (Levy, Cawley, & Foti, 1998). The importance of complete information emphasizes the need for individual interviewers to improve their own interviewing and information-gathering skills rather than relying upon any one specific technique.

Earlier in this chapter, various problems surrounding performance appraisals were discussed. Although certain appraisal methods may give the interviewer an edge in one dimension or another, all appraisal interviewers should be aware that the employee's perception of fairness of the process is equally, if not more important, than the methods used (Stano, 1992). John S. Adams (1965), an early motivational theorist, referred to this concept as *equity theory*.

Equity theory (Adams, 1965; Walster, Walster, & Berscheid, 1978; Kabanoff, 1991) is based on the assumption that individuals evaluate their relationships by comparing the contributions they make with the benefits they receive, comparing this ratio with the corresponding ratio of another person or standard. Thus, according to equity theory, the employee's perception of equity will determine his or her level of motivation. Basically, Adams believes that inequity will lead to employee dissatisfaction.

It is important to note that equity does not mean that everyone gets the same thing. It means that everyone wants to get what they feel is their fair share, depending on their own contribution. For this reason, employees of similar status and position often compare salaries, raises, and bonuses to see if anyone is getting too little or too much. The problem for the manager is that the feeling of equity is just that—a feeling. Because people tend to overestimate their own importance in the workplace, it is difficult for managers to actually achieve equity. However, the theory provides a nice conceptual framework for conducting better appraisal interviews. Organizations can take a number of steps to ensure a fair evaluation process:

1. *Standardize the process.* Whatever method of evaluation is employed, the evaluation process should be standardized so that managers use the same evaluation process for each employee. This requires the organization to have a clear understanding of what characteristics are to be evaluated, which is an important component of both the behavioral and outcome methods of evaluation. Further, the interviewees should have a clear understanding of that process; employee knowledge of the performance appraisal process is directly associated with the effectiveness of such systems (Williams & Levy, 2000).

2. *Increase the number of items.* By increasing the number of items that are evaluated, the chance that one or two items will unreasonably skew the results of the evaluation is lessened (Nunnally, 1967). Increasing the number of items effectively increases the reliability and validity of the appraisal (Lindell, 2001), even if multiple raters are involved in the evaluation (Saner, Klein, Bell, & Comfort, 1994).

3. *Use multiple evaluators.* By increasing the number of evaluators, interrater and intrarater reliability is increased. It also decreases homophily-related validity prob-

lems. Software programs are available to ease the process of computing ratings and to evaluate the reliability of the process (Berry & Mielke, 1997). However, employee satisfaction with the process will be highly dependent on the credibility of the evaluators involved (Albright & Levy, 1995). Although multiple raters may reach agreement on a single-item rating scale (Szalai, 1993), the effectiveness of the rating increases if multiple items are used (Saner, Klein, Bell, & Comfort, 1994).

4. *Increase frequency.* A recent study of over 2,000 workers found that less than one-third had been evaluated in the last year. To be effective, performance appraisals should be done in a timely manner. Whether they are done weekly, monthly, or quarterly will depend on many factors, but employees need feedback in order to improve their performance. Further, even those workers who were evaluated once a year say they prefer more frequent evaluations (Manshor & Kamalanabhan, 2000).

5. *Focus on components of job performance.* As discussed earlier in this chapter, there are growing legal concerns over the fairness of performance evaluations. For this reason alone, managers should be concerned with focusing solely on the components of job performance. This will also mitigate stereotyping and halo effects. Further, focusing on job performance reduces the use of words with strong emotional overtones (Timmreck, 1999).

6. *Deal with anxiety.* Carol's anxiety over her first performance appraisal interview was to be expected. She was facing a new communication encounter, and had little experience to handle it. Her supervisor may have had similar anxieties, particularly if he or she was new to the performance appraisal process. The problem with both situations is that the level of anxiety can interfere with the communication processes (Bartoo & Sias, 2004). It is to the advantage of both participants to address such anxiety early so that it will have minimal impact on the interview.

The hallmark of any effective performance evaluation will be equity and fairness. Regardless of the technique, the manager must approach the interview with an open mind and a desire to do an equitable job. Re (1987) suggests that the following maxims of equity should be the hallmark of any evaluation:

■ *He who seeks equity must do equity.* It is important for management to communicate clearly and fairly with employees. This starts with the performance appraisal process itself, which must be viewed as fair by all participants. Further, that perception of fairness must exist both within and outside the interview setting. Employees will base their assessment of the appraisal on elements within the appraisal system, such as its structure and evaluation policies, but they also will be influenced by appraisal-related interactions that will occur at other times during the year (Giles, Findley, & Field, 1997).

■ *Equity aids the vigilant, not those who slumber on their rights.* The organization should take specific actions to maintain an atmosphere of equity. This is an underlying principle of affirmative action.

■ *Equity follows the law.* To be equitable, managers must stay abreast of their legal obligations.

■ *Equity regards substance rather than form.* It is not enough for a manager to say that he or she "meant well." Managers must establish legal, reliable, and effective methods of appraisal and stick with them.

Employee Responses

Thus far, the bulk of this chapter has focused on the appraisal interviewer rather than the interviewee. The assumption in most cases is that if the manager does a good job then the performance interview will be successful. This, unfortunately, is not the case. As stated in Chapter 1, interviewing is a two-party interaction. Therefore, the behavior of the interviewee, or in this case the employee, must be examined. Those conducting performance appraisals should be aware of how employees may respond, especially when they are faced with an unfavorable review. Monroe et al. (1989) identified several ways in which subordinates give equivocating responses that can be misleading:

■ *Apparent compliance.* Often the employee will seem overly polite or apologetic. The employee may make promises or be reluctant to offer his or her side of things. In many cases, the employee's words will not be followed up by actions. A manager should set a very clear set of goals and expectations when faced with such a response.

■ *Relational leverage.* Some employees may try to talk about who they know, their length of service, or what they know about the subject rather than their job performance. This typically becomes apparent when the employee offers too much information in the way of defense. The employee may claim to know more about the subject than the supervisor or justify his behavior on the basis of his tenure with the organization ("I've been doing it this way for 15 years."). This type of behavior is used more frequently by veteran employees who are being interviewed by a new or relatively young supervisor. The manager must be confident in his or her evaluation. This is where training and preparation will pay off.

■ *Alibis.* The employee may offer excuses related to his or her health or overall workload. This is a delicate situation for the manager, because the alibi may in fact be valid. The manager must be an effective listener. The use of multiple evaluators can help in this situation.

■ *Avoidance.* Some employees will cancel meetings, not answer e-mails, and avoid telephone calls to avoid an appraisal. By having regularly scheduled and frequent appraisals, managers can reduce employees' ability to avoid the situation.

The Exit Interview

An employee–employer interview that is conducted more for the benefit of the organization than the employee is the *exit interview*. Exit interviews are conducted when an

An Interview with Marjorie Allen

Marjorie Allen is vice chapter leader and counselor in the Women's Division of Soka Gakkai International (SGI), an American Buddhist organization. She directs a number of volunteer members in their efforts to support SGI in Albuquerque, New Mexico.

Q. How would you describe the people who you supervise? What do they do?

A. This is a faith-based volunteer organization, where women, and sometimes men, come to me for counseling about nearly all aspects of their life. They also can be and have been responsible for any number of tasks, including, but not limited to, such things as running our bookstore, newspaper collections, special-event planning and execution, regular-meeting planning and execution, member contact, transmission of information both ways, transportation, and other responsibilities that help the organization function.

Q. Since you are directing volunteers, describe the authority you have over these people.

A. In some ways, I have no authority at all. This is a volunteer organization, and anyone who wanted to could simply stop doing anything I requested anytime he or she wanted. Nonetheless, those appointed authority within areas of faith—priests, bishops for example—tend to carry even more weight with an individual who chooses to follow that faith, than any boss or government leader possibly could. The reason is simple. When dealing with secular authority, a person can easily keep an internal distance from the reigning personality, whereas, the nature of seeking spiritual answers demands that a person open internally with a childlike vulnerability to the designated authorities of that particular faith. Once a person has made the internal decision to embrace that faith, his or her life naturally opens to other practitioners, especially those with titles or position.

Q. So your authority springs from their commitment to the organization?

A. Right, the authority that someone in my position can exercise over someone's life is very powerful and can have far more long-reaching effects on that person's life than authority in any other realm.

Q. It sounds as if your role as spiritual counselor and volunteer supervisor are intertwined?

A. Yes, decisions like who a person marries, how they raise their children, how they conduct their daily affairs, as well as what they need to do to improve the results of their efforts and how they think of themselves are all on the table, and the person seeking to lead a spiritual life of this faith is already trying to embrace my direction by the time they come to me. They are already open and vulnerable to my point of view. With little effort, authorities in the realm of faith can lead people to follow whatever direction they choose, even to the point of causing the followers to completely self-destructive, other destructive, or even lethal behavior.

Q. Since you can't fire anyone, what types of things do you do?

A. Inspire them. I make them laugh. I present a dream that comes from my life of how things can be. I embrace them as folk just like me in many ways. I don't feed peoples' fear or feelings of separation.

Q. When you do an appraisal, do you focus on specific behaviors or on general outcomes?

A. Both. If I have an organizational request of them I explain first the importance of the project, and second how the good outcome with this project will help them gain good out-

(continued)

Continued

comes in their personal life, using my own example or that of others. I also indicate my trust in them. In appraising the results, it becomes clear through the course of the project, which problems are symptomatic of a need for a process change. Most problematic outcomes are the result of a need for process change. However, the behavior of the person performing the task often reflects that person's level of confidence or even the suitability of that person's talents for that particular project. For example, I had a woman doing the mathematical tallying of a district's newspaper subscriptions and money collecting. This was a brilliant woman who simply could not do math. The outcomes were wrong every month. Finally, we changed the process. But before that, I found someone else who was good at math to help her. That person really needed the confidence that she had any value, so the interim solution helped both of them as well as the outcome of the task itself.

Q. Are the reviews formal, or informal? Do you review everyone you're responsible for?

A. For a period there were both formal and informal reviews. At this time because of the changing structure and new process approaches being tried, there are no formal reviews and few informal ones, which are only self-sought. During the time of our formal reviews, they would center on the outcomes of that person's responsibility. Informal reviews have always been self-sought by the person and for the sake of training and encouragement in confidence.

Q. How much of an open mind do you need?

A. Completely and not at all: one must be completely open and eager to understand the nature and life of the person with whom one is dealing. At the same time you must be completely immune to the influence from that person's life that reflects that person's negativity. One must go in knowing that that force is there within everyone and that our job is to help that person gain control in his or her life over the devastating effects of that force. So it is imperative they we ourselves are not swayed by it.

Q. Do you mostly talk about what has happened, or what needs to happen in the future?

A. We want to focus on the past only so far as it can teach us what we can do better. The far more important thing is to keep an eye to the future goal. That is the way human beings build hope and trust in community.

Q. What advice would you give other people who have to do appraisal with volunteers and other nontraditional workers?

A. Don't judge them. Listen to find how they have judged themselves and help them resolve that judgment in a positive way. Occasionally, challenge them; everything depends on the nature of that person, so find out who they are and what they respond to . . . If you really watch them and hear them you can immediately tell if what you are saying is reaching them. Keep the focus on helping them resolve the doubts within their own minds about their ability to achieve the desired outcome and away from external judgment.

Q. How do you deal with someone who refused to listen to you?

A. Generally, again due to the nature of this sort of position the people listening to me listen openly. But occasionally they refuse to hear what I am telling them. It is not my job to force anyone to do anything. I will recommend they go to someone else; if they don't want to, then I find usually in time the issue will return for them and they will find the correct answer themselves.

employee leaves an organization. Many organizations interview departing employees (Giacalone & Duhon, 1991). In addition, many educational institutions interview departing graduates (Doll & Jacobs, 1988). Exit interviews serve two major functions: (1) they provide closure for the departing employee and (2) they help the company understand why the employee decided to leave (Roberts, 2003). In addressing the first, organizations can reduce the chance of having disgruntled former employees who speak ill of the company (Sandberg, 2004). Addressing the second can improve the efficiency and morale of current employees with the organization.

Kinsman (2001) notes that effective exit interviews have two essential components. First, the departing employee must be candid and honest, and their comments should be expressed with the intent of making life better for the workers who remain. Sometimes this may be difficult; employees may be reluctant to address and discuss some issues (Knouse & Beard, 1996) or reluctant to give honest answers to others (Giacalone & Knouse, 1997). In many cases, workers simply say that they are leaving for a better-paying job, avoiding discussion of reasons why they were seeking another job in the first place. Further, employees may have trouble verbalizing the source of their dissatisfaction. As Kinsman noted, "someone who thinks they're leaving for a bigger challenge or higher salary might simply be dissatisfied with they way they are treated" (p. 2G).

Sometimes, though, the departing employee may be quite candid about the organization and the reason for leaving. A departing employee has little to gain from expressing hostility. However, if the interview degenerates into a venting session for the departing worker, the worker may feel better, but little will have been achieved from the organization's perspective.

The second component of effective exit interviews, according to Kinsman (2001), is that the criticisms generated must be well received by the company. Candid comments from former workers accomplish little if the company is not receptive to improving the work environment. As Kinsman notes, "it is incumbent that the company be realistic in its assessment and courageous enough to improve its own business operations . . ." (p. 1G). Smart companies hear and respond. In so doing, the organization can increase the morale of those still on the job (Murray, 2004) and reduce retention problems (Use exit interviews . . . , 1999).

Summary

In general, employer–employee interviews provide an effective feedback tool for employees as well as for employers. Regardless of techniques or methods used to conduct such interviews, managers and supervisors should be well prepared and approach them with an open mind.

Performance appraisal interviews are used by the organizations as a means of making decisions regarding pay raises and promotions, providing the employee with feedback, and assisting in overall organizational development. Such interviews also have legal implications, particularly in the areas of discrimination and harassment. There are legitimate issues related to the reliability and validity of the rating process in appraisal interviews, but they continue to be used even as researchers seek ways to increase their accuracy.

Exit interviews are conducted when an employee leaves an organization. They serve two major functions: (1) to provide closure for the departing employee and (2) to help the company understand why the person decided to leave. When handled properly, exit interviews can make the employee feel better about the departure and provide the organization with information for improving its internal processes.

FOR FURTHER DISCUSSION

1. What type of performance appraisals (behavioral or outcome) are used by your college or university to assess your performance? Are they reliable? Are they valid?

2. What makes you especially defensive during a performance appraisal?

3. What stereotypes have you been a victim of? What have you done about it?

CHAPTER

7 Interviews on Radio and Television

One of the authors, while being interviewed for a local news segment, found himself answering each of four questions with a series of clichés and generalities. After the fourth question, the reporter offered his thanks and started putting up his equipment.

"I should apologize," the author said. "I only gave you broad generalities and few specifics."

"That's all right," the reporter responded. "This is television. All we need are broad generalities."

Although the reporter was speaking with a little self-directed sarcasm, he had a point. Both newspaper and television reporters conduct journalistic interviews, but they use different techniques. The newspaper reporter is looking for quotes and information that can flesh out the details of a story. The television reporter is looking for a sound bite that can illustrate a point. These two different goals result in two different interviewing situations.

The Sound Bite

A television reporter may interview a source for 10 minutes, but little of that interview will actually be broadcast. Most stories will run for 1 minute or less, and the reporter rarely has time to include much of the interview. Instead, the reporter will summarize the story with a limited number of quotes (usually just one), typically using only about 10 seconds of what the speaker has actually said (Jones, 1988). Dramatic statements may run for as long as 12 seconds, but that is rare. Ten seconds is typically the top range, a guideline consistent with written quotes for a newspaper story, which are usually limited to one or two sentences. These short quotations are called *sound bites* or *actualities*. They are short statements that illustrate the story. They must be short, to fit within the broadcast format. After all, when you consider that most broadcast stories average between 20 to 70 seconds in length, any sound bite longer than 10 seconds will dominate the story.

Reporters use sound bites for four purposes: (1) to provide credibility to the story, (2) to provide factual information, (3) to add visual realism to a story, and (4) to reveal something about the speaker. Jones (1987) calls these four factors the *FACE* formula for

Rick Journey: On Conducting Live Interviews

Rick Journey is a veteran newsperson and co-host of Good Day Alabama, *a morning show on WBRC-TV (Fox, Birmingham, Alabama). His regular features on the show include live interviews with local and national guests.*

Q. What is the biggest problem in doing live interviews for TV?

A. Time. Time tends to run out on you. What we usually end up with is about four and a half minutes for an interview. That's a lot of time for TV, but many times you don't feel like you've gotten into it as much as you could, particularly if it's a meaty topic. You end up thinking, "I could have done a lot more with that if I hadn't run out of time."

Q. How does the news interview fit within the format of your show?

A. At the top of the show is the hard news part of the show. Typically those interviews get about four and a half minutes, which is about as much as you can hope for in a two-hour format. They're going to get that time because it's a meaty subject and that gets a priority. Occasionally, we'll have a special project that will get more time.

Q. What about feature interviews?

A. If it's a standing segment, a regular part of daily coverage, where you talk to an expert—those are usually a little shorter. Example: If we talk about topics such as money matters, fitness, or nutrition, those interviews are about three and a half minutes. A lot of those are formatted to get information, and we know where the expert is going to go with it. You can keep those tighter. With a hard news interview, typically you don't know where it's going to go. They may say something that calls for a follow-up. That's why we want to have a little extra time. We want the time to have a follow-up.

Q. How do you prepare for those interviews?

A. Say we're talking about something on nutrition. Our nutrition expert and I will talk earlier in the week, trying to figure out something timely. I may brainstorm with her regarding how can we deal with this, but she's the expert. I try to tap into her knowledge of the subject. I'll ask her to give me some bullet points, and she'll e-mail several paragraphs of information to me. I'll go through it and try to hammer out two or three bullet points. Then I let her know what I'm working on and what I want to hit on. When she comes on, she knows what we're going to go over.

Q. How does that differ from a hard news interview?

A. With a hard news interview, we know what we're looking for. The guest will know the general topic and what we want to focus on. But something else may come up that's the news of the day and we may focus on that more. You spend more time on getting their reaction to the arising issue.

Q. Either way, you give the guest advance notice, right?

A. To a certain extent. On the news-maker segments, the harder news, they know the general idea or topic of the interview. When we book somebody for a news topic, they'll usually ask us what we want to talk about it. I'll give them the topic. If it's a politician, that's where I try to keep it. If it's an expert, someone who provides analysis or observations about a news story that's developing, I will try to give them a better idea. That gives them more time to think about it in terms of how they want to respond.

Continued

Q. Earlier you mentioned using bullet points as part of your preparation. Why the emphasis on bullet points?

A. It helps you to know where your interview is going, and it helps to structure it more. Shows like the *Today* show do a good job of using bullet points when they talk with an expert. Let's say they're talking about how a family should save their money. Instead of having an expert just answering questions and saying things that may not stay with the audience, they use that one line or one phrase that people can remember. We are TV, and we are a visual medium. Being able to put bullet points on screen reinforces what you're saying. That's very helpful. It's very helpful to guide your interview if you've got several points you want to make.

Q. It sounds like the bullet points are both an organizational technique and a communication tool.

A. They are, especially for morning shows. In the morning, a lot of people are getting dressed or getting their children off to school, and they're not watching the screen so much as listening to it. We almost become radio to a certain extent. If they're not watching the screen, they're hearing what we're saying in that bullet format during that three or four minutes. If they glance at the screen, they see it and it's reinforced.

Q. Do you do pre-interviews?

A. I like to start asking questions, particularly if it's someone who's apprehensive about going on TV, I want to start a conversation with them and ask some questions as if we were on the air right then. I listen to them and try to get a feel for how they're going to respond on the air. It's a pre-interview for me because I'll know the direction they're going. I'll be prepared when we go on the air. Sometimes I realize that they're saying nothing new, and I'll take things in a different direction. Some people say that's preparing the news, but it still keeps the door open. I know that's been said a hundred times. A lot of times they don't realize that they are in a pre-interview, particularly when you're talking with them on the phone. Sometimes when I'm with somebody who's apprehensive, I'll say, "Look everything you've just said is what we want to discuss on the air." They'll think, "My gosh, that was easy." That also helps to cut down on that long conversation and gets it down to what you need.

Q. How do you handle people who speak too long?

A. Everybody has their own way of dealing with that. When I see them reach a complete thought, I try to step in at that point. A lot of times, I'm not on camera at that point, and I may raise a finger, like in normal conversation when you indicate that you want to make a point. There are rare times that I just have to step in and say we're out of time. You try to find that good stopping point and just jump in. I think it comes with experience after you get used to the time element on TV.

Q. What advice would you give to people who will be interviewed live on TV?

A. They should know, going in, what the interview is about. That doesn't mean the journalist is going to give you the questions they'll ask. But they should have a broad sense of what they're going to be talking about. It makes them better prepared for the interview, and it makes the interview go better. You need to have a good idea going in of what's the topic and what is the journalist wanting to get out of it.

describing what the reporter is seeking. The FACE acronym stands for the following four elements:

F—*Feelings*. To let the audience know what the source is feeling

A—*Analysis*. To provide an assessment of the situation in one phrase or sentence

C—*Compelling Cs*. A catastrophe, crisis, conflict, change, crime, corruption, or color

E—*Energy*. A dynamic delivery that conveys emotions

Redmond et al. (2001) argue that credibility should be the primary goal, i.e., that the sound bite should provide either expert and/or authoritative support for the story or provide the viewer with a first-person view on an incident. Similarly, Shook (1982) notes that "The sound bite . . . is the point of emphasis that proves the story and what's been said about it both visually and in the reporter's narrative" (p. 67). As such, the four purposes for doing a story often are interrelated, with each effective sound bite adding both credibility, factual information, visual realism, and information about the source.

Sound bites have become such an integral part of television news that they may sometimes be overused. The sound bite merely should assist the reporter in illustrating and telling the story. Further, not all stories require sound bites. Sometimes the reporter can summarize the story more succinctly himself, rather than relying on a rambling statement from an interview. The sound bite should enhance the story, "adding a dimension that the script could not" (Redmond et al., 2001, p. 172).

Getting the sound bite is a two-step process of (1) eliciting the statement from the source and (2) selecting the portion of the interview that provides the most impact. This means that the statement is selected based on its impact, not on its effectiveness as a summary. Redmond et al. (2001) argued that the reporter should not rely on the sound bite to tell the story, but merely to enhance the story or to give the viewers "any sense of 'being there'" (p. 172). To increase the chance of getting a sound bite that conveys this feeling, they also suggest that a reporter should be willing to ask a source to explain a point again, particularly if the first response was rambling or too long. The reporter needs to get a short but clear answer that will be understood easily by the television viewer. The source is more likely to provide such a statement when asked the same question a second time. A source's first answer to a question often is a planned summary. Asking the same question a second time is more likely to elicit the same information but in a more conversational manner.

Types of Broadcast Interviews

Redmond et al. (2001) identify four distinct types of broadcast interviews: (1) live interviews, (2) spot interviews, (3) public official interviews, and (4) celebrity interviews.

Live Interviews

Television reporters use live interviews to provide interest and capture a mood. As Redmond et al. (2001) note, "It is one thing to hear the reporter's account of an air disaster and quite another to hear an observer's still strong impressions of a mid-air collision" (p. 243). Such interviews are staples of cable news networks such as CNN (Robinson, 2002) and are a frequent element in network coverage. They enhance the story by provid-

Tips for Being Interviewed for Television

1. Know what the story is about and how it relates to you.
2. Identify the reporter's intent. Are you being interviewed to provide information, insight, or a viewpoint? Or, is the story intended to make you look bad?
3. Suggest a place for the interview. You'll feel more comfortable on your home turf.
4. Arrive early. Don't irritate the reporter by being late.
5. If you're the target, have a witness present or record the interview for your own records.
6. Disregard the microphone and the camera and just talk to the reporter. Assume that only one or two people are listening in their living rooms.
7. Body posture is important. Sit erect or lean forward, but don't lean back.
8. Speak at a normal pace; avoid the temptation to speak rapidly.
9. Use short simple sentences. Start with a concise one-sentence statement of your feeling or opinion followed by your explanation of why.
10. Don't be evasive. Be honest and answer the question as directly as you can.
11. Treat the reporter like a jury. Argue your position.
12. Don't memorize your answers. Instead, memorize key words that represent the main points you wish to make.
13. Anticipate that the reporter will ask you a follow-up question—"Why?"

Source: Jones, Clarence (1988). *How to speak TV*. Tallahassee, FL: Video Consultants.

---

ing details, insights, and credibility. At their best, they also can contribute to the mood of the story while enhancing the authenticity of the situation. For maximum effectiveness, though, the interviewee should be adept at summarizing points quickly. As Jones (1987) notes, "If you're interviewed during a live shot, the pressure to condense what you say is greater than in any other interview form. . . . There's no chance to edit . . ." (p. 52).

Live interviews can be problematic. First, both the interviewer and the interviewee may be uncomfortable in front of the camera, and the reporter has little time to make them feel at ease. The reporter must be able to meet people easily and help them feel comfortable despite the pressures of the moment. At the same time, though, many television reporters are uncomfortable with the live format (Tuggle & Huffman, 1999).

Second, the reporter has no way to guarantee that the interviewee will provide a concise and effective answer. If an interviewee does not want to answer a particular question, he or she may become evasive or ambiguous. The best the reporter can do is to identify the evasiveness and move on.

Third, in some cases, a live interview may deteriorate into a substitute for true reporting. Immediately following the initial terrorist attack on the World Trade Center on September 11, 2001, all of the networks went to extensive live coverage (Reynolds & Barnett, 2003). With so much time to fill, and information sometimes slow to develop, some reporters turned to speculating about events on which they were not prepared to report. Once a reporter arrives on the scene of a breaking story, he might be forced to go on the air quickly. He needs something to put on the air, even if he has had little time to gather information and summarize his thoughts. In the face of such a predicament, the report often falls back on the "easy out," i.e., he finds someone to interview, gives them a brief introduction, and lets them talk. When the source reaches a stopping point, the reporter can then shift the story back to the studio. The approach offers a simple solution to the reporter's immediate assignment. Still, even when such an approach works, it usually results in an incomplete story. Fourth, the use of a live interview may turn into a plea for action, particularly when it is associated with saturation coverage of a real-time event (Robinson, 2002). Finally, the live interview is highly susceptible to the "Reporter as Story" syndrome. Redmond et al. (2001) note that television reporters are on the air so frequently that they often become celebrities. If they start thinking of themselves as celebrities, though, it can alter their interview technique, particularly in live interviews. This becomes apparent most frequently when the reporter's questions are longer than the source's answers. The more effective response takes an opposite approach: ask a short question that gets a quick and immediate reply.

Shook (1982) suggests that the reporter make plans to control the interview prior to going on the air. This involves establishing a predetermined cue—usually a hand signal, touch, or predetermined final question—that indicates to the interviewee that the interview must end within 15 seconds. Further, the reporter must be prepared to interrupt a source who spends too much time on a single question. To avoid this, the reporter must have another question ready to ask whenever the person might pause. In some instances, the reporter may have to interrupt the source in mid-sentence (politely, of course). Finally, the reporter must have a final exit line planned in advance. The exit line serves to conclude

More Tips for Broadcast Interviewers

1. Avoid "yes/no" questions. Such questions and answers impart little information to your audience.
2. Avoid leading questions. Leading questions (e.g., "Do you think . . . ?" "Were you scared . . . ?" and so on) should be replaced by questions that begin with "Why" or "What do you mean . . . ?" Questions that require an articulated response almost always result in the strongest interviews.
3. Don't ask and answer your own questions.
4. Avoid saying "I see" or nodding your head after each response. The interviewee may interpret this as agreement.
5. Avoid asking two-part questions. Either your interviewee or your audience will forget one part of the question.
6. Avoid obvious questions. You don't learn anything new by asking questions for which you already know the answers.
7. Avoid asking questions of bad taste (e.g., asking insensitive questions to accident and disaster victims).

Source: Redmond, J., Shook, F., & Lattimore, D. (2001). *The broadcast news process* (6th ed.). Englewood, CO: Morton, p. 174.

the live interview while also serving as a cue for the director to zoom off from a tight shot and be ready to cut back to the studio.

Spot Interviews

Spot interviews often occur around breaking news. They are used so that eyewitnesses can describe what they saw and felt as witnesses to a dramatic event such as a house fire or automobile accident. This approach allows the audience to get a firsthand sense of the emotions and the drama faced by the participants at that event. This approach is not without its critics. The most obvious problem is that the reporter can be insensitive and intrude on the private grief of an individual who has just faced a tragic loss.

Reporters who do spot interviews with victims or their families are always subject to crossing ethical and legal lines between the public's right to know and the victim's right to privacy. Editors and reporters constantly grapple with ethical questions about privacy (Hanson, 2002). Sometimes, however, such questions may go beyond the ethical dimension and become legal issues. If a reporter releases improper information, the reporter could be subject to possible legal action (TV Newsman can be sued . . . , 1995), in addition to potentially alienating the television audience (Seamans, 2001).

Public Official Interviews

There is some debate regarding the extent to which television effectively covers local public officials, but the city hall beat is a staple of local television news (Coulson & Lacy, 2003). Redmond et al. (2001) argue that the goal of public official interviews should be to expose the sincerity or hypocrisy of an official who speaks on public issues. *Expose* may be too harsh of a term to describe all public official interviews; *reveal* might be more accurate. Ideally, the public official interview should be one in which the reporter asks questions that the public would ask if given the opportunity. The reporter becomes a surrogate interviewer for the public, seeking information that the public will find useful. In other words, broadcast reporters should ask the questions that the viewers would ask, if they had the opportunity. That requires the reporter to keep the interview on track, seek clarification when an answer is incomplete or equivocal, and guide the interaction through an exchange of information that leads to an understanding of the issue.

An *ambush interview* is a controversial form of the public official interview in which "reporters who are unable to schedule an interview with an individual often stake out the person's home or office until they are able to ambush the person as he or she comes into or goes out of the building" (White, 2002, p. 371). Ambush interviews are remarkably easy to do, given recent advances in camera and microphone technology. A television crew has the same access to public places and freedom of movement as anyone else, causing Jones (1988) to note that "In a public place, you have almost no right of personal privacy" (p. 168).

Because of their invasiveness, such interviews are ethically questionable; however, they are sometimes necessary. Lesley Stahl (1999) of CBS calls it "an opportunity for reporters to relinquish their dignity. . . ." Although the technique has always been available to broadcast reporters, Stahl argues that its popularity exploded during the Watergate era, when such interviews were the only effective way to get comments from some of the scandal's participants. Since then, the technique has been used more frequently. The reporter's ethical dilemma is deciding when an ambush interview should be used. ABC News correspondent Barry Serafin has argued that an ambush interview is justified only when there's "a genuine public accountability involved" that relates to the public interest.

Jones (1988), writing from the interviewee's perspective, describes the ambush interview as a "heads they win, tails you lose" situation (p. 123). He recommends that public figures should politely refuse to do them by making an appointment for a full interview at a later time (e.g., "I don't have time now, can you come back at three this afternoon?"). Another option is to first request an off-camera interview to set the rules regarding what will be off and on the record before the ambush interview takes place. Both approaches give the interviewee time to prepare for the interview.

Celebrity Interviews

The celebrity interview is a growing television phenomenon. Celebrities like the publicity that comes from broadcast appearances; the broadcast outlets like the entertainment and star value that comes from interviewing the celebrity. As a result, a number of network and syndicated shows (*Jay Leno, David Letterman, Regis and Kelly*) feature such interviews as major segments of their programming. At the local level, celebrities who pass through town to promote a new movie or book often find themselves doing interviews for local stations.

Such interviews rarely generate major news stories, but that is not their purpose. From the station's view, the goal is primarily to provide entertainment. If the interview is above average, it will also provide the audience with an intimate look at the celebrity. The reporter's guideline here is that "The reporter is not the story" (Shook, 1982, p. 66). The focus of the interview should remain on the celebrity—not the reporter.

Jean Bodon: On Interviewing Celebrities

Jean Bodon, a member of the director's guild, has worked in the film industry over three decades. His film credits include work as producer of the French film Seven Sundays *(starring Rod Steiger) and director of the 1993 film* Hidden Fears *(starring Meg Foster). His television credits include a year of working as director/producer of the HBO/Encore series* The Directors—*a documentary show in which each episode focused on the work of an individual film director.*

Q. You interviewed dozens of celebrities for your work on *The Directors* series. What is it like to interview a celebrity?

A. It's easy to be intimidated by the celebrity, because you, the interviewer, think of them as a celebrity. You have to tell yourself that you're interviewing a normal person.

Q. What kind of special problems do you face?

A. The biggest problem is reaching them and getting them to do the interview. Celebrities are well protected. You have to go through all kinds of processes to reach them. For *The*

Continued

Directors series, we were interviewing movie stars. To reach those kind of celebrities, you have to go through their agents—sometimes more than one agent. In each instance, we had to explain very carefully—using a lot of faxes and e-mail—what the project is about. So you need a lot of proof to show that you are legitimate.

Q. How do you prove your legitimacy?

A. We started by telling the agents that we were members of the Directors Guild of America. That organization is well respected by Hollywood actors. And, we were affiliated with HBO, which added to our credibility. But what really worked best was that we had the support of the directors we were working with. The directors would tell us about working with a particular actor. Then we'd contact the actor, saying we had the support of the director. After that, it was usually easy. If a director spoke well of them, they were usually willing to be interviewed about that director.

Q. Did you have to do any background research before conducting the interviews?

A. For the directors, we did. You cannot interview a celebrity without knowing what they've done. If you're not familiar with their work, they won't respect you or the purpose of the interview. You need to know enough about them to ask good questions. We read about the movies they had made, watched some of their movies, and watched scenes from others. We wanted to have a good feel for the director's work before we asked them any questions.

Q. What about the interviews with the actors?

A. The interviews with the actors were often brief. The questions we asked were based on the information that we got from the directors. We usually tried to interview the director first. If he mentioned something involving one of the actors, we would later try to get the actor to comment on that incident. Then we could edit the two interviews into the same segment of the show. One exception was Sylvester Stallone. We interviewed Stallone for Rocky after we had interviewed director John Avildsen. But he was also in a film with Richard Donner, whom we had not yet interviewed, and another with Norman Jewison, whom we had also not interviewed at that point. Rather than having to bring them back and ask the same questions again, we went ahead and did the interviews for those shows at the same time.

Q. What was the toughest part about doing the interviews?

A. The logistics of going from place to place. We interviewed people in Wyoming, Montana, Los Angeles, and New York. We were constantly on the plane going from place to place. It sounds glamorous, but it wasn't glamorous. And it was easy to make a mistake on the details. We were interviewing at a Los Angeles hotel one time, and I had scheduled four people at the same time. I was interviewing one person, while Martin Landau, Charles Coburn, and Samuel Jackson were all waiting in the hallway. Sometimes you had to improvise. We had scheduled an interview with Morgan Freeman in New York at the office of the Directors Guild of America. We got there on a Sunday morning, and I had to give the security guard twenty dollars to let us in. Even then, he didn't have the keys to Morgan Freeman's office, but he let us into Bill Murray's office. So we interviewed Morgan Freeman in Bill Murray's office.

Q. Did the interviewing influence the structure of the final documentary?

A. It did after the first. It took us about two weeks to edit the first show, working eight hours a day. After that we realized that the format was so easy that the creation of

(continued)

Continued

the following shows was almost instinctive. It became almost automatic. The interview with the director provided the blueprint. When we edited, we used what the director said as the framework of the show. Every time the director talked about an actor, we would cut to the actor. When he talked about a scene, we would cut to that scene. We tried to have as many people telling the story about the same event. The anecdote question was particularly effective for that, because we found that most of them told the same story, although from a different perspective. And many times they had different stories.

Q. Who was the easiest person to interview?

A. Jack Lemmon. He was a remarkably nice man, and he gave us an extra hour to set up the camera and to get the proper lighting. You want the interview to look good on camera, and you want the actor to look good. To do that, it takes time to set up properly. In that case, it only took 30 minutes, but he gave us an hour. If you see that interview on the show, you'll notice that he looks comfortable, as if he's sitting and talking to us in his home. Also, he was superb at doing interviews. If we didn't ask the right question, he knew what we wanted and he would give us what we needed. He told us stories that he had never told before, and that made the show more interesting.

Q. Who was the hardest person to interview?

A. Kirk Douglas, whose office was just down the hall from Jack Lemmon. I did my best interview and my worst interview on the same day. There were two problems. First, he didn't give us any time to set up. If you see the show, it looks like we were rushed when we did his interview, which we were. The lighting isn't as good. And, he had just written a new book and he wanted to promote it. He kept checking the frame on the camera to make sure the picture was in the frame. Of course, that would have been inappropriate, and we kept changing the frame after he looked at it. And third, he refused to let us ask questions. "I know what you want," he said, "just let me tell you my story." He is a professional though, and the sound bites he gave us were very good.

Q. Any other problems?

A. We had a similar problem with Sylvester Stallone, but the problem there was his agent. The agent changed the location for the interview one minute before we were supposed to start. Like Kirk Douglas, we didn't have time to set up properly, and you can tell that when you see the interview. Also, we were interviewing for the show on John Avildsen, and Stallone refused to mention his name. Our understanding was that Stallone and Avildsen didn't get along very well. So Stallone agreed to talk about the movie Rocky, but he wouldn't talk about Avildsen. That made the editing more complicated.

Q. How would you summarize the role of interviewing celebrities, particularly for documentary purposes?

A. A documentary is basically a discovery process. You need to be well informed on the subject matter, but you need to let them tell the story.

Tricks of the Trade

The goal of most broadcast interviews, as ABC's Ted Koppel (2000) notes, is "extracting information from a guest" (p. viii). Most standard interview techniques also apply to broadcast interviews. However, broadcast reporters do use some "tricks of the trade."

Spontaneity

The best broadcast interviews are spontaneous interactions between a reporter and a source, not rehearsed scripts between two amateur actors. To encourage this approach, most reporters avoid prewritten questions and instead work from a *key word question list* that identifies topics to be covered in the interview. Even then, the list may not cover all potential topics in detail, since—once the interview starts—the spontaneity of the exchange often will lead to new topics. Such a situation means that the best interviewers are good listeners, paying attention to what the source says and using those responses as the basis for additional questions that allows the interview to develop naturally. To increase spontaneity, White (2002) suggests that the reporter's question list should not be obvious to the interviewee, and should be referred to "only when necessary" (p. 258).

Nonverbal Behavior

As discussed earlier in the text, providing positive nonverbal feedback is an important interview skill. In television interviews, the reporter's control over his or her nonverbal behavior is twice as important. Reporters must remember at all times that both the interviewee and the television audience are observing their behavior. White (2002) notes, "Television reporters must be concerned about their facial expressions and head movements during an interview, particularly in a studio situation when two or more cameras are being used. . . . a reporter cannot be shown expressing agreement or disagreement" (p. 265). Effective use of movement and nonverbal behavior increases audience attention and knowledge acquisition (Ravaja, 2004).

Nonverbal behavior also is used to induce responses from the interviewee. As such, expert interviewers use nonverbal behavior to enhance interviewee responses rather than to express their own positions, attitudes, or values. As ABC's Ted Koppel (2000) notes, ". . . my tone or apparent mood or facial expression has little or nothing to do with what I really think" (p. viii). Instead, a raised eyebrow or shift in tone of voice is used to induce the interviewee to continue speaking. The most common technique for doing this is silence. For example, when an interviewee completes an answer, the reporter may continue his or her gaze and point the microphone in the interviewee's direction. The nonverbal behavior tells the interviewee to continue talking. The advantage of this technique is that most individuals will continue talking, believing that they need to provide more information.

The nonverbal behavior of the interviewee is also critical. As White (2002) notes, "Many people interviewed by reporters are shy by nature or intimidated by microphones and cameras" (p. 257). A person who is tense on camera can make the audience feel uncomfortable and ruin an otherwise good interview. Reporters must use their own nonverbal behavior to prepare the source for the interview and make the interviewee more comfortable, a process that White (2002) calls "warming up the head" (p. 258). That includes maintaining an open and relaxed position while maintaining constant eye contact with the interviewee. White notes that eye contact will also enhance the listening skills of the reporter because "It's easier for reporters to concentrate on what people are saying if they look them right in the eye" (p. 258). The crew can help in that endeavor by not shining lights in the interviewee's eyes and by putting the microphone in an inconspicuous place.

Icebreakers

Putting the interviewee at ease continues with the first few questions of the interview. The first question a reporter asks should be a formal one, for example, "Could you say and spell your name for the camera?" This makes it easier for the editor to put titles on screen with a character generator for airing of the interview. Such a question is then followed by a series of other simple questions that the reporter has no intention of using. Their sole purpose is to make the interviewee more comfortable and allow the interviewee to acclimate to the broadcast environment. As Redmond et al. (2001) note, "Once people start talking, they settle down a bit" (p. 175).

Listening

One problem facing most interviewers, even the professional, is the tendency to spend so much time planning the next questions that they don't listen to the source's response to the previous question. The problem, of course, is that the reporter can focus so much on the next question that she misses an important statement by the source that warrants more clarification. Further, when reporters fail to listen, interviewees pick up on their lack of interest, and the interviewee's responses become monotone.

Handling this problem is relatively easy. The reporter simply must remember that the initial list of interview questions is only a guide. Those questions are useful to get the interview started and serve as a checklist of topics to be covered, but the best material from the interview is likely to come from the spontaneous questions that arise because the reporter has been listening to the source's responses. That's why Redmond et al. (2001) noted that, without listening, the reporter may "miss the follow-up opportunity that could lead to an Emmy-winning disclosure" (p. 176).

White (2002) notes that failure to listen may create embarrassing situations for a reporter: "Many inexperienced reporters are so intent on asking their prepared questions that they fail to listen to the answers." He writes, "They often do not realize that their previous question was not answered fully, or at all. Sometimes, to the embarrassment of all, the reporter asks a question that already has been answered" (pp. 257–258).

Repeating Questions

Unlike some other types of interviews, it is perfectly acceptable for a broadcast reporter to repeat a question and give the interviewee a second chance at answering it. This approach often is used whenever the first answer provides the information needed for the story, but is too long to use as a sound bite. White (2002) recommends eliciting a second response by saying, "That was great, but could you cover that same ground again in about half the time?" (p. 261). Redmond et al. (2001) recommends simply asking the interviewee to explain the answer again, noting that the approach not only provides clarification but also typically causes the source to relax and respond with a more conversational answer.

Testing Equipment

A broadcast interview is worthless if the reporter doesn't have a sound or an image of broadcast quality. This means that both the audio and video equipment must be tested before the interview begins. The camera should have a fresh battery; the room should be lit so that a good visual image is obtained. Microphones must be pretested, because different types will pick up different sounds.

The most common forms of microphones used for broadcast interviews are the lavalier, the shotgun, and the wireless. Each has its own advantages and disadvantages. The lavalier is attached to the interviewee's clothing; it will pick up the interviewee's responses, but little else. The shotgun microphone can be used at greater distances (up to 30 feet), but it may pick up outside noise that may detract from the quality of the recording. The wireless microphone is a small inconspicuous lavalier-style microphone that broadcasts to a receiver a few yards away; it allows the interviewee more freedom of movement and is thus used with "walking" interviews. Each type of microphone has different levels of audio sensitivity. One may record the interviewee's voice, blocking out other noises, whereas another may pick up the hum of an air conditioner in the background. The crew must test the mike in advance of each interview to see how it will perform in that setting.

Establishing Rapport

White (2002) notes that different reporters have different views on building rapport with the news source. Some like to ask a few questions before beginning the interview, giving the source an overview of the questions that will be asked. As White notes, "The advantage of *warming up* the head is that it gives the person time to collect his or her thoughts, usually ensuring a smoother interview. . . . Warming up an interviewee also tends to put the person more at ease" (p. 258). However, in some instances the reporter will not want the interviewee to know all of the questions that will be asked. If the source anticipates difficult or surprise questions, that anticipation can alter the interviewee's responses. Still, in those instances in which the reporter is not seeking controversial information, the warming up procedure is fairly common.

Asking Questions

Broadcast reporters use a variety of different types of questions when conducting an interview.

Open-ended Questions

Broadcast reporters use carefully phrased open-ended questions that will discourage a yes-no response. Most reporters use carefully phrased *open-ended questions* that will

An Interview with Jeff Mohnen

Jeff Mohnen is a reporter/cameraman with WVTM-TV, the NBC affiliate in Birmingham, Alabama.

Q. What's involved in your daily routine?

A. My day starts with a meeting to determine what story a reporter and I will be working on. Once the story is determined, we set up interviews by making calls. For example, if there was a murder the night before, the first thing you've do is call the PR (Public Relations) or PIO (Public Information Officer) contact for the area where the murder happened. If it happened within the last 12 hours, there probably isn't going to be much information. I would ask if there were any suspects, what time it happened, how many people were involved, and do we have a motive. We might also talk with somebody out in the neighborhood, maybe a friend or family member. Once you have your sound, I will shoot video to go with the interviews and the reporter's voice track. Once that is completed the story can be put together. That's basically my day.

Q. Would that be two stops for the story, then?

A. You usually try to get at least three elements—an official (they usually don't want to give out too much information as not to jeopardize their investigation). Two other interviews might be a family member of the victim, and a neighbor. These are three general areas to start with.

Q. How long are these interviews?

A. It depends on the story. In this case, they're not going to last that long. The family members don't really want to talk; they're going to be too upset. The PIO for the police department probably will only be able to give you general info and no specifics of the murder itself. The neighbors might talk and usually they will tell what kind of person he or she was. Those interviews are relatively short. The longer interviews are for something closer to home, the warm and fuzzy stories, something everybody can relate to. The Columbia Shuttle crash is a great example of a story that hit home with everyone. You could get so many angles on that story. There's just no way you could lose on that story. Everybody knew about it. Everybody felt the pain; everybody had something to say about it. That would be an easy interview.

Q. You still have to edit it down, though. The story itself is still relatively short.

A. About a minute and fifteen seconds is the typical length of a news story. Special feature stories can be anywhere from two to five minutes. Sounds bites are about 4 to 15 seconds.

Q. That is a relatively small proportion of the interview. How do you select what you will use?

A. You select bites that go together with the whole purpose of your story. Obviously, you don't want to make the interview sound untrue by cutting the interview bite off short. You also don't want the interview to be one sided. If you weigh your interviews on a positive side or a negative side, you're being biased.

Q. How do you know when you've got a good sound bite?

A. You just know. You know that interview, you know that bite. It's hard to say what it is, but you know it when you hear it. You know this person has just told me everything I

Continued

wanted to know about what I'm looking at. If they answer everything—Who, What, Where, Why, How, and When—in one sentence, you have the perfect sound bite.

Q. Have you ever been criticized by somebody on the way you portrayed them on camera?

A. Not afterwards. It's usually when you're asking a question during the interview that you get criticized. "Why are you asking this question?" "I don't think it is appropriate to ask this." This would be the kind of ridicule you would get. For example, if a child drowned in the family pool, how would you confront that family and ask questions. "How are you feeling at this moment?" The answer to that would probably be, "How do you think I feel. I just lost my child." The question sounds horrible and to ask it but, the way you ask it makes the difference. I would first try to make friends with the family and subtly help to feel their pain and then tactfully ask for an interview in the most sincere way. The point is that we have to ask these questions and it is not fun to do. This is not the highlight of being a journalist. I would much rather be interviewing kids and parents at the circus.

Q. What advice would you give a PR person who deals with the media?

A. If you're a PR person, massage us. Not talking to the media is the worst thing you can do in your career. If you can't talk to us, we may go with what an employee tells us, and the employee may have damaging information that is not supposed to be leaked. Your job as a public relation person is to defuse a situation that is causing your company or organization to run and hide. If you run and hide with them, you're adding to the situation, making things worse, and making the media burn you at the stake. On the air, we'll say, "We tried to contact the Company but were told that no comment was available." If the company is accused of something minor it would be stupid not to comment. Diffuse the problem.

Q. What about the average person who finds himself or herself interviewed for the news?

A. Relax. Try to ignore the camera. Just talk with us like we're having a conversation. Don't make them uncomfortable by putting them on the spot. A more relaxed person is easier to talk with.

Q. And what about a person who's on camera a lot, such as a public official.

A. Work on your interviews. You've done so many, and by now you should be better, but you're not.

---

discourage a "yes-no" response. The reporter wants a one-sentence summary of the person's belief, not a one-word response to an idea. Further, the reporter should avoid the temptation to use leading questions. This can be difficult, particularly because reporters are often looking for emotional reactions. Still, it is not considered proper for reporters to use leading questions to trigger emotional reactions. Therefore, the reporter should ask, "What did you think when you first returned home?" rather than "Were you upset when you first saw how badly your home had been damaged?" The goal is to restrict the questions to those that gather information about what the person knows or thinks about the topic.

Tough Questions

Tough questions are those that the interviewee will resent. Because of the potential reluctance of the interviewee to answer such questions, they often are held until the end of the interview. Some reporters, in fact, will avoid asking them at all rather than risk their relationship with the interviewee or risk offending the audience, if such questions are asked without sufficient cause. However, tough questions are appropriate in some situations. White (2002) suggests that it helps "to blame the tough questions on other people" (p. 259), such as the source's critics (e.g., "Some of your critics say . . ."). Redmond et al. (2001) note that the reporter isn't required to ask tough questions of all interviewees, but such questions are appropriate when the interviewee intentionally avoids answering the questions that need to be addressed in the interview.

Even when tough questions are asked, the interviewee may avoid answering. If so, the reporter should point out that the question was not answered. White (2002) suggests that this be done politely by saying, "I'm sorry, but you still haven't answered my question" (p. 261). If the interviewee still avoids the question, that response in itself can be newsworthy. As White (2002) notes, "When the response is, 'That's all I'm going to say on the subject,' that in itself makes a statement" (p. 261). If the interviewee's response is to say nothing, the resulting silence can be particularly devastating when replayed on television.

Surprise Questions

The *surprise question* is a specific variation of the tough question that is designed to ". . . catch the interviewee off guard" (White, 2002, p. 259). It requires advance preparation and research on the part of the reporter. The reporter should not ask the question unless he or she already knows the answer. If the source tries to avoid the question, or gives an inaccurate response, the reporter must know the question and probable answer well enough to ask a quick follow-up for clarification (e.g., "But that's not what you said last week? Have you changed your mind?").

Jones (1988) warns his readers about responding to surprise questions, particularly those that the interviewee considers unfair. "Controlled anger is the key here," he writes, "A seething resentment that the reporter would stoop so low. And a clear, positive statement, delivered with deep feeling . . ." (p. 131).

Closing Questions

The *closing question* for most interviews is usually the same: "Did I forget something?" or "Is there anything else you'd like to add?" The pressures to conduct the interview and to get it completed in time to edit and air it will often cause the reporter to overlook something important. A simple final question to address that possibility easily solves that problem. And, that final question often provides the best sound bite. The open-ended nature of the closing question allows the interviewee to essentially interview him or herself. The interviewee often will respond with a statement that honestly and accurately reflects his or her feelings and beliefs. The result can be an effective sound bite.

Another crucial skill for the interviewer is knowing when to stop. White (2002) notes that "Reporters just entering the field tend to ask too many questions, usually because they are understandably insecure" (p. 262). However, the television journalist has a limited amount of time available for the sound bite. Asking too many questions leads to too much material, and too much time being spent on a single project. A quote from a different source will be more valuable than extending the time interviewing a single source.

The Other Side of the Microphone

Part of the job of a broadcast reporter is conducting interviews. Most broadcast journalists are adept and skillful, the by-product of years of training and experience. The participant who is likely to have less experience and training is usually on the other side of the microphone—the interviewee. Many people who appear on camera may do so during the only television interview in which they will ever participate. They have little chance to build up experience and are often at a disadvantage in the interview situation. Others, however, may find that part of their job includes frequent media interviews. In the entertainment industry, interviews are a normal part of the job (Murphy, 2002). Professionals from such diverse fields as politics (Powell & Cowart, 2003) and medicine (Jud, 1999) often have to face the camera and answer a reporter's questions. An entire consulting industry has developed to help businesspeople deal with and schedule TV interviews (Novotny, 2000). Many new authors find that broadcast interviews are a key element in promoting their latest work (Jud, 2003). Still, as Jud has noted, "What makes a good guest for a show doesn't always make a good show for the guest." Experienced interviewers work to ensure that the interviewee tells his or her story, not just the story that the journalist wants to be told.

Different experts have made a variety of suggestions for being effective on camera. Hyde (1999) places a priority on remaining calm. Jud (1999) suggests that interviewees use what she calls "The seven C's" as their goals for the interview—try to come across as Creative, Credible, Current, Convincing, Complete, Clear, and Concise. Jud (2003) also emphasizes the need to identify ahead of time the key points to mention during the interview. Myers (2000) notes the importance of sincerity in influencing the public's perception of the interview. Jones (1988) suggests that, for live interviews or press conferences, the interviewee should get the tough questions out of the way first so that "Then you have the rest of the show to counter with a brighter side" (p. 50).

If the interviewee expects tough or controversial questions, a copy of the interview should be requested. Reporters have been known to take quotes out of context, thus conveying something that was not representative of the interview. Reporters also have been known to do reverse shooting—getting a response from an interviewee, subsequently taping a different question, and then editing it into the presentation as if it were the original question. Keeping a complete tape of the interview provides evidence if such techniques are used.

Chris Matthews (2001), host of MSNBC's *Hardball*, believes that passion is a key factor for a political reporter: "If someone has no passions, he or she has no business either running for office, standing on a downtown corner holding a bullhorn, or hosting a political talk show" (p. 214). Bill O'Reilly, host of the Fox News Channel's *The O'Reilly Factor*, has a similar view. O'Reilly (2000) notes that one reason conservative talk show hosts are more successful than liberal ones is because liberal talk show hosts "are usually nonjudgmental," which limits their ability to take a strong position when interviewing others (p. 51).

Matthews (2001) hopes that his guests bring their own passion to his show. Specifically, Matthews identifies five things he looks for in his guests: facts, spontaneity, honesty, feistiness, and laughter (p. 215). The goal, he adds, is to provide information, viewpoints, and entertainment. "This isn't the inquisition," he writes. "No one really gets hurt. In fact, guests usually want to come back for more" (p. 215).

Jones (1988) notes that the importance of the sound bite means that people who are interviewed for broadcast news must develop "a stopwatch in your head" (p. 67). Any statement that the interviewee wants to be included in a broadcast should be limited to 10 seconds. White (2002) gives a similar time estimate, saying that interviewees should "usually try to express their views in about 12 seconds to make sure their answers are not edited" (p. 261). Conversely, a source can limit the chance that the station will air an answer to an adverse question by simply spending 20 seconds or more answering it. As Shook (1982) notes, "the people who are the most important newsmakers often have become television performers over the years. They know the clock is in their favor and they can talk for three minutes and still not give meaningful answers to the reporter's questions" (p. 68).

Jones (1988) also suggests that interviewees should use their interviewer's name when answering questions. This acknowledges the reporter's role while building rapport, which can make both participants feel more comfortable during the interview. That comfort level is important. As Jones notes, "The camera detects phonies" (p. 28). Any indication of tenseness can be interpreted as insincerity, thus damaging the interviewee's cause. To ensure that sincerity is present, Jones also advises against memorizing answers: "The first thought that comes to your mind is usually the best, the brightest, and the most sincere" (Jones, 1988, p. 31).

Sincerity must be supported by honesty. Some interviewees are so tempted to paint themselves in a positive light that they stretch the truth in some of their replies. Such actions almost inevitably create problems. As Jones (1988) notes, "If you're caught in an on-camera lie, television will never forget. It will be played over and over. You can't say you were misquoted" (p. 127).

Another approach is for interviewees to view broadcast interviews as interpersonal conversations rather than public speeches. Jones (1988) calls this the "living room" mentality, recommending that interviewees "Talk as if only one or two people are listening . . . [because] . . . There may be half a million people out there listening—but they're not all together in one place" (p. 27).

Perhaps the major tool available to the interviewee, though, is the topic shift. A topic shift occurs when the interviewee takes a question and then rephrases it into one on a different topic. Brian Jud (2003), host of the television show *The Book Authority*, offers two suggestions for handling topic shifts. First, if the interviewee believes the question slants material in the wrong direction, he or she can say, "That's a good question, but if you look at it from a different perspective . . ." Another option, particularly if the question is actually a statement about the interviewer's beliefs, the guest can reply, "Most people think that's true, but look at it in the context of . . ."

Summary

The essence of an effective television interview is the priority that broadcast reporters place on the sound bite. The reporter should always remember that the purpose of the interview is not to gather information, but to elicit a sound bite from a credible source. That sound bite should then be used to help the reporter tell the story. Live television interviews enhance coverage of ongoing events, and prerecorded sound bites can be used to flesh out the details of a story. Meanwhile, those who are the subjects of broadcast interviews must remember that the audience is both listening and looking at them.

FOR FURTHER DISCUSSION

1. A reporter approached a witness of an accident and asked when it happened. "About ten minutes ago," he responded. "Did you see it happen?" she continued. "No," he said, "I was looking the other way." What's wrong with these questions? What's wrong with the responses?

2. Suppose you had a chance to interview your favorite celebrity—movie star, musician, or sports star. What would you need to do in terms of research for the interview? What type of psychological preparations would be necessary to get into the proper frame of mind for the interview?

3. Executives in the XYZ manufacturing company have just discovered that one of their products poses a potential hazard to children. The company has issued a recall notice to encourage consumers to return the defective product for a free replacement. Your job as public relations director for the company included setting up interviews for the company executives with the media. What advice would you give to those executives? How would you handle the logistics of setting up the interviews?

CHAPTER

8   Newspaper Interviews

Ellie is the executive assistant to the company's chief financial officer (CFO). She knows that the Securities and Exchange Commission (SEC) is investigating the company, but she does not concern herself too much with it. One night, while out with friends, she is approached by a reporter from a local newspaper who starts asking her questions. At first she tries to avoid the reporter's questions. The reporter then tells her, "Look, I just need to get some background here, I don't have anyone to tell your boss' side of the story. If you don't talk to me, I'll just have to print what the critics are saying."

Ellie agrees to answer the questions, and—to her horror—she sees that she is quoted by name in the paper the next day. Many of Ellie's comments were presented in such a way as to show her boss' guilt. Although she tells her boss that she was ambushed and that the quotes misrepresent her comments, she is fired anyway. Ellie's problem was that she was not prepared for the interview and did not understand how reporters work.

Examine a typical story in a daily newspaper; most of the articles are a combination of facts and quotes. The facts may be statistics or recountings from public records. An article based solely on such facts would be dry and dull. Quotes are needed to make the article more interesting.

Most quotes used in newspaper articles are generated through journalistic interviews. Historians continue to debate as to when the first journalistic interviews were conducted, but the practice goes back at least to the 1860s (Schudson, 1994). Journalistic interviews share many characteristics with other types of interviews (Brady, 1976). However, the results of journalistic interviews are used by reporters to create a written story that conveys useful information to the reading public (Metzler, 1977; Raugust, 1994). In addition, journalists do not use the term *interviewee*; they prefer the term *source*.

The Importance of Accuracy

One of the authors is occasionally called by reporters to comment on local and state politics. The resulting stories usually quote the author and identify him as being with the communication studies department at UAB, the University of Alabama at Birmingham. The quotes usually are accurate, but the attribution sometimes is not. The author is frequently identified as being either with the political science department or with the University of Alabama. Minor mistakes, perhaps, but unnecessary ones. Such mistakes

An Interview with Hugh Merrill: Gathering the News through Interviews

Hugh Merrill is a journalism instructor and former reporter who has worked for major newspapers in Georgia, Florida, and Alabama. He has written several books, including The Red Hot Typewriter, *a biography of novelist John D. MacDonald.*

Q. What role does interviewing play in the journalistic process?

A. Everything. Journalism is really all about interviewing. In academic writing, and most other forms of writing, you use print sources. But in journalism it's all interviewing.

Q. Does the interview structure the story, or does the story structure the interview?

A. The interview probably structures the story more. You always go in with a preconceived notion—that's the reason you call. But you must be prepared to change. You can fish for the story you thought was there, but the real story may be something completely different.

Q. Is interviewing a matter of preparation or one of responding to what's going on at the moment?

A. Both. You have to be prepared to ask good questions, but—at the same time—you have to read the person when you talk to them. You have to recognize when they get bored and want to move on. When they're avoiding a question, you have to be smart enough in your head to say "Alright I'll leave that alone for now, but come back to it another way later."

Q. What can a reporter learn in an interview that you can't learn any other way?

A. One thing you learn is when they're telling the truth, particularly because of the body language. If they start drumming their hands, shuffling through papers, clearing their throat—there are all kinds of things that let you know that they're nervous.

Q. What else can you learn?

A. You learn more about the people themselves. People—particularly celebrities—tend to have a formal picture of themselves, but if you can convince them that they want to talk to you, you can go beyond that and find out stuff about them. It's not that they're keeping it a secret, it's just the sort of self that they don't tend to reveal.

Q. How do you get someone to break their guard down?

A. The first thing I do is try to tell them that I'm their friend—that I'm not there to hurt them. Then, I try to turn it into a conversation. You know and they know that you're there for a reason. But if you can make them forget that, you can turn it into a conversation where they feel comfortable talking. If I have the time, I usually try to allow at least 15 minutes to talk about things that have no relationship with anything you're doing. Just make them feel comfortable talking to you.

Q. How do you do that?

A. Try to identify any hint of interests, of friends that you might have had. For example, I interviewed Norman Mailer once, and he was being sort of standoffish. But I got him to talk about boxing for about half an hour. That had nothing to do with what I was interviewing him about. But once he found out I was a regular guy and could talk about boxing, he loosened up. Actually, I didn't know much about boxing, but I knew that he liked it. So I made it a point to talk about something he liked, and it worked.

(continued)

Continued

Q. How quickly can you get to your major questions?

A. I always save the really hard questions for the very end, because, at least if they throw you out, you still have a story. You don't want to go in and get thrown out after five minutes.

Q. Do reporters often get thrown out?

A. Not really. I've only been thrown out one or two times. Nonetheless, it is a possibility that you might. I once interviewed a Country Western singer who was rumored to have an affair with their duet partner. I didn't ask about that until the end; I thought I might have literally gotten picked up and thrown out, but in actuality all they did was clam up.

Q. When would you do a telephone interview rather than an in-person interview?

A. You do phone interviews when you can't get a face-to-face interview. If the telephone is all you've got, you use it. But you can't see their reaction. You can't watch them and whether you've said something that caused them to look away. You can't understand how they are as a person.

Q. Is it an efficient way to verify information?

A. Yes, it's also good for the two-minute interview like "How does it feel to know your son is a serial killer?" You'll also do it if you have deadline pressure. And sometimes it's all you can do. But for a major story, there's no substitute for a face-to-face interview. Also, they can hang up on you easier than throwing you out.

Q. How do you deal with someone who uses technological language you don't understand?

A. I tell them "I've been sent to interview you, but I don't understand much of this, so you'll have to help me along, so that I don't look stupid."

Q. What advice would you have for someone who isn't experienced but who was going to be interviewed?

A. Understand the questions. If you don't want to answer something, just say so. What a lot of people don't understand is that you may be interviewed for an hour and only one or two sentences may appear in the story.

Q. If only two sentences are going to appear, is there anything an interviewee can do to control which two sentences are going to appear?

A. No, because you have no idea that only two sentences will appear. I was interviewed for the *Columbia Journalism Review* a while back, and I thought a lot of the story would be about me and what I had to say. They only used two sentences. They won't tell you in advance.

Q. If I really want to make a point, and highlight something I'm going to say, is there a way to say something to give it a good shot at getting into the story?

A. Repeat yourself. You answer the question, they ask another question, you answer that and then you say "But as I was saying earlier." Another thing you can do is start by saying, "I really believe . . ." That gets into the interviewer's head. The more times you can get back to something, the better chance you have of getting it into the story.

result from poor interviewing techniques that disregard basic elements of journalistic interviews.

Journalists must remember what Fedler (1989) calls "The importance of accuracy" and the corresponding "need to be fair" (pp. 186, 189). They should make every effort to ensure that their stories are both fair and accurate, even with regard to small details. Spelling, for example, must be perfect, and checking spelling is a relatively easy task. Before completing an interview, the reporter should verify the spelling of the source's name and position. Further, important facts elicited in one interview should be confirmed against at least one other source. Verification is essential. Accuracy must be foremost in the reporter's mind before, during, and after an interview.

Even if the journalist makes every attempt to be accurate, problems may still arise. Gordon and Kittross (1999) argue that journalistic interviews are "an unreliable, often invalid, and even harmful way of obtaining information for the media" (p. 291). They point to three factors that can negate the usefulness of journalistic interviews. The first is the unreliability of eyewitness accounts. Even trained observers have been known to give inaccurate accounts of events.

Second, they argue that many reporters use the interview as an easy alternative to sifting information from documents. Documents can often provide "smoking gun" evidence for the misdeeds of a public figure, for example, but reporters must sift through reams of paper to uncover such evidence. It is often easier simply to get a quote from someone. Good reporting, Gordon and Kittross argue, should involve both forms of research. For example, the Watergate scandal uncovered by Bernstein and Woodward (1994) is best known for their interviews with an unknown source referred to as "Deep Throat" (Garment, 2001). However, much of the story was based on information obtained from official and unofficial documents.

Third, Gordon and Kittross note that quotes from interviews may be used as a substitute for a reporter's own opinion. When a reporter has a specific view of an event, he or she may be reluctant to express that individual view in print. If the reporter can find a source who will provide a supportive quote, however, it likely will become part of the story. The journalistic interview should be used to confirm, illustrate, or assist the readers with evaluating a story (Nylund, 2003).

The importance of accuracy means that reporters have an ethical responsibility to approach their interviews differently than most other professional interviewers. If that accuracy is attained, a reporter can feel satisfaction in getting the job done, generating a story, and holding people accountable for their actions (Rothstein, 2002).

Before the Interview

Reporters need to establish rapport with an interviewee, ask questions in a systematic manner to elicit the desired information, and conclude the interview in a manner that provides closure. However, before the interview even starts, the reporter needs to do some homework.

Se Habla Espanol

The Latino population in the United States is growing more than three times the national average, and generating ad revenue topping over $850 million (Grow and Sager, 2004). In the United States, there are more than 600 Spanish-language daily newspapers, more than 400 magazines, and more than 400 other Spanish-language publications (Halperin, 2004). It is no wonder that more and more newspapers are looking toward the Latino community to make up for general circulation declines. The ability to speak and write Spanish is now a definite asset to any would-be reporter.

Sources: Grow, B., & Sager, I. (2004). Rising tide of edociones espanolas. *Business Week, 3894*, p. 135; Halperin, K. (2004). Training the next wave of Spanish-speaking reporters. *Criticas, 4(3)*, p. 2.

Pre-Interview Research

Pre-interview preparations include researching the topic and the person to be interviewed. Journalists can begin the research process with a simple Internet search (Prochnau, 2002), by gathering information from official sources, and by talking with others about the topic. The goal of this research is to maximize the information that will be obtained from the interview and to prepare a list of questions and identify information that will need to be obtained from the interview.

Pre-interview research is important. As Stephens and Lanson (1986) note, ". . . there is a direct relationship between how much the reporter knows *before* an interview and how much that reporter will find out *during* the interview" (p. 229). Goodman (2002) suggests that reporters ask themselves the questions they want answered before the interview as a means of starting pre-interview research. Pre-interview research also increases the ability of the reporter to adapt questions as the interview progresses. Rivers (1992) writes, "If you have done your homework, you will know enough about the interviewee to modify your approach in the direction of more or less formality, respectful deference, or cheerful camaraderie, carefully framed speech or streetwise jargon . . ." (p. 146).

Effective pre-interview research makes the interview more efficient. One of the authors was once asked to do a 2,000-word newspaper profile of a singer who would be performing a concert in the city. The deadline for the assignment was on a Thursday— three weeks away. That left plenty of time for preparation and the interview, which was scheduled for a week later.

A change in the artist's recording schedule disrupted this plan, though. When the interview was rescheduled, it was for the day before the deadline. This left the author with less than 24 hours to write and polish the 2,000-word article.

The author handled the problem by intensifying research for the piece. Previous profiles of the artist were examined to identify relevant topics and to provide a better understanding of the subject of the story. Most of the article was essentially written in advance, with gaps left in so that the relevant quotes could be inserted once they were obtained.

Portions of the article still had to be rewritten. A preliminary draft had included a reference to the singer's position on a social issue. The author asked the singer a question about this issue, and anticipated a similar response. When the question was posed, though, the singer responded with an unanticipated answer. A follow-up probe referred to the quote from the earlier interview: "Yeah, I know that's what he wrote," the singer said, "But I don't know where he got that from."

Pre-interview research sometimes can lead to questions that might otherwise have been overlooked. While researching an article on singer Mark Chesnutt, the author came across an earlier article by *Billboard* that called him "Country Radio's Stealth Superstar," based on Chesnutt's ability to rack up radio play with little publicity. When the author referred to that article during the interview, Chesnutt replied, "They hit it right on the head. . . . *People* magazine and *Entertainment Weekly* did interviews with me, but neither ran a story. They said I wasn't interesting enough." That story and quote became the lead of the article (Powell, 1994).

These anecdotes illustrate how reporters can use research to develop questions, identify needed information, and provide background for probing during the interview.

Selecting Sources

The sources used for a story may influence the slant of a story or show the bias of the individual reporter or newspaper. Source selection can influence local (Berkowitz & TerKeurst, 1999; Gant & Dimmick, 2000), state (Wasserman, 1999), and national news coverage (Viser, 2003). Source selection can be influenced by such factors as race (Domke, Garland, Billeaudeaux, & Hutcheson, 2003) and gender (Armstrong, 2004; Craft & Wanta, 2004; Zoch & Turk, 1998). Gender seems to be a particularly important variable; male editors generally have a more negative focus than women (Craft & Wanta, 2004). Female reporters are more likely to use women as sources for news stories (Armstrong, 2004).

Generating Questions

Once pre-interview research has been completed, the journalist identifies the questions to be asked during the interview. Exactly how that is done varies from reporter to reporter. Fedler (1989) recommends that reporters "write their questions in advance, then check off each question as they ask it so that they do not run out of questions or forget to ask an important question" (p. 511). Others work from a list of topics to be covered, listing the most important topics first.

Even if working from a list of written questions, the reporter generally uses the list only as a guideline. As Stephens and Lanson (1986) write, the written questions ". . . rarely will be used exactly as they are written out or exactly in the same order— good interviewers always are open to new avenues of questioning should they present themselves" (p. 230).

Depending on the situation, the journalist may use open- or closed-ended questions, but the open-ended format dominates. Open-ended questions are more likely to elicit quotable responses. The best open-ended questions are short, simple, specific, and relevant. Such questions generate details and provide useful information to the reporter.

One technique used by journalists that is not frequently used with some other form of interviews is the use of *repetitive questions*. Reporters may ask the same question two, three, or four times. As Fedler (1989) notes, this technique is effective because "Each time a source retells a fact, he or she may add a few additional, and sometimes important, details" (p. 512).

Reporters should ask questions without arguing or debating issues with their sources. Reporters gather and report information. Debating the issues with their sources is not part of their job. In fact, it can hinder their effectiveness. A good reporter remains objective; it is that objectivity that makes the information useful. When a reporter appears to take a particular side, it damages the journalist's ability to conduct the interview. Further, anything that indicates a lack of objectivity can inhibit the answers that the reporter will obtain. This is particularly true if a reporter indicates a bias toward an opposing side or if the reporter disagrees with the source. As Felder (1989) notes, "Few sources will continue to speak freely after reporters disagree with them" (p. 512).

The reporter should avoid asking vague questions. As Fedler (1989) notes, "Vague questions elicit vague answers" (p. 512). Long questions also should be avoided. It is difficult for sources to answer long questions because they are hard to understand. Using long questions increases the likelihood that the source will not answer. Oftentimes, the maxim against long questions is ignored because many topics are complex and not easily summarized into simple questions.

Unless the reporter is seeking a specific admission, a denial of guilt, or a specific behavior, yes/no questions should be avoided. Such questions limit sources' responses to answers that are rarely quotable. Instead, the reporter should use open-ended questions that start with phrases such as "describe," "why," "tell me how," or "explain." Rivers (1992) adds that ". . . you should frame questions that are responsive to the natural flow of conversation but open-ended, implying that no right or wrong answer exists" (p. 147). Such an approach is more likely to elicit responses that will be useful in writing the story.

The Interview

The interview process begins when the journalist sets up the interview. The location of the interview is often chosen at the convenience of the interviewee. Many interviews are conducted over the phone—a process that is less disruptive to the schedules of both participants. Telephone interviews are particularly popular for breaking news stories or those that face a daily deadline. Reporters may not have the time to travel to several different locations for short interviews with several different people related to the same story. A few quick phone calls will suffice. In-person interviews are used for feature stories and profiles.

Telephone Interviews

Most journalistic interviews are done over the phone. Topics often arise quickly, with deadlines approaching. The reporter must quickly obtain quotes on an issue. The journalist may not have much time to prepare a list of questions or plan a lengthy interrogation. Often, a quick telephone interview is oriented around one question. The reporter will ask

Newspaper Lingo

Like any profession, journalism has developed its own special jargon. Aspiring reporters should begin learning the lingo as soon as possible. Here is a sampling:

AP. The Associated Press; one of the major wire services that provides stories to news organizations. See also, *the wire*.

Art. Any picture, graphic, illustration that goes with a story. Essentially, anything other than text.

Banner. A headline that runs across an entire page. Usually used for the lead story of a section.

Beat. The topic area covered by a reporter.

Body. The main part of the story.

Box. A border around a story. Borders are used to call attention to certain stories.

Broadsheet. The standard size of most daily newspapers.

Budget. The size of a given section. It does not refer to money. When an editor asks for a bigger budget, he or she is asking for more space, not more cash.

Bulldog. An early evening newspaper or edition. Usually timed with the close of the stock exchange so that closing prices can be published.

Bullet. A black dot next to an item in a list. Popular in business writing.

Byline. When the reporter's name (and often picture) appears with the story.

Cold type. Text that has been produced photographically or as an image.

Column inch. One vertical inch of space per column. Can be used to measure the amount of coverage or for advertising sales.

Copy boy. The newspaper equivalent of a gofer.

Copy desk. The editing area.

Copy editor. Edits all the news stories and writes headlines.

Correspondent. An out-of-town writer.

Cover. Getting all the facts for a story.

CP. Canadian Press, a wire service.

Cut line. A caption.

Dateline. A line that identifies the location of a story at the beginning of an article.

Dingbat. Typographical material used as ornamentation.

Dummy. A mock-up of the newspaper that shows where everything will go.

Ear copy. Small items of information put in the upper-right corner (or ear) of a front page; usually the weather or a joke.

Filler. A story of little news value.

FIOA. The Freedom of Information Act.

Gutter. Space between facing pages.

Hard news. Urgent, serious news.

Jump. A story continued on another page.

Kill. To delete.

Lead. First part of a story, usually with most of the important information.

Market. Readership.

Morgue. Where the newspaper keeps old stories, photos, and other information.

Play. Emphasis that a story gets on a page.

Rim. All the copy editors.

Scoop. An exclusive story for the newspaper and/or the reporter. Newspapers frequently hype

(continued)

Continued

their scoops, but the concept has come under attack from those who argue that scoops focus less on reporting and more on preventing others from reporting news (Kinsley, 1999).

Sidebar. Text that accompanies a story (also used in textbooks; you are reading a sidebar now).

Trip. A story that goes across the whole page.

Stringer. A part-time reporter.

Tab. Refers to a tabloid, a paper that is half the size of a broadsheet paper.

Takeout. A long story, not breaking news, often used in support (background) of current news.

UPI. United Press International, a wire service.

Wire. News provided by various wire services.

---

the question and then ask the source to respond (e.g., "The mayor just announced that he's not running for re-election . . . what's your response to that?"). The advantage of such an approach is that it is quick and efficient. The interview is conducted at the same time as that of the initial contact.

Most sources eagerly participate in these quick, informal interviews because the process is mutually beneficial. The reporter gains information for a story, and the source gets exposure. As Stephens and Lanson (1986) note, "Most people who participate in public life, or who find themselves in the news, will be glad to talk with a reporter (because) they want a chance to state their case or to gain a little publicity" (p. 230). During the 2000 presidential election, for example, Republican senator John McCain gained the respect of the national press by his accessibility and willingness to bluntly answer questions (Mitchell, 1999).

One-on-One Interviews

Telephone interviews comprise the bulk of a reporter's interviewing channel, but some stories require one-on-one interactions. As Fedler notes, "Telephone calls . . . are not a very satisfactory means of obtaining in-depth interviews about controversial or complex issues and personalities" (p. 511). Stephens and Lanson (1986) add that while the phone is fast, it provides the reporter with less feedback for monitoring the source's responses (p. 230). Such feedback can be critical on in-depth stories, which is why in-depth stories require in-person interviews.

If a reporter wants to conduct an in-person interview, an appointment must be set up with the source for an appropriate time and location. Proper etiquette requires that the reporter provide his or her name and that of the newspaper to the source and explain the purpose of the interview. The source also needs to know the deadline under which the reporter is working.

Conducting the Interview

Once the interview begins, the reporter must adopt an open attitude and be receptive to new information. As Stephens and Lanson (1986) write, "Reporters should enter any interview ready to learn" (p. 229). Openness to new information is essential, for it may reveal a crucial story angle that the reporter has not anticipated.

Keeping a Record

Before the interview starts, the reporter decides how he or she will keep a record of the interview. The two most common methods—note taking and audio recording—both have pluses and minuses. Alfino (2003) recommends using both, but note taking is the most common technique. As Fedler (1989) notes, most reporters (68 percent) prefer note taking and never use tape recorders.

With the note-taking method, reporters make detailed notes, recording more information than could ever be used because they are never sure what information will be useful. Statements that will make potential quotes are written out using the source's exact words. Once the interview has been completed, the reporter immediately reviews and transcribes the notes while the interview is still fresh in his or her mind.

The problems with the note-taking approach are twofold, though. First, there is a question of accuracy. Sources who claim they were misquoted often point to faulty reporter notes as the reason. Second, the note-taking process can be intimidating to some sources. As Rivers (1992) notes, taking notes simply "scares some subjects" (p. 151). Still, the note-taking approach is the most commonly used technique, particularly for reporters facing daily deadlines.

The audio recording is more accurate, but also more time consuming. The reporter, in effect, goes over the interview twice—once when it is conducted and a second time when the interview is transcribed. If the reporter does not transcribe the entire interview, using it only to review needed quotes, it may be difficult to locate the quote on the tape. The result is more loss of time. For this reason, audio recording is often reserved for feature stories or magazine articles—stories that do not have immediate deadlines. However, Stephens and Lanson (1986) note that audio tapes may be useful for legal reasons because, "In investigations, tapes may provide evidence needed to protect the newspaper's and the reporter's credibility" (p. 231).

Asking Questions

The reporter's first questions should be general, easy, and make the source feel comfortable. Most reporters generally do not start by asking for specific information, but instead begin with more general questions that are easy for the source to answer. These might include such open-ended questions as "What happened?" or "What did you see?" The reporter should not open an interview with tough questions. As Stephens and Lanson (1986) note, there are many different ways to open an interview, "But one that almost never works is to open with an accusatory question" (p. 231).

As the interview progresses, the reporter will move to more specific questions. As Biagi (1986) notes, "Reporters are after specifics" (p. 232). The general questions get the source to talk, but the specific questions provide the most useful information. As noted earlier, specific questions should be developed in advance based on the reporter's goals. As Stephens and Lanson (1986) write, "Reporters have a much better chance of getting what they want from an interview if they know what their goal is" (p. 231). Achieving this goal requires that the reporter (1) actively listen to the source's answers and (2) ask follow-ups that ensure that source's answers are understood. A topic should not be abandoned until the reporter feels comfortable with his or her understanding of the source's answer.

During the entire interview process, the reporter should attempt to talk with the source rather than simply ask a barrage of questions. As Rivers (1992) notes, "The ideal interview strikes a balance between monologue and dialogue" (p. 152). If the source dominates the interview, he or she will control the topics that are discussed and the reporter may miss major issues. If the reporter does too much talking and asks too many questions, the source will become annoyed with the direction of the interview. Both extremes are to be avoided.

Closing the Interview

Some of the most effective quotes come in the closing stages of the interview, after the formal interview has been completed. A reporter often closes an interview by asking a simple overview question such as "That's all my questions, is there anything I've left out that you think needs to be covered?" or "Do you have anything else to add?" The source may then offer an idea that the reporter had overlooked, or, more frequently, add an unrehearsed comment that summarizes the point more vividly than some of the "prepared" responses elicited by earlier questions. As Biagi (1986) notes, reporters sometimes get the "best material after the formal interview is over" (p. 235). Wilkerson (2002) says that this wealth of material from the final question occurs because "the source feels free to say almost anything" (p. 17).

One of the authors, for example, was interviewed by a newspaper regarding the 2000 presidential election between George W. Bush and Al Gore and was asked to predict the winner. His response was that it was too close to call. When the interview was completed, the reporter asked if he had anything else to add. "Not really," the author replied, "but anybody who says they know who will win is either a psychic or they're faking it." It was this last, spontaneous comment that was used by the reporter as a quote in the story.

The close of the interview may also be the time to ask the most sensitive question. Biagi (1986) advises reporters to "end tough," because, "At the end of the interview you have less to lose by alienating subjects, and after a long interview they might be more inclined to let down their guard" (p. 235). Similarly, Rivers (1992) notes that the use of a final tough question may obtain information that may be difficult to get otherwise.

If the source is helpful and not antagonistic, the final question should be directed toward future interviews. Some questions may have gone unasked or new developments may occur that cause the story to be rewritten before the day's deadline. Thus, the reporter should close every interview by asking the source how they can be contacted should another question come up. As Biagi (1986) notes, this approach works with even reluctant sources, because "Most sources will be impressed rather than annoyed by a diligent reporter who calls back to clarify points" (p. 235).

Interviews for feature stories, in particular, often require more than one interview—either with the source or the source's friends and relatives. If another visit with the source will be required, that interview can be scheduled then. If friends and relatives are needed to provide more insight, their names and phone numbers should be obtained.

Types of Journalistic Interviews

There is no one single type of journalistic interview. Interviews are conducted for a variety of reasons and in a variety of contexts. Generally, interviews are conducted as (1) news/feature, (2) press conferences, or (3) roundup interviews.

News/Feature Interviews

Most of the information provided in this chapter so far has focused on the standard journalistic interview; that is, those conducted for the purpose of writing a typical news story or feature article. Such interviews are the bulk of those conducted by reporters during a typical workday. As Stephens and Lanson (1986) note, ". . . not every journalistic interview is an attempt to make a person sweat, twitch, tremble, and break down and admit guilt. In fact, the majority of interviews are just friendly attempts to get some helpful information and some usable quotes" (p. 331). However, some types of news stories, such as round-up stories and those involving reluctant sources, may require a different interview technique.

Press Conferences

The second most common form of journalistic interview is the *press conference*. The press conference is a semi-formal arrangement in which the source speaks with several reporters at the same time. Politicians often hold press conferences to make major political announcements. Coaches and players hold press conferences after games, so that sports reporters can get their comments on winning or losing. The approach is highly efficient, if somewhat impersonal. As Fedler (1989) notes, "Most press conferences . . . are more convenient for sources than for reporters" (p. 518).

Still, the press conference offers reporters a chance to ask questions, just not as many as they would in an individual interview. At a large press conference, any individual reporter may have the opportunity to ask only one or two questions. However, the source's response to any question—whether asked by the reporter or not—are considered fair game for quoting. The principal interviewing strategy is to focus on topic priority. Given that the reporter only may be able to ask one question, he or she should be sure that it is the right question—the one needed to flesh out the angle for the story.

One problem with press conferences is that they sometimes foster an adversarial relationship between the press and the interviewee. Clayman and Heritage (2002) examined presidential press conferences from Dwight Eisenhower to Ronald Reagan and detected an increasingly adversarial relationship over those 40 years of press conferences. The interviewee has considerable power in that the person holding the press conference gets to select whose questions they will accept. Not surprisingly, President George W. Bush is known to prefer recognizing foreign journalists who are usually deferential with their questions (Stevenson, 2004).

Roundup Interviews

With most interviews, one individual is asked a number of questions. Roundup interviews take the opposite approach—asking a single question of a number of different people. The purpose of a roundup interview is to study a single question or issue from different perspectives. Diane Osen (2002), for example, was interested in identifying which books had influenced the lives of successful authors. The result was a book, *The Book that Changed My Life*, which answered that question from the perspective of writers who had successfully competed for national book awards.

Reluctant Sources

Investigative interviews pose complex and potentially frustrating problems for reporters (Lieberman, 2004), often placing them in situations requiring careful ethical consideration (Berkowitz & Limor, 2003). The interviews are essential, because the reporter needs information from an inside source to reveal an heretofore unknown problem. However, the people who can provide the necessary information are often reluctant to do so because of fear of retribution or because they are the subjects of an investigation. Reluctant sources are not necessarily dishonest people. President Harry Truman, for example, who gets high marks from historians for the integrity of his presidential tenure, often had a contentious relationship with newspaper reporters of his day (Mitchell, 1998).

Interviews with reluctant sources must be preceded by extensive research, and the questions must be limited to a highly specific area. Only then should the reporter approach the reluctant witness, confront the person with the research information, and ask for a comment. In this situation, even the "no comment" reply becomes a useful quote.

A variation of this approach is used when the reporter catches the source without advance notice and confronts him or her with the information. This approach, the *ambush interview*, is useful if no other means has been successful in getting a response. However, it can create ethical dilemmas for the reporter who confronts a source with new information without giving him or her the chance to review it. The source, caught off guard, may respond angrily, even if the information is to his or her advantage.

Sometimes the source's hostility is based on a distrust of the media (Arpan & Raney, 2003). As Fedler (1989) notes, some people are merely nervous around reporters and some "may distrust reporters and fear that a topic is too complex for reporters to understand or that reporters will be inaccurate or sensational. Hostile sources frequently complain—sometimes justifiably—that reporters have misquoted them and made embarrassing errors in previous stories" (p. 513). Reporters can increase source receptivity by understanding why the source may be reluctant. The reporter also can try to convince the source that it is to his or her advantage to speak. After all, a "no comment" line in a news story looks bad on the source. It could be less damaging if the source explains his or her side of the story.

Proximity may be important to the success of the interview with a reluctant source. Stephens and Lanson (1986) note that "The closer a reporter can get to a potential source, the harder it is for that person to turn down an interview" (p. 230). During the Iraq war, this principle was taken to the extreme; some reporters were embedded with the military units they were covering (Pfau et al., 2004). In other instances, getting close to the source sometimes means interviewing associates of the primary target. If so, it is essential that the reporter treat those associates in a highly professional manner. If the target feels that his or her associates have been subjected to a fair interview, the source may be more likely to speak with the reporter.

A fourth approach to investigative interviews is the use of deception, or what Stephen and Lanson (1986) call "the trap." In may seem ironic that journalism, a profession that ideally seeks the truth, frequently uses deception as a technique for obtaining it. Deceptive techniques used by reporters include impersonations, nonidentification, and fabrication. However, such techniques are justified according to the pragmatic harm–benefit framework, which basically balances the harm done by the benefits gained (Lee, 2004). Sometimes a reporter may approach a source and request an interview on an unrelated issue. Once the interview begins, most of the questions will focus on the unrelated issue. Later though, the reporter can bring up the investigative issue and ask the source to explain some details about it. Fedler (1989) notes that this approach can be effective in eliciting both new information and confirming the accuracy of one's research information.

Biagi (1986) suggests three different techniques for "trapping" reluctant sources: the funnel interview, the covertly sequenced interview, and the machine gun interview. The *funnel interview* uses the standard funnel technique of moving from general to specific questions. For reluctant sources, though, the technique is revised slightly in the latter stages. As the questions become more specific, the reporter hones in on the controversial elements. In this instance, then, the goal of the funnel technique is to force the source to respond to a general question first. Once the source has answered the general questions, it becomes harder to evade the specific questions that follow.

The *covertly sequenced interview* takes a different approach. Rather than saving the tough questions for last, this approach spreads the tough questions throughout the interview. After asking a few general questions, the reporter tosses in a tough, specific question. Assuming that the source responds, the reporter then follows with more general, easy questions. Then abruptly, the reporter sprinkles in another tough question. The goal of this interviewing strategy is to surprise the source and/or possibly catch him or her in contradictions. Its potential weakness, though, is that the source may try to evade each difficult question and wait for the reporter to return to safer topics.

The *machine gun interview* is the third alternative. Again, the reporter starts with general questions. However, at some point during the interview, the reporter tosses in a series of tough questions—one quickly followed by another. The goal here is to put the reluctant source on the defensive, asking specific questions that leave little room for evasion. It has the advantage of reducing evasiveness, but it also can increase the number of defensive responses. This technique generally is not effective if it is done early in the interview.

Another situation in which a reporter may encounter a reluctant source is an interview with a victim of tragedy. In this instance, the source is not defensive about the topic or accused of doing anything wrong. Still, the very nature of the tragedy may make the source unwilling to talk with the press. Any attempts to impose on the source's mourning, in fact, will cause the reporter to be viewed as insensitive and crude. Still, information may be necessary to provide others with a sense of the suffering caused by the incident. In such instances, the reporter must approach the victims "gently, without hassling" (Stephens & Lanson, 1986, p. 230). Bucqueroux and Carter (1999) recommend explaining to the victim the goal of providing breaking news to the public. Still, sensitivity to the source's feelings must be a top priority.

Levels of Confidentiality

Most journalistic interviews are straightforward, question-and-answer exchanges in which the source provides the reporter with information that can be used in a story. Sometimes, though, special rules can apply in terms of the level of confidentiality for the interview. For example, the source may feel comfortable providing the reporter with the information, but be uncomfortable being quoted on the topic. In such instances, one of four levels of confidentiality may be applied to the interview through mutual consent of both the source and the reporter. Four different levels of confidentiality are possible: indirect quotation, off the record, not for attribution, and background. These levels of confidentiality are critical to the journalistic process. Without confidentiality, many sources would not provide the information needed for a story—particularly for investigative pieces.

Indirect Quotation

An *indirect quotation* is when the reporter summarizes the substance of a source's information without providing a verbatim quote. This is the lowest level of confidentiality. In many cases, in fact, the source of the information is identified. However, the indirect summation allows the journalist to simplify complex ideas without using the technical language of the source.

Not for Attribution

Not for attribution refers to information that the reporter can use in the story but that should not be attributed to a named source. Such information often appears in stories attributed to "a reliable source," "a longtime friend," "a source close to the president," and so on. Usually, the source is not named for fear of embarrassment or professional retaliation. In other instances, though, this approach is used by government officials who may want to leak information that officially is supposed to remain confidential.

Background

Background information refers to information that may be used by a writer to find or support other information and that is not attributed to any specific source. The source providing the information cannot be identified in the story. Typically, the writer presents the information as if it is based on original research. It is frequently used in situations when even a general reference to an unidentified source may reveal the source's identity.

Off the Record

Off the record is the highest level of confidentiality. At this level, the source expects the reporter to hold the information in complete confidence. The information is not published. Why would reporters want such information? Sometimes off-the-record information is useful in providing writers with information that will orient them to future events that will require special handling.

The reporter should make sure that the source knows the rules at the beginning of the interview. The source can ask to go off the record at any point in the interview, but the request has to be made before the source answers the relevant question—not afterward. Changes in the level of confidentiality cannot be made on a *post hoc* basis. As Fedler (1986) writes, "If a source grants an interview and—at the end of the interview—says it was off the record, reporters are not obliged to cooperate" (p. 517).

Summary

Journalism interviews must place a priority on (1) accuracy and (2) fairness when interviewing a news "source." That begins with small details such as accurate spelling of the source's name and title. It continued with the use of quotes from the interview that fairly represent the person's views. Reporters must be careful when gathering information through interviews, because the process is subject to the same problems that plague any information gathered from witnesses of an event—the potential for inaccurate perceptions.

The purpose of the reporter's questions is to gather information. Thus, the questions should be asked without arguing or debating the issue with the source. A wide range of question types should be used, including broad, open-ended questions to elicit unprompted responses (e.g., "Tell me what you saw") to specific questions designed to get more details (e.g., "Did you say you saw two men or three men?").

Journalistic interviews can occur in numerous formats. News/features interviews are standard; soft interviews are designed to obtain quotes and information for use in a typical news story. Press conferences act as a semiformal group interview in which the source speaks to several reporters at one time. Roundup interviews are those in which a single question or topic is addressed by a number of different people.

FOR FURTHER DISCUSSION

1. Review a newspaper article and identify the quotes. What questions and interviewing techniques do you think were used to elicit the quotes? Now review other portions of the story. Can you identify any other paragraphs or sentences that were probably based on the interview, even though those sections are not quotes?

2. Assume that you have been assigned to write a newspaper article on a city council meeting. You would start by reviewing what actions the council has taken in its past few meetings. Then you would make sure that you attended the meeting so that you could cover it properly. Finally, you would plan to interview some of the people at the meeting. Who would you interview? The council members? Those in the audience? What questions would you ask? Why?

9 Interviews in the Political Arena

It started out as a routine news conference. John, a candidate for governor, was leading in the polls and seemed headed to victory in the statewide contest. He had called the news conference to discuss his new plan for lowering the state's crime rate, something that would likely be another boost to his campaign.

After presenting his plan to reporters, he opened the floor for questions. After a few follow-up questions on the candidate's crime plan, one reporter brought up a different issue—rumors that the candidate was having an affair with a subordinate and using state vehicles to ferry her to their liaisons. The reporter closed by noting another rumor—that a local newspaper had photos documenting the indiscretion. John replied quickly and angrily, saying there was no truth to the rumors and condemning the use of a rumor campaign against him. He also denied the possibility that a newspaper had photos that would prove anything and dared the news organization to print them if they had them.

The next day, John's responses to the rumors dominated press coverage of the campaign. Two days later, the newspaper ran the incriminating photos. John eventually lost the campaign by a narrow margin. This example reflects the importance of interviews in today's political arena. Interviews with the press or with representatives of government bodies are a daily activity for many public officials, and nearly all eventually find themselves in interview situations.

Interviews often are critical both to the careers of the public officials involved and to the public that they represent. Quotes from interviews may become fodder for news coverage that can make or break a political career. Most career politicians know this and are well trained at handling the political interview. Their training, however, sometimes emphasizes equivocation and topic shifting (i.e., techniques aimed at avoiding a direct response to a question).

This chapter examines interview situations that occur in the political arena: media interviews, debates, and interviews before legislative committees. The role of each type of interview will be discussed and the techniques used by the participants, both the interviewers and interviewees, will be described. Hopefully, those who plan on entering the political arena will benefit from the information presented here. However, this chapter is meant to provide the average citizen with information on political interviews in today's media environment. By understanding the process of political interviews, we believe that citizens (particularly voters) will be better able to make more sense of the communication that occurs in this context.

The Press Secretary

A key figure in any political interview is the press secretary. The press secretary serves as the major conduit of news and information between the public official or candidate and the news media. As Perloff (1998) notes, "It is a dicey job" (p. 69), one in which verbal missteps can have serious consequences. Not surprisingly, then, the press secretary not only plans and works on interviews for the public figure, but also engages in day-to-day interviews with reporters on his or her behalf.

In political campaigns, the press secretary's role is separate from other campaign functions, with the press secretary acting as both manager of the message and as the "messenger boy" (Grossman & Kumar, 1981, p. 130). The press secretary serves as a conduit for information to the press, informing reporters of the candidate's schedule, scheduling press conferences, and writing press releases for standard announcements. The press secretary serves as a gatekeeper between the candidate and the press, managing which reporters get interviews with the candidate or public official. Using this "gate" to control access to the candidate requires careful balance. Too much access can be detrimental, offering too many opportunities for negative press; too little can be even worse, creating an antagonistic relationship that also leads to negative coverage.

The extent to which the press secretary interacts with the press often depends on the extent to which the press seeks interviews. One factor that can influence interview requests, particularly for political candidates, is the financial strength of the campaign. Journalists cover candidates in rough proportion to their spending (Powell & Cowart, 2003). The more money a candidate spends, the more the press wants to cover the campaign, and the more likely that reporters will seek interviews with the candidate or other campaign representatives. Thus, campaigns often work to enhance their campaign reporting status, knowing that the release of a positive fundraising report will trigger an increased number of interview requests from the media.

Although approaches to the role may vary, depending on the personality of the individual, most press secretaries aim for a positive working relationship with the press and seek to maintain that relationship through the ups and downs of the campaign. As a result, some campaigns use the campaign manager and the press secretary in "good-cop/bad-cop" roles. When the campaign feels it is necessary to criticize the press, the criticism is more likely to come from the campaign manager; that way, the criticisms do not hinder the press secretary's working relationship with reporters.

The press secretary has several options for passing information to the press. These options are essentially the same as the levels of confidentiality discussed in the chapter on newspaper interviews. Interviews can be *on the record* (comments may be quoted and the name of the source identified), *not for attribution* (information can be used, but not attributed to a named source), *on background* (the quote can be used but the source can be identified only by status or position, not by name), or *off the record* (the information cannot be used at all; it is provided merely to help the reporter understand the larger context of an issue or situation). Some information may be *embargoed*, in that the information is provided to a reporter in advance of a planned event, but the information cannot be used until the event occurs.

Some information may bypass the press secretary entirely because of news *leaks*. Leaked information is information that the source wants the press to have, but which the source is unable to disclose through normal channels.

Scott Mauldin: Interviewing Politicians

Scott Mauldin is an award-winning television reporter who heads political coverage for WVTM-TV, the NBC–owned station in Birmingham, Alabama. His coverage has been featured nationwide on MSNBC, CNN, and in top media markets, including New York, Los Angeles, and Miami. Mauldin's notable interviews include President George W. Bush, Secretary of State Colin Powell, former presidential candidate Bob Dole, plus a long list of national and state political leaders.

Q. Whenever you're interviewing politicians for a news story, what do you have to consider?

A. Reporters have to realize their unique access to public officials and ask questions that the public would ask if they could talk with politicians. The general public doesn't usually get a chance to ask questions of elected leaders, while reporters enjoy those freedoms all the time, so our audience relies on us to find out what they want to know from politicians. I consider both my knowledge of an issue, along with what I hear from the public, when I interview politicians. You have to put yourself in the public's shoes and remember that they can't just walk in and talk to elected leaders very often, while we can do it all the time.

Q. How do you decide which questions to ask?

A. That's the tricky part. It comes in two steps for me. I try to step into the mind-set of an inquiring public citizen. That means asking questions that I think my viewers want answered. To do that, reporters must stay informed as to what is important to the public. I also pick questions with the goal of getting below the surface of an issue. I want the interview subject to explain an answer, not simply react with a sound bite. What's more, I try to form questions so that the response comes in a complete thought, not a short reaction.

Q. Sometimes public officials don't want to reveal much. What do you do to push them to reveal more information?

A. Public officials usually have a specific message that they want to communicate. The challenge becomes asking questions that get them off topic, or at least results in more details. I do it by asking broad, open-ended questions. I'll ask questions like, "This means what?" I'll ask for examples. I'll ask them to list benefits that they see in the issue. To uncover more information, I ask questions that require detailed answers. Those kinds of questions and answers give me more meat to the story. The deeper questions require politicians, or any subject, to flesh out their message, adding information that's more meaningful to real people.

Q. You still don't have a lot of time as far as the sound bite that you're going to use. How do you select the sound bite out of all of those answers?

A. Picking the perfect sound bite is the toughest part of television journalism. You have to pick a sound bite that is meaningful, succinct, informative, and one that supports the message that you as a reporter have chosen for the story. For example, a politician may explain a tax program three different ways. You have to pick the explanation that best applies to real people. If a sound bite can't stand alone, for timing reasons or context, you have to set it up with your own words, then include the usable fragment of the bite that does make sense. The simple goal is to air a sound bite that supports what you want viewers to know.

Continued

Q. You've also done in-depth, sit-down interviews with public figures such as President George W. Bush, the governors, and U.S. senators. What's different about preparing for those types of interviews?

A. In a daily news interview, a reporter can start with general information and use that quick interview as a learning process for a quick story. The sit-down interview is very different, because the reporter must begin by knowing as much or more than the political leader about the topic to be discussed. The rapport between the subject and the interviewer is just as important as the questions. You have to be prepared about that person's background, their stance on issues, and about what's important to that elected leader and their constituency. A sit-down interview is a back-and-forth discussion, and the reporter leads the direction. I use a checklist so that I'm prepared for a formal sit-down interview. First, I consider what I want to know or ask. Next, I form written questions, and then decide the best order to present those questions. I keep in mind the flow of a logical conversation. Finally, I decide how to begin, realizing that if I want to conduct a meaningful sit-down interview, I want the subject to be very comfortable with me. To keep it all on track, I am never afraid to use notes during a sit-down interview. While following my notes, it's important not to get into a question–answer rhythm. If the politician is not responding the way I want, I'll rephrase questions, touching the same topic several different ways—approaching that politician on several different fronts to really get a meaningful answer. And, in addition to the questions, the answers are also different. There's more time for lengthy responses—responses that go beyond the typical sound bite seen on television.

Q. What about the press conference?

A. I call them "news" conferences. There's no "press," as in printing, in a TV newsroom. A news conference can be a tricky, disorganized event with so many reporters and cameras and microphones. When the public official approaches that group, they are often on edge, and become inclined to stay on message more than they would in an individual interview. Public officials usually approach groups of reporters with one specific message that they want to communicate. The biggest challenge for reporters is turning that official message into a meaningful response. I tend to do that with open-ended questions after the initial statement. I'll simply ask, "This means what?" or "How does this affect people?" Also, I'm not afraid to be very basic in trying to get an explanation. It's not the reporter's place to sound like an expert. It's the reporter's place to learn and to engage the responses that news consumers will find most relevant.

Q. So news conferences are approached from an entirely different perspective than the other forms of interviews.

A. Yes, and it's really a two-phase process. The initial phase starts with the statement from the public official and some questions aimed at getting some sound bites. But there's a second phase that's the informative stage. It's usually a flurry of questions from the reporters to learn the background of that initial message. These questions are just as important as the others, but instead of that nice sound bite, you're looking for the nuts and bolts of the story to give you an understanding of the background on which the story is based. So the gang interview really has two different categories. On one hand, you're seeking the message and a clear meaning of it. On the other hand, you're really learning about the story as you go along.

(continued)

Continued

Q. How do your questions interact with the questions of other reporters at the news conference?

A. Reporters feed on each other in those news conferences. Many reporters may have the same questions in mind. When one reporter asks a question, it may jog something in the memory of another reporter who may present a follow-up, which furthers the issue. In many cases, more reporters are better than few because there's a collective approach to learning information about that story. It's not uncommon for one reporter's question to feed a follow-up, and for that follow-up to feed an entirely new line of questioning, that wasn't considered to begin with. Even your competitors can prove helpful in a news conference.

Media Interviews

The press has a long history of covering political campaigns and politicians. Press coverage of politics goes back to the beginning of active campaigning. However, coverage of politics intensified in the twentieth century as the mass media expanded to include newspapers, radio, and television. The nature of the relationship between the press and public officials has varied depending on the public figure involved. President Franklin Roosevelt, for example, had a close relationship with many reporters in the national press and would often give impromptu interviews. In contrast, Richard Nixon was openly hostile and skeptical of the press (Crouse, 1974).

News Interviews

The most frequent form of coverage available to politicians, candidates, and campaigns is that of straight news that will appear in a newspaper or newsmagazine. A story is reported in an unbiased manner and presented as information to inform the public. Public officials make conscious efforts to gain such coverage (Ansolabehere, Behr, & Iyengar, 1994). Typically, success in achieving news coverage is referred to as *free media* or *earned media*.

Politicians typically enjoy doing interviews for straight news. They may avoid such interviews, though, when coverage turns to scandals, controversy, or the personal lives of the public officials. The news media, however, often seems to be most active when covering such topics.

During the 1884 presidential campaign, Grover Cleveland was beset by accusations that he had fathered an illegitimate child. Cleveland's only response to reporters who approached him about the issue was "tell the truth," and most reporters did not pursue the matter. Not so today. Modern campaigns often represent a "politics of intimacy" (Parry-Giles & Parry-Giles, 1996) in which a candidate's personal life is considered fair game. During the 2000 presidential campaign, candidates were asked a multitude of questions that had little to do with the issues of the office, but a lot to do with what they did in private. During Hillary Clinton's campaign for the U.S. Senate in New York, a radio talk show host in Buffalo asked the first lady if she had been "sexually unfaithful" in her marriage (Hu, 2000). Clinton called the question "out of bounds," but answered it anyway (she denied the charge).

This type of political reporting raises two issues. At what point do reporters cross the line, delving into matters that are none of his or her business or the public's? To what extent does such intrusion keep quality candidates from even running for public office? The latter question is difficult to answer. During the Clinton–Lewinsky controversy, Texas governor George W. Bush speculated that he might not seek the Republican nomination for president if he and his family would be subjected to such scrutiny, but he ultimately decided to run anyway.

Topics considered appropriate by reporters range from the sometimes controversial to the mundane, including questions about a person's sex life, religious views, physical and mental health, income, advisors, friends, favorite books, movies, and political philosophers. Right or wrong, the press seems intent on examining candidates' private lives, and the pressure to do so increases with the increased visibility of the office being sought. Candidates who run for public office today have to expect some news coverage of their private lives.

Sometimes public officials will try to use an interview as a means of diffusing a potential scandal. During a 1987 congressional primary in Tennessee, front-runner Bob Clement was sued for alienation of affection by a man who claimed that Clement had an affair with the man's wife. Clement denied the allegations, but reporters had more questions. Rather than holding a news conference to address the allegations, Clement and his wife met with reporters in individual interviews held at their home and answered reporters' questions on the charges. Despite the stress associated with responding to such charges, Clement was perceived as being at ease and honest during the interview, and the press shifted its attention to whether his opponents were behind the allegations. It was subsequently revealed that one of Clement's opponents had indeed been behind the charges, and Clement went on to an easy win in the campaign (Powell & Cowart, 2003).

On other occasions, however, this strategy may backfire. In 1972, Senator Edward "Ted" Kennedy was considered a major Democrat candidate for president, but he was dogged by questions concerning a major scandal—the Chappaquiddick incident (Tedrow, Tedrow, & Tedrow, 1980; Lange & DeWitt, 1993). To have a realistic chance at winning the Democrat's nomination, Kennedy needed to address the situation. In an attempt to do so, Kennedy agreed to an in-depth interview with the CBS program *60 Minutes*, knowing that questions about the incident would be raised during the interview. When asked about the incident, however, he responded in a highly defensive and agitated manner. The subsequent broadcast of the interview doomed his chances for the nomination (Lester, 1972; Lippman, 1976).

The Press Conference. Public officials make frequent use of the press conference, an interview situation in which a public figure speaks with several reporters at the same time. As noted in an earlier chapter, "Most press conferences . . . are more convenient for sources than for reporters" (Fedler, 2001, p. 518), which is why public officials are so fond of them. The White House generally holds press briefings on a daily basis. During times of major crises, they will occur even more frequently than that. The speaker at such press

Analyzing Political Interviews

How does the average citizen evaluate quotes from political interviews? After all, most of these quotes are relatively short and only part of a longer interview or press conference. Given those limitations, how should the people evaluate political quotes? Here are a few guidelines for evaluating political quotes.

1. **What is the political environment?** What is happening in the world that created the need for the interview? How is this interview part of a larger story?
2. **What is the context of the quote?** Was the quote a planned statement given in response to an anticipated question or topic? Or was it a spontaneous response to an unanticipated topic? How does it fit within the context of other statements from the same public figure at the same time? Other sources, such as newspapers and the Internet, can provide more context information than can typically be obtained from television coverage.
3. **Who is the target audience?** Sometimes an interview may be used to send a message to another nation or another public figure, particularly if there is limited contact between the parties. On other occasions, the response may be aimed at a particular demographic or geographic target group.
4. **What was the speaker's purpose?** This involves some supposition, but a trained observer can usually identify several potential purposes. A Republican who makes a positive statement about racial diversity may be reaching out to minority voters or trying to appeal to political moderates. A Democrat who speaks of fiscal responsibility may be reaching out to moderate Republicans who are skeptical of the image of Democrats as big spenders or they may be trying to inoculate against later attacks from opponents on this issue.
5. **How do you feel about the statement?** Does the quote change how you feel about the speaker? Is it the type of statement that you will use as an anchor (i.e., something that you will always remember when you think of this person)? Do you consider this a typical or atypical remark from that person? Does the statement reflect your values?

---

briefings is usually the press secretary or another administration official—not the president. Most public officials only attend major press briefings; their press secretaries handle those held on a daily or weekly basis.

Public officials sometimes use press conferences to diffuse controversial situations. They typically do this by presenting a prepared statement on the controversy before opening the floor to questions. The prepared statement will be designed to preempt the toughest questions, allowing the individual to define the issue in his or her own terms before the questions begin. Even when such tactics do not succeed fully, some of the reporters' questions will be answered in advance, reducing the likelihood of an extensive debate on the topic with reporters (Rowley, 2003).

Personality Profiles.   An increasingly popular form of news coverage of politicians is the personality profile. A personality profile is a story that attempts to allow the public to get a better understanding of the public official as an individual. Some public figures use personality profiles to increase awareness of issues that are of interest to them.

Sometimes personality profiles can lead to major news stories. During his 1996 campaign for president, Jimmy Carter made national headlines when he did an interview with *Playboy* magazine and said that he had sinned at times by having "lust in my heart" (Schram, 1976).

Editorial Interviews.   Editorials and op-ed (opinion) pieces in newspapers often have little direct impact on election outcomes (Powell & Cowart, 2003). Few people read the editorials, and those who do tend to be politicos who have already decided how they will vote. Still, endorsements can have an impact. Being able to cite a newspaper brings instant credibility to a television ad, and candidates love to use headlines as a visual association for a verbal message. That's why most public officials willingly go through a process known as the editorial interview.

Before offering an endorsement, most major newspapers conduct a series of panel interviews with the candidates. Candidates are typically invited to meet with the editorial panel on an individual basis. The panel is composed of the paper's editors and political reporters, and each member of the panel can ask the candidate questions about his or her policies. Most candidates readily agree to subject themselves to this grilling, even those who do not expect to get the paper's endorsement. An endorsement becomes a plum that can be touted in other campaign venues. Even if an endorsement is not obtained, the interview provides the candidate with the opportunity to explain his or her positions to the gatekeepers of the newspaper, hopefully enabling those editors and reporters to provide more accurate coverage of the campaign.

Broadcast Interviews

Broadcast news coverage of politicians falls into two distinct categories: recorded interviews and live interviews.

Recorded Interviews.   Recorded interviews for broadcast news programs are similar in many ways to newspaper interviews. From the reporter's view, the purpose of both interviews is the same—to use quotes from the interview as part of a news story on the public official. However, broadcast interviews and newspaper interviews differ in a few important ways. Interviews with newspaper reporters are usually more casual than those with broadcast reporters. The newspaper reporter may have a tape recorder, but will not have television cameras, lapel microphones, or other equipment that will be distracting to the interviewee. Further, in a newspaper interview the interviewee is allowed more leeway in his or her responses.

Consider, for example, the following question: "What will be the impact of this piece of legislation on the public?" In a newspaper interview, the public official can use "hedges" (statements that delay or qualify the response) before giving an answer. The interviewee may respond to such a question by saying, "Well, in my opinion, when you look at all the factors, I think you'll see that most of the public will be better off under this new law." This statement is boring and wordy and would not come across well on television. However, it works well for a newspaper interview. The newspaper reporter can simply edit the statement and report the quote as: "I think . . . most of the public will be better off under this new law."

With recorded broadcast interviews, it is important to remember that only a small portion of the interview will be aired. The interview itself may take several minutes, with the interviewee answering several questions. When the interview is aired, however, only about 12 seconds of the person's comments actually will be used. The reporter will choose the sound bite that makes the story look good and allows for presentation of the story in a narrative format (Grabe & Zhou, 1999, 2003). From the public figure's perspective, it is important that the sound bite be the right 12 seconds. The public figure's goal is message consistency; the sound bite used by the reporter should convey the message that he or she is trying to convey. This can be remarkably easy to do, but it takes a little advance preparation.

1. **Decide in advance what the sound bite should be**. In the brief amount of time before the interview starts, the public official usually decides what the sound bite should be. The public official will formulate a single statement that can be spoken in 12 seconds or less that reflects the desired message.
2. **It is okay to mumble and be monotonic, as long as it is not during the sound bite**. Most novice television interviewees do not realize that it is not a big deal to make mistakes, such as mumbling or stumbling over words. Recorded broadcast interviews are very forgiving of such mistakes. Most of the interview will never be aired, and such mistakes are routinely edited out of the story.
3. **It is okay to start over**. If the interviewee gets into a sentence and begins to stumble over words or phrases, it is acceptable to simply stop and start over. Stopping in mid-sentence kills that part of the interview as a potential sound bite. The interviewee can then tell the reporter, "Let me say that again," and repeat the answer in a coherent manner.
4. **Emphasize the sound bite**. Many public officials have learned to pause before saying the sound bite and then, when they say it, they say it with passion. This is what the reporter is looking for—a distinct statement that effectively and dramatically summarizes the story.

Live Broadcast Interviews.   Live broadcast interviews differ from taped interviews. The audience sees and hears everything done or said. All mistakes are seen by the public. Consequently, to be effective in this situation, the individual must be well-informed on the topic (so they can speak freely and knowledgeably) and have the self-confidence to express themselves in an authoritative manner. Not everyone has those attributes. Still, since their comments are not edited, some public figures are more comfortable doing live broadcast interviews than taped news interviews. During the early stages of his 2000 presidential campaign, for example, George W. Bush seemed uncomfortable when responding to reporters' questions, but was more adept at one-on-one interviews. Some reporters noted that in his early TV appearances, questions from reporters ". . . caused him to send a panicky look into the camera" that contrasted sharply with the "easy charm" exhibited during his first appearance on CNN's *Larry King Live* (James, 1999). Much of the difference was due to the location of the camera; instead of speaking at a press conference, where Bush often felt like an open target, the Larry King interview was conducted in "the warm, woody setting of a Nashville saloon."

Priming

The goal of spin is message priming—establishing expectations for judging political messages. This process goes back to an academic concept known as *news priming*. Iyengar and Kinder (1987) argue that news priming is part of the news process in that the media establishes standards that voters use to evaluate the government, the president, and political candidates. Those standards serve as expectations for the public; they use those expectations to make judgments about what they see and hear in the media. This theory has been supported by research on the extensive media coverage in 1986 of the Reagan administration's covert diversion of funds to the Nicaraguan Contras. The attitudes of those voters who subsequently had negative opinions of Regan were strongly linked to the amount of coverage the issues received (Krosnick & Kinder, 1990).

The news-priming function is the main reason that elected officials and candidates attempt to control the media agenda (Perloff, 1998). Spinning is one way to influence news priming. The spin process is particularly active just prior to and after major public performances, such as televised debates. Spin doctors typically participate in the process by trying to deflate expectations prior to an event and making positive comparisons with the expectations on a post-hoc basis. During press interviews, spin doctors may try to lower expectations of upcoming performances ("Our candidate doesn't have as much debate experience as our opponent, but we expect he will do well") or try to encourage reporters to look at particular points of a candidate's performance ("The important thing is what he had to say on the economy").

Framing

Message framing is news priming on a holistic level. If the media accepts the way a politician frames an issue, then subsequent coverage of that issue tends to be beneficial. Most research on framing has focused on news coverage, with the results indicating that the way the media frames an issue can have a major impact on public opinion and voter behavior (Devitt, 1997; Gamson, 1996; Gitlin, 1980; Graber, 1987; Iorio & Huxman, 1996; McCombs & Shaw, 1993; McLeod & Detenber, 1999). More specifically, framing can have in impact on candidate credibility by framing voter attributions of blame or praise (Iyengar, 1996). Framing works because political attitudes are expressions of underlying arguments recalled from memory (Kelly, 1983; Zaller, 1993; Chong, 1993; Chong, 1999).

Campaign themes are often used to frame a political campaign. Miller (1999) notes that campaign themes attempt to construct a reality by framing the interpretation of external events and providing a suggestion as to how the electorate should decide the election. The theme expresses an attitude, defines the rhetorical situation, and provides a mechanism for responding to reporters' questions. Thus, a campaign theme acts as a controlling concept, naming and revealing attitudes toward events and providing a "strategic answer" to questions posed by situations (Burke, 1973, p. 1). The frame simplifies external events, defining them with decision-making cues. Bill Clinton's 1996 campaign theme, "Bridge to the 21st Century," framed the election context as a decision about the future. It simultaneously expressed confidence in his earlier programs and optimism and excitement about the ambiguous future of the next millennium (Miller, 1999). Ronald Reagan's "common culture" evoked benevolent capitalism and civic virtue as elements of the cornerstones of the American myth (Patterson, 1999). When he needed a political scapegoat, Reagan often framed the federal bureaucracy as a "benign political scapegoat" that he could target with verbal assaults (Braden, 2001).

Word Choice

Framing is influenced by word choice. Public officials carefully choose the right words or phrases to use during an interview. Words can simultaneously create labels, convey a speaker's feelings on a topic, and signal emotional distance between the speaker and the issue (Fraser & Gordon, 1994). The official's goal is to select the "right" word; that is, "the word that does exactly what you want it to do, and nothing else" (Perlman, 1998, p. 129). The spokesperson usually tries to avoid long words that may be difficult to pronounce and hard for the audience to understand. As Noonan (1998) notes, ". . . big things are best said, are almost always said, in small words" (p. 54). Once a word or phrase is identified, it may be used repeatedly—part of the process of staying "on message" (Norris et al., 1999). The authors worked on one campaign in which the guidelines for a candidate's radio interview included working in the phrase "fiscal conservative" three times. During the 2000 presidential election, George W. Bush never talked about spending "cuts" to reduce government expenditures, but always used the word "savings" (Bruni, 2000). During the 1980 New Hampshire primary, Ronald Reagan's consultants countered concerns that Reagan was too old (he was then 69) by using the phrase "oldest and wisest" in speeches and in conversations with reporters, thus putting a positive spin on the age issue. Deborah Tannen (2000) notes that George W. Bush's campaign rhetoric was filled with words that would appeal to women voters, including references to "children," "dreams," "hope," "love," and "hearts."

Sunday News Shows

In national politics, some of the most influential news television is broadcast on Sunday mornings (when few people are watching television) on interview shows such as NBC's *Meet the Press*, CBS's *Face the Nation*, and ABC's *This Week*. As TV commentator Roger Simon (1987) notes, these shows are all based on the assumption "that important political and government figures, faced with vigorous questioning, just might slip and commit news" (p. 4).

The format of these shows is similar. Each has a reporter or reporters directing questions at public officials or other newsworthy individuals. In most cases, the guests are either high-ranking administration officials or people who are in leadership positions in Congress. The oldest of the Sunday news shows, *Meet the Press*, made its debut in 1951. For the remainder of that decade, the questions were gentle, with reporters typically showing respect toward their guests. Simon (1987) notes that, in the beginning, "persistent follow-up questions were somehow considered bad manners" (p. 5). Today, tough questions are the rule, not the exception. Further, appearances on the shows may offer little opportunity to reach undecided voters; the audience tends to be made up of active voters (Hofstetter et al., 1994), most of whom have already made their voting decision.

So why do politicians agree to participate? First, they want to get exposure for themselves and their ideas. Despite the small audience, all of the Sunday interview shows generate a great deal of spin-off coverage. Comments made on the show are reported on the evening television news and distributed in print to all of the major newspapers. An effective interview on any of the shows can dramatically increase recognition of an issue, pushing it to the forefront of the media's agenda. Second, most of the guests are not afraid of the tough questioning. Most, if not all, have been interviewed thousands of times before they make their first Sunday-morning appearance. Their interview-response skills are often just as well developed as the interview-questioning skills of the reporters. As Simon (1987) notes, "if they don't want to say something, it is hard to make them say it" (p. 6).

Campaign Debates

Perhaps one of the most critical interview situations in political campaigns is the televised debate. Debates have been major components of every presidential campaign since the Ford–Carter debates of 1976 (Hess, 1988), and they are regular components of most gubernatorial campaigns. They are now such an institutionalized and ritualistic part of campaigns that voters expect them to occur (Kraus, 2000), even though they are not legally required. Further, despite concerns over political malaise and lack of interest among voters, televised debates typically have a large viewing audience—larger than any other presidential campaign event (Buchanan, 1991).

Presidential debates are truly critical events. They offer candidates a chance to enhance their credibility while addressing issues that the media may have overlooked (Hellweg, Pfau, & Brydon, 1992). Further, although such elements are merely one of several sources of voter information, debates typically have some type of impact on the voting public (Chaffee, 1978). Debates enable candidates to show their personalities, highlight differences in political philosophies, and focus attention on their campaigns (Glenn, 2001). Debates can increase voter interest and participation in a campaign (Delli Carpini et al., 1997; Buchanan, 1991), increase knowledge of a campaign (Becker et al., 1978), enhance ability to discuss the campaign with others (Miller & MacKuen, 1979), and trigger increased interpersonal communication about the campaign (Jamieson & Birdsell, 1988). In addition, debates offer reporters access to the candidates in a situation that allows for cross-examination questioning, thus allowing voters to see how the candidates respond to pressure situations (Glenn, 2001).

Debates often have a short-term impact on the salience of issues (Swanson & Swanson, 1978; Atkin et al., 1989). In the immediate aftermath of the debate, the issues addressed by the candidates are likely to receive increased coverage from the news media and an enhanced perception of salience by the voting public. Debates also can influence the image and perceptions of the candidates, although the impact does not typically alter voters' intentions (Abramowitz, 1978).

However, debates are not perfect forums for candidate–voter communication (Jamieson & Birdsell, 1990). Media questions may be superficial, and even persistent questioning may reveal little information. Candidates often resort to repeating segments from their stump speeches or use the debate as a forum for attacking their opponents (Glenn, 2001).

Voter response to a debate is often affected by three factors: (1) the expectations of the candidates, (2) the performances of the candidates, and (3) the political ideologies of the voters.

The public's expectations of a candidate are often formed from other elements of the campaign—the image that the candidate projects and the issues he or she discusses (Hellweg, Pfau, & Brydon, 1992). In the 2000 election, George W. Bush entered the debates following a series of campaign misstatements that had raised doubts about his ability to perform well during the debates. While his resulting performance was not particularly stellar, it was not bad either. He subsequently came out of the debates with an improved image with the voters.

The performance of the candidates also affects the voters' response. Debates present voters with a longer and more intense view of the candidates than news or advertising do, giving the public a chance to familiarize themselves with the candidates (Jamieson & Birdsell, 1988). Vancil and Pendell (1984) note that presidential candidates can use debates as an opportunity to demonstrate a presidential image. The candidate who appears most presidential typically will be perceived as the winner of the debate.

Finally, a voter's impression of a debate is based heavily on the voter's political ideology, position on the issues, and prior support of a candidate (Martel, 1983). Despite the secondary impact that debates can have on the information available to voters, they typically have little impact on voter decisions (Abramowitz, 1978). Decided voters typically declare their candidate to be the winner. For them, the debates are more like a pep rally. Rather than changing their vote, it merely reinforces their support of the candidate, particularly if the candidate meets their expectations. Even the positive impact of increased knowledge and information is tempered by the voters' predispositions. Although they generally increase their knowledge of the issues in the campaign, the voters' pre-existing attitudes still serve as filters through which they process the information obtained in the debate. As a result, they still may misunderstand some of the issues (Jacoby et al., 1986). Ultimately, debates play a pivotal role in campaigns, but their impact can be muted by other campaign factors.

Debate Preparation

Candidates frequently prepare for debates through role-playing. Campaign staff members play the role of reporters, asking the candidate tough questions and follow-ups. At least one person may play the role of the opponent, seeking to throw the candidate off balance with an unanticipated question or challenge.

Lawrence (2000) notes that debate contenders also typically rehearse a few "gotchas." Noonan (1998) traces the trend to 1984 when Walter Mondale criticized the substance behind Gary Hart's positions by asking "Where's the beef?" "After the success of Mondale's line," Noonan notes, "the word went forth: candidates needed to be supplied by their staff with zippy sound bites before they went into a debate or an interview" (p. 98).

Preparations for the candidate may include both verbal and nonverbal training. In an analysis of the 1992 and 1996 presidential town hall debates, Goodman and Gring (1999) note that Clinton often repositioned himself so that each television image of him either included the American flag in the background (in 1992) or pictured him with the audience (in 1996). They conclude that Clinton ". . . made a conscious effort to maximize his visual impact during the town hall debates . . . ," a factor that implied that he had planned and practiced the positioning in advance of the actual debate.

A few other rules often are used in debate preparation:

1. **Don't start sentences with "I think" or "I believe."** Public officials often have a tendency to preface their answers with hedge statements such as "I think" or "I believe." The problem with these phrases is twofold: they are too egocentric and they are too weak. Notice the difference, for example, between saying "I think we can lead the nation to a great future" and "We can lead the nation to a great future." The second version is stronger, whereas the first version is a tacit admission that the speaker might be wrong.
2. **Don't worry about time**. Many forums are framed around rules that specify that the candidate has a specific length of time to answer a question, usually about two minutes. Some candidates feel obligated to speak for the entire two minutes—a perception that can adversely affect their responses as they try to "stretch" their answer to the appropriate length. In reality, it doesn't matter how long or how short their answer might be, as long as the answer is a good one. The audience is looking for an answer, not a two-minute long answer. If the answer is a good one, it doesn't matter if it is 15, 30, 60, or 90 seconds. The audience pays attention to what the candidates say, not how long they speak.
3. **Answer the question in the first sentence**. Sometimes candidates will answer a question, but only after they explain why. In essence, their answer comes at the end of their statement. By then, many of audience members will have quit listening. The audience listens to the first sentence, using it to judge whether the speaker is truly answering the question or merely trying to avoid it. If the audience doesn't hear the answer in that first sentence, they may label the candidate as indecisive—even if the candidate eventually answers the question later in the response. Therefore, the first sentence in a response should leave the audience with the impression that the candidate is decisive and knowledgeable on the topic.
4. **Offer support for the answer immediately after giving it, preferably in a bullet-point format, and end with a "bookend" that reinforces the main idea**. Combined with the above recommendation, the ideal format for answering a debate interview question is (1) answer the question in the first sentence, (2) explain why, including at least one fact to demonstrate knowledge of the topic, and (3) end by referring back to the first sentence. Thus, if the question is, "What will be your top priority as governor?" the answer should be something along the lines of:

We must turn around the economy so we can raise the standard of living for everyone in the state (ANSWER TO QUESTION). Our economy is so bad right now that we're losing thousands of people every year who move out of state in search of jobs. Further, the current administration is doing nothing to actively recruit new industry (EXPLAINS WHY). I'll be the leader who'll change that (BOOKEND).

This approach to debate preparation is not universal. Different political consultants have different strategies. Still, the goal is essentially the same regardless of which style of preparation is used—that the candidate is perceived as a knowledgeable and intelligent person who understands the needs of the public.

Legislative Hearings

As a sitting member of the U.S. Supreme Court, Justice Clarence Thomas is in a position to rule on the constitutionality of numerous cases that come before the court. Before he could take his position, though, he—like all of the other justices on the Supreme Court—had to go through a rigorous interview process in which he was questioned about his qualifications by a legislative committee.

The legislative review interview is required for a number of executive appointments, both at the federal and state level. The purpose of the interview is to enable the committee to make a decision regarding the appointee's qualifications for the position in question. The nominee appears before the committee that oversees the office to which the person has been appointed. The committee will be composed of both Democrats and Republicans, and each committee member is allowed to ask the nominee questions. Such questions are usually limited to a specific length of time (usually about 10 minutes), but additional questions can be submitted in writing.

Sometimes these hearings are perfunctory in nature, with the U.S. Senate committee convening merely to meet the candidate and to confirm the president's judgment. In fact, the Senate has confirmed 89 percent of the judicial nominees sent to it by all presidents (Yalof, 2001). In other cases, however, such hearings can be brutal. In those instances, the committee members often break into two groups—usually along party lines—in terms of support and opposition for the nominee. Supporters usually use their time for two purposes: (1) to ask "softball" questions that allow the nominees to talk about their strengths and (2) to ask question that will refute points raised by the opposition. Opponents usually approach these interviews as if they are cross-examining a witness in the court case. They are usually well trained in this approach, because many politicians start out as lawyers.

Opponents usually try to impeach the character of the nominee. Robert Bork, nominated to the Supreme Court by Ronald Reagan, was turned down by the committee after Democrats on the Senate Judiciary Committee raised questions about his legal ideology (Simon, 1992). Similarly, Clarence Thomas, who was nominated to the Court by President George H. W. Bush, was subjected to intense questioning about his professional behavior in an office setting (including charges of sexual harassment) before he was nominated (Simon, 1992; Thomas, 2001). In Thomas' case, his professional behavior became a bigger issue than his legal philosophy (Gerber, 2002).

The most common technique used by the opposition is to question the nominee about inconsistencies in his or her record. Any person nominated for a high government post will have a lengthy public record that can be examined—and it will be. The opposing legislators will have their staff sift through and research the nominee's background. This material will be supplemented by research done by special interest groups who oppose the nominee.

The questioning process is similar to that of a courtroom cross-examination. The legislator reads something that the nominee has written in the past and tries to get the nominee to confirm the statement or fact ("Did you write a friend-of-the-court brief in which you supported the defendant in that case?"). The legislator then identifies an inconsistency about the fact ("Weren't you the only person out of 35 who filed such briefs to support the defendant?"). The nominee, to have any chance to pass, must respond positively and aggressively to such questions ("Yes I was, but I was also the only one who was right. The court agreed with me").

Meanwhile, supporters of the nominee, particularly those who have yet to ask any questions, are listening to each question and answer. They also have had their staff conduct research on the nominee and are supported with material from special interest groups. As opponents ask questions that hurt the candidate, the supporters plan questions that will refute the allegation implied by the opponents' questions. Further, these questions will be part of an organized campaign aimed at gaining support for the nominee. Some critics have charged, in fact, that Clarence Thomas won his nomination despite strong opposition from the Democrats on the Judiciary Committee because the Republicans were better organized than their Democrat opponents (Mayer & Abramson, 1994).

A second type of interview done by legislative committee is the witness hearing. In most instances, the goal of a witness hearing is to gather information. The legislative committee meets to discuss a topic being considered for legislative action. Experts in the field are asked to meet with the committee so that the committee can learn more about the topic before presenting its recommendation to the full legislative body. The process typically starts with the witness making a formal presentation of his or her basic ideas. After the witness presents a statement, each member of the committee can then ask questions of the witness. The witness's presentation usually is intended to be persuasive; the expert argues for a change in the law that supports his or her position ("Smoking is dangerous to one's health, and we must do more to curtail smoking by teenagers"). The committee members' questions are usually probes intended to gather more information ("Is there any evidence that tobacco companies are targeting teenagers?").

Sometimes witnesses also will be interviewed during nomination hearings. During the Clarence Thomas hearing, for example, opponents brought in a former Thomas co-worker—Anita Hill—to testify against him (Hill, 1997). Her testimony—that Thomas had subjected her to sexual harassment—triggered a public counterstrategy from the Republicans that included an attempt to impeach her character as a witness (Brock, 1994).

Sometimes, witness hearings are held to promote the agenda of a group or an individual politician. The most infamous legislative hearing to fall in this category would be the congressional hearings of the House Committee on Un-American Activities headed by Senator Joseph McCarthy the mid-1950s (Reeves, 1997). McCarthy used the Congressional hearing as a stage for interviewing those suspected of being Communist spies (Fried, 1997). The concern over spying in the United States was real; the Soviet Union had established an extensive spy network using Communist sympathizers (Buckley & Bozell, 1977; Herman, 2000). McCarthy's ability to tie into that issue and the fears that surrounded it made him a national political figure (Herman, 2000). As the hearings progressed, though, the questions presented during the hearings shifted from interviews to interrogation. The questions used in the interrogation were designed to elicit guilt by association or by reluctance to answer—particularly for those witnesses who were associated with the Hollywood film industry. Those who refused to testify soon found themselves blacklisted from future film work (Schrecker, 1998).

Summary

Public officials and candidates must have solid interviewing skills if they are to succeed in their careers. Interviews with the press or with representatives of government bodies are daily activities for many public officials. Interviews often are critical both to the careers of the public officials involved and to the public that they represent. This chapter has outlined some of the interviewing situations that apply to the political arena: media interviews, debates, and interviews before legislative committees.

Media interviews include news interviews, press conferences, and broadcast interviews. Such interviews may become particularly intense if a controversy about the official's career emerges. Interviews also are important during political campaigns, particularly in debate formats in which journalists ask each candidate questions about his or her policy positions. Finally, interviews are important inside the political arena, particularly when public officials have to appear as witnesses or nominees before legislative committees.

FOR FURTHER DISCUSSION

1. Watch a televised presidential news conference. What process is used to determine which reporters get to ask questions? Is each reporter allowed a follow-up question? How does one question relate to the one that follows it, or are the two questions unrelated?

2. Watch one of the Sunday morning political interview shows. Who asks the questions? What techniques are used to encourage interviewees to be open with their responses? Would you describe this as an easy or a tough interview for the interviewee? Why?

3. Analyze a televised political debate. Who asks the questions: reporters, candidates, or both? What question–answer format is used? Are some of the questions too long? Are some of the answers too short?

CHAPTER

10 Qualitative Research Interviews

Before writing a book on the religious rituals of rural Appalachians, an ethnologist spends six months in the foothills of Appalachia, interviewing the local residents regarding their lifestyles and religious beliefs.

A sociologist visits maximum security penitentiaries across the nation to interview criminals on death row. The sociologist's goal is to understand why some people become mass murderers.

A historian interviews the widow of a war hero. Her answers provide insights into the historical figure's private life and offer information as to where the historian can find written sources pertaining to the hero's life.

Each of these examples represents an instance in which interviews are used as a research methodology. Researchers have used interview techniques to investigate such widespread topics as local politics (Mullen, 2003), national politics (Olsen, 2003), family relationships (Boose & Flowers, 1989), and nonprofit organizations (Gutgold, 2003). By asking questions, researchers gather information that then becomes research data. Researchers compare data from multiple interviews to draw conclusions about an event or group of people.

Quantitative interviews tend to be highly standardized and qualitative interviews are less structured; both techniques can be used by researchers to gather meaningful data. Researchers have found that qualitative research interviews can be used to explain and supplement data obtained from quantitative interview research (the topic of the next chapter). Such an integration of interview techniques has contributed to our understanding of aggression (Bushman & Anderson, 1998) and intercultural communication (McKinley & Jensen, 2003). The potential for integrating qualitative interviews with other forms of research offers a dramatic opportunity to expand our collective understanding of the human condition.

Three major approaches are used to conduct qualitative interview research: (1) in-depth interviews, (2) focus groups, and (3) informal interviews done as part of participant–observation research.

In-Depth Interviews

In-depth, or extended, interviews are one-on-one sessions in which an interviewer explores a topic in detail with one interviewee. In communication research, such interviews are frequently face-to-face. Many pollsters and market researchers conduct in-depth interviews over the telephone.

The goal of the in-depth interview, as Brenner (1985) notes, is to gain an "intimate familiarity" (p. 148) with the points of view of the person being interviewed. Stacks and Hocking (1999) note that the approach is particularly useful in studying research questions that are either value- or policy-oriented. Researchers have used the technique to examine social problems (Bandy, 2004), social activism (Moore, 2003), depression (Loewenthal et al., 2002), and psychiatric recovery (Smith, 2000). Historians sometimes use in-depth interviews as a way to learn about a person's life from the perspective of those who knew him or her.

The Retrospective Interview Technique

One in-depth interview technique that is used in academic settings is the *Retrospective Interview Technique (RIT)*, which aims to help individuals reconstruct events and circumstances in chronological order (Huston, Surra, Fitzgerald, & Cate, 1981). With this technique, both participants graph and discuss changes that have occurred over time in some aspect of their relationship. As a research methodology, it has been used to study romantic relationships (Baxter & Bullis, 1986; Baxter, 2001), post-divorce changes (Graham, 1997), parent–child relationships (Golish, 2000), behavioral patterns of children (McVeigh, Norris, & de Wet, 2004), blended families (Baxter, Braithwaite & Nicholson, 1999), occupational therapy (Eklund, Rottpeter, & Vikstrom, 2003), career paths (Allen & Pickett, 1987), teacher–student interaction (Norby, 2002), marital conflict (Erbert, 2000), child abuse (Bifulco, Brown, & Harris, 1994), and intercultural communication (Adams & Stadler, 2002).

Known Associate Interviews

Another in-depth interview technique is the *known associate interview*. In the known associate interview, the researcher interviews individuals who are known to be friends, family, and/or business associates of a particular person. The researcher's goal is to gain some insight about an individual who is the focus of a larger research project. Such information can be invaluable in doing a thorough investigation into the individual or topic. Scott Berg (1999), for example, won a Pulitzer Prize for his 1999 biography of Charles Lindbergh. The biography would have been much less successful without the cooperation of Lindbergh's widow, Anne Morrow Lindbergh. By talking with her, Berg was able to gain an understanding of Lindbergh's private life, his private thoughts, and the public aspects of the man that warranted additional investigation.

Field Interviews

Another in-depth interview technique is *field interviewing* (Ives, 1995). Field interviewing is a semi-directed conversation in which the researcher seeks to elicit the participant's point of view on a topic. The interviews are typically conducted in the participant's environment, or *field*. By conducting the interview in the participant's field, the participant will be more comfortable. In addition, the context also will help provide the interviewer with cues for directing the conversation. The interviewer starts out with a general idea of the topic to be covered but draws on comments and issues raised by the participant to direct the discussion.

In many instances, field interviews turn into extended conversations rather than true interviews. Once a topic is raised, a few probes keep the conversation flowing. Sometimes the conversations can be rather lengthy, resulting in some researchers referring to them as *long interviews* (McCracken, 1988). Lindsley (1999), for example, spent four hours on some of the interviews she used to study cultural themes in American-owned businesses in Mexico. Similarly, Chen and Chen (2002) used in-depth interviews with 16 Hong Kong business people who did business with the People's Republic of China to identify cultural factors that affect business negotiations.

Because the participant controls so much of the conversation, the researcher may elicit details that could not be obtained with any other methodology. This is one reason why Berger (1998) notes that the approach is a highly effective tool for understanding how people view the world. Although the entire event or topic in question may be difficult to understand, the interview allows the researcher to at least understand it from the participant's perspective. Further, such interviews may point the researcher toward other people who can provide important information (Peterson et al., 1994).

A field interview starts with the traditional interview approach. Early questions are intended to orient the participant to the purpose of the interview and to put the person at ease. The interviewer may ask some biographical questions at this stage to get the participant to talk about a familiar topic while providing the interviewer with an understanding of the context (McCracken, 1988). Questions should be designed to allow the participant to tell his or her own story. Open-ended questions, combined with a

---

The Seven Objectives of a Field Interview

1. To learn about events and interactions that cannot be directly observed
2. To understand a communication event or process from the participant's perspective
3. To develop a relationship with the participant to infer communication properly and processes
4. To verify or validate data obtained from other sources
5. To test hypotheses
6. To uncover the distinctive language and communication style used by participants in their natural communication environments
7. To collect data efficiently

Source: Lindlof, T. R. (1995). *Qualitative communication research methods*. Thousand Oaks, CA: Sage.

liberal use of probes, are most commonly used. Closed-ended questions are used as fol-low-ups to clarify information.

Use of In-Depth Interviews in Market Research

Market researchers sometimes use extended telephone interviews as an alternative to focus groups. Because of the length of extended interviews, the sample size used usually is smaller than that used for a full survey or poll. The goal of such interviews is to gather qualitative data that can provide a more complete answer to a research question. Because each interview is conducted on an individual basis, the extended interview eliminates any group influence on an individual's opinions and statements. The individual's opinions are then entered into a database for the purpose of drawing research conclusions. The disad-vantage of this technique, particularly when compared with focus groups, is that it is time consuming and may be expensive. Further, because the total sample for such interviews may be small, the generalizability of the results may be limited.

To counter this problem, in-depth interviewers often go to great lengths to ensure that the people they interview are representative of the types of individuals that they wish to study. Some researchers use demographic screening questions, much like those used for focus group recruitment. Others use the "snowball" technique in which one interview par-ticipant is asked to help identify others who fit the desired profile. If the study is investi-gating the communication behaviors of diabetics, the interviewers may first talk to friends who are diabetic. They may then ask those participants to suggest other diabetics who would like to participate in the project. Still others use convenience sampling by going directly to groups whose membership reflects the target audience. A study into coping behaviors among women who have suffered from breast cancer, for example, might look to cancer support groups for potential participants.

Advantages and Disadvantages of In-Depth Interviews

The advantage of an in-depth interview is that it allows the researcher to get heavily involved with a single aspect of a research project. The interview may actually be a series of interviews conducted over days, weeks, or months. The researcher often has time to explore different angles, different topics, and different directions related to the topic. This level of involvement allows for a more complete understanding of the other person than could ever be achieved through survey research or through focus groups.

However, in-depth interviews do have disadvantages. First, they are very time con-suming—so much so that in-depth interviews with all of those knowledgeable on any one topic usually is impractical. Second, only one perspective can be obtained at a time. Although the researcher may gain insight into an individual's perspective, it can be diffi-cult to verify if that perspective is accurate and objective. Third, the individual's limited perspective necessarily leads to questions about reliability and validity. Reliability arises because the opinions of the interviewee may not be representative. Validity questions arise from the possibility that the researcher may impose his or her opinions on the data. Even the most objective researchers will examine the data in light of their own experiences; because only one view is being analyzed, there are no counter-balancing sources of infor-mation to help maintain the researcher's objectivity.

Focus Groups

A focus group is a group of people who are gathered together at a common location to discuss a topic under the direction of a moderator (Merton, Lowenthal & Kendall, 1990; Stewart & Shamdasani, 1990; Wellner, 2003). In most cases, the size of the group is small (usually 10 to 15 participants). As a result, data from focus groups lack the generalizability of similar responses obtained from a poll or survey. That weakness aside, in-depth information often can be obtained from focus groups.

Johnson (1996) argues that focus groups offer a radically different approach for researching social relations. In essence, polls and surveys provide a "quantitative" assessment of a public's opinion on an issue. Focus groups can go "beyond surveys" (Bullock & Jones, 1999, p. 38) and provide "qualitative" data about the same issue (Morgan, 1997). Nayyar (2003) describes focus groups as "a window" into how the participants "think and feel" (p. 6). Or, as Joseph Glick (1999) notes, "The strength of the focus group is that it allows people to be people" (p. 121). Surveys can tell a researcher what is happening, but focus groups can tell them why. As Hansen et al. (1998) note, the semi-structured nature of the focus groups allows the researcher "a potentially much richer and more sensitive type of data" (p. 258).

Critical Success Factors for Focus Groups

Three factors are critical to the success of a focus group: a good research question, a good facilitator, and the recruitment of a good sample.

The Research Question. The research question is essential, because it is unlikely that the researchers will elicit useful information if they do not know what they are seeking. Developing focus group questions requires advance planning and thoughtful consideration (Betts & Baranowski, 1996; MacDougall, 2001; Tiberius, 2001). The research question guides both the development of the group discussion and the selection of the participants, who are usually selected on the basis of some demographic or psychographic criteria. Thus, inadequate planning as to the research question can doom the success of the project (Morgan, 1995).

The Facilitator. The facilitator is critical to the success of a focus group (Glick, 1999). The role of the facilitator is so critical that some authorities recommend using a professional moderator for the role (Shoaf, 2003). The moderator's job is to encourage discussion by all participants and guide the discussion along the topic of interest but not influence the discussion in any manner. Facilitators often have an outline guide or a questionnaire to remind them of the information being sought, yet they must use their personal research skills to guide the discussion without letting the questionnaire become an artificial part of the process (Keyton, 2001).

The Interview Process

The focus group interview will begin with broad opening questions that are designed to encourage participation. As the interview progresses, a funnel technique is used to

Moderating Focus Groups: An Interview with Jim Jager

Jim Jager is owner of New South Research, a public opinion research company that conducts focus groups on behalf of clients across the United States. Mr. Jager has conducted hundreds of focus groups in varied industries, including retail, health care, financial services, package goods, legal services, automotive, utilities, and education.

Q. Why do you do focus groups?

A. To understand the why behind what people think. To have an interactive process where someone who understands the clients' goals and objectives—the reasons behind what the client is trying to achieve. Having a trained moderator who understands that and can then interact with respondents on the client's behalf. It's a dynamic process as opposed to descriptive process or quantitative research.

Q. When it doesn't work, what goes wrong?

A. When something goes wrong, most of the time it's the recruiting that's wrong. The people in the room don't qualify. You're trying to recruit Bruno's grocery shoppers, and you end up with people who go in Bruno's once in 10 trips, so they're not regular shoppers there. You end up with the wrong respondents for what you were trying to discuss. That's usually evident by their lack of ability to discuss the topic. That can happen because the screener was wrong. I've seen screener's where I've thought, "They're not getting who they're trying to get." That can also happen because the respondent misunderstood on the phone when they were being recruited. I've had respondents cheat because they wanted to participate.

Q. As long as you're getting only one or two of those per group, it's really not a big problem, is it?

A. That's right. And I'd say that in a usual group of 10, there's nearly always one person in there who shouldn't be in the room. I do groups coast-to-coast, and it's pretty rare that I look around the table and every single face at the table is exactly what I expected when the screener was written.

Q. What other things can hurt the research?

A. The moderator doesn't spend the time necessary to understand it in the dialogue that goes back and forth with the client. Or, the client keeps changing the objective. That happens, too. The moderator can try his or her best, and the client just keeps changing.

Q. You said earlier that it requires a "trained moderator." What type of training and skills are required to be an effective moderator?

A. The most important skill is a persona or personality that people find it easy to get comfortable with. For example, if you put an intimidatingly attractive female or a bullyish or intimidatingly attractive male, it's going to put some people off. The personality type of the person leading the group is a huge issue. They must be a person that people feel comfortable with and approachable to. That's number one.

Q. What else?

A. An understanding of group dynamics is also critical. There's going to be a leader in the group, and you must know how to close the leader down without insulting them or

Continued

totally shutting them out, but making sure that everybody else in the room can talk, too. You also need an understanding of human behavior and why people do things that they do.

Q. Give me some examples.

A. What motivates people. For example, convenience is not an innate motivator, but in our modern society, convenience is a huge motivator in most decisions. The moderator must search for that, understand that people want acceptance, and they want to be comfortable.

Q. What are some of the techniques that you use to elicit their comments?

A. Ultimately what you're trying to do is ask a question and get an answer. That's the bottom line. There are a bunch of ways to go about that. One is to use projective or associative techniques. You ask, "If this entity were some kind of animal, what would it be?" And you let them draw a picture. You've got to make them comfortable with doing that. The idea that they're not all there because they're artists. Drawing a stick dog is okay. But it's amazing how people will reveal things about what they perceive about that company—things that they wouldn't say if you just asked, "What do you think of this company?" I may give them a long list of words and just have them pick words out of the list that they would use to describe it. I'll do that if it's a group that—educationally—may need a little more leading along. We may lay a series of pictures and say, "Pick from these pictures what the personality of this organization would be like. Pick two or three pictures and tell me why you chose those pictures." All of those things get people to associate or project things that ultimately gets them talking. It reveals things that just a direct question—"Tell me about that"—wouldn't do it. I've seen it enough to know that it works when you take people around the corner instead of going directly at them.

Q. What about techniques for ensuring that everybody participates?

A. I have somebody that I know is going to be a leader or a talker—someone who always wants to be the first one to speak—I will go to them last. I'll go to the other people first. If I've got one who I think is thoughtful and into the process, but is kind of shy, I'll go to them first. Occasionally I will play the Devil's advocate—not necessarily taking my own position—but taking a position that's different from theirs so that they will explain and defend it. And there is the occasion when you simply have to ask someone in the group to "hang on, let everyone else talk first." That is a risky moment, because you may offend that person and turn them off for the night.

Q. What is your goal in writing the report?

A. There are two goals. First, you want to summarize what you heard. Second, you look for insights that will help the client understand their objective and look for opportunities for new ideas. When I'm in the group, I'm not good at summarizing what I've heard. I've got to go back to a tape or a transcript to get the big picture. But ultimately the goal is to summarize what we heard and to look for insight that will help the client.

Q. Some focus group researchers work in two person teams—the moderator and the observer. Is that a good idea?

A. That's a good idea. When I can, I do that. The second person is behind the two-way mirror taking notes for me. They will also be involved in writing the report. We always have two people working on the report. Always. Sometimes it's somebody who watches the tape.

(continued)

Continued

Q. What about observations from the client themselves? How often does that occur?

A. There are always observations from the client themselves. Most of the time, I agree with those observations. At times, we have to refute those observations because they were out looking for what they wanted to hear.

Q. How would you summarize the process?

A. My analogy is that it's a chain. Any weak link can cause a break. It starts with the first link, the moderator trying to understand the client's objectives and assuring that groups are the proper methodology. The next link is writing a good screener and recruiting the participants. Follow that with an effective job of moderating. The next link is understanding and analyzing the discussion, while the final link is providing a written report that is clear, addresses the client's objectives, and is insightful. If anyone of those links breaks, the entire chain is gone.

narrow the discussion to the specific research question. This technique requires a skillful moderator.

The group format generates discussion (Carey & Smith, 1994) and conflict that allows new ideas to emerge (Morgan & Krueger, 1993). As Glick (1999) notes, "When nonconsensus and disagreements are encouraged, two things generally emerge in group discussion: opinion becomes nuanced in ways that begin to reveal underlying thought frameworks, and people often invoke powerful images" (p. 117). If the group moves too much toward consensus, the moderator has to play the role of the "devil's advocate" and generate discussion from a counter viewpoint (MacDougall & Baum, 1997).

Facilitators often use materials to stimulate discussion. The most popular of materials are copies of television ads, with group participants serving as critics and explaining their responses to the ads. The researchers typically monitor the entire process. The monitoring occurs at the same time as the discussion, with the researchers observing from behind a one-way mirror. In addition, the entire process usually is videotaped, providing for frequent viewings at a later date to verify conclusions.

How Focus Groups Are Used

In most cases, the researcher is not looking for generalizable answers from the focus group. Instead, the goal of focus group research is to obtain new insights into the target audience and its views, which works to supplement other forms of research. Marketers often use focus groups when preparing a media campaign. Focus groups have contributed to the development of advertising campaign slogans, which use terminology provided by the focus group participants. Or, marketers may edit ads based on participants' comments. Other times, it can lead to the development of new ideas or messages that are subsequently tested with survey research (Wimmer & Dominick, 1994).

Focus groups are increasingly being used as a tool for academic study. Janesick (1998) recommends it for those situations in which the research is a new area of study or the target group is well defined. Keyton (2001) notes that focus groups are particularly useful in gathering comparative data, "information about the same topic from different types of people" (p. 307).

Focus groups have a wide range of applications. Swenson and Griswold (1992) recommend their use in journalism and in any troubled organizational program that uses some form of intervention to address its problems. Political campaigns use focus groups to pretest television ads, monitor audience response to presentations, and identify audience language habits that can be used in campaign messages (Williams, 2004). One Republican pollster, Richard Wirthlin, provided data for former President Ronald Reagan. Every time Reagan gave a televised speech, Wirthlin had focus groups watching and using hand-held devices to record their responses to the speech, second by second. Wirthlin used the resulting data to identify what worked and what did not work for each speech. The information was then used in preparing the next speech (Taylor, 1990).

Limitations of Focus Groups

Focus groups have some major limitations (Morgan, 1995). Wimmer and Dominick (1994) argue that, considering the small sample size and qualitative methodology, it is inappropriate to gather quantitative data from a focus group. Several observers note that focus groups lack the statistical validity and reliability of quantitative research methods (Hunter, 2000; Carey, 1995). This problem may be particularly acute if the group has one or two dominant members who quickly lead the other participants to a false consensus (Morgan, 1997). For this reason, most academicians argue that focus group data should be viewed as preliminary data that should be verified with more in-depth research.

Another problem with focus groups is their representativeness. The sample for a focus group essentially consists of volunteers who often are provided monetary incentives to participate. Such groups may not be representative of the overall population from which they were selected. This is particularly true if the participants are "professional subjects" who are constantly used by research organizations for a number of projects. Once someone volunteers to participate in a focus group, the research organization often keeps his or her name (complete with phone number and demographic data) on file. When the research organization needs a participant, it may first call people who have participated before, creating a sample of people who are frequently used for similar research. Constant repetition of this process leads to focus groups composed of unrepresentative samples.

An additional problem with focus groups has to do with the role of the researcher and his or her ability to conduct an impartial analysis (Weinberger et al. 1998). It is remarkably easy for a researcher to let personal biases enter the resulting report. Analysis of any focus group discussion requires that the researcher view the data from three different perspectives—that of the individual, the group, and the group interaction (Duggleby, 2004).

Sim (1998) notes that, regardless of researcher's impartiality, the focus group process limits a researcher's ability to obtain some information. It is impossible to infer attitudinal consensus, because any view expressed by the group may be a result of the group interaction rather than individually held attitudes. For the same reason, researchers often have trouble assessing the strength of group opinions which, in turn, makes it more difficult for the researcher to make comparisons between groups. Reed and Roskell (1997), for example, note the importance of following the sequence of the discussion and the social context of the discussion. That is, it is important to observe and record group dynamic issues such as to whom comments are directed as well as who seems to be leading and influencing the actual comments and other factors. Similarly, Kitzinger (1994) notes that the interaction of the group is a key attribute of focus groups, and yet researchers rarely include the impact of that interaction in their reports. Traulsen, Almarsdottir, and Bjornsdottir (2004) suggest an added level of analysis—an interview with the moderator—to address the issue of impartiality. Still, even this may not totally eliminate researcher bias.

Stockdale (2002) suggests that some researcher bias can be eliminated if the researcher relies more on quantitative analysis of the resulting group discussion, using spreadsheets to analyze and compare the resulting data. Others suggest using online focus groups, noting the advantage of this approach in providing a written record of the discussion (Schneider et al., 2002; Murray, 1997).

Participant–Observation Research

Participant observation is a formal method of observing the actual communication behaviors from within the environment. It is a comparison of what the behaviors should be and what they actually are. Participant–observation research is "a combination of a first-person and a second-person account, that takes place in a naturalistic setting, of the actions and behaviors of a specific group of people" (Hocking, Stacks, & McDermott, 2003, p. 195). The researcher uses participant–observation research to examine communication activities as they naturally occur, looking at those activities from the perspective of both a participant and an observer (Spadley, 1980). Ideally, this research technique allows for both a subjective and objective view of the topic or event. The goal of such an approach is ethnomethodological (Garfinkel, 1967); that is, to determine "how people make sense out of the situations in which they find themselves" (Hocking, Stacks, & McDermott, 2003, p. 197).

Participant–observation research has been used to examine a number of diverse topics, including social norms of southern rednecks (Roebuck & Hickson, 1982), nursing home residents (Brown, 1990), communication problems in a government bureaucracy (Powell & Hickson, 1977–78), urban neighborhoods (Phillipsen, 1975), organizational communication (Hickson, 1974), and political campaign strategies (Powell & Shelby, 1981).

Interviews conducted as part of a participant–observation study can be useful in generating discussion on topics of interest to the researcher. However, researchers conducting participant–observation interviews may face obstacles that are not presented by other forms of research. In particular, participant–observation researchers who use interviews face two problems. First, the interviewer cannot do anything during the interview that disrupts the normal activities of the event being observed. Thus, if the interview itself is disruptive, that in and of itself may reduce the value of the data obtained. Consequently, participant–observation interviews are usually conducted in informal situations. The interviewee, in fact, probably will not consciously realize that he or she is being interviewed.

The topics discussed are elicited during an interaction that could be described as a typical conversation.

Second, the researcher usually cannot record the interview. As Hocking, Stacks, and McDermott note, there often is "a fine line between participant–observation and violating another person's right of privacy" (p. 201). Although laws vary from state to state, most states require the consent of the second party before any interview can be recorded. Requesting permission to record a participant–observation interview inevitably disrupts the nature of the study. Even if the interview occurs in a state where people can be recorded without their permission, ethical questions regarding the person's right to privacy remain.

Consequently, the general rule is that participant–observation interviews (conversations) are not recorded. Instead, participant–observation researchers rely on note-taking (if they can do so without being noticed) or the use of a reflective log following the observation. The latter—the reflective log—is perhaps the most common method of recording observations, with most researchers recording their observations on a daily basis. Such a log usually incorporates the researcher's observations of the situation and the behavior of the participants, interpretations of what happened, the typical and atypical elements of the event, an assessment of how the participants were influenced, and an assessment of how the researcher was influenced by the event. By recording such impressions on a daily basis, the researcher gradually can develop a database of impressions from broader conclusions may be drawn.

Participant–observation research can be used to study some communication behaviors that cannot be researched from other perspectives. For example, participant observations provide the easiest access to some of the normative pressures that are difficult to observe from the outside of a group, simply because most groups hide this information from outsiders. Further, although it requires some training, participant–observation research requires less training than most other forms of communication research. The skills needed to conduct such research are fully within reach of most undergraduate students (Hickson, 1977). Still, one obvious weakness of participant–observation research is that it is time consuming. For some projects, it many take months or years to gather and analyze data. In some cases, the researcher may stop once he or she realizes that the accumulated data is beginning to become repetitive. In doing so, the researcher may miss subsequent changes in the way the group being studied behaves and interacts. Still, through an extensive process of interacting and talking with individuals in the group, the researcher can develop an understanding of the participants in ways that would not occur in other forms of communication research.

Data Analysis

The qualitative interview is the means by which the researcher collects the research data. To be useful, however, that data must be subjected to some type of systematic evaluation, with the interview questions serving as the "raw material" for the analysis (Krueger, 1998). The most common means for this is some form of *content analysis*. In its purest form, content analysis involves "the systematic study and quantification of the content or meaning of communication messages" (Stacks & Hocking, 1999, p. 163). It is *systematic* in that the researcher analyzes the data in terms of categories related to the topic being studied. It involves *quantification* to the extent that instances of communication that fall within each category can be identified and counted.

Krueger (1998a) identifies three key elements of content analysis: the analysis must be systematic, verifiable, and timely. The extent to which it is *systematic* usually depends on the categories used for the analysis. The extent to which it is *verifiable* depends on the researcher's ability to base his or her conclusions on specifics within the data. *Timeliness* refers to having sufficient time to do a thorough analysis without taking too much time, which would jeopardize the validity of the conclusions.

When done well, content analysis can be used to give either a description of a particular communication event (e.g., "Among young adults 56 percent said the political issue that concerned them the most was education"), an explanation of a communication behavior (e.g., "Sixty percent of the people who voted for Candidate A said they did so because they were dissatisfied with the incumbent"), or a comparison of opposing opinions (e.g., "Women in the group generally liked A, while men were more likely to support B"). The specific units used for a content analysis will vary, depending on the purpose of the research.

Berelson (1952) identifies five major units that serve as broad guidelines for conducting a content-analysis. Four of the units—words or symbols, themes, character, and time and/or space—frequently are used in content analysis of interviews.

When researchers use words or symbols as the analysis unit, they only look at specific words within the interview. Powell and Kitchens (1975), for example, studied student interviews with each other and coded the summaries of those interviews in terms of personal pronouns. They found that women typically summarize their conversations with joint pronouns ("We talked about . . . "), whereas men usually use first and third person pronouns ("He said . . . and I answered . . . ").

Researchers use thematic analysis to find common topics and ideas. Thematic analysis is a common approach for both in-depth interviews and focus groups. With thematic analysis, the researcher reviews the conversation, looking for topics that are mentioned by more than one person. Further, the analysis will include the responses of other people to that topic (e.g., whether people agree or disagree when the topic of higher taxes is mentioned).

Analysis of time and/or space involves the quantitative measurement of discussion topics. Researchers may combine this technique with thematic analysis. Suppose, for example, that a researcher found that an interviewee made an equal number of references to education and to taxes during an in-depth interview. Which issue was of more concern to the individual? The thematic analysis would not offer insight into the answer; however, the question could perhaps be answered by measuring how much time the person spent discussing each issue or how much space was devoted to each topic in the written transcript.

Other options for content analysis are usually left to the individual skills of the researcher. Typically, for example, a researcher will also look for consistency or inconsistencies among the remarks provided by the group or individual. Does the person say one thing that is inconsistent with other remarks he or she has made? Or, does one individual say something that is consistent with several other views that have been expressed? If so, how specific is the individual's complaint or praise?

Krueger (1998a) recommends that content analysis include two key elements. First, the researcher should look for the unspoken idea—"what was not said" (p. 37). Things that are not articulated may reflect common assumptions that all of the participants made about the topic or identify taboo topics that the participants did not feel comfortable approaching. In addition, it is essential for the researcher to "find the big ideas" (p. 38). After the first analysis of the data has been completed, the researcher must review the data again, looking for overall ideas that represent the primary results of the groups' comments. Only then does the researcher have data that is useful in explaining the discussion.

Summary

Qualitative interviews provide researchers the opportunity to engage in extended conversations with individuals. Such interviews provide insight into the lives of those individuals and allow generalizations to be drawn regarding larger research issues. Retrospective interviews are a form of in-depth interview that helps individuals reconstruct events and circumstances in chronological order by asking the interviewees to graph and discuss changes that have occurred to them over time. The known associate interview is a technique in which the researcher interviews individuals who are known to be friends, family, and/or business associates of a particular person. The goal of this approach is to gain insight on that person as part of a larger research project. Field interviewing is a semi-directed conversation in which the researcher seeks to elicit the participant's point of view on a topic; such interviews often are conducted in conjunction with participant–observation and ethnology research.

FOR FURTHER DISCUSSION

1. Develop a discussion guide for a focus group on a topic of your choice. How would you open the discussion so that everyone feels comfortable? How would you lead into the main topic of discussion? What would you do to ensure that everyone participates?

2. Take the topic you used in the previous question and divide it into smaller subtopics. For which of these subtopics would quantitative research methodologies be appropriate? Which ones would require another research approach?

3. Choose a commercial product and analyze its sales campaign. Can you identify any elements of that campaign—including slogans and sales pitches—that may have been developed with the help of focus groups?

4. Assume that you want to investigate the communication behaviors of sales workers at a local retail outlet through the use of in-depth interviews. Construct an interview guide for the interviews. How many different people would you need to interview to fully understand this subject?

11 The Quantitative Research Interview

A research group representing a politician conducts a political poll in the days before an election. A restaurant owner wonders if his customers like the restaurant's new menu items and commissions a market survey to find out. A radio station tests a new format by gathering some of its listeners and asking them to rate a list of songs being considered for the play list.

Each of these examples represents a form of research interview; that is, an interview conducted to gather data that can be used to draw conclusions and/or make decisions about some target audience. In other words, research interviews are a systematic form of audience analysis. While qualitative interviews allow for great depth of information, the primary goal of quantitative interviewing is to achieve a high level of reliability and consistency across a number of interviewees and between multiple interviewers. Therefore, the consistency of the interview itself is of primary concern. The interviewer talks with people from a target audience for the purpose of understanding that group. Although a number of different techniques can be used for this purpose, most fall within two distinct categories: (1) public opinion surveys and (2) convenience/intercept surveys.

Public Opinion Surveys

The use of surveys and polls to measure public opinion began in the late 1930s, a development that coincided with a nationwide increase in the use of scientific approaches to study communication variables. By the 1970s, public opinion research was a staple tool of consumer market researchers and political campaigns. By the 1980s, it was a standard tool of media outlets covering political campaigns and other public opinion issues (Taylor, 1990).

Although most people use the terms interchangeably, polls and surveys differ. A *poll* is a relatively short questionnaire with a descriptive purpose. Its intent is to describe attitudes and behavioral intentions, and it does so with relatively simple questions. A survey uses a longer questionnaire and seeks more in-depth information about audience attitudes and predispositions. Both approaches fall within a broader category of *cross-sectional research*; that is, research that analyzes a cross section of a population at *a given time* (Stacks & Hocking, 1999). Though the term *pollster* often is synonymous with those who conduct polls for political campaigns, it is used here in the broader sense of referring to anyone who conducts survey interviews.

Deborah Diehl: Training for Survey Interviews

Deborah Diehl is a partner with TDM Research, a research company that conducts political surveys and market research for a variety of polling firms throughout the country. TDM has offices in Austin, Texas, and Birmingham, Alabama, with a total of 120 phone lines, and has conducted more than 3,000 surveys, the majority for Democratic pollsters, since its inception in 1989.

Q. What process do you use in training workers to do surveys?

A. The hiring process begins with an extensive interview, reading test, and participation in a sample poll to test for comprehension and the ability to follow the directions needed for conducting an accurate interview. If the person is hired they go through a three-hour training session. We go over the rules and regulations of what to do and what not to do. Of course, since you cannot cover everything that may come up in three hours, they are also given a packet of instructions and procedures to read and sign.

Q. What happens when they start to work with the phones?

A. Once they're put on the phone, they're monitored during a probationary period to make sure that they are conducting the interview correctly. This means reading the questionnaire exactly, word for word, not omitting a single "the." Sometimes it takes some reiteration to get that through to them. That is so critical. We must make sure that they do not vary in any way from the precise phrasing of the pollster.

Q. Do you have to retrain for each individual survey?

A. Yes. Sometimes, with routine surveys, which have the same survey components that the interviewers have done literally hundreds of times, we just have to go over any candidates' names that might have difficult pronunciations. When the survey is more complex, for example when there are some skip patterns to execute or unusual screening criteria that have to be met to qualify to do the survey, there is additional training that stresses those points.

Q. Do you have the capability of allowing clients to monitor the calls themselves?

A. Yes, but it requires the intervention of one of our supervisors to patch them through. The supervisor will look for an interviewer who is beginning a survey, and they can then switch over to that person to be monitored. All the person who is monitoring has to do is call in.

Q. What's your biggest problem?

A. The proliferation of telemarketing calls and the entire technology of call block and caller ID has made our job so much more difficult in the 14 years that we have been doing this. We have to make more phone calls to get few completed interviews. That's making our jobs harder.

Questionnaire Development

The polling process begins with the development of a questionnaire. Typically, the researcher and the client discuss the research questions and the issues and circumstances surrounding the issue in question. Based on this discussion, the researcher develops a first draft of a questionnaire. This is followed by subsequent rounds of discussions and revisions until all parties are satisfied that the questionnaire will provide the needed information.

Guidelines for Writing Questions.   When designing the questionnaire, the pollster will need to carefully construct and write each question. Questions must be direct, clear, and unambiguous. Further, unless the researcher is interested in testing for audience bias, the questions should be phrased in an unbiased manner. This can be difficult, because many clients prefer to phrase questions from their own perspective. The researcher should convince the client that the results will be of little use if the questions are biased.

Most quantitative researchers use some version of forced-choice options or Likert-type questions. Forced-choice options are closed-ended questions that limit the respondents' responses (e.g., "Yes" or "No"). Likert-type questions offer more options (e.g., "strongly agree, somewhat agree, undecided, somewhat disagree, or strongly disagree"), to cover a broader continuum of responses.

Zaller and Feldman (1992) oppose both Likert-type scales and alternative scales such as the feeling thermometer, arguing that attitudes on issues are particularly difficult to measure at precise preference points, because such positions may be based on a number of considerations that might compel respondents toward various positions on that issue. These "considerations" are underlying arguments that are recalled from memory and may vary with time (Chong, 1993). Zaller (1990) also argues that responses to political survey questions are influenced by the political sophistication of the respondents; when counted, though, the responses of uninformed voters are weighted equally with those of political sophisticates. The only way to counter this, they argue, is to measure attitudes in terms of a range of possible responses that are either acceptable or not acceptable to the voter.

Conducting the Survey

Several techniques often are employed when conducting a survey. These include (1) the greeting, (2) the screen, (3) attitude questions, (3) projective questions, (4) open-ended questions, and (5) demographic questions.

The Greeting.   The greeting is a brief statement that introduces the interviewer to the telephone respondent and leads to a question about his or her interest in responding to the survey. Typically, the greeting starts with (1) an introduction ("Hello, I'm John Doe") and (2) identification of the research unit (". . . and I'm calling from JLP Research"). As Stacks and Hocking (1998) note, these two elements serve "as a credibility inducement and provides indication that the project is important" (p. 251).

The interviewer then offers an explanation of the project (e.g., "We're conducting a public opinion survey on issues facing the state") coupled with a request for assistance (e.g., "Would you mind taking a few minutes to answer a few questions?"). Typically, before the person can answer "yes" or "no," an additional *inducement* is provided by mentioning (1) the short amount of time involved and (2) the importance of the call (e.g., "The questions will only take about five minutes, and your answers could help us understand the state better").

The Screen.   If the respondent agrees to participate, the interviewer must then determine if he or she qualifies for the survey. This qualification element is operationally defined by the survey's screen, a question that verifies the respondent's eligibility. For marketing surveys, the screen often involves demographic descriptors of the target audience (e.g., "Are you at least 35 years old?"). For political polls, the minimal and most basic screening question is one that asks whether the respondent is a registered voter; if not, the phone call should be terminated.

Most political pollsters add additional screens depending on the nature and circumstances of the campaign. For example, political polls may include questions regarding whether the respondent plans to vote in the election and his or her likelihood of doing so. Due to the possibility of embarrassing a person who does not vote, these questions often are asked in a manner that makes it socially acceptable to say they will not vote. Thus, instead of asking, "Are you going to vote in the up-coming election," the screen is instead phrased as, "As you know, the state will be holding its election for statewide offices in November. Do you currently plan to vote in that election, or do you expect that you will be unable to vote in that election?" If the person qualifies under the screen, and agrees to participate, then the rest of the survey can be completed.

Research Questions.   The research questions comprise the bulk of the questionnaire. These are primarily closed-ended questions that represent those items to which the researcher is seeking answers.

From a structural view, the first few questions should be relatively easy. If the respondents can answer the first few questions easily, it tends to create interest in the survey and increases the chances that they will participate for the duration of the questionnaire (Wimmer & Dominick, 1994). Conversely, if the survey starts off with questions that respondents feel they cannot answer, they will often hang up.

Attitude questions are a specific form of research question often used in surveys. Attitude questions are intended to measure public reactions to statements that represent various views on public issues. Although the format of such questions may vary, the most common techniques for measuring attitudes toward an issue are in terms of (1) support or opposition of an issue, (2) agreement or disagreement with a position on an issue, or (3) forced choices of major positions.

Support/opposition questions generally use a Likert-type approach, for example, "Do you strongly support, somewhat support, somewhat oppose, or strongly oppose requiring a three-day waiting period for the purchases of handguns?"

Agree/disagree questions identify an expressed position on an issue and ask if the respondent agrees with the position. Again, such questions typically use a Likert-type approach, for example, asking respondents if they "strongly agree, somewhat agree, somewhat disagree, or strongly disagree" with the statement "Any attempt to limit handgun purchases interferes with the public's constitutional right to bear arms."

Forced-choice questions offer a variety of positions and ask the respondents to pick the one that is most closely aligned with their own, for example, "Do you support efforts to require a three-day waiting period for the purchase of handguns, or do you consider such efforts an infringement on the public's right to bear arms?"

Projective questions are short "what-if" scenarios that are intended to give the pollster some idea as to the respondent's reaction to a specific message. Although this form of question is frequently used in public opinion research, the validity of such questions is highly questionable. Often the respondents themselves do not know how to answer such questions and provide a response only because they are required to do so. The past is more knowable than the future, and people are more likely to make judgments on retrospective rather than prospective information.

Open-Ended Questions.   One problem with most survey questions is that the respondents can only provide answers to what is asked. Because most questions use closed (or forced) options, the pollster has no way of analyzing what other issues or factors may be influencing the respondents. One way to counter this problem is through the use of open-ended questions that allow the respondents to express an opinion with no guidance from the pollster. The "Most Important Factor" question is based on this approach (e.g., "Overall, what do you think is the most important factor you consider when deciding to choose a restaurant for dining out?"). The open-ended format of such questions allows for a range of responses that can go beyond the scope of the closed-ended questions in the survey.

Open-ended questions also are used as probes when more information is needed to explain a response to a forced-choice question. For example, a market survey may ask people to say whether their next automotive purchase is likely to be a car, an SUV, or a truck. When the respondent makes a choice, the interviewer may then probe with an open-ended question—"Why do you prefer an SUV?"—to get more insight into the respondent's decision. The disadvantages of open-ended questions are that they generally provide less information than can be gained from structured questions and the results are less reliable in assessing the impact of attitudes on political campaigns (Rahn, Krosnik, & Breuning, 1994). Miller and Shanks (1996) note that structured survey questions provide a clearer picture of voter preferences because they are not hampered by the ambiguity of open-ended questions and the uneven or incomplete data that often results.

Demographic Questions.   *Demographic questions* measure respondent attributes such as age, income, gender, and ethnic background. They are usually delayed until the end of the survey, and they serve three purposes. First, they allow the pollster to stratify the sample and verify its representativeness. Second, cross-tabulations of the results based on demographic factors are the primary statistical analysis for many surveys. Third, demographic breakdowns provide crucial targeting information.

Sampling

The accuracy of any poll or survey depends on the extent to which the sample chosen by the pollster represents the intended target group. For this reason, the use of random sampling is essential, and a variety of techniques have been developed for this purpose.

With *random-digit dialing,* a computer uses a randomization process to generate telephone numbers. Researchers who lack a computer with this capability can substitute a *random numbers table* and achieve the same effect. This process has two advantages: the researcher cannot deliberately bias the sample in any manner and households with unlisted numbers can be included in the sample. Its disadvantage is that many middle- and upper-income households now have multiple phone lines, whereas lower income households only have one; this creates a risk of biasing the results against lower income households.

Another common approach is to use *computer-generated lists* of randomly selected telephone numbers. To increase efficiency, lists generated with this approach use some multiple (usually ranging from 10 to 20) of the projected sample size as the basis for the list generation. Thus, if the target sample size for the survey is 600 registered voters, then a list of 6,000 randomly selected telephone numbers (if a multiple of 10 is used) is generated. The multiple numbers allow for efficient calling, because many of the calls cannot be completed for a variety of reasons (no answers, phone machines answering, disconnected numbers, etc.). The disadvantage of this approach is that it does not reach unlisted numbers.

The most common approach, regardless of how the list is generated, is to use a process called *stratified random sampling.* In this approach, the pollster predetermines how many people need to be called in an identified demographic category (usually geography), and then respondents are randomly selected within each of the subgroups of that category. This approach is the preferred choice of most professional pollsters, because it guarantees that certain groups within the population will be sampled. Or as Hansen et al. (1998) notes, stratified random sampling "allows for the appropriate representation of different groups in the population" to ensure that the sample represents the population under study (p. 241).

A variation of stratified random sampling is cluster sampling. *Cluster sampling* involves the development of computer-generated lists of clusters of people with similar demographic characteristics based on the stratification criteria. Thus, a pollster conducting a statewide survey of 600 registered voters would create a computer-generated list of 600 clusters of voters (with 10 to 25 names matched with phones per cluster), and each cluster would correspond with the stratification criteria of the survey. One name from each cluster would be surveyed.

Completion Rates

Not everyone reached by telephone will agree to respond to the survey. Yu and Cooper (1983), in an analysis of surveys reported in academic journals, found that the average completion rate for telephone surveys was about 72 percent. Phone banks that specialize in political polling often reach response rates of 80 percent when dealing with lists of registered voters, but their success drops if a general population list is used.

The completion rate decreases as the length of the interview increases. Wimmer and Dominick (1994) recommend that telephone surveys be limited to a maximum of 20 minutes in length, because there is a significant increase in the break-off rate (hang ups) when interviews exceed that length. Electronic surveys should be even shorter, because it is easier for people to hang up on a machine than on another human (Havice, 1990).

What Can Go Wrong

Any number of things can confound the results of a poll and lead to unreliable poll numbers. The most common problems are (1) sampling errors, (2) question framing, (3) ordering effects, and (4) interviewer effects.

Sampling Errors.   *Sampling errors* are perhaps the most common source of mistakes. For example, if a survey sample is not representative of voters *who will vote on election day*, the survey results will likely be inaccurate. It is relatively easy to generate sampling errors. In some instances, the respondent-selection process may not be truly random, leading to skewed results. Other times, the pollster may use a stratified random sample based on turnout patterns of previous elections; if those turnout patterns are altered in future elections, the survey will be inaccurate.

The sample also may be affected by the use of improper screening questions. Some marketing surveys, for example, screen only for "head of household." Most marketing surveys would want to screen for income level and demographic factors that reflect the target audience. Most political pollsters believe that more accurate samples are generated when a "tight" screen is used, such as when only "probable voters" are selected for the survey.

Question Framing.   *Question framing* also may affect survey results (Hansen et al., 1998). Ideally, survey questions should be clear and simple, requiring a minimum amount of effort on the part of the respondent. Lengthy questions create confusion; respondents may forget the first few options by the time the last ones have been read (Wimmer & Dominick, 1994).

Biased questions use words and phrases that have positive or negative connotations. For example, consider the following question: "Do you favor or oppose spending more money on welfare?" This question often receives a majority of negative responses, due to the negative connotations that some people have of the word *welfare*. Conversely, if the question is phrased with a positive connotation (e.g., "Do you favor or oppose providing more money to the poor and needy?"), an undue number of positive responses will be generated. The goal of the pollster is to use neutral language to obtain an unbiased response (e.g., "Do you favor or oppose increasing the budget for health and human services").

Leading questions also are problematic. Some leading questions may be based on a defined frame of reference, which will influence the response. For example, "Would you agree that national security is the most important issue facing America today?" would encourage respondents to agree with the statement. On the other hand, asking "What is the most important issue facing America today?" is much more neutral and would probably lead to a more reliable set of responses. Kinder and Sanders (1990) note that in political polls a person's response to a candidate can be altered by manipulating the priority that the respondent gives to different arguments or considerations. Such processes frame political issues to the advantage of the candidate, creating favorable poll results that may be used to mobilize current constituencies (Jacobs & Shapiro, 1994). A similar bias may be created for a product or service, with the researcher framing the question in such a manner that it leads the respondent in a specific attitudinal direction.

In addition, *double-barreled questions* should be avoided. Double-barreled questions are those that contain two parts, creating a situation in which the voter may respond to either or both ideas separately. For example, the following is a double-barreled question: "Do you support the president's efforts at gun control and his attempts to fight crime?" The voter might have different reactions to the president's efforts on gun-control and his anti-crime program, even if one is part of the other. The result may be poll numbers that reflect some unknown combination of the two attitudes.

Ordering Effects. A third factor that may influence survey responses is the ordering effect. *Ordering effects* are the impact of question placement on responses. As Hansen et al. (1998) note, ". . . where a question is placed both in a numerical sense, but also in a contextual way, can impact on the meaning of the question and the results" (p. 246). Wimmer and Dominick (1994) call this problem "question contamination" (p. 120) in reference to the impact that the presence of one question may have on subsequent questions. For example, suppose a survey included a series of questions aimed at voter attitudes toward education; if those questions were followed by another asking which issue the respondent considered to be the most important problem facing the state, an undue number of respondents likely would answer "education." Another example of an ordering effect was reported by Morrison (1986) in his study of public attitudes toward the BBC, in which response differences were attributable to the ordinal placement of the questions. As noted earlier, favorability ratings and test ballots are typically placed in an early ordering position on the questionnaire. This helps minimize the impact of follow-up questions on general favorability questions. For instance, a client might be interested in how members of a community generally feel about his restaurant, and be concerned with specific aspects of his service (cleanliness, friendliness, etc.). Focusing the respondents on the specific issues will likely color the overall rating, so it's best to get to that first. Conversely, demographic data and personal/sensitive questions are generally placed near the end of the questionnaire; this allows time for the interviewer to establish a rapport with the respondent. In addition, the other responses have already been obtained should the respondent choose not to answer those questions.

Interview Effects. *Interview effects* refers to those responses that are produced as a result of the behaviors of the interviewer. Research has indicated that face-to-face interviews may be influenced by the type of clothing worn by the interviewer (Hickson & Stacks, 1992; McPeek & Edwards, 1975), and any number of other nonverbal cues (e.g., nodding, smiling, tone of voice) may influence responses.

Most marketing and political surveys are conducted by telephone. Although telephone interviews are not immune to interview effects, they do eliminate those that are related to the personal appearance of the interviewer.

With political polling, interview effects can be further diminished by using professional interviewers who are not connected to the campaign. Preferably, the telephone personnel who are actually conducting the survey should not even be aware of which candidate is paying for the survey, thus limiting their ability to influence the results. The polling company may also use interviewers who are unfamiliar with the candidates. This is frequently done by subcontracting the phone calls to a phone bank in a state different from that of the campaign.

One common demonstration of how interviewer effects can alter a poll can be seen with the use of volunteer polling. To save money, a new business may use its own staff to conduct a poll. This approach invariably overinflates support for the product or service. Even if extensive training is conducted for each worker, it is still impossible to eliminate all of the subtle cues that they will give to respondents. Consequently, the survey results will be altered.

Mall Intercepts

The most common commercial form of intercept interview is the *point-of-purchase*, or *mall intercept*, interview (Sudman, 1980; Gates & Solomon, 1982; Bush & Hair, 1985). The term *mall intercept* is based on the fact that a number of research companies have offices located in major consumer malls. Their staff interview consumers at the mall, often testing products offered by one of the mall's retail outlets. Such interviews are used to gather consumer preference data on topics such as food products, tourism, and a variety of other products and services (e.g., Robinson, Smith, Murray, & Ennis, 2002; Litvin & Kar, 2001; McCullum & Achterberg, 1997).

Exit Polling

Another type of intercept interview, one frequently used by media outlets during political campaigns, is *exit polling*. Exit polling is sometimes used by media outlets to make early projections about the winners of an election (Grossman, 2000). Exit polls are on-site interviews conducted with voters on the day of the election after they leave the voting booth. The purpose of the interview is to identify (1) for whom they voted and (2) what factors influenced their voting decision. This data can be very useful to media outlets that are covering the election. It allows them to project winners before the voting is completed to provide some type of insight as to why one candidate won and another lost. Media outlets use the information from exit interviews to shape election night coverage and to manage technical resources.

Individuals who do exit interviews must be highly adept at (1) approaching strangers in a public environment, (2) quickly establishing rapport, and (3) asking political questions without offending the interviewee. Most exit poll interviews are relatively short. The questionnaire is usually limited to one typed page so that it easily fits on a clipboard. The responses are recorded directly onto the questionnaire, so that results for each individual interview can be quickly recorded and added to the total database. Research indicates that the exit interview response rates are higher if the interviewee is provided with self-administered "secret ballot" questionnaires rather than having to answer questions in a face-to-face encounter (Bishop & Fisher, 1995).

A problem with early exit polls is that they can be inaccurate. Individuals who vote early in the day often represent different demographic and income groups than those who vote later in the day. Thus, exit polls based on interviews with early voters may not be representative of the entire universe of voters (Busch & Lieske, 1985). Indeed, the use of early exit polls to project winners has produced a number of embarrassing incidents for media outlets. The most famous, perhaps, is the mistake made by the national television networks in projecting Al Gore as the winner of the presidential vote in Florida in 2000 (Abramowitz, 2001). All of the major networks made the same mistake, an understandable

James T. Kitchens: Interviewing for Market and Political Surveys

James T. Kitchens (Ph.D., University of Florida) is owner of The Kitchens Group, an Orlando-based political and market research company. Dr. Kitchens has conducted hundreds of surveys for a range of political clients that have included governors and members of Congress.

Q. What role does interviewing play in the research process?

A. Interviewing is the most important part. That's where we get our data, the information that we must have to advise our clients. If you make a mistake on the interviewing, the data is bad. Further, it's the one mistake we can't correct. If we get the sample wrong—have too many men or too many women—we can always go back and do more interviews to correct a problem like that. But if the interviews are wrong—if the questions are poorly worded or the interviewers have biased the responses—there's nothing you can do about it.

Q. What do you mean when you say the questions can be poorly worded?

A. The questions have to be easy to understand. Remember, we're asking these over the telephone, so the person doesn't get to read the question themselves. We read it to them, and they have to be able to understand it after hearing it once. That means it can't be too long either or, by the time you get to the end, they'll forget the first part of the question. And the respondent shouldn't think that the questions have a right or wrong answer. The questions must be worded so that any of the answers would be considered socially acceptable. If you ask a question that points toward the answer you want, you'll get that answer but you'll never know for sure if they were telling you the truth or merely saying what you wanted them to say.

Q. What about the interviewer—how can they influence the interview?

A. We call them the phone workers, not interviewers, but it's easy for them to bias the results. A slight shift in tone of voice, or a little more enthusiasm when they're reading responses—things like that can tip off the respondent as to what you're testing. When that occurs, the data is not reliable.

Q. How do you handle that problem?

A. We start with the construction of the questionnaire. We try to write the questionnaire in such a manner that it doesn't give away the purpose of the study. The phone workers will know the topic of our research, but they won't know its purpose and they shouldn't be able to figure that out by reading over the questionnaire.

Q. How does the client know that the interviews are being conducted professionally?

A. Most of them trust us, because we've been working with them for years. But, you occasionally have new clients who ask about that. When that occurs, we arrange for them to monitor the calls themselves. With today's telephone technology, it's no problem to hook them up to the interview. They can monitor it from their own home using their own phone.

Q. Do you find that many people are reluctant to talk to you?

(continued)

Continued

    A. Not really. Our biggest problem is with people who think we're selling something. Once we convince them that we're not selling anything—that we just want their opinion—they're usually eager to cooperate. Most people are quite willing to give you their opinion on things—particularly politics.

    Q. And a final question—do you think there's been too much polling and surveying—particularly in political campaigns?

    A. Not at all. I know you hear that complaint a lot, but the truth is that few people are ever actually called. Remember, we work with relatively small samples of people. Political surveys may be conducted all during an election campaign, but it will still be a relatively small number of people who are actually involved. If you go out in your neighborhood and ask your neighbors if they have been polled, most will say they haven't. Polls may get a lot of publicity, but they actually involve small numbers of people.

---

problem when one realizes that they were all sharing data from the same research organization—a joint effort known as the Voter News Network (Buell, 2001; Shepard, 2001). Still, although the 2000 election may be the most famous exit poll blunder, it is far from the only one in American history. For example, in the 1989 gubernatorial campaign in Virginia, exit polling predicted that Gov. Douglas Wilder would win re-election by a 10-point margin—a number proudly touted by the state's media. Wilder did win, but by a razor-thin margin of 0.2 percentage points (Traugott & Price, 1992).

Convenience Interviews

Another variation of the intercept interview is the convenience interview. With the convenience interview, a researcher gathers a group of people at one location and asks each person to respond to a questionnaire. The most common use of this technique is in the academic setting. University professors frequently ask their students to help them with a research project by responding to a questionnaire. The technique also is useful in a number of other research situations. For example, an organization that has noticed a decrease in member satisfaction may gather a group of members together to measure satisfaction levels. A fast-food restaurant may ask its customers to give their opinion of a new menu item. Thus, the convenience interview may be used in a quantitative research model whenever a group that would make for an appropriate sample is gathered in one place.

Mystery Shoppers

Another variation of the intercept interview is the *mystery shopper*. The mystery shopper technique is something of a reverse intercept. Instead of selecting a location and interviewing those who approach the location, the mystery shopper visits the store being tested to see how sales personnel handle their interviews with customers (Lipke, 2000). Basically, the mystery shopper is an interview evaluator whose job is to assess employee behavior toward customers (Helliker, 1994). Mystery shoppers are used by a variety of retail outlets, including fast-food restaurants, banks, and the travel industry (Del Leung, 2001; Hudson et al., 2001; Steinhauer, 1998). Several research companies primarily focus on providing mystery shoppers to retail clients (McDonough, 2004; Greco, 1994; Helliker, 1994; Brokaw, 1991).

In many cases, the use of mystery shoppers is an ongoing program that provides a company with a way of measuring customer service. Many organizations use the compiled responses as a way to reward employees and improve service. The shoppers themselves typically undergo a two-to-three hour training session before working their first assignment. Details of the training will vary, depending upon the nature of the product or service, but two general rules typically apply. First, the mystery shoppers must limit their comments to things that they can observe. A mystery shopper at a restaurant, for example, could observe and report on the behavior of the servers and the quality of the food, but would probably not be in a position to report what occurred in the kitchen as the food was being prepared. Second, the shoppers must record their observations on the provided report form surreptitiously, so that employees of the establishment will not realize that they are being evaluated. When employees spot a mystery shopper, they will give the suspected mystery shopper special treatment, thus destroying the intent of the research project.

The Ethics of Audience Analysis

Polls and surveys are essentially a sophisticated form of audience analysis—a way of measuring and identifying the public's perception toward any number of individuals, issues, products, and/or services. However, several observers question the ethics of using these techniques.

Some are critical of the polling process—particularly political polling—because of its potential impact on elections. Many of the major critics of quantitative research do not attack the methodology, but rather its role in political campaigns and market research. Specifically, some argue that such research has too much impact on campaigns and candidates. Taylor (1990) argues that polling has had a negative impact on the political process because "politicians have become increasingly dependent on the technologies of political market research . . . to guard against ever uttering an unpopular word in public" (p. 218). Taylor quotes Democratic pollster Stan Greenberg as saying, "The dialogue has become more sterile because the campaign ads are designed to repeat back to voters what they already know" (p. 218).

Ryan and Wentworth (1999) argue that polling has had a negative impact on news coverage of political campaigns, with the media "focusing more on who is ahead and who is behind than the substance of political issues" (p. 81). One reason for this is that many reporters are not well informed on the issues themselves, and poll results are easier to cover. Others argue that the public is more interested in the ups and downs of political careers or relative changes in candidate positions in the polls than they are in specific issues. Regardless of the cause, though, today's media (newspapers and TV) do indeed have a strong focus on "horse-race" coverage. The trend has grown to such an extent that many media outlets now conduct their own surveys, in essence creating their own news to cover.

Former Democratic pollster Paul Maslin believes polling has contributed to an increase in negative campaigning. As quoted by Taylor (1990), Maslin said, "It's like taking a shot, because you can see the way they (negative ads) move the numbers. The techniques have gotten so refined, the weapons so powerful, that if you don't use them, you'll lose . . ." (p. 218).

Maslin's comment seems to echo the pragmatics of polling in modern political contests. Polls will be used. The issue to be addressed is not whether to use them, but how to use them in an ethical manner. Polling is just a sophisticated form of audience analysis—a basic skill taught in nearly all communication courses. If audience analysis is important for other forms of communication, then why not for political communication? Political candidates have a right and, ideally, an obligation to consider the beliefs and values of the people they represent. In a time when a single individual may represent thousands or millions of people, polling provides a means of assessing those beliefs and values.

One of the authors once met a local political activist who opened the conversation by saying, "I don't believe in polls." She then recounted a local tax referendum in which she had been involved, noting that she campaigned in the wealthy section of the community by talking of how the area would benefit from a better school system. When campaigning in the low income areas, her message focused on the structure of the tax—one that would be paid by wealthy families. She summed up her story by smiling and saying, "We passed that without ever doing any polling."

No polling? Perhaps. But she did engage in audience analysis. With a small local electorate, one with which she was highly familiar, she was probably correct to reject formal polling. Her narrative indicates, however, that she did adjust her message to different target audiences based on her perceptions of those two audiences. Had she done a poll, the pollster would probably have recommended the same strategic approach that she used. She did not need a poll, though, because she already understood her electorate well.

Candidates in major campaigns lack that capability. A person from a wealthy family from Texas may run for President, but it is unrealistic to expect that person to understand the problems faced by Hispanics in California, low income white voters in Kentucky, or African-American voters in Mississippi. Polling provides a way for the candidate to analyze large and diverse audiences within the electorate.

Market researchers receive less criticism about their use of polls, but they face some of the same issues (e.g., the extent to which they use market research information to influence cultural and consumer responses).

Summary

Polling and survey research have become an integral part of modern public opinion research—both in market research and in the political arena. Because quantitative interviews tend to stress replicability and reliability, their standardized formats allow for their results to be generalized more readily than qualitative interviews. In its most essential form, polling is merely an extended form of audience analysis with the goal of providing the communicator with an understanding of the attitudes and values of the audience to be addressed. The reliability of polls and surveys is usually based on sampling techniques;

their validity is usually based on the questions used to collect the survey data. Good questions and good interviewers lead to good research results. Poor questions and biased interviewers, though, lead to unreliable and invalid research data.

The ethical questions surrounding quantitative research interviews must be addressed for each research project. The problem is intensified by those who use push polls for unethical purposes. It is also complicated by the frequent use by the media of pseudo-polls, which can cause the public to question the legitimacy of true research interviews.

FOR FURTHER DISCUSSION

1. The next time you are asked to participate in a public opinion survey you should agree to do so and note the following: How do the questions progress? Is the order of the questions important? What answer options were you offered? Did you feel that you were asked questions that you did not understand? Did you feel that you knew the purpose of the survey once it was over?

2. Search your local newspaper for a published public opinion poll or survey. Analyze the quality of that poll based on the information provided in the story. What was the sample size? The margin of error? What screen was used to ensure that the poll was based on interviews only with those individuals who were appropriate for the study?

CHAPTER
12 Oral History Interviews

The grandfather of one of the authors used to tell stories of growing up in Oklahoma, of losing his parents while he was still a teenager, and taking a stage back to Alabama to live with relatives. Details of those narratives largely have been lost, though, because no one ever recorded them. Such recollections came naturally to him. He was born in the nineteenth century and grew up in a world without television and radio. He grew up in a narrative tradition in which his family spent their spare time gathered around a fireplace exchanging stories.

That tradition is making a comeback in both the academic and family arenas. Academic disciplines have taken notice of the role of narrative traditions in modern life. The communication field, in particular, has looked at Fisher's narrative paradigm (1984, 1987) as a way of using stories to understand how people explain their lives. Meanwhile, as computers and the Internet have made genealogical information more accessible to family history researchers, an increasing number of genealogists have turned to oral history as a way to flesh out the details of family traditions. Pulitzer Prize-winning writer Rick Bragg (1997) argues that every life has a dignity that makes its story worthwhile, regardless of the person's health or financial status. Best-selling author Studs Terkel agrees; one of his best works, indeed, is an oral history of working people in the United States (Terkel, 1997).

The primary research tool of the oral history field is the interview. One or more interviewers sit down and record a one-on-one conversation with someone else. For the academic researcher, these conversations serve as primary data to record the history of a person or event. For genealogists, oral history records the traditions of a family by recording the stories of that family. Jerome Bruner (1987) describes oral history as "life as narrative."

Nor is the technique limited to military history. Oral history can provide insight into any number of historical events. Oral history interviews can be used to study organizational culture, intercultural issues, and an entire host of other topics. Howell Raines (1983), for example, conducted a series of interviews with participants of the civil rights struggle in his recounting of those events. Similarly, oral histories have been used to record memories of former slaves (Hurmence, 1989), military heroes (Smith et al., 2003), those who experienced the Great Depression (Terkel, 2000), and those affected by the tragic events of September 11 (Fink, 2002). Several authors have used the oral history approach to study the history of sports. Ballew (2002) used the oral history technique to look at major league baseball during the 1970s; others have used oral history to study individual

An Interview with Waddie Mitchell: Oral History and Storytelling

Waddie Mitchell is a cowboy poet and storyteller. Some of his audio CDs include: Buckaroo Poet, Lone Driftin' Rider, The Bard and the Balladeer: Live from Cowtown, That No Quit Attitude, *and* Prairie Portrait. *Mitchell captures the history of the American West by capturing stories from the era and converting them into narrative poems.*

Q. In one sense, it seems like you're recording an oral history of the West. Is that correct?

A. I'm not recording a history *per se*, other than stories from that history. I really don't think that what I'm doing would be called historical. But I do collect stories.

Q. How do you collect them?

A. They're getting harder to come by. For years, I used to meet people with like interests and trade, barter, borrow, or buy the stories.

Q. How many do you get from individuals, people who passed the story down within their own family for generations?

A. After I do a show, it's amazing how many people will come up to me and say, "I've got a story about my granddad." One out of a hundred will actually have something that really sparks my interest, but I'll listen to all one hundred. I'll sit and listen to them because I've sparked a memory in them about a story their granddad told them. If I'm not real interested in taking that story and writing it, I try to get them to write it. If it goes no further than the family—the grandchildren and the great-grandchildren—do you realize what a present you've given them? At some point in their life, they're going to want to know where they came from. Hopefully, that does some good.

Q. Why is storytelling so effective?

A. The best way to really learn something is through a story. When somebody's crafted a story, it takes you from point A to point B, and you finish there. In life, you often miss B or some of the things that happened in A to get to B. It's like going to history class when you're a kid, and having to learn the date when a battle happens. It's all dates and facts, and it doesn't really enthuse anybody. But somebody can make a movie of that same battle, and you can get into it on a human level and see the conflict. Although the dates are important in the classroom, they're not nearly as important as the why's, where's, and how's of the conclusion that we now hold as part of our history.

Q. Can you give me an example of such a story?

A. You bet. A guy came up to me after a performance, and said, "My dad spent his last year in bed. For the last six months, he didn't want to watch TV—he wanted to listen to the old cowboy music and your poetry. But he had a story I thought I'd want to tell you." He told me a story about a fellow who delivered mail for rural parts of Nevada. Often it might be an hour's drive from one place to another. When he would show up on his biweekly or once-a-week trip, he would always have pie or something waiting for him. This guy told him a story about going to a dance with his daughter and having to wait in line to get a dance with her. He thought before the night was over that he wouldn't get a dance with her. But she'd saved the last dance for him. Although this happened in the 1920s, it moved me because I had a 16-year-old daughter at the time. I was seeing

(continued)

Continued

her switch from a little girl to a young lady. I had to go write that story. It moves people—it doesn't matter where you're at. Although I put it in a Western setting, it's not a Western story. It's a human story. As I get around to storytelling festivals, I find myself completely drained at the end of a weekend—completely drained—because the storyteller can capture me and put me there.

Q. How does storytelling fit in with oral history?

A. An oral history—even if it's just an elderly grandparent telling her grandchildren about her grandparents, her parents, and her life—that is a gift that most people will cherish more so than reading their journals. If she can make her granddaddy come alive to her grandchildren, that means they know a little about their great-great-granddaddy as a person.

Q. How do we get people to value these family stories?

A. I'm afraid it comes from life. I lost my Dad in October, and I had the opportunity to spend the last eight months caretaking. We talked more in those eight months than in my 55 years prior to that. Although he was quite a storyteller, and I knew many of his stories, he was the kind of storyteller who rarely had himself involved in the story. Somebody else was always the hero of his stories. I learned what a big part of the stories he actually was. It was an amazing epiphany about the guy I knew as Dad. I make it a big point, when I'm around my kids and stories start getting told, I really make a point of how it all came about. They knew we lived at this ranch or that ranch for a while, but they didn't know the stories of what took us there, or why we left there. As kids, they just weren't involved with that. I'm seeing an awakening of understanding of why we moved from ranch to ranch sometimes. I'm seeing more questions about my time in the military, and why I allowed myself to get drafted during Vietnam—those kind of stories that I don't think they'd ever wondered about or asked about if I had not made it so accessible to them.

Q. What advice would you give to people who're involved in doing oral history?

A. The person telling the story has the responsibility to tell the story good enough that the listener has a chance to appreciate what the story is about. He should take the time to craft that story, to find his own voice.

---

baseball teams (Golenbock, 2000a, 2000b; Eisenberg, 2001) and players (Powell, 2002). Oral history also has found some utility in counseling, particularly in the field of marriage counseling (Buehlman, Gottman, & Katz, 1992; Honeycutt, 1999). Further, journalists routinely use oral history to illustrate news stories, supplementing their presentation of facts and figures with the stories of individuals affected by the story.

Oral history also is becoming increasingly popular as a means of recording the local history of a community. Typical of this approach is the work of the Pell City Oral History Committee in Pell City, Alabama. With this project, sponsored by the local city government, researchers conducted interviews with 30 older citizens in the community who had been identified as "historical treasures whose stories should be captured for future generations" (Ray, 2003, p. 20A). Interviewees included 94-year-old Jessie Armstrong, who talked about the city's first car and Franklin Roosevelt's 1934 visit to the city on a

A Quick Guide to Oral Histories

Need a quick reference for conducting oral history interviews? Here's a quick review.

- Ascertain willingness of person to participate.
- Research the person's background.
- Prepare and send the interviewee an outline.
- Schedule the interviews.
- Obtain a signed release agreement at the first interview.
- Ensure that all equipment is functioning properly.
- Take an outline, photos, and clippings to interview.
- Tape-record the interviews.
- Develop rapport with the interviewee, but remain neutral.
- Ask who, what, where, when, why, and how.
- Remain polite but firmly in control.
- Listen carefully; pursue new topics as they emerge.
- Use silence.
- Ask for examples and anecdotes as illustrations.
- Label tapes with the names of the interviewer and the interviewee, the date, and the tape number.
- Transcribe the interviews.
- Review the transcript, then get interviewee to review it.
- Deposit corrected transcripts, tapes, and release agreements in the appropriate library, archives, or historical society.

Source: Hicke, Carole (1997). *One-minute guide to oral histories*. Berkeley, CA: University of California at Berkeley Library.

whistle-stop tour. Completed interviews were transcribed and published either on CD or in manuscript form and made available to the public through the local library.

Elements of Oral History

As with other forms of interviewing, the interviewer should conduct background research before conducting an interview. The researcher should learn as much about the interviewee as possible before the interview.

For public figures, such as professional baseball players, written sources provide a means of doing preliminary research. The interviewer can consult old newspapers, magazines, books, or other publications for information about the person. These sources can then be categorized into topics, with those topics serving as the interview outline. For research into family histories, the interviewee often conducts preliminary interviews with other people, such as other family members or friends of the subject (e.g., "Has grandma ever told you anything about how she and granddad first met?"). These preliminary interviews also can be used to construct a topic list to guide the interview.

Books on Oral History

The following are several "how to" books on oral history.

Ives, E. D. (1995). *The Tape-recorded interview: A manual for field workers in folklore and oral history* (2nd ed.). Knoxville, TN: University of Tennessee Press.

Baum, W. (1987). *Oral history for the local historical society*. Thousand Oaks, CA: Sage.

Yow, V. R. (1994). *Recording oral history: A practical guide for social scientists*. Thousand Oaks, CA: Sage.

Ritchie, D. A. (1995). *Doing oral history*. New York: Twayne Publishers.

The important guideline here is that the interviewer should not conduct preliminary interviews with the person who is the subject of the research. Any attempt to do so will likely lead to a number of interesting stories, but none that will be recorded. Further, once someone has told a story to an interviewer, it can rarely be repeated with the same enthusiasm and attention to detail that would have been captured in the person's first interview. Interviewers should keep the story fresh, letting the person tell his or her story to the interviewer and the tape recorder at the same time.

Technical Preparations

The primary tool of the oral historian is the tape recorder (Ives, 1980; Yow, 1994; Zimmerman, 1992). An oral history interview is ruined if the tape recorder does not work. It is the interviewer's responsibility to avoid such problems. Problems can be prevented by preparing in advance for any technical disasters that may occur.

The interviewer should know how the tape recorder operates, records, stops, and erases. The latter is particularly important, because one does not want to inadvertently erase hours of hard work.

In the past, most interviews were recorded onto audio cassette tape. These tapes are easily transportable and adaptable to a number of recording systems. However, the popularity of digital video cameras has led to their increased use for oral history interviews. The video image has the advantage of both recording the person's words while conveying the nonverbal expressions that accompany his or her stories.

The Oral Interview

After gathering information and making technical preparations, the researcher is ready for the first oral interview with the subject. The key term here is "first" interview, because a successful oral history often involves a series of interviews. The participant rarely will recall all of the key details of a story in one sitting. However, that initial interview should be the most productive of all of the interviews that may be conducted.

The interviewer should use work from an outline of questions prepared in advance. Samples of potential questions are presented elsewhere in this chapter, but each interview

Practical Tips for Oral History Interviews

Pre-interview Tasks

- Contact the person you want to interview. Use your "ins" and explain significance of your study or project.
- If possible, hold a pre-interview session to establish rapport, discuss taping session mechanics, and explain the legal agreement form.
- Prepare a proposed topic outline. Ask the interviewee to add to the list if he or she wishes.
- Prepare specific questions for each topic, but do not submit them to the interviewee.

Question Techniques

- Start with easy, noncontroversial background questions that will elicit expansive answers.
- Save controversial questions for later, after you have established rapport.
- Ask short questions.
- Ask one question at a time.
- Avoid questions that will result in "yes" or "no" responses.
- Keep your opinions to yourself; never "lead" the interviewee.
- Encourage the interviewee with continual and constant attentiveness; employ facial expressions, eye contact, and occasional short verbal responses.
- Never turn off the recorder except to change tape and to avoid recording telephone calls, doorbells, or emergency calls of nature. Do not turn off the machine in order to go "off the record."
- Take notes. Write down reminders for later questions or to ask for clarification of details.
- Do not interrupt the interviewee.
- Do not fret over seemingly endless pauses; give the interviewee time to think and then speak.
- Ask the interviewee to clarify the time and place of specific recollections when he or she finishes answering a question.
- Probe! Always ask why and how. Ask for opinions and feelings.
- If interviewee's recollection of an event seems to disagree with facts as you understand them, rephrase and repeat the question later. Do not challenge interviewee's veracity; if the interviewee persists with the questionable version, refer to an anonymous source that disagrees with the remembrance and ask for a response.
- When concluding the interview, ask an obvious wrap-up question that will permit the interviewee to reveal anything that questioning may have missed but that he or she thinks is important to include.

will have a progression of questions designed for that particular person, preferably with the questions arranged by keyword topics. If the interviewer is familiar with the individual, these keywords should be enough to guide the interview. Thus, the outline of questions should be a flexible guideline that ensures that all major topics are covered.

The success of the oral history interview often hinges on the trust developed during the interactions between the interviewer and interviewee (McMahan & Rogers, 1994). McMahan (1989) describes the effective oral history interview as one of cooperation and coherence in which the trust between interviewer and interviewee leads to eliciting coherent narrative information. The process occurs, she says, "as a social event. As such it reflects the social relations of the moment—those between interviewer and interviewee— and those of the larger culture . . ." (p. x).

Like most interviews, the interview process begins prior to the actual recording of the conversation. The interviewer should chat with the interviewee while setting up the recording equipment and getting prepared for the interview. This offers an opportunity to establish rapport before the questioning begins.

Once the interview starts, the first questions should be easy, open-ended inquiries that offer the interviewee a chance to talk. The best oral history interviews are really a series of short monologues, rather than a series of quick questions and answers. The goal of the questions is to trigger memories that will result in an extended narrative from the interviewee.

The Written Transcript

In some ways, the term *oral history* is misleading. True, one goal of the research is to get participants to give an oral account of their lives or of some event in which they participated. For maximum effectiveness, though, that oral account must be transcribed. McMahan (1989) notes that the construction of a written text is essential to the development of an oral history autobiography. Consequently, after the first interview has been conducted, the interviewer should return to his or her home and office and transcribe the interview. Two things are accomplished by doing so. First, it ensures that a written record of the interview is generated. Cassette tapes may be easy to make, but they are still awkward for others to use on an everyday basis. Family members may become bored having to sit around and listen to a lengthy taped interview; they may more willingly and more quickly scan a written text of that same interview. Second, the transcription provides the interviewer with an opportunity to review the entire interview. As the interview is transcribed, the interviewer can identify those narratives that require more information or clarification.

The transcription is perhaps the single most time-consuming aspect of oral history research. Although voice-recognition software has made the job somewhat easier, the technology still needs to be improved before most people can easily use it for their interviews. In most cases, a person transcribes the interview. Typically one hour of tape-recorded interview equals about 50 pages of typed transcript and represents about eight hours of work. Some researchers choose to hire professional dictation stenographers to handle this job. Others transcribe only parts of the interview; they review each tape individually and use the digital counters on their recorders to identify those segments that they wish to transcribe. This latter approach, however, runs the risk of losing some key details that are important to the individual's story.

Back to the Library

Memories are faulty. Sometimes stories become ingrained into a family's narrative history, but do so with such elaboration that some element of truth is lost. The author once interviewed a relative of country music legend Hank Williams who recounted how Hank had written one of his hit songs while visiting her. A great story, but subsequent research revealed that Williams was not the person who wrote that song. She had confused a hit song that he did not write with another song with a similar title that never received much radio play. Similarly, Harry Walker recounted a story in which Dizzy Dean struck out one player four times in a single game, with the last strikeout coming after Dizzy knocked the catcher down to keep him from catching a pop-up foul. When the researcher tracked down the game, though, he discovered that Dizzy did get the final strikeout following two foul balls by the batter, but neither of those fouls was playable by the catcher. The researcher has a responsibility to verify as much of the information obtained in the interview as possible. Discrepancies can become a topic for subsequent interviews, as the interviewer and interviewee work together to form a coherent account of the person's life.

More Interviews

The process of interview, research, and more interviews is repeated as often as necessary. More interviews provide more information. The questions asked in subsequent interviews differ, however. Most of the subsequent interviews focus on providing details or filling in gaps created by the information in the first interview. As questions are asked, other memories are frequently triggered that will, in turn, necessitate additional research by the interviewer. This may sometimes trigger entirely new lines of questioning on topics that had not initially been anticipated by the researcher. McMahan (1987) describes this process of exchanging and learning new information as "speech and counter speech," a give-and-take process in which language is used to elicit the details of a person's life. Similarly, Harris (1985) describes it as a process in which ". . . memory, myth, ideology, language, and historical cognition interact in a dialectical transformation of the word into a historical artifact" (pp. 6–7).

Any discrepancies identified during outside research should be investigated with more questions that ask for specific details of the event. This process of probing is called *reality monitoring*. Reality monitoring works under the assumption that memories for real experiences are richer in sensory details and with contextual attributes than memories for imagined events (Johnson & Raye, 1981; Johnson, 1988). Subsequent research on this topic has generally supported this theory (Anderson, 1984; Johnson, Foley, Suengas, & Raye, 1988; McGinnis & Roberts, 1996). The practical application of the research is to probe the topic—particularly those with potential discrepancies—for more details about how the person felt at the time and their memories of the context in which it occurred.

Editing the Narrative

The collection of interviews that comprise the oral history of any one individual will be a hodgepodge of stories that ramble in no particularly sequential order. All of the transcripts should be compiled and then edited into a coherent narrative form. The original transcripts should not be discarded; they should be retained in their original form for reference purposes. However, the final product itself must be an edited version of the materials.

The easiest way to edit oral history materials is to order all topics by chronological, spatial, or topical sequence. If the oral history is on the life of an individual, the chronological organizational pattern usually works best. The topics will usually be categorized as early years, young adult, career, and elderly years. Under each topic area, appropriate subtopics can be developed. For example, a person's early years might include subtopics related to their parents, siblings, hometown, early schooling, and childhood activities. Each of the interview transcripts are scanned for material that would fall into each category and then the materials are cut and pasted to organize the various segments. The narrative is then edited further to ensure that the story is a coherent one. The interviewer must take particular care to tell the story in the words of the interviewee—the narrative is the person's story, not the interviewers.

Oral History in Academic Research

Oral history is perhaps the world's oldest academic discipline. Before the development of written languages, people maintained their cultural identity and passed information to the next generation through the telling and retelling of oral histories. Over time, many of these stories became myths or legends that eventually found their way into our written culture. Was there once a great flood that covered massive parts of the earth? The story of the flood is part of the oral tradition of several cultures and was eventually written down by a few. However, verifying such stories is difficult.

In modern academic communities, oral history first found its home in the discipline of history. Historians found that extensive use of oral history could provide details and insight into a historical event. A written record may provide an objective account of an event, but personal impressions provided an understanding of that event. As mentioned earlier, Cornelius Ryan recorded the oral histories of combat veterans for his historical account of three World War II battles. Similarly, a number of researchers have used oral history to examine historical events related to the Civil Rights movement of the 1960s. Diane McWhorter (2001) won a Pulitzer Prize for her account of Civil Rights battles in Birmingham, Alabama, during the 1960s. Culpepper Clark (1995) narrowed his topic to a single event—George Wallace standing in the schoolhouse door at the University of Alabama—and examined it through oral history interviews.

As illustrated by these examples, the most common use of oral history in academic research is to examine one event or topic from the perspective of its participants. From the communication perspective, this line of research is a subcategory of a specific form of communication research—*critical events analysis*. The focus of critical events analysis is the study of major, discrete events that test the relationship between media and politics (Kraus, Davis, Lang, & Lang, 1976). A number of researchers have used this approach to look at high-profile political debates (Kraus, 1962) or provocative events, such as the assassination of President John Kennedy (Greenberg, 1964; Mendelsohn, 1964) and the attempts on the lives of candidate George Wallace (Steinfatt, Gantz, Siebold, & Miller, 1973) and President Ronald Reagan (Gantz, 1983; Weaver-Lariscy, Sweeney, & Steinfatt, 1984).

Oral history differs from pure critical events analysis because of its focus on the interview technique. For purposes of a broad study of a critical event, a variety of research methodologies would be used. Interviews with participants would be one of the methods used, but only one of several. Typically, critical events analysis might also include survey

Oral History Web Sites

Numerous Web sites are devoted to oral history, and new ones always are being created. The following are some useful oral history Web sites.

- *www.dickinson.edu/oha/*—The homepage of the Oral History Association. Includes general information about the association, its membership requirements, and a list of its publications, including the *Oral History Review*.
- *www.library.ucla.edu/libraries/special/ohp/ohpdocs.htm*—The Web site of the Oral History Program at UCLA. The site includes instructions and guidelines for conducting oral history interviews.
- *http://members.aol.com/_ht_a/famjustin/usnoentry.html*—The online Navy Oral History Collection contains stories from Navy veterans and their family.
- *www.history.navy.mil./faqs/faq66-3.htm*—The Navy Historical Center contains a collection of oral history by topic. This specific URL directs visitors to a collection devoted to oral histories of the attack on Pearl Harbor on December 7, 1941.
- *www.personalhistorians.org*—The Web site of the Association of Personal Historians.
- *http://sunsite.berkeley.edu:2020/dynaweb/teiproj/oh/warren/*—UC Berkeley maintains an extensive collection of interviews with people who knew and worked with former Supreme Court Justice Earl Warren.
- *www.jewishgen.org/infofiles/quest.txt*—A list of questions, summarized elsewhere in this chapter, that can be used to prompt memories from people who are the subject of oral history interviews.
- *www.usd.edu/iais/oralhist/ohc.html*—The Web site for the South Dakota Oral History Center, which includes more than 5,000 interviews in the oral history collections of the Institute of American Indian Studies.
- *www.gcah.org/oral.html*—Oral history Web site of the General Commission on Archives and History for the United Methodist Church.

data, analysis of media output, and analysis of general public opinion responses. Oral history primarily uses one method—the in-depth focused interview—to develop an understanding of an event.

Oral History as a Family History Narrative

A nationwide interest in family history research has led to a wider interest in oral history interviews as a way for people to record family histories. The desire to engage in an oral history project immediately shows the subjects of such interviews that someone cares about them and their personal history (Zimmerman, 1992). Oral history offers a way for individuals to understand their family's past. It also can fill in gaps that might not be revealed by documents that merely record births, weddings, and deaths. As Linda Spence (1997) notes, "As we move through our lives, we carry with us the stories of our childhood.

We may change them, forget or deny them, smile or cry over them, but, like charms or spells, they bring back a sense of who we were and how we came to be the people we've become" (pp. 3–4).

For a really effective family history, rule number one is to start early. Genealogists recommend that researchers not wait until the last minute or insist that everything be perfect before beginning a project (Xiong, 2002). Every day lost is another potential memory that will never be recorded. One should start by asking the oldest members of the family—grandparents, great aunts, and great uncles—to talk about their lives. Family gatherings such as birthdays, holidays or anniversaries are particularly good times to do the first interviews. Such events may trigger a number of memories.

A number of oral interview guides are available to the novice interviewer, including those presented in this chapter. The specific questions included in each guide vary; Spence (1997), for example, includes nearly 400 possible questions that can be used to trigger a person's memory. However, the interviewer should not feel compelled to answer every question in one sitting. Such an attitude will produce frustration on the part of both the interviewer and the interviewee. Multiple interviews may be needed to fully cover all of the desired questions.

One option is to schedule interviews around major topics. However, in all likelihood, the interviewer will not be able to stick entirely to the schedule. Any question can prompt memories from multiple stages of the interviewee's life. Still, some broad areas can serve as a general outline for the interviews. Spence (1997) recommends organizing the interviews around nine different life stages:

1. *Beginnings and Childhood.* This starts with having the interviewee list as many names as possible from the family tree, telling what he or she knows about those ancestors. It can move from there to where he or she was born, earliest memories, descriptions of the childhood home, pets, games played, schooling, weekend activities, holiday rituals, childhood chores, heroes, adults who were present, and family rules.

2. *Adolescence.* This is a key phase in identity development, one that many people remember vividly. Have the interviewee describe the scene in terms of where he or she lived and went to school and what he or she did at school. What activities was he or she good at? What activities were difficult? Did the interviewee have a good relationship with his or her parents? Did the interviewee ever get into trouble or participate in risky behaviors?

3. *Early Adult Years.* Those first steps into the real world can be memorable. What were the significant milestones in the person's early career? What was happening with his or her family during this time? How did the person's values change during early adulthood?

4. *Marriage.* Not everyone in modern society includes this stage in their own personal life, but marriage still plays a major role in the lives of most people. The key here is getting the individual to talk of how he or she was attracted to his or her partner, how they met, and how their courtship progressed. How about details of the wedding? What obstacles did the couple have to overcome in the early years of the marriage, including those in their careers? Ask the interviewee to recall some of the good times and bad times of those early years together.

An Interview with Sandra Sleight-Brennan: Preserving the Memories of a Community

Sandra Sleight-Brennan lives in the Appalachian region of Ohio (Athens County) and is a 20-year veteran of oral history research. Her work has included the "Countdown to the Millennium," an oral history project to record the history of coal-mining communities in Ohio; "Deep In Our Hearts," a radio documentary about four women in the Civil Rights movement, as well as other oral history projects. She has won 18 state, national, and international awards for her work.

Q. Can you give me some background on your "Countdown to the Millennium" project?

A. I started that project in 1997. It had several different levels. One of the ideas was to get people to share their memories of living in the twentieth century. We have many old, coal-company towns in the area that are dying. We felt that the best people to do the interviews in those areas were high school students. If I had gone in to do the interview, I would have been an outsider. But people rarely turn down an interview with a local high school student.

Q. How did you make it work?

A. First, we taught the kids the basics of oral history interviewing, how to use video cameras, and asked them to find people in their home town to do the interviews with. That worked very well. We've got about eighty that we've done the transcripts for and put on the Web site.

Q. What was the second layer?

A. Once they collected all those interviews, I looked through them and worked with a historian to look for the main themes that would chronicle the twentieth century. We identified the individuals who could best represent those themes. I then went back and interviewed them with better quality equipment and put together a radio series called, "Countdown to the Millennium."

Q. What do you think the students got out of this?

A. They worked in groups of three. Often they interviewed someone who was a relative of one of the three. I was amazed at some of the questions they were asking their grandparents that they had never bothered to ask them before. They were finding out things about family history that they had never bothered to ask. A number of these people were elderly and have since died; in a number of cases, people have asked me for copies of the tape after their family member has died. Another experience I had was one time when I went to the local high school and happened in on a class. They were all sitting there, watching one person's interview. They were just entranced by it. It was holding the attention of these 17-year-old kids.

Q. Why is oral history so interesting?

A. It's the stories that don't get written down. People tend to think that history is written by the conqueror, by the people in power. In this case, it was the story of people in Appalachia—the people who had never been in power. These are the stories that tend to be forgotten. In fact, it's often the case that when you go to interview people, they'll say, "Oh, you don't want to interview me. I've never done anything." They don't feel they're important enough for an interview. Yet, when you interview them—particularly older

(continued)

Continued

people—and get them to talk about things that are important to them, they're kind of reevaluating their whole life. It's a way of honoring people, and they've very grateful that you're taking the time to listen to them.

Q. How does it work?

A. You should really work on letting people tell their own story in the way that they want to tell it. Don't use too many questions. I do tell them to go into an oral history with a list of questions that they want to ask. But they should really have a good sense of history before they go in. If the person is 70 years old, when were they born? Gauge your questions based on their age, but try to let them tell it in their own words as much as possible. What happens when you do that is they tend to focus on events that were personally important in their lives. Somebody gave me an interview that was done in the 1960s, a man who at the time was 106 years old. He could remember the Civil War. He was five years old when the war started. Morgan's Raiders came through this part of Ohio, and the area was afraid that the Raiders would come through. He told in incredible details of how they cinched quilts and the family's featherbeds on their horses, and stuffed their hats in around the girth strap so that when they went over the hill to hide, they wouldn't run and hurt the horses too much. He talked about all the horses he took to the county fair over the years. At the end of this 45-minute interview, you realize that he told you the name of every horse he ever owned. He also had 14 brothers and sisters, but he doesn't tell you the name of one single sibling. From that, you infer that the horses were more important to him than his siblings. He worked day in and day out with those horses. The siblings grew up, moved away, and he probably saw them a few times a year. But that kind of thing comes out when you let someone tell it in their own way. You find out what's important to them. The things that people choose to remember reflect the rhythms of their lives. And the way they tell it tells something about their values.

Q. Do you concentrate on doing stories of communities?

A. Not just communities. I've just finished an hour-long radio documentary on the lives of four white women who were involved in the Civil Rights movement. But most of my stories deal with the area I live in.

Q. Is there anything you'd like to add?

A. Oral histories are really interesting and a really important way of interviewing people, for many different purposes. If somebody wanted to do a character study for a character in a play, novel, or movie, it's a wonderful way to get the essence of a person. By letting people tell their own stories, so many personalities emerge. It can be spellbinding. I always walk out of an oral history interview feeling privileged that this person gave me the time to talk to them.

---

5. *Being a Parent.* Children change the dynamics of family life as both parents have to adjust their lives for the new family member. Start with the basics—name, date, and place of birth of each child—and move on to the feelings, dreams, and behaviors of the child and those around them. How did the interviewee react to parenthood? What memories does the person have of the children's childhood? What activities did he or she share with the children? How did the parent's relationship with the child change as the child grew older?

6. *Middle Adult Years.* Spence (1997) notes that one's middle years are those where "we see the results of the time and energy we've given to our family, work, community, self" (p. 101). This stage in one's life provides an opportunity for assessing everything that came before and preparing for what will come later. What was the interviewee's family like during this time? What was the routine on a typical workday? What friends were parts of the interviewee's life? Was the interviewee active in the community? What was the most difficult part of these years? What was the best part?

7. *Being a Grandparent.* Grandparents often have special relationships with their grandchildren. Getting grandparents to talk about this stage of their lives is usually easy, particularly when they talk about their grandchildren. The interviewer, though, should also get them to talk about their role as grandparents and how they felt about that role.

8. *Later Adult Years.* Individuals who are in their eighties or nineties can aptly be described as "today's pioneers" (Spence, 1997, p. 119), but their memories often are overlooked. Questions from any previous life stage can be used here, but these individuals also can provide insights that younger interviewees do not have. They can compare the modern world with the one in which they were born and lived. They can recall how lifestyles, means of transportation, and communication methods have changed. And, they often can speak passionately about changes in values and culture. Each of these ideas provides insights into the person and his or her times.

9. *Reflections.* Spence (1997) lists this category as a distinctly different topic, but it could also easily fit as a subcategory or topic for "Later Adult Years." It simply refers to a specific type of question in which the interviewee is encouraged to recall critical phases of his or her life and to make comparisons between the past and modern life. Is life more difficult for people today? What did the interviewee learn from life that was important? What were the fears and uncertainties that the interviewee faced? Were there any lost opportunities?

By using this nine-stage process, the interviewer—over time and through the use of multiple interviews—will be able to elicit some extended narrative stories that will provide insight into the individual's life. Both the interviewer and the interviewee are likely to enjoy and be surprised by what they discover.

The Few Disadvantages of Oral Interviews

Oral history interviews have one major weakness—reliability. Memories are notoriously faulty. As time passes, people forget some details, accentuate others, and new—and inaccurate data—may become part of the story as it gets embellished. This is why the interviewer must verify as much information as possible. Not only does research increase the accuracy of the final text, it can produce written records that can reinforce or corroborate the narrative, and perhaps trigger additional memories.

Oral histories also can be time-consuming. Rick Bragg (2002) spent three years working on an oral history of his grandfather. A. Scott Berg (2003) spent 20 years interviewing actress Katherine Hepburn before the publication of his memoir about her. Although not all oral histories require such a lengthy time commitment, the oral interview is substantially more time-consuming than other types of interviews. Thus, the person who embarks on conducting an oral history must be committed to seeing it through. If not, both the interviewer and the subject of the interview will be disappointed.

Summary

Oral history interviews offer a rich opportunity for both academic and popular communities. For academicians, oral history provides a means of viewing history from the perspective of the participants. Battles are studied in terms of their human turmoil and suffering, rather than as strategic activities. Social history is viewed by those who lived it rather than as a summation of demographic descriptors.

At the popular and personal level, family oral histories provide individuals with a chance to learn more about themselves and their families. Recording such an oral history helps to bridge the gap between generations, as the stories of one generation are passed on to another. Further, these oral histories provide a lasting record of the lives of older Americans, one that can be passed on to future generations.

As such, oral history interviews have the capability of making major contributions to both the academic community and to the lives of individuals. All they require is a tape recorder, a little patience, and a desire to record someone's story so that others can know what he or she has experienced.

FOR FURTHER DISCUSSION

1. Choose a historical topic of interest to you. Read a book on that topic that uses the oral history technique. What questions were asked? How were the interviews used to develop the topic?

2. Design an interview guide for an oral history project. Who would be the subject of your interview? What initial research would be necessary? What questions would you ask?

CHAPTER
13 Police Interviews

Two police officers spot a car weaving on the highway. After pulling the car over and speaking with the driver, they soon come to believe the driver is inebriated. The officers' questions become more focused as they look for signs of slurred speech and confused thinking. After asking for permission to search the driver's car, the officers find a sizable amount of drugs and $30,000 in cash. They call in for detectives who then take the driver in for interrogation.

Lawyers gather together for a deposition because the plaintiff in a lawsuit seeks more information before going to trial. The plaintiff's lawyer hopes to learn as much as possible without giving away too much of their courtroom strategy. The defendants want to say as little as possible while always telling the truth. The dialectical tension in the room is mild, but apparent.

Inside a courtroom, a prosecution witness is examined at length by the district attorney as the state's case is presented, bit by bit. When the district attorney sits down, however, the defense attorney rises, intent on discrediting as much of the witness's testimony as possible.

These scenarios present the four types of interviews that occur within the U.S. legal system: (1) police officers question those they encounter on their beats in their efforts to reduce crime and capture criminals (Langworthy & Travis, 1994); (2) detectives interrogate suspects to gather information about felonies that have been committed; (3) lawyers use a structured form of interview known as the deposition to gather information from the opposing side; (4) and prosecution lawyers, defense lawyers, and judges interview those involved in civil and criminal court proceedings. An understanding of police interviewing techniques is important for police officers, those involved in the judicial process, and reporters.

With regards to police interviews and other legal interviews, most of the interviewing rules presented in this text do not apply. Whereas most interview formats emphasize the need to be open and trusting, policemen are more likely to be suspicious, less trusting, aloof, and secretive (Westley, 1970). Officer attitudes can have a direct impact on the officer's behavior when interacting with individuals at the scene of a crime (Black & Reiss, 1967). People who are interviewed by the police, including average citizens with nothing to hide, may find that they are uncomfortable and their resulting interactions are somewhat unnatural (Piliavin, 1973). Therefore, to learn about police interviews and other forms of legal interviews, it is necessary to start over.

How Police Interviews Differ

The most important factor influencing whether a case is solved is the information obtained by the patrol officer who initially responds to a complaint (Smith, Moracco, & Butts, 1998). Initial interviews with victims, witnesses, and suspects can help investigators determine what crime has been committed and identify possible suspects (e.g., Smith, Moracco, & Butts, 1998). Sometimes an arrest can be made immediately; other times, the information from those initial interviews is broadcast to other officers who can watch out for suspects or suspicious vehicles. If patrol officers can identify witnesses or suspects who can be interviewed, a case is more likely to be solved (Greenberg, Elliot, Kraft, & Procter, 1975). In fact, the resolution of approximately 80 percent of all cases can be traced back to information obtained from the initial interviews conducted by police officers (Greenwood, Chaiken, & Petersilia, 1977). What is often overlooked is that many of the techniques taught in typical university interviewing classes do not apply to the legal environment. Consider the following differences:

- *Most interview situations place a value on openness and a willingness to communicate about oneself.* In a legal interview, such behavior could land a person in jail. Criminal suspects have constitutional protection against self-incrimination. If they do not want to answer questions, they do not have to.
- *Most interview training stresses the need for honesty and integrity.* In a police interrogation, it is considered ethical for the police to lie in order to gather information related to a crime. As of this writing, the Supreme Court has placed few limits on the use of deception in the interrogation room. As a result, police often use deception for interrogation purposes (Skolnick & Leo, 1992). As such, the police often treat interrogation as a "confidence game" in which they attempt to trick the suspect into confessing (Leo, 1996, p. 259). Officers may use a variety of deceptive techniques, such as misrepresenting the seriousness of the offense or presenting fabricated evidence to elicit a confession (Skolnick & Leon, 1992). Magid (2001) argues that virtually all successful interrogations involve some form of deception.
- *The effectiveness of most interviews is enhanced if the participants adopt a collaborative style in which they seek to help each other.* In a police interrogation, the police and the subject have an adversarial relationship. The police want a confession from a guilty suspect, or at least information that would incriminate the suspect; however, the suspect wants to stay out of jail.
- *Police interviews can be highly stressful for the officers who conduct the interviews.* The nature of the officer's job can place high levels of stress on individual police officers. The norms of their profession requires that they remain calm and in control, constantly guarding their emotions, as they conduct interviews to gather evidence and interrogate suspects. The result can be repressed feelings that build up over time. Research indicates that the stress of the job is enormous. Further, regardless of any stress management techniques that may be used to combat stress, the emotional strain and tragedy associated with the job takes an emotional toll on police officers (Pogrebin & Poole, 1995).

■ *Police interviews may involve complex intercultural interactions.* Police often work among and with diverse cultural groups. To be effective in such situations, effective police work requires a recognition and understanding of intercultural communication (Cornett-DeVito & McGlone, 2000).

Interviewing Witnesses

Police interviews police fall into two broad categories: interviews of witnesses and interrogations of suspects. Witnesses to a crime tend to fall into three distinct categories: victims, eyewitnesses, and others with information related to the crime. Typically, the police use different interview techniques with each type of witness.

Interviewing 911 Calls

The initial contact that a citizen may have with the police when a crime occurs is often via emergency 911 calls in which a person calls to report a crime. The 911 operator's job is to get essential information from the caller that can be used to direct a police response to the emergency (Zimmerman, 1984, 1992).

In many places, automated 911 enables the operator to identify where the call is being made from; however, additional information is still needed (Whalen, Whalen, & Zimmerman, 1990). The problem, to the dismay of many 911 workers, is that the person reporting the crime often resists answering questions (Tracy, 2002). Tracy found that 911 operators often pose questions in such a manner that the callers think the operator is questioning their trustworthiness, their intelligence, and their moral character. When these feelings are combined with the stress of the situation, callers resist further questioning from the operators.

Tracy notes, "callers occasionally have trouble answering open-ended questions such as 'Which way did the suspect go?'" (p. 153), but generally do better if the 911 operators use short closed-ended questions. Tracy recommends that call-takers use polite language when phrasing questions, using embedded questions such as "Can you tell me if . . . " rather than "Tell me if . . ." Such wording is less threatening to the caller. Another technique is to preface the question with a statement indicating urgency, such as "We need a description of the suspect so the police can identify the assailant." Although such wording takes slightly longer than a direct question, it provides a distraught caller with motivation to calm down and answer the question.

Interviewing Victims

Interviewing victims requires a high level of tact and skill. While being interviewed, crime victims typically respond either with feelings of anxiety or feelings of being respected, with the response highly dependent on the demeanor of the interviewer (Holmberg, 2004). Speaking with victims as soon as possible after an incident ensures a more vivid recollection of the event (Cordner, Greene, & Bynum, 1983). At the same time, the trauma of the event may still have the victim in such a state of shock that the interviewer must proceed

Interview with Bob Berry

Robert L. "Bob" Berry is Chief of Police in Hoover, Alabama. A 28-year veteran of police work, Berry is also an instructor in the Justice Sciences Department at the University of Alabama at Birmingham, where he teaches undergraduate and graduate courses in law enforcement.

Q. How important is interviewing in police work?

A. Very important. Most crimes are solved by "information," whether it's information gathered from a witness or suspect, or information gathered at the scene, or from scientific investigation. Very seldom and mostly in movies do you see the cops roll up with the crime in progress. That's good TV stuff.

Q. How do you gather that information?

A. It depends on whether you're doing an interview or an interrogation. Generally, you interview witnesses. You interrogate suspects. A witness has information that you need to get out of them; often they're willing to give it, if they're able. A suspect often has information that you need, but they're usually not willing to give it up.

Q. How does the process operate?

A. Let's say it's a bank robbery. The first officers on the scene will gather what information they can. That's done with quick interviews with witnesses, asking what did you see, what did you hear, describe the person. It's amazing how those descriptions will change. You may have three different descriptions of the suspect put out over the air within five minutes.

Q. How do you resolve the conflicting descriptions?

A. You try for corroboration. If you've got five people out there, and they all saw the same thing, you may go with that. Or you look for some other evidence—videotape, or something like that—that can corroborate the witnesses. Often that corroboration can tell you whether the person you've interviewed is a witness or a suspect.

Q. What's the next step?

A. Then you move into a true interview situation. You'll usually have somebody else—a local detective or investigator assigned to the case—who'll come into a controlled environment, sit somebody down and get their story. You always try to interview as quickly as you can after they've calmed down.

Q. What do you mean by a controlled situation?

A. Anytime a violent crime happens, the first question that the officers will ask is "Is everyone OK?" Is it safe for everyone, including the officers? Secondary to that is "Now give me the information." You ask, "What'd you see?" "What happened?" You may take someone away from the scene where they can gather their thoughts, maybe into a closed office—a place where you can limit phones ringing, doors opening, other disturbances. Anytime you're interviewing someone, you want to control the environment and limit the distractions. Any distractions should be preplanned by the investigator, but the person you're interviewing shouldn't have that luxury.

Q. What about interrogating suspects?

Continued

A. Same thing. A controlled environment is very important. You may question someone on the scene, and not even know they're a suspect. Or the officer on the scene may grab somebody who fits the description. They're going to do a basic interrogation right there on the scene. If they decide it warrants going further, then they will try to take them out of that environment and put them in an environment that they can control. When you're interviewing a witness, you may interview them in their home or where they work. That's alright, because you want them to be comfortable and responsive. But when you're interviewing a suspect, you want them in your territory. The interviewer must have control.

Q. How does the interviewer control it?

A. Limit distractions—phones, doors opening, even pictures on the wall—anything that would give the person something else to focus on. The type of attitude and type of personality that the interviewer has makes a huge difference in the case. You've got to first make them understand that they're in your ball park, on your turf. It may be little things in a subtle way. You tell them they can't smoke. Or tell them to sit. Or no, you can't sit in that chair, sit in this chair over here. It's often very subtle. There's none of that slamming people down into the chair that you see on TV. But you've got to get control and try to maintain control of the conversation, because they're going to try to get off on a tangent and run off into left field on you. You've got to get control of the conversation and bring it back to the topic that you need to talk about. You need to be able to read the type of personality the person you're interrogating has also. There are numerous techniques to utilize based on demeanor, personality, attitude, etc. Interview style has to fit both the suspect and the interviewer.

Q. Are all interviews done immediately after the crime?

A. Sometimes you may interview people about something that they saw that happened a day or two ago. There may also be times when you interview people about something that happened a year ago—their name may have just come up. That happens a lot. You've got to go and get more information out of them. The tone and intensity may be different. They've had a chance to calm down. And you can talk to them in a controlled situation. Usually, the sooner after an event the better. Our memories tend to fade with time, and also with outside influences. You may hear what someone else said they saw or heard and decide maybe they were right and not you.

Q. What specific techniques are used?

A. There are a lot of standard techniques that you read about and are taught to officers— from body language to psychological reactions. But the personality of the interviewer is the critical factor. It takes finesse. You've got to have patience and endurance. Sometimes these things will take hours and hours, so patience is critical.

Q. What about the legal requirements?

A. You never want to lose a case on a legal technicality. Those are so rote now, that they're not as big a factor as they once were. Today, having a case thrown out because somebody screwed up a Miranda warning is not too common. The officers are trained for those things. There's a lot of legal case law that goes into when, where, whether or not they should be interrogated, but well-trained officers know what they can do and what

(continued)

Continued

they can't do. And there's all sorts of exceptions. Let's suppose they've caught someone robbing a bank, and the person had a gun. The officer can ask the suspect, "Where's the gun?" without giving a Miranda warning, because it deals with a public safety issue. You know there's a gun somewhere that you need to locate.

Q. Is there any general guideline that they follow?

A. A lot depends on the situation. Often, officers are told not to Mirandize every suspect that they apprehend. They may detain him, put him in the car, and bring him to the station. If they Mirandize him at the scene, and he lawyers up—asks for a lawyer—detectives don't even get a shot at a real interview with him before contacting an attorney.

Q. Do they have to read the suspect his rights before they talk to him at all?

A. No. There is a misperception that you have to tell every suspect his rights, but—like I said—there are plenty of exceptions. There's a lot of latitude if the person is not under arrest or in custody.

Q. When do you have to read the Miranda rights?

A. The general rule is that they have to be in custody and interrogated by the police. If you and I were standing on a street corner, I don't have to do a thing. It's just me and you. If I had coerced you into talking to me, for example, I order you, "Stand right there, I want to talk to you," then in essence, you're "in custody"—you do not feel that you have the freedom to leave, and it is not my intention to let you leave whether you want to or not. But as long as you're free to leave, and you understand that, there's no mandate for the Miranda rights. If it becomes clear that they're a suspect, and I don't intend to let you go, well then, time out. It's probably time to read you your rights.

Q. What's the major factor in getting someone to confess?

A. The interrogator. Sometimes that means being his friend. Sometimes it means being his enemy. Whatever it takes. Oftentimes they won't talk. Then sometimes, if you shut up, they'll talk. Most people have an inherent desire to talk. You often have to lead them in the right direction.

Q. How do you lead them in the right direction?

A. That's when training plays such a critical role. You watch for subtle signs. You watch for body language. There's a world of different things you look for, because you have to know if you're getting truthful information.

Q. What do you look for?

A. Myriad things. No one thing is going to do it. Body posture. Locked hands. Eye shifts. Sweaty palms. Nervous ticks. Toe tapping. Coughing. Throat clearing. Stalling tactics to give them time to think of an answer. Some people look one way when they're lying and one way when they're telling the truth. You can't take any one thing. Take sweat, for instance. Some people may sweat a lot when they're lying. But maybe he has a medical condition, or maybe it's just hot. Who knows. It's a sign of something to look for, but you can't hang everything on it. And facial color. Sometimes people face will blush when they lie, but that may also be a normal reaction for some people when they're asked certain questions that are normal in an interview. Or the pallor face. Sometimes their face will drain if they're surprised. I put more faith in that. He may get flushed because he's mad at you. But when you make his face drain, you're usually onto something. You may

Continued

not know what it is, but you know you've hit a hot spot anyway and you need to dig some more. Still, there are a thousand little things you have to look for.

Q. What about implicating other people?

A. As a general rule, if you're not guilty of something, I don't think you'd mind giving me a name. You may not like implicating someone you know, but as an honest person you'd probably be helpful in answering questions about someone you know. Generally the guilty aren't as inclined to snitch on their buddies unless they get something for doing so. I think that's just human nature.

Q. Assuming that you get a confession, what's next?

A. Verify it. Even though they've confessed to it, you've still got to corroborate it. You can confess to a murder, but if we can't find a body or at least verify that a murder occurred, we can't do much. Confession is just part of it. You always want that. If you've got the guy's fingerprint or DNA, you still would like a confession. Just because you got a person's print from a crime scene, it doesn't necessarily mean he committed the crime you're investigating. You need evidence that does more than just place a suspect at the scene.

Q. What's unusual about police interviews?

A. You often catch people at a disadvantage, at a bad point in their life and sometimes at a weak point in their life. And yet, you have to talk with them, because you need the information. It's not often that police get to interview people about something nice that happened in their life—unless it's maybe a background check on a friend who listed them as a reference. Unfortunately, by the time law enforcement is involved in the interview or interrogation stage, somebody's already not a happy camper.

slowly and carefully. Research on attribution theory has demonstrated that, as time passes, witnesses rely less on what they saw and heard during an event and more on their *attributions*; that is, their theory of what must have occurred. Thus, the sooner the interviewer is able to talk with the victim the more accurate the victim's statements will be. Later, inaccuracies that may creep into a victim's statements may unwittingly point the police in the wrong direction.

Interviewing Witnesses

The key to building a case is gathering evidence. Witnesses, particularly eyewitnesses, may have information relevant to a case. However, officers must be careful in gathering eyewitness testimony. Investigators must gather information that can be used in court without doing anything that would prohibit its use as evidence. This is not always easy to do. Witnesses are notorious for providing inaccurate testimony, because they may describe what they thought they saw rather than what actually happened (Stephen, Allen, Chan, & Dahl, 2004). A witness's first impulse may be to describe his or her holistic impression of the event (e.g., "Everything was crazy") rather than what actually happened (e.g., "I heard an explosion and turned around to see a dozen people running toward me"). Investigators must frame their questions in such a manner as to move the witnesses toward the latter type of information.

Several demographic variables also can affect the accuracy of witness testimony, including age (Memon, Bartlett, Rose, & Gray, 2003; McCarron, Ridgway & Williams, 2004), gender (Butts & Mixon, 1995), and ethnic background (Natarajan, 2003). For example, children have trouble articulating what they have seen using adult terminology. Men and women often focus on different attributes of the same event. Members of most ethnic groups are less adept at identifying facial differences among members of other ethnic groups than of their own group.

Social Remembering.   One approach used with multiple witnesses to an incident is called *social remembering*. With social remembering, witnesses are interviewed in dyads or groups. Instead of treating recall as an intrapersonal phenomenon, proponents of this approach assume that the recall process is enhanced by interpersonal cues. The investigator relies on cues from the responses of one person to trigger additional recall elements for another person. Research has found that this approach generally creates more accurate recall of events, but may also lead to overconfidence in inaccurate elements of those memories (Clark & Stephenson, 1990).

Cognitive Interview Technique.   Another approach to witness interviews is the *cognitive interview technique* (Gieselman, Fisher, MacKinnon, & Holland, 1985, 1986; Fisher, Geiselman, Raymond, Jurkevich, & Warhagtig, 1987; Fisher & Geiselman, 1992; Memon & Wark, 1997). With this approach, context restatement and social techniques for increasing rapport are used to enhance witness recall. Context restatement involves the use of probes to prompt the witness to provide more specific information. For example, when a witness says, "I saw a man with a hat," the investigator follows up with "What color was the hat?" "Did you see his face?" "What was he doing?" and so on. Each probe is intended to spark more memories of the event. The technique is remarkably effective at increasing witness recall. Unfortunately, it can sometimes be too effective—it may trigger inaccurate memories. Numerous studies have demonstrated that extensive probing can introduce errors into witnesses' statements (Memon & Wark, 1997). The problem seems to be particularly acute when the witness is a child (Goodman, Aman, & Hirschman, 1987).

The Use of Mug Books.   One approach used with witnesses who could potentially make an eyewitness identification of a suspect is the use of a "mug book," which is a collection of photographs of individuals who have a record of committing previous offenses of a similar nature. The advantage of using a mug book is that the witness quickly can filter through most of the photos. The problem, though, is that witnesses may have trouble identifying individuals based on mug shots and may make a false identification after looking at too many of them. This problem has led some police departments to ask the witness to fill out a form describing the facial features of the suspect before looking at the mug book. The witness is then shown the photographs in order of decreasing resemblance to the facial features the witness described (Lee et al., 2004).

Professional Witnesses

Another problem faced by investigators is that they often find themselves questioning *professional witnesses*, "people who every time you investigate a crime are either (A) involved somehow, or (B) were mysteriously present to witness what happened" (Dillingham, 1995b, p. 33). Detectives often find themselves interviewing such people when investigating several unrelated crimes. Such witnesses present the investigator with a dilemma—whether such a person is a legitimate witness, someone seeking personal glory, or a suspect in the case. Dillingham notes that investigators must take information from such people "with a grain of salt." He adds, "Naturally, in the course of multiple interviews, these people learn things about our investigative and interview techniques. This puts us at a disadvantage, since we must then adapt our techniques accordingly" (p. 33).

Interrogating Suspects

During the first half of the twentieth century, the police frequently used questionable techniques to induce confessions from suspects. One early study (Hopkins, 1931) found that

You Have the Right to Remain Silent . . .

In 1963, Ernesto Miranda was arrested for the armed robbery of a bank worker. Miranda, who had a prior arrest record, not only confessed to the robbery, but also signed a confession to robbing, kidnapping, and raping an 18-year-old woman who was mentally retarded. Miranda was subsequently charged, convicted, and sentenced for these crimes.

On appeal, Miranda's lawyer argued that Miranda did not fully understand his rights to not self-incriminate himself that sprang from the Fifth Amendment of the Bill of Rights in the U.S. Constitution. In 1966, the U.S. Supreme Court agreed with Miranda's lawyers and overturned his conviction and ordered a new trial. Miranda was retried and reconvicted. He was paroled in 1972 and died four years later after being stabbed in a bar fight. Miranda was 34 at the time of his death. Since that time, it has become common practice for police to inform suspects of the following rights before they are held and interrogated:

- They have a right to remain silent.
- Anything they say can be used against them in a court of law.
- They have the right to have an attorney present before any questioning.
- If they cannot afford an attorney, one will be appointed to represent them before any questioning.
- They are asked if they understand their rights.

Sources: Brandt, C. (1991). *The right to remain silent.* New York: St. Martin's Press; Cassell, P. & R. Fowles (1998). Handcuffing the cops: A thirty-year perspective on Miranda's harmful effects on law enforcement. *Stanford Law Review, 50,* 1055–1069.

more than 20 percent of all suspects had suffered some abuse at the hands of police—a finding that led one authority to describe interrogation techniques of the time as the "detective as inquisitor" (Gaines, Kappeler, & Vaughn, 1997, p. 166). Fortunately, this is no longer the case. Laws now protect the rights of suspects.

Still, the key to solving many crimes is the interrogation of key suspects. Inbau (1999) calls the interrogation process a "practical necessity" in modern police work (p. 1403). Indeed, without the information gained from interrogations, many cases would be difficult to solve. Leo (1996) notes that the strength of the evidence prior to the interrogation was the key factor leading to a successful interrogation in one-third of the cases he studied.

The format of an interrogation differs from that of other interviews in that there is a definite adversarial relationship between the interviewer and the interviewee. The reason for the antagonistic situation is that the interviewee is a suspect in a crime. As such, the interviewer must either confirm or disconfirm the investigator's suspicion. If the investigator's suspicions are confirmed, then the interviewer tries to go one step further—obtaining a confession. As Dillingham (1995a) notes, "A confession is the biggest hurdle a defense attorney must jump when trying to absolve his client" (p. 8). Getting a confession may not be easy, though. Like any good interview, an interrogation takes preparation, skill, and (usually) rapport with the suspect.

Preparation

Police prepare for interrogations by (1) learning about the crime, (2) researching the suspect, and (3) choosing a location for the interrogation. The first factor—knowing about the crime—is critical for three reasons. First, the investigator must know the key details of the crime in order to ask relevant questions and elicit new information from the suspect. The investigator can use this information to feed the suspect bits of information, pretending that he or she knows more than is actually the case. The second reason is credibility. As Dillingham (1995a) writes, "If it appears during the interview that you know nothing about the crime in question, the suspect will figure out that you cannot prove he committed the crime" (p. 8). The third reason has to do with the weight of the evidence. The Supreme Court has consistently ruled that a confession cannot consist simply of an admission of guilt. Instead, the confession must contain "facts about the crime that only the suspect or victim could know" (Dillingham, 1995a, p. 8). The investigator can verify this only if he or she also knows key details of the crime.

The second key pre-interrogation element is learning as much as one can about the suspect. Doing so helps the investigator establish rapport with the suspect and choose what approach to take during the interrogation. With today's modern computer systems, such research can be relatively easy to accomplish. As Dillingham (1995b) notes, "Recidivism is a wonderful thing" in that suspects in a current case often have criminal records that can be used to gather information about them and their habits. Some professional investigators go even further, maintaining their own databases to track all of their interviews.

The third key pre-interrogation element is the selection of a location for the interrogation. Professional investigators prefer to interview suspects in a controlled situation at the police station. Doing the interrogation on "their own turf" gives the investigators a psychological advantage over the suspect that they would not have at the suspect's home or workplace. Further, they take great care to control the nonverbal elements of the immediate environment, that is, the interrogation room. The typical interrogation room is painted a neutral color and has soft lighting. It is usually about 10-feet square, just large enough for two chairs and a small table. One of those chairs, the one the suspect uses, is in a fixed position, whereas the interviewer's chair is unfixed and may have wheels. The rest of the decor is best described as "traditional stark." The walls are bare; there are no clocks, radios, telephones, televisions, or any other item that may distract from the interview. The design is intended so that the suspect will focus on the investigator's questions and nothing else (Dillingham, 1995a). The only thing in the room that has any similarity to decoration is the two-way mirror that allows others to monitor the interrogation from another room.

A few other factors have to be considered during this pre-interview stage. The investigators must decide when to conduct the interrogation, which usually is as soon as possible. The sooner the interrogation can be planned, the less time the suspect has to create an alibi. Dillingham (1995a) advises investigators to be prepared to conduct the interview immediately.

The investigators must also request an interview. Most requests for interrogations are made in person. Calling on the telephone makes it easier for the suspect to decline. If the suspect agrees to be interrogated, he or she should immediately be taken to the police station.

Finally, the investigator must be prepared for the physical rigors of the approaching investigation. An investigator should not go into an interview hungry, sleepy, or tired. Interrogations are rarely as brief as they appear on *Law and Order*. In reality, they are often lengthy and tiring. The general guideline is that the investigator should be prepared to spend as many as four hours completing the interrogation.

Conducting the Interrogation

Professional police interrogators usually approach the interrogation as a fluid process in which their actions and goals change as the interrogation progresses. Thus, it is a multistage process that involves (1) establishing rapport, (2) information gathering, and (3) the closing. The information gathering stage accounts for the bulk of the process. It has four major subdivisions: (1) kinesic interviewing, (2) key question interviewing, (3) reaching a decision point, and (4) the confession. The goal of each stage must be met before the interrogation can productively progress to the next.

Establishing Rapport.   In any good interview, the interviewer's first goal is to establish a positive relationship with the person being interviewed. With interrogations, this goal is somewhat more complicated. Both participants in an interrogation recognize that they are in an adversarial situation. The interviewee understandably will be skeptical of any efforts to establish a relationship. However, skillful investigators usually can develop some degree of rapport. When rapport is achieved, the suspect will find it more difficult to lie.

The techniques that interrogators use to build rapport fall into two broad categories: verbal and nonverbal. The most common verbal technique is for the interrogator to start a conversation on a topic unrelated to the crime. Any topic is appropriate, but the one most frequently used in actual police interrogations is the criminal history of the suspect. Police departments will have extensive information about any past crimes the suspect may have committed. Further, the suspect knows that these crimes are part of his or her criminal record. In some cases, the suspect may already have served prison time for these crimes. As a result, such suspects frequently discuss their past crimes freely and openly, particularly when talking to the police. After all, no harm can come from discussing what the police already know. So why discuss such topics? According to Dillingham (1995a), "... once a suspect begins talking to you about one subject ... it is more difficult for him to not talk about other subjects. This includes crimes the suspect has committed" (p. 9). Such discussions create a momentum of truth that benefits the investigator.

The nonverbal aspects of establishing rapport are traditional ones—using open positions and gestures, smiling, and leaning toward the suspect. These behaviors convey openness on the part of the investigator and indicate that the interviewer is not a threat to the suspect but is interested in hearing his or her side of the story. The suspect's response to such behavior is typically a relaxing of his or her own defensive posture. As this relaxation occurs, the interrogator typically moves closer in proximity to the suspect.

Kinesic Interviewing.   As the interrogator establishes rapport with the suspect, the interrogator also begins to monitor the nonverbal behavior of that suspect. That behavior becomes a baseline as the questioning moves into the second stage—kinesic interviewing. The basis for the kinesic interviewing stage is similar to the concept that guides the use of lie detectors. Lie detectors are used in relatively few interrogations because they increase the cost and time of the interrogation and they require the permission of the person being interrogated. Still, an understanding of how a lie detector operates can help to explain the

Tips for Police Interviews

Tips for Witnesses

- Tell the truth, the whole truth. This includes details that you may think are unimportant. Such details may be useful to the police.
- The stress of the incident will make your adrenalin flow. Do not let the police interview make it worse. Remember that the police officer is on your side, trying to capture someone who has done harm to you or your community.
- In the stress of the moment, you may forget something important. Keep the name of the interviewing officer so that you can call if you remember something else.

Tips for Suspects

- If you need a lawyer, ask for one immediately.
- If you are innocent, cooperate. Provide what information you can that will assist the police in identifying the real culprit.
- Name someone else who would be a better suspect and tell the police why. Innocent people are usually eager to point the finger at others. Guilty parties are reluctant to mention that they have any association with the case.

principles of kinesic interviewing. When a suspect takes a lie detector test, the operator of the machine first asks a series of baseline questions for which the answers are already known. Thus, the first questions that are asked may be simple biographical questions for which the suspect has no reason to lie (e.g., "Are you 38 years old?" "Do you live in Cleveland?" "Are you married?"). Later, the major question of the investigation is asked (e.g., "Did you kill your business partner?"). To determine whether the suspect's response is a lie or the truth, the lie detector operator compares the response to the important question with the suspect's responses to the mundane ones. In essence, the early questions provide a baseline of physiological responses for each suspect by which the truth is evaluated.

Kinesic interviewing is based on the same principle. Early in the interview, typically during the rapport stage, the suspect is asked a series of easy questions. The investigator monitors the suspect's response and uses those observations as a baseline for their normal behavior. Later, the interrogator asks a stressful question, one that might cause a guilty person to lie. If the person does lie, the stress of lying may be exhibited in kinesic behaviors that differ from the baseline, such as poor eye contact, turning away from the interviewer, covering the mouth, or stuttering. Suspects who are being deceptive will often engage in other noticeable behaviors, including a reluctance to be forthcoming and a tendency to provide stories with fewer imperfections and placed in fewer unusual contexts than will truthful suspects (DePaulo et al., 2003). Generally, investigators assume that any guilty behavior of this type occurs more frequently just before a suspect gives a verbal answer. Therefore, the suspect's behavior must be constantly monitored, not just before he or she answers. Dillingham (1995a) gives examples of three questions that may be used to create stress in a guilty person, along with the responses for which the investigator should look:

- *"We are investigating a (name crime). Let me ask you right up front, did you do this?"* Innocent people will firmly deny the accusation; those who are lying will exhibit uncomfortable kinesic behavior prior to answering.
- *"Tell me about your alibi?"* Guilty people tend to have two responses to this question: they give a ridiculous alibi or they become visibly dejected.
- *"Is there any reason or any type of evidence that would show you were at the scene when this crime was committed?"* Again, innocent people answer firmly; guilty suspects will exhibit uncomfortable kinesic behavior.

Key Question Interviewing. Jack was recently arrested on a drunk-driving charge. He was picked up during a routine traffic stop. When the officer asked if he had been drinking, Jack acknowledged that he'd "had a few beers" earlier in the night, but insisted that he was not drunk. He was arrested anyway, but the case was subsequently dismissed when he was able to verify his story. Later, he wondered why he had even been arrested.

The answer is simple. When asked if he had been drinking, he gave the answer of a guilty person. Perhaps, subconsciously, he felt guilty for having "a few beers" even if he was not drunk. The guilty response in this instance is the vague response—"a few beers." In a similar situation, an innocent sober person would say "I had two beers" or "three beers." The innocent person gives a precise answer; the guilty person gives a vague answer. Jack's vague response of "a few beers" was enough to make the officer suspicious.

Such an incident reflects the importance of *key questions* during the interrogation. Key questions are those that are typically answered by innocent people differently than by those who are guilty, or at least those who are being deceptive. Unlike witness interviews, which often use close-ended questions, key questions often are open ended. Their purpose is to help in identifying deception; it is easier for a suspect to lie when answering a closed-ended question. Open-ended questions require longer answers and offer more opportunity for the investigator to identify deceptive responses.

The advantage of key questions is that, unlike kinesic interviewing, which requires the interrogator to monitor the suspect's nonverbal behavior, key questions only require that the interrogator know how innocent and deceptive responses differ. Here are some examples of key questions, along with the innocent and deceptive responses (Dillingham, 1995a):

1. *"Do you know why I asked you here today?"* Innocent people answer correctly ("You're investigating this crime . . ."), sometimes recognizing that they may be a suspect (". . . and you've got to eliminate me as a suspect"). Guilty suspects usually answer "No," typically because admitting that they are a suspect is too close to confessing to the crime.

2. *"Who do you think committed this crime?"* Remember the TV detective Columbo? This was one of his favorite techniques, except that he usually got the process reversed. In the show, the guilty person always pointed to somebody else. In real life, the opposite typically happens. Innocent people usually express their suspicions and offer suggestions for looking further. Guilty suspects usually will offer no suggestions for solving the crime.

3. *"Why do you think this crime was committed?"* Innocent people typically blame the crime on deviant behavior (e.g., "It must have been some nut with a grudge"). Guilty people typically will not suggest a motive or will give self-serving reasons that they feel are acceptable.

4. *"Do you think this crime actually occurred, or do you think something else is going on?"* This question does not fit every crime, but it has occasional utility. Innocent people are usually sure that a crime was committed and someone should be brought to justice. The guilty are more likely to say that they are not sure a crime has been committed.

5. *"Do you think the victim caused this to happen, even slightly?"* Guilty suspects often are quick to blame the victim for the crime (e.g., "She shouldn't have been there"). Innocent people are more likely to blame the person who committed the crime.

6. *"What should happen to the person who did this?"* Innocent people tend to support harsh punishments. Not so for the guilty. They often suggest either an apology or, for a serious crime, a rather minor punishment.

7. *"Will you take a polygraph or lie detector test?"* Innocent people quickly agree, whereas the guilty often refuse.

8. *"How would you do on that lie detector test?"* Innocent people are sure of their innocence and confident that they will pass the polygraph. Guilty suspects, even if they agree to the polygraph, are more likely to say they do not know whether they will pass.

9. *"How do you think this investigation will come out for you?"* Innocents are sure that they will be exonerated. The guilty tend to express doubt, sometimes simply saying "I don't know."

The Decision Point

As the interrogation progresses, the investigator will reach a point at which he or she has deduced whether the suspect is telling the truth or being deceptive. At this point, a decision must be made whether to continue the investigation. Before making this decision the interviewer typically leaves the room. The departure will allow the person conducting the interview to compare notes with those observing the interrogation from behind the two-way mirror.

If those observing the interview share the investigator's assessment, the investigator reenters the room. If the suspect is free to go, he or she is told to leave and the interview is terminated. However, if the general conclusion is that the suspect is being deceptive, the investigator will return and try to get a confession. Dillingham (1995a) recommends that the investigator return to the room with a file folder that has the suspect's name clearly visible and confidently say, "Joe, our investigation clearly shows that you did this crime. I'd like to sit down and talk to you about this."

The Miranda Warnings

If the evidence is strong enough, the investigator may officially arrest the suspect at some point. If an arrest is made, the law requires that the suspect be read his or her rights as stipulated by the *Miranda* warnings—that the suspect has the right to remain silent and the right to an attorney (White, 2001a). As long as the interrogation is for the purpose of gathering information, the investigator is not required to read the Miranda warnings (Pepinsky, 1970; Schulhofer, 2001; White, 2001b). A suspect must be read his or her rights prior to custodial interrogation (Tubbs & Sloan, 2002); it is not required for noncustodial interrogations. However, if a suspect asks for an attorney at any time during an investigation, the interrogation must stop until an attorney is present. Generally, interrogators prefer to hold off on reading the Miranda statements as long as possible, because their introduction interrupts the interrogation process. Once a suspect knows his or her rights, they have the right to say nothing, and many do just that—they clam up. Most suspects know that they have these rights, but few choose to invoke them until the Miranda warnings are read to them.

Some scholars question the relevance of Miranda warnings in modern police investigations—mostly due to overexposure. Thomas (2000, 2003) argues that schoolchildren are more familiar with the Miranda warnings than they are the Gettysburg Address. Leo (2001) argues that they have become so well known that they have little relevance to confessions by suspects in modern police investigations.

The Confession

If the suspect agrees to keep talking, the investigators will attempt to elicit a confession from them (Dillingham, 1995a). The first step in getting a confession is for the interrogator to offer the suspect a face-saving confession. Typically, the interrogator will suggest an

What to Do If You Are Stopped by the Police

Traffic stops are becoming increasingly more and more dangerous for police officers. More and more incidents of violence are occurring in these encounters, and most officers do not have a partner in the car with them. Many police departments now publish "What to Do When Stopped" brochures to help ease tensions between the police and civilians during traffic stops. The following is an excerpt from one such brochure provided by the New York State University Police.

- Stay in your car unless the officer advises you otherwise.
- Keep your hands on the steering wheel so the officer can see them.
- Try to stay calm. Getting agitated with the officer or with others will not help the situation.
- Avoid making sudden movements, especially toward the floor, rear seat, or passenger side of the vehicle.
- Do not reach for your license or other documents until the officer requests them. (NYS law requires drivers to show their license, registration, and insurance card upon request.)
- If the stop occurs at night, put on your dome/interior lights so the officer can easily see that all is in order.
- If the officer issues you a ticket for reasons that are unclear to you, ask the officer for information, but do not become argumentative or antagonistic. Accepting a traffic ticket is not an admission of guilt. You can contest the ticket in court.
- Patrol cars often are staffed by only one officer. However, given the inherent dangers of traffic stops, officers often request backups when stopping a vehicle. Therefore you might see two or three police vehicles involved in a traffic stop.

Source: New York State University Police. (2001). What to do if you are stopped by the University Police. Available at *http://police.binghamton.edu*.

---

acceptable reason as to why the suspect committed the crime (e.g., "You probably just meant to borrow the car for a little while, not steal it"). This approach makes it easier for the suspect to admit to the crime while also protecting his or her ego. Effective investigators have a number of face-saving confessions in their repertoire. When one fails, they bring up another one (e.g., "It was probably Jack's idea, and you just happened to be there," "Somebody else probably made you do it," etc.). In another tactic, the investigator may shift the primary blame away from the suspect and toward another person until the suspect shows some interest, typically by giving the appearance of listening intently. When that occurs, the investigator focuses on that theme, repeating it again and again. At some point, the suspect will likely give a nonverbal indication that they are ready to confess. Dillingham (1995a) notes that this is often observed by "the suspect suddenly bowing his head, leaning forward, and resting his arms upon his knees" (p. 10).

The skill of the investigator is crucial at this point. If signs indicating a "readiness to confess" are observed, most investigators will offer the suspect a forced-choice, either-or question, asking the suspect if he or she committed the crime for a good reason or a bad reason (e.g., "Did you rob this guy to get some money for your family, or did you just want some cash for another high?"). The suspect will either accept the "good" reason or shift back into denial. If the response is denial, then the interrogation must regress as the investigator continues to seek a face-saving justification for the crime. If the suspect acknowledges that he or she did it for the "good" reason, the investigator immediately asks for details of the crime.

Closing

Once the confession has been obtained, the interview is not over. Three things must be achieved before the interrogation is complete: (1) outside confirmation must be obtained, (2) the suspect must write or sign a written confession, and (3) the interrogation must be officially closed. For high-profile cases, confirmation may be obtained by simply videotaping the entire interrogation. In this case, there is visual and auditory evidence of the confession (Leo, 2001). However, this approach is rarely a complete solution to the problem of confirmation, because the suspect may claim that he or she was intimidated off-camera (Westling & Waye, 1998). Instead, confirmation is typically achieved by having the investigator leave the room and quickly return with another person. The investigator then addresses the second person and tells him or her about the confession.

For example, the main investigator may leave the room and return with a colleague. The investigator would then say something like "Bob, this is John. John wants us to know that he robbed the store because his family was hungry." Bob, the second investigator, should then seek confirmation (e.g., "Is that true, John?"). Such a question triggers the second telling of the confession. It simultaneously provides outside confirmation of the confession while reinforcing the suspect's admission of guilt. As Dillingham writes, "The suspect, now having made admissions to two people, will find it hard to retract those admissions" (p. 10).

At this point, the second person typically leaves the room again. Because the initial confession was given to one investigator, the one who spent some time establishing rapport with the suspect, the suspect will find it easier to make a full confession to that one person. The full confession is written out and the suspect will then sign it. The investigator often encourages the suspect to provide a written version of the confession by saying that such paperwork is required by the police department. Or, the investigator may tell the suspect that the written version is necessary to protect the suspect from those who might say that the crime was committed for a different reason. Either way, the investigator pushes for a written and signed version of the confession.

Once the confession has been confirmed and a written statement has been signed, the investigator is ready to close the interview. Most investigators typically close the interrogation by thanking the suspect for being honest about the crime and/or praising the person for taking responsibility. As Dillingham writes, "You'll want the suspect to feel good about confessing." This attitude solidifies the confession even further and encourages the suspect to take full responsibility for the crime.

Verification

Even if a suspect confesses, the information must be verified. Verification also is a key element in gathering information. Although the investigator may rely on nonverbal cues to detect possible deception, the easiest way to detect deception is to seek confirmation from third parties or from physical evidence at the scene. This idea is supported by contemporary research that indicates that most people rely on third-party information and physical evidence to detect lies (Park et al., 2002). Checking the validity of any information provided by a witness or suspect may be a lengthy process, one that may take days, weeks, months, or longer.

False Confessions

One problem often faced by interrogators is the possibility that a confession elicited from a suspect is a result of their interrogation skills rather than the actual guilt of the suspect. In other words, it is possible for an interrogator to elicit a confession from an innocent person. As noted earlier, a skillful interviewer watches the nonverbal behavior of the suspect with signs of deception and focuses on the topic that created the suspicious behavior. However, research indicates that such suspicious behavior may simply be the suspect's reaction to the nonverbal behavior of the police officers. Specifically, the movements and nonverbal behavior of the interrogators may make suspects appear to be more suspicious (Akehurst & Vrij, 1999). The result can be false confessions that lead to the incarceration of an innocent person.

False confessions may be more common than most people expect. Leo and Ofshe (1998) identified 60 cases in which an innocent person had confessed to a crime and unjustly gone to jail as a result. Most of the false confessions could be attributed to the use of deceptive interrogation techniques or—more frequently—the use of psychological techniques in which the police induce a confession from a person who tries to provide the police with the response he believes they want (Kassin, 1998; McCann, 1998).

Perina (2003) notes that false confessions can be a major problem with three classes of suspects: (1) suspects with below-average intelligence, (2) suspects with highly compliant or suggestible personalities, and (3) suspects with anxiety disorders. For such suspects, confession to a crime that they did not commit is easier to endure than continued interrogation. Those who are particularly vulnerable may doubt their own memory, particularly if the police use a deceptive technique, such as presenting them with false evidence. Either way, the police interrogator must constantly be aware of the possibility of eliciting a false confession—even if the officer does not intend to do so.

Summary

Some features of police interviews are common to most interview situations. Others are unique to the particular form of information gathering that relates to police work. One basic element of commonality is the threefold division of the interview: the opening phase in which rapport is established, a work period in which information is gathered, and a closing phase that is aimed at providing closure. Investigators may use open-ended or closed-ended questions, depending on the information needed. In addition, the investigator must carefully monitor the interviewee's responses.

Police interviews fall into two distinct categories: interviews of witnesses and interrogations of suspects. Interviewing of witnesses typically involves talking with people who have information about the crime. Because they are not suspects, they will often try to be helpful, even if their memories of the event are foggy. When the interview shifts to the interrogation of suspects, though, the interaction between the interviewer and interviewee becomes adversarial. The skillful interviewer must establish rapport with a suspect whose crime may be repulsive, but such rapport may be crucial to gaining a confession. There is, then, an element of duplicity and deception in police interrogations. The police may engage in deceptive behavior in order to get a deceptive person to tell the truth. As a result, the interrogator must always be alert to the possibility that they can elicit a false confession from a vulnerable suspect.

FOR FURTHER DISCUSSION

1. Tape two episodes of two different television crime dramas and compare how each show portrays police interviews. How do interviews with witnesses and interrogations of suspects differ? How do these dramatic TV interviews compare with the points made in this chapter? Are such depictions realistic?

2. Try to recall the last time that you were stopped by a police officer for a traffic violation. How did you feel? Did the officer's initial comments put you more at ease or make you more defensive? What techniques did the officer use during the incident?

3. Follow a newspaper story that recounts a police investigation of a crime. To what extent was the crime solved through police interviews as compared with forensic evidence? Were the interviews crucial to solving the case?

CHAPTER

14

Interviews for Lawyers

Jason is divorcing his wife. His wife's lawyer calls Jason to provide a deposition. For three hours, Jason is asked more than a hundred questions about many aspects of his personal and financial life. Later at trial, whenever he is asked a question under examination by his wife's attorney, the attorney says, "That's nice, but didn't you just contradict what you said during your depositions?" The attorney then produces the offending statement.

This scenario describes just one example of how litigators use interviews to build cases, support their witnesses' credibility, and undermine the credibility of opposing witnesses. Interviewing is a vital tool in modern legal work. Legal interviews done in the courtroom differ from those conducted by the police. For the police, interrogation of suspects is an adversarial relationship that requires an aggressive interviewing technique. When interviewing witnesses, though, the police generally take a gentler approach that relies on building rapport with witnesses and stimulating their memory. Interviewing witnesses, from the police perspective, is not an adversarial interview situation.

However, anyone who testifies in a courtroom is likely to be subjected to both a supportive and an adversarial interview. The side for which the witness presents evidence will interview the witness politely and confidently. The opposition will then do its best to discredit the witness's testimony. Serving as a witness in a court case can be a high-stress situation in which the interviewee is almost certain to face an adversarial interview.

Communication is a key attribute that influences an attorney's success in the legal profession (Chanen, 1995). Matlon (1988) views the legal interview as a form of dyadic communication that operates according to force-field theory. The attorneys are agents of change who seek to use the judicial process to affect change on behalf of their client or the state. This requires attorneys to follow two steps of the classic three-step interview approach. The first two stages—establishing rapport and gathering information—are consistent with most interviewing situations. However, with legal interviews, attorneys use the information gathered in these first two stages either to provide advice to the client or to generate an advantage for the client. Understanding interviews that take place in the courtroom thus requires an understanding of the role of the interview in that setting. Typically, such interviews are divided into five distinct categories: (1) client interviews, (2) witness interviews, (3) jury selection interviews, (4) direct examinations, and (5) cross examinations.

Client Interviews

Client interviews are those conversations that attorneys have in their offices with clients or with potential clients (Bailey, 1985; Delia, 1980; Fahrenz & Preiser, 1980; Goldsmith, 1980; Thompson & Insalata, 1964). Such interviews involve a range of topics, such as criminal matters, real estate, divorce, domestic violence, or estate planning (Perkins, 1981; Greenwood, 1986; Goldstein, 1992; Lehrman, 1995).

Individuals who need legal services come to a lawyer to ask for advice (Meyerowitz, 1996). Edelstein (1992) noted that this initial contact is critical to the success of the attorney–client relationship. The attorney speaks with the client, gathers information about the case, and offers advice on possible courses of legal action (Perkins, 1981; Greenwood, 1986). The purposes of such interviews are threefold: to gather information, to provide legal advice, and for the lawyer to decide whether to take the case (Baum, 1983; Herman, 1995; Sugarman & Yarashus, 1995). The ability of an attorney to handle these initial interviews can be critical in determining the success of the attorney's legal practice (Lezin, 1987).

An effective attorney must wade through a multitude of barriers that are not always present in other interview situations. People bring a variety of backgrounds and emotions to the legal interview environment. Clients often are from a different social class than that of the attorney; this class distinction may inhibit disclosure, making it harder for the attorney to gather the information needed. Because clients will come from a variety of educational backgrounds, the attorney must be able to converse well with people regardless of whether they possess a Ph.D. or are high-school dropouts (Matlon, 1988). Overcoming such barriers requires the attorney to practice active listening skills (Barkai, 1984; Jenkins, 1990; Lidman, 1998; Keeva, 1999).

The client's need to talk to an attorney may be triggered by a traumatic event, one that may result in the expression of a variety of emotions. The person may have been arrested for a crime, something that can trigger both embarrassment and guilt. He or she may have suffered from an incident that is painful and/or shameful. Lehrman (1995) notes that the attorney may be the first person to hear the client's whole story, because the pain and embarrassment of the situation may prevent the person from sharing it with others. Such factors may inhibit the client's willingness to communicate. Still, if the attorney is to provide assistance, such information must be elicited (Reuben, 1987). Thus, the attorney must assure the client that all information will remain confidential due to attorney–client privilege (Lehrman, 1995).

All of these factors can be exacerbated by environmental factors at the attorney's office. Long waits may intensify the client's concerns about the approaching interview. Once the interview begins, any interruptions may disrupt the client's disclosures. Thus, most attorney–client interviews occur within an area that maintains privacy for both parties; the attorney's staff is instructed to minimize or eliminate disruptions such as telephone calls.

Stages of the Client Interview

Client interviews tend to occur in three stages. The first two stages—developing rapport and gathering information—are similar to the standard interview format. However, client interviews differ with regards to the third stage—providing legal advice and counsel.

Developing rapport is particularly important in establishing a working client–attorney relationship (Earl, 1993). If rapport is not developed, the client will not trust the attorney and the value of future interactions will be nullified. To establish rapport, the opening elements of the initial interview rely heavily on a dialogic approach in which the client is encouraged to talk while the attorney listens (Haskins, 1985).

The second stage—information gathering—should be the attorney's top priority. This is the work stage of the client interview. The success of this stage determines whether the attorney will be in a position to offer effective advice and counsel. Thus, this stage continues until the attorney has all of the information needed to provide legal advice. Some attorneys use a *direct approach* in which they ask a series of specific closed-ended questions related to the legal issues in the case (e.g., "Were you driving when the accident occurred?" "What part of your car was damaged by the accident?"). Others prefer an *indirect approach* in which the attorney begins by asking a series of broad and general questions (e.g., "Tell me what happened"). Nonleading questions at this stage allow the attorney to become familiar with the language a client uses and thus develop an understanding of how he or she will tell the story in court (Abramson & Flaste, 1997). A third approach is to use the *funnel interview* technique, whereby the attorney begins by asking broad, open-ended questions and moves toward asking a number of closed-ended questions that address specific legal issues.

In addition, the effective legal interviewer will use probes to encourage the client to provide information. These may include requests for elaboration (e.g., "Can you tell me more about that?"), clarification (e.g., "Did you see his car before or after you were hit?"), mirror questions (e.g., "So you experienced some pain in your right side?"), and silence. Such probes are intended to get the client to continue talking.

Once the attorney has gathered sufficient information, the focus of the interview shifts to the third stage. The attorney stops asking questions and begins to provide advice and counsel (Freeman & Weihofen, 1972; Goodpaster, 1975; Watson, 1976; Hingstman, 1983; Binder, Bergman, & Price, 1990). The format of this stage is simple: The attorney makes a suggestion and refers to the specific piece of information that warrants the suggestion (e.g., "This isn't a legal issue. It happened too long ago to bring it before the courts now").

During the second stage, the attorney will ask specific questions to gather needed information. Those questions will help the attorney identify the facts of the case, clarify whether any potential conflict of interest is present, and make a determination of whether the problem is one that the legal system can address (Earl, 1993). If it is a situation that requires legal counsel, the discussion during the third stage will focus on (1) the legal issues/principles involved, (2) whether the client has a provable case, and (3) an assessment as to whether the case is worth pursuing in the legal system (Herman, 1995; Sugarman & Yarashus, 1995).

Witness Interviews

To prepare for a trial, an attorney will interview a number of witnesses who can provide information about the case in question. Some of the information generated will support the client's side and some may benefit the opposition (Harrigan, 1986; Reuben, 1987;

McElhaney, 1997). Background research for such interviews will include reviewing police files and identifying people who may be able to provide relevant information about the case.

The attorney must be able to ascertain the reliability of the information provided. People may withhold information because they do not want to get involved. Others may interpret events in light of their particular biases in the case. And some people will simply not remember things accurately. Because of this, Frank (1973) estimates that witnesses are probably correct only half of the time. Schum (2001) goes even further, arguing that nearly all such evidence is inconclusive, imprecise, and vague.

Matlon (1988) notes that witnesses tend to remember four things well: (1) events that have been observed frequently, (2) intense events, (3) recent events, and (4) events that evoke experiences of pleasure or pain. Thus, it is important for the attorney to interview any witnesses as soon as possible, when they are still eager to talk about the incident and their memories are better. In addition, Matlon (1988) notes that there is a psychological advantage to being the first attorney to interview a witness, because "they tend to remain more loyal to the first party who interviews them" (p. 60).

The interview should be conducted in a comfortable and isolated location. Except for those instances in which the witness has his or her own attorney, others should not be in the room because they may influence the witness's response. The attorney should be polite. The attorney should take special care to use simple language that minimizes the use of legal jargon. As with most interviews, establishing rapport must be an early goal, but intent in this situation often is to increase the witness's rapport with the victim rather than the attorney. People are often reluctant to reveal information to attorneys unless they are sympathetic toward one of the parties in the dispute (Keeton, 1973, p. 311).

The attorney also should be prepared to ask useful questions (Powell, 1994). That will require that the attorney review all elements of the case prior to conducting the interview, so that he or she will know what elements of the case need to be clarified by the witness. As Matlon (1988) notes, "Familiarity with the scene makes it easier to determine accuracy of accounts and lets the attorney help a witness remember some details" (p. 63).

As the interview progresses, the attorney must do two things—assess the value of the information obtained and evaluate the impression the witness will have on a jury. The attorney can do some things to enhance some elements, such as making suggestions as to how to dress. McElhaney (1993) suggests that the attorney consider a full range of options if the witness needs rehabilitation, including redirect (i.e., a third round of questioning by the attorney that follows the cross-examination by the opposing attorney), asking simple questions, reminding the witness not to bluff, and calling on corroboration witnesses. Still, some personality elements may still influence the jury's perceptions. When considering testimony, the jury often considers the demeanor of the witness (Imwinkelried, 1985).

Attorneys use a variety of techniques to jog witnesses' memories (Cope, 1989). Many attorneys using a variation of the cognitive interviewing process used by police investigators (Fisher & Gieselman, 1986; Gieselman & Padilla, 1988; Barney & Coughlin, 1996). See Chapter 1.

Most eyewitness testimony is limited by the impact of the selectivity process. The *selectivity hypothesis* provides an explanation of how distortion, inaccuracy, and incompleteness creep into a person's perceptions of events. Specifically, it attributes memory distortions to a combination of four factors: (1) selective exposure, (2) selective attention,

(3) selective perception, and (4) selective retention (Egeth, 1967). *Selective exposure* refers to the idea that people tend to choose from a variety of perceptual stimuli at any given time. Even if a witness was on the scene of a crime or accident, he or she may not have been looking at the event when it occurred.

Even if a person saw a two-car accident, that person may have been paying attention only to one of the cars. Further, people are easily distracted by noise or other stimuli in their perceptual field (Smith, 1991).

However, returning to the car accident, what if the witness had a good view and paid close attention to the entire incident? That person's impression of the event may still be distorted through the process of *selective perception*. A person's past experiences, attitudes, and expectations will influence his or her view of any event. Finally, even if the witness perceives the event accurately, there is no guarantee that it will be remembered for any extended period of time. The principle of selective retention states that people more accurately remember messages that are favorable to one's self-image than those that are unfavorable (Levine & Murphy, 1943).

The problem, of course, is that the attorney must determine whether the witness is telling the truth. And, if the witness is inaccurate, are the inaccuracies deliberate or the result of selectivity distortions? Is the witness telling the whole truth? As Malton notes:

> Some potential witnesses appear to have poor memories; they claim they do not know or remember certain information. Such claims should not be taken at face value. What the respondent may really want is more time to think. The best communication strategy for an attorney to use in that situation is to give the person time—say nothing and wait. . . . follow with gentle probe. If still nothing, don't press. (p. 64)

An additional problem may occur when witnesses are asked to make visual identifications of a suspect or other party or object involved in an incident. Note that inaccurate eyewitness identification often is unintentional. Sometimes ethnic factors may interfere with the identification process, because members of one race often have trouble identifying members from another race (Malpass & Kravitz, 1969; Meissner & Brigham, 2001). Identification also may be compromised if someone provides the eyewitness with incorrect information. Mudd and Govern (2004), testing viewer memories of incidents on the television series *Cops*, found that misinformation provided by a confederate became incorporated into the memories of those viewing the show in a group setting. Further, this effect increased in over time, with individuals becoming more confident of those false memories after a two-week delay.

Depositions

Depositions are a form of legal interview used to gather information during pretrial preparations. It is an adversarial interview in which a potential witness for one side of a case is interviewed by the attorney for the opposing side prior to a trial (Blumenkopf, 1981; Harrigan, 1986; McElhaney, 1997). Ruvoldt (2001) describes the deposition as the key to an effective cross-examination. Matlon identifies four reasons why depositions are needed:

- To assist the attorney in investigation and preparation for a case
- To evaluate a case for possible settlement
- To gain information to use in impeaching a witness during cross-examination
- To appraise the performance of the opposition's witness

Depositions are conducted under oath and are subject to the same rules of perjury that apply in the courtroom. Anything said during a deposition must be consistent with later testimony in court, or the individual could be subject to prosecution for perjury. Any questions that trigger an angry or evasive response during a deposition may warrant further inquiry during cross-examination.

Despite the strict legal requirements, depositions are relatively mild legal interviews. Although such interviews are naturally adversarial, because they are conducted with the opposition's attorney, the opposing attorney rarely becomes hostile or confrontational. On the contrary, depositions are usually casual and conducted in a relaxed atmosphere. They are usually conducted in the office of the supporting attorney. The opposing attorney asks enough questions to ascertain the gist of the witness's testimony and to gather information that can be used to later discredit it. Tough questions are usually avoided. The opposing attorney does not wish to ask anything that may enable the witness to be better prepared for cross-examination. The really tough questions are reserved for that latter interview.

Attorneys approach the deposition slightly differently from other legal interviews. They prepare in advance by developing an outline of key points and topics to be covered (Blumenkopf, 1981). Each topic is covered thoroughly before moving to the next (Morrill, 1972). Questions are broad and open-ended to encourage the witness to ramble as much as possible so that they'll get away from prepared and practiced responses (McFigg, McCullough, & Underwood, 1974). A few key questions, particularly those that the attorney may want read aloud during cross-examination, are written out and read verbatim (Barthold, 1975).

A skillful attorney can gain useful information during a deposition. Even if the witness tries to be evasive, the attorney can repeat or rephrase the question and continue probing until the desired information is obtained (Kornblum, 1971). When that information is obtained, follow-up questions should be avoided; attorneys usually do not want to give the witness an opportunity to "dilute" a previous response with more information (Vetter, 1977).

Before the deposition, the witness is prepared by his or her attorney, who reviews each major point that may be addressed (Hickman & Scanlon, 1963). Although witnesses are required to tell the truth, they do not have to provide any information that is not requested by the question. Thus, the witness is advised to think through each question carefully and respond truthfully, but in a concise manner that only answers the question asked—not other unasked questions. The golden rule for the witness, according to Matlon (1988), is to "Never volunteer information unless it is specifically asked for" (p. 73). The second major rule is that a witness should never answer a question if he or she does not know the answer. The witness must be willing to admit deficiencies in knowledge and insist on explanations for questions they do not understand.

Jury Selection Interviews

The legal term for jury selection interviews is *voir dire*. Matlon (1988) defines the term as the "oral face-to-face questioning of prospective jurors by judges and lawyers for the purpose of determining the jurors' competence to serve" (p. 114). In theory, the goal of voir dire is to seat a jury that will be impartial and objective. In reality, attorneys for both sides try to use the interviews to enhance their chances of getting a jury that will be favorable toward their side of the case (Sannito & McGovern, 1999). The attorneys' goals are threefold: (1) to get a jury that will be favorable toward their side of the case, (2) to establish credibility with the jury, and (3) to sensitize the jury toward their side of the case (Matlon, 1988). Broeder (1965) found that most of an attorney's time during voir dire is spent on the sensitization goal, with the selection of favorable juries ranking last. The credibility goal seems to take up about 40 percent of the jury-selection process (Balch et al., 1976).

Mauet (1988) recommends outlining open-ended background questions in advance to voir dire, with probes added to identify specific attitudes that may be related to the case. If a bias against the attorney's case can be identified, the attorney can challenge the right of the prospective juror to sit on the jury. Typical screening questions used for this purpose are those asking if there is anything that would prevent the juror from being impartial; whether the potential juror knows the judge, the lawyers, or any of the parties; if the potential juror has had prior jury duty (if so, what kind of case); whether the potential juror has ever been sued; or if the person has ever been the victim of a crime. For example, attitudes toward capital punishment are relevant on murder cases. If the case is a civil trial, attorneys may ask prospective jurors whether they work for an insurance company and how willing they are to compensate a plaintiff.

An attorney can gain credibility by being friendly and conveying a sense of professionalism. The attorney also must be careful to do nothing that would make the jurors dislike him or her. As Mauet (1988) notes, "Never embarrass a juror. Make sure you never force a juror to reveal anything about his job, family, home, education, or background that may embarrass him" (p. 34).

Attorneys also seem to take personality under consideration when selecting jurors. Individuals who get excused from jury duty by attorneys tend to have higher levels of verbal aggressiveness, dominance, and contentiousness than empaneled jurors (Wigley, 1999). Thus, a potential juror who makes a favorable impression on an attorney is more likely to be empaneled.

As mentioned earlier, most of the attorney's focus typically is on jury sensitization or, as Holdway (1968) defines it, indoctrination. As Mauet (1988) notes, an attorney's questions should familiarize the jury with the legal and factual concepts that are related to the attorney's side of the case. At the same time, the jurors' responses will help the attorney assess the likelihood that they will accept arguments based on those principles. These questions are *leading questions*—those that provide cues as to what answer the interviewer is expecting (McElhaney, 1989). As a result, little true information is obtained. However, as Mauet (1988) notes, "they serve a valuable purpose by introducing the jurors to legal and factual concepts pertinent to case" (p. 37).

Direct Examinations

A direct examination is when an attorney asks questions of his or her own witnesses during the presentation of a case in court (Packel, 1982; Rubinowitz & Torgan, 2002; Wood, 2003). Matlon (1988) defines *direct examination* as oral testimony that "is given when witnesses are brought to court in person to present information" (p. 60). The direct examination process has two stages: preparation of witnesses, adding of witnesses, selection and order of witnesses, and the courtroom examination.

Preparation of Witnesses

Attorney Leslie Abramson notes that the role of the attorney is to prepare witnesses to tell their own stories—not to create their stories for them—a distinction she makes by comparing the attorney's role to the "stage manager" of a production rather the "playwright" (Abramson & Flaste, 1997, p. 107).

Abramson recommends that an attorney begin preparing a witness for direct examination by using information from the initial interview to go over the witness's probable testimony. This way, the attorney can verify that the witness is providing the same responses offered in the initial interview. "More often than I care to remember," she writes, "they didn't" (Abramson & Flaste, 1997, p. 107). Abramson's comment illustrates the need to go over witness testimony for both truth and consistency. The first step in preparing for a courtroom case is for the attorney to review his or her own witnesses and the testimony they can provide. To do this, attorneys typically prepare their witnesses in advance (Hamlin, 1985b; Harley, 1995; Allison, 1999; Silver, 1999; Gutheil, 2003). Such advance preparation serves two purposes: (1) it gives the attorney a sense of what and how the witness will answer a question and (2) it prepares the witness to be a better witness in court.

The attorney will review all of the topics to be covered with the witness. The witness's response to each topic provides the attorney with an understanding of what the witness's final testimony will be, thus helping the attorney to develop a strategy for the presentation of the case and the order of the questions. The process of reviewing these topics also will serve to "minimize the effect of courtroom tension" for the witness (Matlon, 1988, p. 214). The exchanges between the lawyer and the witness can help both refine their questions and answers.

Mauet (1988) argues that witness preparation "involves both evidence selection and testimony preparation" (p. 11). He recommends several rules for ensuring that each witness receives sufficient preparation:

1. *Prepare witnesses individually.* Mauet notes that each witness should receive individual attention from the attorney. The questions the attorney plans to ask should be outlined on a separate sheet of paper for each witness and the "witness sheets should reflect what exhibits the witness will qualify and the location of all prior statements" (p. 11).
2. *Review all previous testimony by the witness.* This usually means that the attorney reviews all of the depositions given earlier in the case. It is essential that the

testimony in court is consistent with the testimony in the deposition. Consistency is important to the attorney's case. Inconsistency could result in a charge of perjury against the witness.

3. *Review all exhibits with the witness.* The witness needs to know which of the exhibits the attorney will ask him or her to identify and discuss. Further, the attorney should explain to the witness how a particular exhibit fits the overall strategy for the case.

4. *Review the probable testimony of other witnesses.* The attorney should identify potential inconsistencies, identifying anything in the witness's testimony that may be contrary to what someone else will say in court.

5. *Prepare and review direct examination.* The attorney will review each question and the order in which it will be presented in court. The goal is to make the witness comfortable with the process and confident as to how to handle each question. However, the attorney typically does not show the actual written questions to the witness. The opposing attorney may specifically ask if such an exchange occurred and use an affirmative response to imply that the attorney attempted to influence the witness's testimony.

6. *Anticipate cross-examination.* Cross-examination techniques are discussed later in the text. However, the attorney typically tries to anticipate what the opposing attorney will ask the witness during cross-examination and prepare the witness to handle those questions better.

Advising the Witness

Attorneys often will provide suggestions to the witness for enhancing the impact of testimony. The following are several areas in which attorneys may advise a witness (Packel, 1982):

1. *Recommendations for courtroom appearance.* Nonverbal factors can impact a witness's credibility. Many attorneys advise witnesses on what to wear to court. Sometimes the advice will be specific, such as telling the witness to get a haircut or to trim a beard.

2. *Remind the witness to tell the truth.* Lying is a questionable moral behavior in the real world, but in the courtroom, it is perjury. Further, a witness who is caught lying will hurt the attorney's case (McElhaney, 2003). As defense attorney Leslie Abramson notes, "It's so much more dangerous for the defense to put on a witness who lies than for the prosecution to do it . . . . It will be the excuse to convict, because no matter what the rules say, the impulse is to convict" (Abramson & Flaste, 1997, p. 107).

3. *Emphasize the importance of listening.* The most effective witnesses listen to every question and then answer only that question. They do not ramble on to other issues or topics or volunteer information that is not requested.

4. *Be polite.* Juries are more responsive to witnesses who are polite to the attorneys, to the jurors, and to the judge. A rude response may be rejected, even if it is accurate.

5. *Ask the lawyers to rephrase any question that is not understood.* During cross-

examination, the opposing lawyer may ask complicated questions. Asking the attorney to simplify such a question is both acceptable and recommended.

6. *Don't speculate.* Witnesses can testify only to what they personally did, saw, or heard. The latter may not be allowed if it is from a secondary source, that is, from a third party. Such comments are considered *hearsay* and usually are not accepted as evidence in court.

7. *If either attorney makes an objection, wait for the judge to rule.* If the objection is sustained by the judge, then it officially was never asked, and an answer is not required. Further, the witness who answers too soon may say something prejudicial to one side or the other, which could lead to a mistrial.

Selection and Order of Witnesses

Part of the attorney's preparation for trial includes identifying witnesses and determining the order in which evidence should be presented to the jury (Maggiano, 1998). The general rule, according to Mauet (1988), is "Don't overprove your case" (p. 17). When several witnesses will testify to the same thing, all of the witnesses are not needed. The attorney typically will choose only one or two of them—those who will make the best impression—to present that information to the jury. Other witnesses may have information that is irrelevant to the attorney's theory of the case. In those instances, the attorney must remember that he or she is "not required to prove everything, only the elements of your claim or your defenses" (Mauet, 1988, p. 17).

The order in which the witnesses are presented is based on three principles: (1) start with a strong and important witness, (2) present the case in a manner that presents the evidence in a chronological or logical manner, and (3) finish with a strong witness. Mauet (1988) argues that "effective direct examinations that clearly, logically, and forcefully present the facts of the case will usually have a decisive effect on the outcome of the trial" (p. 75).

Strong introductions and strong conclusions enhance the impact of any message. If the case is a lengthy one that lasts for several days, the attorney will typically space the witnesses so that each morning and afternoon session begins with a strong witness. Weak or adverse witnesses usually are called during the middle of the case. Technical information usually is presented in the middle of the case, calling several successive witnesses if it is necessary to explain and simplify the information. Corroboration witnesses—those that testify to the same thing and support each other—are called in succession, with the second witness immediately adding credence to what the first witness said.

Conducting a Direct Examination

In court, the attorney will follow a few general principles when conducting the direct examination (Paine, 2000; McElhaney, 2003). Variations may be used, depending on the particular type of witness being addressed. Most attorneys use the *witness narrative method*, whereby the attorney asks broad questions that allow the witness to tell his or her story. The general rule here is that "the witness is the star," so the attorney uses open-ended questions that put the witness at the center of attention (Matlon, 1988).

The attorney guides the direct examination by eliciting "from the witness, in a clear and logical progression, the observations and activities of the witness so that each of the jurors understands, accepts, and remembers his testimony" (Mauet, 1988, p. 75). Questions are crafted to elicit relevant information and evidence that is beneficial to the client's case (Stuart, 1999). The attorney has to elicit information without using leading questions, because such questions usually are not allowed in direct examination. Mauet (1988) describes the resulting interview as "a creative art, one which allows you to tell a story to the jury in a way that is most advantageous to your party" (p. 76). Some witnesses will be used to establish facts in the case (Bossart, 1998); others may be asked to provide expert testimony (Malone, 1988; Lubet, 1993; Parker, Mills, & Patel, 2001). Regardless of the purpose of each witness, most direct examinations follow the steps presented below.

Step 1: Put the Witness at Ease.   Most witnesses experience at least some mild form of anxiety when they first step into the courtroom. The attorney's first job is to calm down the witness. This is done by opening the interview with preliminary, nonthreatening questions, such as asking the witness his or her name and background (Matlon, 1988). Most witnesses will feel more comfortable if the attorney uses conversational English rather than legal jargon when asking questions (Anderson, 1990).

Step 2: Establish the Witness's Credibility.   Once the preliminary questions have been covered, the attorney moves to a series of questions that establish the witness's credibility on the topic. This may include an extension of background questions, particularly for expert witnesses, and other questions that explain to the jury why this witness is qualified to provide evidence for this particular case. Mauet (1988) notes that "Witness credibility is determined by who the witness is (background), what he says (content), and how he says it (demeanor)" (p. 75).

The attorney's job is to ask preliminary questions that enhance the witness's credibility on each item. This is achieved by asking questions that tell the jury why the witness is there and shows them why the witness should be believed. Exhibits may be necessary at this point to help orient the jury. Meanwhile, the attorney must be a good listener and pay attention to the witness's responses. Not only does this ensure that all vital information is covered, but it also monitors the interview for unexpected answers and increases the witness's credibility. Some members of the jury will be looking at the attorney to be sure the attorney is interested in the testimony.

Step 3: The Key Question.   Typically, each witness is brought to court to testify to one key question related to the case. Once the witness's credibility on that question has been established, the attorney is poised to ask that key question. To emphasize its importance, Matlon (1988) recommends that the question be preceded by a "punch line" so the jury will know that the focus of the testimony is about to come. The punch line may be a preliminary question that emphasizes the importance of the approaching testimony (e.g., "Did you see anything unusual at that time?"). The attorney then follows up with the key question, which is then presented in an open-ended narrative format (e.g., "Could you tell us what that was?").

Mauet (1988) calls these punch lines "orientation questions" that let the jury know what to expect, noting that technically they are leading questions that are permitted by the court because of their preliminary nature. Mauet (1988) also recommends dividing the key question into two subtopics: scene description and action description. The ideal action questions elicit flowing descriptions in which the witnesses "paint a picture that the jury can actually visualize" (p. 86). Either way, using an open-ended format is critical. Research has demonstrated that the use of closed-ended questions with specific answers triggers more errors by the witness than does the request for an open-ended narrative (Cady, 1924; Stern, 1939). Further, the narrative approach increases the witness' credibility with the jury; the more complete and detailed the story, the more believable it is (Loftus, Goodman, & Nagatkin, 1983). Conversely, the use of closed-ended questions during the direct examination hurts the attorney's credibility (O'Barr & Conley, 1976).

Stage 4: Inoculation Questions   There are no perfect witnesses and no perfect cases. As Mauet (1988) notes, perfect cases are settled in advance and rarely go to trial. Each witness will have some weakness in his or her testimony. Most attorneys prefer to bring out those weaknesses in their direct examination and present them in a favorable light so that the witness's credibility will not be damaged during the cross-examination. Mauet (1988) recommends this approach, but suggests burying the relevant questions in the middle of the direct examination.

Dealing with Special Witnesses

Some witnesses, by the very nature of their testimony, require special handling. The most common special witness is the *expert witness*. An expert witness is "someone in any field of endeavor who has achieved a high level of education, a great deal of experience, and a high degree of skill enabling him to render an opinion on matters that fall within his expertise" (Hurowitz, 1985, p. 222). Matlon (1988) notes that the attorney should explain the case in detail to the expert witness in advance to learn his or her views on it. The attorney must spend time preparing such witnesses, with a strong focus on "helping experts to use lay language in their answers" (p. 67). Abramson notes that it can be more difficult to elicit information from an expert than to elicit eyewitness testimony (Abramson & Flaste, 1997). After all, the purpose of expert witnesses is to "get their opinion about events they haven't witnessed" by "calling upon their specialized knowledge and training to tell you something about the evidence that you, as a layman, can't see or understand" (Abramson & Flaste, 1997, p. 106). Thus, the first step of dealing with an expert witness is to ask questions that demonstrate expertise. After that, the attorney can get into the expert's analysis of the case.

With the growing popularity of television shows that employ scientific investigation teams, many juries may be placing a growing emphasis on expert witnesses. This phenomenon is called "The CSI Effect"; some authorities suggest that television series such as *CSI* have raised jurors' expectations of what scientific evidence prosecutors should produce at trial. This may make it more difficult for prosecutors to get a conviction if scientific evidence is missing; some defense lawyers say that jurors rely too heavily on testimony from scientific experts (Willing, 2004).

Another problem witness is the *hostile witness*, one who "is hostile to the attorney who calls that witness to testify" (Mauet, 1988, p. 237). Hostile witnesses usually are friends or allies of the other side, but they have information that is damaging to that side (Munday, 1989). Although some risk may be involved, direct examination of a hostile witness may be the only way to get some evidence entered into court.

Attorneys can be more aggressive when interviewing hostile witnesses. Mauet (1988) describes the tone of this interview as "somewhere between the approach for a friendly witness and ordinary cross-examination" (p. 237). Direct examinations of hostile witnesses are not as aggressive as cross-examinations, because the attorney does not need to destroy the credibility of the witness. Instead, the attorney's goal is merely to obtain some specific information that is important to the case, and the questioning is limited to that information.

In some cases, the attorney may use leading questions, but permission must be granted by the judge to do so. Leading questions may be used to lead up to the key question, because "if the witness were to be asked a vital question, point-blank, his answer would likely be unfavorable," whereas, if the attorney asks a friendly question, "an admission may be obtained which may logically or necessarily lead to a concession upon the principal issue" (Bodin, 1976, pp. 559–560).

A particularly delicate special witness is *the child as witness* (Geiselman & Padilla, 1988; Bull, 1994). Attorneys must keep the child calm in court, simplify their questions for the purposes of their testimony without asking leading questions, and simultaneously keep the child's parents from imposing their views on the child's testimony (Goodman & Michelli, 1981). Such situations require both sensitivity and empathy on the part of the attorney.

Juvenile witnesses represent a specific variation of the child as witness. As Abramson notes, juveniles who get into trouble with the law are often "graduates of the grunt-and-shrug school of communication" (Abramson & Flaste, 1997, p. 107). The attorney must ensure that the witnesses—many of whom may be functionally illiterate—can tell their stories coherently.

Mistakes to Avoid

Attorneys must elicit the witness's testimony while avoiding mistakes that damage the witness's credibility. Two mistakes are fairly common: (1) eliciting too much testimony and (2) not spending enough time on critical information (Mauet, 1988). The attorney must constantly remember that the jury has never heard the information in the case before. The jurors are hearing it for the first time, and it is essential that the attorney not overwhelm them with too much information. Keep the interview simple and to the point. As Mauet says, "Too much clutter bores the jury, detracts from central points, and provides the opposition with material for cross-examination" (pp. 80–81). If major time is spent on any one topic, it must focus on information that is vital to the case. This can be done by letting the witness explain as much as possible in a narrative format.

Cross-Examinations

The opposing attorneys have just finished their direct examination of a key witness. It is now the other attorney's turn as the trial moves to the cross-examination stage. Cross-examinations are follow-up witness interviews in which a witness for one side of the case is interviewed by the attorney of the opposing side (Stuart, 1999; Ruvoldt, 2001; Valdespino, 2004). Such interviews typically serve three purposes: to clarify direct testimony, to elicit more testimony, or to weaken or impeach the direct testimony (Matlon, 1988).

The nature of the cross-examination varies depending on the legal rules that apply to the court in question (Mauet, 1988). The *English rule* of cross-examination allows the opposing attorney to address any issue relevant to the case. The *American rule* is stricter, limiting all cross-examination questions to those facts and circumstances that were covered in the direct examination. A compromise approach is the *Michigan rule*, in which the opposing attorney can ask questions related to burden of proof but cannot raise new questions that are only related to that attorney's theory of the case.

Preparation

Preparation for cross-examinations begins before the trial. The attorney reviews the probable testimony of each opposing witness by reviewing their depositions, statements, and any exhibits that will be presented with their testimony. Mauet (1988) recommends that the attorney do preliminary interviews with every opposition witness, including those from whom depositions were not solicited. Such interviews should preferably be conducted in the presence of a third person, just in case it becomes necessary to have a witness for later impeachment purposes. All potential information offered by the witness should be reviewed in terms of (1) information that is favorable to the attorney's position, (2) information that appears improbable, and (3) information that can be used for possible impeachment of the testimony. Such a review will allow the attorney to identify those areas of testimony that will be most beneficial to his or her side.

After this review, the attorney prepares a witness sheet for each person who will be subjected to cross-examination. The sheet will contain three main elements: (1) a short summary of the witness's probable testimony, (2) a listing of up to three key points to be made, and (3) the key questions to be asked to elicit those points (McElhaney, 1988).

Eliciting Favorable Testimony.   Often the credibility of the witness is so high that the attorney will be unable to discredit the witness's testimony. In those instances, the attorney typically will examine the witness's testimony for anything that could be used to bolster the attorney's own theory of the case. When the attorney does find information of use in the witness's direct testimony, during the cross-examination the attorney will typically ignore all of the facts presented during the direct examination and focus on getting the witness to agree with those facts that help the attorney's side of the case.

Hinck and Hinck's (2000) politeness theory argues that violating expectations of politeness can have a negative effect on persuasive efforts. Their approach expands on the work of Brown and Levinson (1987), who argue that politeness is a universal value that operates across cultures. It certainly appears to operate in the courtroom, particularly when trying to elicit favorable testimony during cross-examination. Eliciting favorable testimony requires that the attorney be pleasant and courteous to the witness. The attorney must approach the witness in a natural and relaxed manner, because as Hamlin (1985) notes, "The jury has a nose for phony friendliness" (p. 244).

The actual technique is relatively simple. Instead of reviewing the entire direct examination, the attorney simply identifies those elements of the witness's testimony that were favorable to his or her side. The attorney asks questions that simply ask the witness to repeat portions of his or her testimony.

Note that this approach can be used even if the material is not mentioned during the direct examination. If the witness said something during an earlier deposition or had made other prior statements that would be favorable, the attorney can get them to go over that portion of his or her previous testimony.

The technique can be effective even if the witness does not fully state what the attorney is seeking. As Matlon (1988) notes, "If the witness does not admit what you believe he should, the testimony will probably not be accepted by the jury either" (p. 225).

Another possibility, if the witness is a friendly one, is to use leading questions to stimulate a memory or fact (Taylor, Buchanan, & Strawn, 1984). However, this approach usually only works if the attorney politely asks for the information. Conversely, the attorney who is viewed as rude or who engages in impolite behavior is likely to diminish any chance of a positive response from the jury.

Creating Doubts About the Facts of the Testimony.   One of the attorney's goals may be to create doubt about a witness's testimony. In this case, the purpose of this cross-examination is not to destroy the credibility of the witness, but to create sufficient doubts about the testimony such that the jury will either dismiss it or minimize its effect. Matlon (1988) describes this approach as having the goal "to demonstrate or suggest that the testimony is less probably true than appeared at the end of the direct examination" (p. 225). The emphasis is not on "destroying the witness" but to demonstrate that "the person may have colored their testimony by injecting their own attitudes and perspectives" (p. 225).

Once again, politeness theory comes into play; the attorney who seeks to discredit such testimony cannot make the cross-examination "a direct assault on the witness' integrity, because the jury will resent and reject this tactic" (p. 226). Instead, the attorney assumes that the witness is honest, but the cross-examination seeks to suggest factors that could have aversely influenced the testimony. The attorney may attempt to raise doubts about the witness's ability to correctly recall certain facts due to (1) deficient perception, (2) deficient memory, or (3) the witness's inability to accurately communicate his or her testimony. With the first approach, the attorney will try to prove that the witness's testimony was influenced by physical problems (e.g., poor eyesight, hearing loss) or confusion (e.g., "There were two dozen other people there as bystanders—could the defendant have been one of them?"). The second approach attempts to raise doubts about the witness's ability to remember what happened at that time. The third approach simply questions the witness's ability to recall and relate the event accurately. Put another way, this approach questions the witness's ability to communicate and testify in a logical manner (e.g., "When you say it was a tall, dark-haired man, aren't you saying you're not sure who it was?").

Impeaching the Credibility of the Witness. This form of a cross-examination is often viewed as a "destructive" cross-exam, because its goal is to discredit the witness so that the jury will minimize or disregard the witness's testimony. Matlon (1988) notes that this approach only should be used when the attorney has a sound basis for doing so. "Unsuccessful attempts are worse than mere failures," he writes, "An impeachment attempt that fails causes opposing counsel's witnesses to look stronger than when they began" (p. 238). Mauet (1988) notes that attempts to impeach the witness's credibility "invariably involve calculated risks" (p. 213) for the attorney and the wrong decision can backfire. A witness who successfully resists attempts at impeachment often will be viewed as more credible to the jury.

The attorney has two approaches for impeaching a witness: (1) focusing on internal contradictions in the witness's testimony and (2) noting the witness's reputation for not telling the truth. The attorney structures the questions around apparent contradictions in one of three situations: (a) statements that are inconsistent with previous statements, (b) statements that contradict known facts, or (3) statements that are inconsistent with the witness' behavior (Brewer & Hupfeld, 2004).

With either approach, the attorney lays a foundation by establishing an inconsistent statement. This statement may be uncovered from prior testimony, written materials authored by the witness, or other legal pleadings. The attorney quotes the exact language of the statement and asks the witness whether he or she said it. The goal is to get the witness to commit to the statement, build up that commitment, and then contrast it with an impeachment question—another statement from the same witness that is inconsistent (e.g., "Which of these is the truth—the first statement or the last?").

When the witness makes statements that contradict known facts, the impeachment question focuses on the inconsistency of the response and other known facts (e.g., "How could you have seen him do that—the defendant was 30 miles away at the time?"). When the witness exhibits inconsistent behavior, the attorney uses a similar approach, with the question focusing on the witness's behavior (e.g., "If that's what you saw, why didn't you run to help?").

The other option for impeachment focuses on the character of the witness and his or her reputation for truthfulness. Matlon (1988) advises that this approach should rarely be used; when it is used, the attorney must use it dramatically and effectively. It cannot be used against a typical witness, but only those for whom a dramatic tendency toward falsehood can be demonstrated. Ladd (1966–1967) notes that it is reserved for those instances in which the evidence can "show that the conscience of the witness would not be disturbed if he falsified" (p. 241).

Four techniques generally are used to elicit such testimony, in many cases using questions that are prefaced with "Isn't it true . . .":

- Show that the witness has a bias or an interest in the outcome (e.g., "Isn't it true, that if the defendant is convicted, you'll take control of the company?").

- Show that the witness has a prior criminal record (e.g., "Isn't it true that you pleaded not guilty to robbery, but were convicted when your accomplices testified against you?").
- Show prior bad acts (e.g., "Isn't it true you were charged with assault for beating someone who didn't laugh at your jokes?").
- Demonstrate that the witness has a reputation for lying. This requires another witness who can testify to such incidents. Questions directed toward a reputation witness usually use the preface, "Have you heard . . ." rather than "Do you know . . ." although the latter is accepted in most courts (Mauet, 1988).

If the decision is made to use the destructive approach, the attorney should use it early during the cross-examination because the witness is more likely to be more nervous. Attorneys usually open cross-examination with a question that is unrelated to where the direct examination ended. The direct examination probably ended on a strong point for the opposition, and the witness will feel somewhat comfortable with that position. Therefore, with the destructive approach the attorney usually will open with a question on a topic that the witness is less comfortable with. The first questions lay a foundation for a specific objective, with the discrediting question coming only after that foundation is established. Bergman's (1979) "safety model," i.e., the less the attorney tries to achieve in the cross examination, the more likely she is to accomplish her purpose. The safety model is sim-

Preparing Witnesses for Cross-Examination

Successful attorneys not only prepare to cross-examine the opposition, they also prepare their own witnesses to be cross-examined. The coaching techniques are relatively simple. Emphasis is placed on several points:

- Be courteous. Politeness theory applies just as much to the witness as it does to the attorney.
- Avoid yes and no answers. Give brief explanations, but keep them brief—as short or possible.
- Answer the question directly. Do not be evasive.
- Do not volunteer information that is not requested.
- Do not guess at answers. If you do not know the answer, say so.
- Listen for facts built into questions to see if they are true.
- Ask the opposing attorney to repeat questions you do not understand.
- Take time to think. Do not feel that you have to answer immediately. Take time to consider the question before answering.
- Don't look at your own attorney for answers.
- Break the steady rhythm of the cross-examiner.
- Always tell the truth. Perjury is a major offense, and the truth is always the best defense.

The witness should expect some standard trick questions. "Have you talked to anyone about this case?" is a standard question used to imply collusion, but considering that most witnesses have talked with the police or attorneys in the case, the correct answer is "Yes." Another favorite is "What did your lawyer tell you to say in court?" which implies that the attorney has tried to influence the witness's testimony. The easiest and most effective answer is always the truth.

ple: "Do not ask a question that you do not know the answer to" (p. 185). McElhaney (2000) expands the concept, arguing that the attorney should never ask a question unless: "(a) You know the answer; (b) The answer doesn't matter; (c) Any 'bad' answer would be absurd; or (d) You can prove the 'bad' answer is wrong" (p. 69).

In addition, when conducting an impeachment cross-exam, the attorney should not ask the witness to repeat any aspect of his or her direct testimony (Mauet, 1988). Further, most attorneys specifically avoid using the same organizational pattern or chronology that was used by the opposing attorney during the direct examination. The witness will feel relatively comfortable if the questioning picks up where the direct exam left off or if the flow of future questions can be predicted; as the witness's comfort level increases, impeachment becomes harder to achieve.

However, if the attorney suspects that a witness has memorized his or her testimony, it is an effective technique to ask some of the same questions that were asked in the direct examination. Witnesses who have memorized their story are likely to repeat their answers in the same manner a second time. As Mauet (1988) notes, "Once this has been demonstrated, you should inquire whom the witness talked to before testifying, to uncover the origins of the memorization" (p. 263).

Another guideline for impeachment cross-exams is to ask short, clear, closed-ended leading questions and to do so in a rapid manner. The attorney uses closed-ended questions to maintain control. As Matlon (1998) notes, open-ended questions are dangerous because "hostile witnesses are always looking for an opening to slip in a damaging answer" (p. 216). The fast pace is used because, as veteran trial lawyer Melvin Belli (1976) once wrote, "A witness answering rapidly is more likely to contradict himself" (p. 172). Closed-ended, leading questions provide the attorney with a better chance of reducing witness credibility (Wells, Lindsay, & Ferguson, 1979). The general formula is for the attorney to (1) make a statement of fact and have the witness agree with it and (2) gradually establish the information that will be used for the impeachment question. The use of short questions will help to maintain the jury's attention. Asking questions in a rapid manner keeps the witness uncomfortable and avoids long pauses that might be interpreted by the jury as doubt.

One approach to this form of impeachment is to use a series of short questions, the totality of which is intended to convey a favorable narrative (Hobbs, 2003). Each question is used as a point-by-point critique of the narrative provided by the witness during the direct examination, with the intent to provide an alternative interpretation of the narrative and the conclusion offered by the witness. Such an approach has the advantage of allowing the attorney to introduce a different interpretation that explains the event.

Timing is important. Sannito (1981) notes that the impact of a perception is about one-quarter of a second, and continuing the cross-examination after that perception has been achieved is counterproductive. The impact can be effective even if the attorney never succeeds in getting a witness to admit to a contradiction. Mauet (1988) notes that the very fact that the witness avoids admitting a contradiction will make the cross-examination effective, and the attorney can intensify this effect by asking the evasive witness if he or she has trouble understanding or hearing the question. As Mauet (1988) writes, ". . . keep in mind that all this evasive activity is making a horrible impression on the jury" (p. 261). This assertion is supported by research. McElhaney (1981) found that watching a witness squirm when being impeached with a prior inconsistent statement was, to the jury, the most impressive part of a trial.

The cross-examination should end on a strong note. Matlon (1988) calls this the "Stop when finished" principle, noting that "Cross-examination continuously tempts you to keep going on. There is always one more question you could ask" (p. 219). Similarly, Mauet (1988) warns against proceeding "past a climax." Continuing past that high point could backfire, triggering what Matlon calls ". . . the one-question-too-many" (p. 218) that hurts the case. The attorney should begin with the intention of seeking only two or three main points from the witness, with one point identified early and the other at the end of the cross-examination.

Interview: Gordon Ball

Gordon Ball is an attorney from Knoxville who handles both civil and criminal cases. His civil litigation has included the high-profile Bridgestone Tire Case.

Q. What do you consider when you're meeting the client for the first time?

A. When I'm meeting a client on a criminal case, I want the client to tell me what he is charged with and his version of what happened. I then explain to him the process of the criminal justice system and the possible consequences that he might face. At the same time, I'm trying to size up the situation in terms of where we're going and whether the client is being truthful with me.

Q. How do you do that?

A. Anything he tells me is under attorney–client privilege, but I explain to him that under no circumstances can we put on perjured testimony. I'm not trying to cross-examine him here, I'm just trying to elicit information from him. I want him to be open and honest with me and tell me how he felt. I want to try to establish a rapport with the client and get him to open up with me.

Q. Can you give me an example?

A. The day before a criminal case years ago, my co-counsel and I were meeting with the client and going over the facts of the case. He gave us a document that my co-counsel reviewed and realized that our client had told us something that was inaccurate. When we asked him about it, he said, "I was lying about it. I just wanted to see if I could get it by you guys. If I could get it by you, I could get it by the jury." That's ridiculous. You've got to make clients understand that they must be truthful to you. To do that, you've got to establish a rapport. In that sense, it's like picking a jury.

Q. What's involved in preparing for a direct examination?

A. I sit down and go through the testimony of each witness. I then take the jury instructions that the judge is going to give at the end of the case. I use those instructions as a guideline of the elements that I have to prove. I will go through those with my witnesses. I will almost write out my direct examination. You want to cover everything that you have to prove in direct examination—including writing the questions out—to be sure that you get everything in to the jury that you have to prove.

Continued

Q. How should the witness act during the direct examination?

A. We always instruct our witnesses to look at the person who's asking the question and then turn to the jury to answer the question. Talk to them, make eye contact. What they wear is very important. A few years ago, I represented a black man charged with running a drug ring. I told him to wear a suit with a white shirt and tie to court. He came in wearing a purple jump suit open to his waist. I leaned over and told him, "Joe, if there was ever any doubt in the mind of this jury about you being a drug dealer, you've certainly removed it." But the suit and tie didn't fit with his image of himself, and he wouldn't do it. And he was found guilty.

Q. What about cross-examination?

A. More cases are lost when you have to put your client or your facts on the stand and subject them to a cross-examination. The witnesses you put on the stand will probably do well in direct examination. It's when you turn that witness over on cross that they have to understand that you're basically out of control. It's up to the witness to answer the questions. They'll probably have to initially answer the questions "yes" or "no," but they have the right to explain their answers. And please turn to the jury when you explain the answers. That's where you lose your cases, when you put your witnesses on the stand so that they can be cross-examined. You win your cases when you cross-examine the witnesses of the other side.

Q. How do you prepare for cross-examination?

A. In most criminal cases, most of the government witnesses have been interviewed by the investigating agency in advance, or they've given a statement to a grand jury. You have that statement, so you have the ability to cross-examine the witness from those statements. Usually the first government witness is crucial to setting the stage of what's happened. I like to take that witness and basically re-create the stage and then use other witnesses to contradict that stage. For example, a few years ago in the Butcher Banking criminal case in Tennessee, the government put on a witness (we'll call Mr. Jones). On cross-examination, I took that witness through each step of his testimony. Then, when I cross-examined the second witness, I got him to contradict some of the things said by the first witness. Finally, after we'd gone through all the contradictions, I asked him, "You know Mr. Jones. Would you believe Mr. Jones under oath in a court of law?" The government objected, but the judge allowed me to ask the question. This guy thought for a long time, and finally said, "No, I wouldn't believe him?"

Q. Can you give another example?

A. A few years ago, the government put on a witness who testified that, on numerous occasions, he had taken money to my client to pay for getting people out of prison. After he testified, the judge called a recess and took me and the prosecutors back to chambers. "Mr. Ball," he said, "It's obvious that your client is guilty. If he will plead guilty now, I'll give him a reduced sentence." My client refused to plead guilty. We went out and continued with the cross-examination. On cross, I was able to destroy his credibility because he had testified earlier before three different grand juries. I had those transcripts, and his story had changed from the first time to the second time to the third time and to his actual trial testimony. When you have the opportunity to review testimony or prior statements, it is much easier.

(continued)

Continued

Q. How do you prepare for that?

A. It's different from a direct examination. As I said, you script the direct examination, but the cross-examination is more like playing baseball. You never know if you're going to be able to hit the pitch until it's thrown. When you throw the question, most of the people in that room—including yourself—don't listen to the answer. The jury listens, but the cross-examiner doesn't hear the answer because they're thinking about the next question and how they're going to ask it. And that's the problem with most people who don't cross-examine well.

Q. What about the general rule that you shouldn't ask a question on cross-examination that you don't know the answer to?

A. On crucial questions, you shouldn't do it. The classic example was in the O.J. Simpson case when the prosecutors asked O.J. to put on the glove. When that happened, O.J. was in control. That glove was never going to fit. When you have a witness on cross-examination, you cannot let them take control. Still, you can't follow that rule all the time. Sometimes you'll ask a question and their response will trigger a question or idea that you had not considered before. Chances are, if the response triggered a question in your own mind, it also triggered one for the jury. You have to ask that question, even if you don't know what the answer is going to be.

Q. It sounds like you believe listening skills are the most important skill that a lawyer can develop for cross-examination.

A. If you could only learn to do one thing, you need to learn to listen. You don't get any training for that in law school. The closest that you come would be your work in moot court. That may be why some lawyers aren't good at cross-examinations—they've never learned to listen. If you listen, you can ask questions that you hadn't prepared that may be crucial to your case.

Q. What's the second most important skill?

A. Knowing when to stop. If you ask too many questions, you can hurt your case. Years ago, I was co-counsel in a case where one of the attorneys kept looking for something positive in the cross-exam where he could sit down. And he could never find it. It was just excruciating to see this lawyer twisting in the wind. The same thing can happen in cross-examination if you have a witness who won't turn you loose—who won't give you that opening to sit down on. But you've got to understand when to quit.

Q. Does that differ for civil and criminal cases?

A. In criminal law, you don't get to question the witnesses before the trial. In a civil trial, if I sue you, I have a right to take your deposition and find out everything about the case before we go to trial. I can find out what you had for breakfast if I want to ask that question as part of discovery. But in a criminal case, in federal court and in most states, you don't have a right to know even who the witnesses are before they take the stand. Technically, they don't have to turn over the prior statements of the witness until they've finished their testimony. That means that in criminal cases you've got to be able to listen and think on your feet. That's crucial to cross-examination.

Q. Do you have an example?

A. Perhaps the best lawyer I've ever worked with is Bobby Lee Cook—a lawyer from Summerville, Georgia. He's probably one of the top two criminal defense lawyers in the

Continued

nation. The TV character *Matlock* was patterned after Bobby Lee Cook. Bobby Lee and I were defending two bankers in the Butcher banking scandal, when the government put on an expert from Arthur Andersen. The government had paid him about $400,000 to audit a bank that had failed. I was just a young lawyer, and Bobby Lee made me cross-examine him first. I cross-examined him for about two hours, and thought I had done a pretty good job and perhaps gotten a draw with the witness. Bobby Lee got up and said, "Mr. Smith, you've been paid about $400,000 to testify here today. You're being paid $300 an hour, and you have two assistants in the audience who are being paid $200 an hour to be here. Could you tell me your assistants' names?" Smith told him the name of one of the assistants, but he couldn't remember the last name of the other one. Bobby Lee was listening, and he seized upon that, and said, "Mr. Smith, I'm going to ask you some more questions, but I'm going to put you to a little test. I'm going to come back in about five minutes and ask you if you've remembered Rick's last name." For the next hour, he would come back every five-to-ten minutes and ask Smith that guy's name. Smith never did remember. Finally, we take a recess and Smith asks someone about the name. When we return, Smith is cowering behind the microphone and he raises his hand like a little child. "Mr. Cook, Mr. Cook. I know his name now." The jury broke up laughing. Any credibility that Smith ever had was destroyed by Bobby Lee Cook and that innocuous question. It had nothing to do with the case, but the $400,000 case went out the window because Bobby Lee knew how to listen. Both of our clients were found not guilty.

Q. How do you prepare your own witnesses for cross-examination?

A. I cross-examine my own clients. I try to do a mock cross-examination to prepare them for what's going to happen to them, what questions will be asked, and how they should react. If I know the prosecutor, I explain his general tendency. Is he someone who will scream at them or is he a low keyed person? They have to remain polite and respectful. Quite frankly, most people have never taken the witness stand. Being a witness is not an easy thing to do, because you tend to want to over-explain things as opposed to just answering the question and explaining your answers. If you try too hard, you cross a very fine line. I've seen people who I thought would be good witnesses, but when they got on the stand, they just weren't very good.

Summary

Interviews within the legal system can occur outside or inside the courtroom. The initial interviews between an attorney and a client occur outside the courtroom; those interviews enable the attorney to gather the basic facts of the case, make a decision whether to pursue the case, and allow the attorney to offer initial advice and counsel to the client. This interview may be followed by witness interviews in which the attorney seeks additional information that may be useful to the case.

Interviews inside the courtroom fall within three broad categories: (1) voir dire, (2) direct examinations, and (3) cross-examinations. Voir dire refers to questions asked during the jury-selection process. Attorneys from each side will interview prospective jurors to see if any of them may have a bias that could affect the jury's decision. The direct examination is an interview within the courtroom in which an attorney interviews a witness for his or her side of the case, using the question-and-answer format to introduce evidence that will be beneficial. The cross-examination is a follow-up interview to a direct examination; it is conducted by the attorney for the opposing side with the intent to weaken the evidence presented during the direct examination.

Thus, the interviewing process plays a vital role in the legal system. It is the process through which attorneys gather information, present their case, and attempt to refute the case of the opposing side. An understanding of the interview process can make both attorneys and the witnesses more effective at presenting their positions.

FOR FURTHER DISCUSSION

1. Analyze the interview behavior of attorneys on a television drama such as *Law and Order*. To what extent do their actions in a direct examination reflect the principles mentioned in this book? What about their actions during cross-examination?

2. Visit a real courtroom and observe the behaviors of the attorneys. Are they similar or different from what you observed from the television attorneys? What was similar? What was different?

CHAPTER

15 Interviews in the Medical Setting

Charlene had taken the day off from work so she could take her mother to the doctor. Soon they would be ushered into a room where a nurse and then a doctor would see them, talk with them, and make some diagnosis regarding her mother's chronic health problems. Would she remember to ask all the questions she had? Would her mother adequately explain all of her symptoms to the doctor? Would the doctor make a quick diagnosis and dismiss their concerns about other issues? Would both she and her mother leave the doctor's office feeling more confident about her mother's health? Frequently, patients and their relatives leave the encounter disappointed, feeling that the doctor has not addressed all of their concerns.

The reason for such feelings is understandable. American medicine has traditionally embraced the "medical model" of disease, an approach that defines disease in biological terms and pays little attention to social concerns. The patient's attitudes toward his or her health, well-being, or health-care provider are not a major concern. However, modern medicine is beginning to embrace a more patient-centered approach to the diagnosis and treatment of disease.

Weston and Brown (1989) argue that patients' attitudes about their conditions play a critical role in identifying and implementing effective treatments. These attitudes include patients' expectations toward the physician and the health-care system, personal meaning and restrictions about their conditions, moral meaning ascribed to their conditions, and attitudes toward lifestyle changes. They argue that "Physicians who ignore these dimensions of sickness overlook a powerful source of information and potent tool for healing" (p. 77). The information-centered model claims that better healing is achieved when doctors and patients achieve a consensus of understanding about the problems leading to the patient's condition, the goals of health-care treatment, and the roles taken by the patient and the caregiver. In short, every step in the wellness process is predicated on a clear understanding of patients' attitudes.

Medical interviews can have a life-or-death impact on a patient. Gaining accurate information about a patient's health is critical in diagnosing diseases and injuries, in making subsequent treatment decisions and establishing and maintaining the doctor–patient relationship (Suchman, Markakis, Beckman, & Frankel, 1997; Marvel & Doherty, 1998; Jones, 2001).

The medical interview process begins when a receptionist interviews a new patient, asking for contact information, past medical history, and insurance information. The process continues when the nurse interviews the patient to get an initial assessment of the medical problem. It moves into full throttle when the doctor arrives. The doctor then examines the patient and asks for more information about his or her medical history and symptoms.

Ideally, the goal of the physician–patient relationship should be that of a collaborative partnership in which both are working to improve the patient's wellness (Young & Flower, 2001). Somewhat surprisingly, medical personnel often feel that their training in all forms of health communication is inadequate (Langille et al., 2001), yet patient satisfaction and compliance is heavily influenced by the physician–patient interaction (O'Keefe, Roberton, & Sawyer, 2001; Ishikawa et al., 2001; Moore, O'Hair, & Ledlow, 2002).

Communication skills are known to have a positive impact on the diagnosis and treatment of a range of medical problems, including Alzheimer's disease (Small et al., 2003), cancer (Ishikawa et al., 2002; Rowan et al., 2003), HIV infections (Roberts, 2002), gerontology-related conditions (Haug, 1996), and treatments in ambulatory clinics (Jackson & Kroenke, 1999). As a result, many medical programs are placing an increased emphasis on communication and interviewing skills (Du Pre, 2001, O'Keefe, Roberton, & Sawyer, 2001; Ogawa, Taguchi, & Sasahara, 2003).

Just as important is a growing recognition that much of the responsibility for providing information during the medical interview lies with the patient (Ballard-Reisch, 1990; Manning & Ray, 2001). Patients who are trained in medical interviewing techniques are more adept at providing information to medical personnel, and medical personnel are more likely to understand their problems (Weaver, 2003). Patients often assume responsibility for relational control within the medical interview, including making decisions about when to let the physician dominate the conversation (Fitzwater & Gilgun, 2001). Patients with low levels of participation are less likely to provide full information about their problems (Robinson, 2003). Thus, training in the techniques of medical interviews is important to both medical personnel and to patients.

The Functions of Medical Interviews

Interviews serve several functions within the medical setting including: (1) information gathering, (2) assessment, (3) relationship development, and (4) credibility enhancement.

Information Gathering

Perhaps the most vital role of medical interviews is to gather information from the patient that will assist the doctor in making a treatment decision (Roter & Frankel, 1992). A variety of information must be gathered—patient history, symptoms, allergies, and current medications, to name a few. Even more important, this information must be accurate. Any inaccurate information can invalidate the suggested treatment and, in some cases, lead to the death of the patient.

Assessment

Marlow (1997) describes the medical interviewing process as one of "data collection" that uses observational and communication skills. That data is then used to make an assessment of the patient's conditions and problem. "In reality, assessment can begin while information is being gathered," she notes. "It differs from data collection in that judgments are made about the information that has been collected" (p. 57).

Relationship Development

The medical interview is a two-way exchange of information that leads to the development of a relationship between a physician and a patient (Cegala 2002). Most of the responsibility for achieving that relationship rests with the doctor (Cegala et al., 1996; McNeilis, 2001, 2002), because the patient rarely initiates such communication. The relationship is manifested in terms the doctor's "bedside manner." It plays a vital role in the development of the doctor–patient relationship. A positive result leads to a relationship in which the patient perceives the physician as understanding his or her problem (Makoul, 2002), increasing the likelihood that the patient will follow the suggested medical regimen to ensure good health (Clowers, 2002).

The interview is an important tool in developing this relationship. In fact, Enelow and Swisher (1979) call interviewing "the key to successful clinician–patient relationships." The key is to provide useful information. The doctors' messages for the patient are more likely to be effective if they provide explicit information while providing an implied message of concern (Cegala, 1997; Levinson et al., 1997).

Credibility Enhancement

For the doctor to be effective, the patient must trust the doctor's expertise. Given that the patient is often relatively uninformed on medical or anatomical matters, much of that trust will be based on the patient's perceptions of the doctor's skills. Granted, the medical degree itself will bestow a great deal of credibility, but often that is not enough. The patient will fine tune his or her evaluation of the doctor based on the doctor–patient interview.

Research has found that a physician's communication skills influence patient perceptions of a doctor's credibility in terms of competence, trustworthiness, and caring for the patient (Richmond, Smith, Heisel, & McCroskey, 2002). Doctors who rush through interviews leave patients feeling frustrated and cheated (O'Hair, 1989). Doctors who ask good questions appear to know what they are doing, and patients will be more satisfied with the care they receive (Wanzer, Gruber, & Booth-Butterfield, 2002; Richmond, Smith, Heisel, & McCroskey, 2002).

Barriers to Effective Medical Interviews

Despite the need to gather and exchange accurate information in medical interviews, several barriers can inhibit the exchange of such information. These generally can be attributed to barriers created by (1) the patient, (2) the doctor, (3) medical jargon, and (4) the situation.

Patient-Based Barriers

Patient-based barriers generally fall into four broad categories: (1) a reluctance to share personal information, (2) a lack of understanding of medical terminology, (3) an inability to objectify symptoms, and (4) an inability to articulate symptoms.

Measuring Physicians' Interviewing Skills

What do people look for when evaluating a physician's interviewing skills? The following statements were developed by Du Pre (2002) as a means of measuring patients' perceptions of physicians' interviewing skills.

1. The physician frequently self-discloses about his or her own health and life experiences.
2. The physician makes frequent expressions of empathy.
3. The physician involves the patient in decision making.
4. The physician and patient talk explicitly about fears.
5. The physician uses many open-ended questions.
6. The physician listens.

Source: Du Pre, A. (2002). Accomplishing the impossible: Talking about body and soul and mind during a medical visit. *Health Communication, 14(1)*, 1–21.

Patient Reticence.   Many medical problems are of a personal nature and require individuals to talk about their body in ways that they rarely do with others. Patients rarely seek
information when speaking with doctors (Cegala, 1997) and ask considerably fewer questions than doctors (Roter, Hall, & Katz, 1988) even though they express a desire for more
information (Waitzkin, 1985). When they do seek information, they often do not ask for
information directly (Beisecker & Beisecker, 1990), preferring instead to use indirect
methods to approach a topic.

Patients can be particularly reticent when it comes to verbalizing their emotional
state. The result is that physicians often ignore such concerns (Suchman et al., 1997).
Sometimes even the most verbose patients become remarkably shy when asked to discuss
their medical problems (Torres et al., 2002). This tendency is most pronounced with sexual disorders, and the effect can be multiplied when the doctor and patient are of different
genders (Hirschmann, 2002). A male with erectile dysfunction, for example, will often feel
uncomfortable discussing the problem with a female nurse or doctor. Patient reticence can
extend into a myriad of other medical situations—the athlete who is reluctant to admit pain
for fear of being released from the team, the factory worker reluctant to admit vision problems for fear that he will be transferred or fired, or the middle-aged man who fears that the
pains in the chest are signs of his mortality. The medical interviewer must gradually break
through such reluctance to gain an accurate picture of the person's symptoms.

Objectification Skills.   Charlotte is particularly adept at pre-interviewing patients and
translating their symptoms into medical terminology that is relevant to the doctor's diagnosis. Doctors frequently ask her to sit in on their interviews with patients so that she can
explain what symptom the patient is trying to describe. Those skills become relatively use-
less to her, though, when she becomes a patient herself. When a nurse or doctor asks for
her symptoms, she frequently finds herself making vague references to aches and pains
without being able to identify the specific source of the complaint. Such problems are
common. Many patients, when placed under the duress of pain and discomfort, are unable

to objectify their symptoms in such a manner as to give a precise description of them to the doctor or nurse. Others engage in lifestyle activities (e.g., lack of exercise, poor eating habits) that accentuate symptoms that may be unrelated to their immediate medical problems (Meredith, Stewart, & Brown, 2001; Street & Millay, 2001). The person who interviews the patient must verbally probe for finer and more distinct explanations of the patient's problems.

Inability to Communicate.   Johnny was admitted to the hospital for surgery to remove a kidney stone. By then, he had been in pain for a considerable amount of time, and his family doctor had administered pain relievers to help with the discomfort. Admission to the hospital, though, required the completion of a pre-admission interview. However, since Johnny was under the influence of pain medication, he was not able to answer the interview questions. This scenario illustrates those instances in which the medical condition of the patient interferes with his or her ability to communicate. Such situations can exist due to the physical or mental condition of the patient (Jackson & Kroenke, 1999). Sometimes an injury or disease can have such a strong impact that the patient is physically unable to describe his or her symptoms to the medical practitioner. When this occurs, the physician has to rely more heavily on direct observation of physical cues (e.g., blood pressure, pulse rate, temperature), and the interview has to be conducted with a person who is familiar with the patient's symptoms—either a family member or a witness to a particular incident.

Doctor-Based Barriers

Not all barriers to effective medical interviews are the fault of the patient. At times, the behavior and personality of the medical personnel conducting the interview also can create problems. As one group of researchers noted, "It is well established that most medical interviews in primary care are characterized by a scarcity of patient-centered interventions . . ." (Del Piccolo et al., 2002, p. 1871). Several behaviors can contribute to this problem.

Insensitivity.   An overworked admissions clerk must deal with dozens of patients and their families every day. The clerk's job is to process information that will ensure treatment for the patient and payment for the medical personnel, transferring information to forms that serve as medical records. Over time, a clerk may increasingly focus on obtaining the needed information while showing less concern for the patients and their families. The clerk is not the only medical worker subject to such problems. Because of increased focus on insurance forms and government reimbursements, it is relatively easy for all practitioners. Doctors, for example, often interrupt their patients' responses (Frankel, 1984), change topics (Frankel & Beckman, 1984), and put off answering a patient's questions (Cegala, 1997).

The opposite of insensitivity is immediacy or empathy, which is the ability to relate to the immediate needs of the other person on an interpersonal basis (Suchman, Markakis, Beckman, & Frankel, 1997). Research has shown that patients who perceive medical personnel as engaging in immediacy behaviors are more satisfied with the medical services they receive (Richmond, Smith, Heisel, & McCroskey, 2001). Further, immediacy is a major factor in patient reaction regardless of whether the medical personnel involved in the interaction is a doctor (Richmond, Smith, Heisel, & McCroskey, 2001) or a nurse (Adkins & De Witt, 2000).

Premature Judgments.   A bigger problem is the possibility that medical personnel will prejudge a condition and, as a result, fail to conduct a thorough patient interview. Although such problems may occur at any time, such prejudging appears to be more frequent during periods in which doctors see a number of patients with similar symptoms. An outbreak of a new flu virus, for example, will result in dozens of patients visiting the doctor with flu-like symptoms. Most of those patients will have the new virus, but some are likely to have different, and possibly more serious, problems. The practitioner must avoid the temptation to think, "Here's another one."

Medical Jargon

Bernstein and Bernstein (1980) point out that "Health care professionals do not share a common vocabulary with most patients" (p. 78). Indeed, the medical community uses a very precise form of jargon. Proficiency with the jargon tends to increase over time; experienced medical personnel find that they use technical language almost subconsciously. In many ways, this is an asset, because of the resulting precision in communication. That precision of word usage allows for an accurate exchange of information in doctor-to-doctor, nurse-to-nurse, or doctor-to-nurse interactions. It is not, however, conducive to effective communication between a medical practitioner and a patient. Words that easily roll off the tongue of a doctor or nurse may sound like a strange, multisyllabic foreign language to the medically naive patient.

The problem may be particularly acute when dealing with children. Children frequently have had little exposure to medical jargon, and many of the words used by the medical practitioner will be strange to them. Further, the euphemisms for bodily functions that they use at home are likely to be different from the euphemisms used by medical personnel. The medical practitioner who asks a child if he or she has had a BM or bowel movement in the past 24 hours will likely be met with a blank stare. The question has to be phrased with a different euphemism, one that conveys the question without embarrassing or confusing the patient (e.g., "Have you been to the bathroom today?"). Or, the physician must work with the parents to obtain an accurate assessment of the child's symptoms and establish a positive relationship for care (Wanzer, Gruber, & Booth-Butterfield, 2002).

The problem also is a major concern with patients from different cultural backgrounds. Patients are growing increasingly more culturally diverse in terms of age, education level, ethnic background, and language. Communicating with people from such diverse backgrounds is a growing problem for the profession (Du Pre, 2002). Age can be a major factor; some older patients are less active in the interview process (Hines, Moss, & Badzek, 1997). Language is another barrier. The physician, in particular, has to be tolerant of patients who mispronounce medical terminology, or risk alienating the patient. Further, patients with lower levels of formal education are often less active in providing information to the doctor (Hines, Moss, & Badzek, 1997), which may require more probing on the part of medical personnel.

Situation-Based Barriers

Some factors unrelated to both the doctor and the patient can adversely affect the medical interview. The two most common are (1) the location and physical environment in which the interview occurs and (2) the presence of other people during the interview.

Location.   Joe was involved in a traffic accident in which an automobile struck a motorcycle. The motorcyclist was thrown 15 feet by the impact of the collision and suffered major injuries. Emergency personnel treated the victim, stabilized his condition, and had him transported to a nearby hospital before turning their attention to the occupants of the car. One child appeared to be sitting in an uncomfortable manner. When the EMTs asked if he was in pain, the child admitted that both feet hurt. The EMTs rolled up his pants and carefully cut away his shoes to get a better look at the injury. As the shoes were removed, the boy sighed and said, "That's better. I tried to tell them those shoes were too small." The point, of course, is that the location of the interview created expectations about the nature of the patient's complaint. Those expectations are not always accurate, and medical practitioners have to be ready to adjust in those situations.

The location also can cause medical personnel to alter their interview style, based on their assessments of the seriousness of the problem. Hospitals sometimes run out of emergency room space during accidents that generate multiple injuries, and some of the injured may end up on cots in the hallway while waiting for an open room. In such situations, medical personnel may assume that the hallway patients are not as badly injured as those already in treatment rooms. This assumption is not always correct. Patients who are strapped to a hospital cot may assume that their injuries are more severe than they would if they were standing or sitting while responding to the interview.

Presence of a Third Person.   Sometimes the presence of a third person (e.g., a spouse or a nurse) during the interview can alter the patient's responses, sometimes enhancing and sometimes detracting from the medical experience (Schilling et al., 2002). Women may be reluctant to speak of pregnancy problems in the presence of a male nurse. Similarly, a husband may be reluctant to discuss symptoms related to a sexually transmitted disease if his wife is present during the medical interview. During such situations, it is the job of the medical practitioner to be sensitive to possible reticence created by the presence of the third person. When such reticence is identified, the interviewer should change the situation so that the third person leaves the room.

Types of Medical Interviews

Northouse and Northouse (1985) identify two distinct types of health-care interviews: the information-sharing interview and the therapeutic interview.

Information-Sharing Interviews

Information-sharing interviews are those that place an emphasis on content. These include admissions interviews, health history interviews, and interviews aimed at symptom identification. These interviews may vary dramatically in terms of (1) the level of information needed and (2) the expertise required to conduct the interview. Admissions interviews, for example, are typically collected by clerical staff workers who gather biographical, demographic, and financial information. Health history interviews may be conducted by nurses who meet with patients before they are seen by a doctor. Information about symptoms may be gathered by the doctor prior to making a diagnosis and a recommendation for treatment.

Although there are several techniques for conducting an information-sharing interview (Rimal, 2001), such interviews are usually divided into at least three distinct stages: (1) a medical history, (2) a physical examination, and (3) a conclusion that includes explanations and treatment plans (Billings & Stoeckle, 1998; Shaikh, Knobloch, & Stiles, 2001). This structure is particularly applicable to the initial interview, in which the primary goal is to gather information that can assist in the screening out of some medical factors (Stiles et al., 1979). The structure typically varies somewhat on subsequent return visits; the doctor will spend less time on the medical history and physical examination, but spend more time emphasizing health behaviors and the active involvement of the patient in his or her treatment (Bertakis et al., 1999).

Therapeutic Interviews

The purpose of a therapeutic interview is to establish a supportive relationship that will help patients identify and work through personal issues, concerns, or problems. Benjamin (1981) calls such interviews "helping interviews," and they may be conducted by social workers, nurses, doctors, chaplains, or psychologists.

Therapeutic interviews tend to fall into two distinctive variations. *Directive interviews* are those in which medical personnel direct and guide the discussion for the purpose of providing prescribed solutions. *Nondirective interviews* use open-ended questions to encourage patients to examine their own situations to find comfort and possible solutions. The directive technique is often used in situations that lend themselves to prescribed solutions. For example, medical personnel may guide cancer patients through a series of options that have worked for others in their situation. The nondirective technique is more likely to be used in emotionally charged situations, such as the death of a loved one. At those times, a chaplain may use the nondirective method as a means of getting the individual to express and confront his or her grief.

Stages of the Interview Process

The stages of the medical interview are similar to those of other interview situations. Northouse and Northouse (1985) identify four stages: (1) preparation, (2) initiation, (3) exploration, and (4) termination.

Preparation

Successful interviews start with anticipating and planning. Anticipating the situation allows the interviewer to evaluate and assess his or her strengths and weaknesses as it

Dr. Patricia Garver: On Talking with Patients

Dr. Patricia Garver (MD, Johns Hopkins, 1985) is an Assistant Professor of Medicine at the University of Alabama at Birmingham and the Director of Internal Medicine at the Kirkland Clinic, Birmingham, Alabama. Dr. Garver specializes in primary health delivery.

Q. What do you try to learn during your initial screening interview with a patient?

A. That depends on the type of visit. If it's the first visit, there's a reason for them being there, a chief complaint. That first visit is probably the most important. That's where you get their past history and a sense for the whole patient—their personal history and social history, too. It might be the number of kids they have, when they went to school, a lot of things that help you in taking care of them in the future.

Q. How is it helpful?

A. Everybody reacts differently to pain, to different problems. Once you figure that out, it gets a lot easier to take care of them. You need to know why certain things bother some people. For example, for some people it's just the pain. For others, they're worried about whether the symptom is cancer. They can handle the pain, but they just want to be told it's nothing serious. And another person doesn't like one little bit of pain, wants a pill for it, and really isn't worried about what's causing it. They just want to feel better.

Some people clearly look nervous when they're telling me something. They might be wringing their hands a little bit, fiddling with their hair, looking down. I've had a few patients that I can always tell when they can't make eye contact, they're looking at their skirt—so then you know you might be on to something important if they're nervous talking about it. It lets you know again what's bothering them, because sometimes a doctor focuses on something they've said. Take chest pain, for instance. You're thinking one thing, they're thinking another, and sometimes it's only in how they're talking about it that you realize that they're scared. I might automatically know that it's not their heart, but they don't know that, and they're really scared about it. So it's how they talk to you that lets you know what their worry is.

Q. What are patients afraid of?

A. They're afraid of dying. They're afraid of having a horrible disease. But sometimes they're afraid of things that surprise you. One lady was afraid she had an inflammation of her thyroid and might be hypothyroid. In my mind, that's not a big deal. Maybe she'll have to take thyroid replacement; if that's the worst that could happen, well, that's not too bad. So what she was afraid of and what I was worried about were two different things. What I wanted to do was make a diagnosis, but sometimes the doctor and the patient aren't on the same page. Usually the patient is a little more worried than the doctor.

Q. Do patients ever try to deceive you?

A. Many try to belittle their symptoms, particularly men. Their wives bring them in because they've been having indigestion for a long time, and it turns out it's their heart. They've been ignoring it and will even tell you that it's just a little heartburn. They really don't want to get tests done. They're worried about it themselves, but they're afraid of the outcome, and so they belittle their symptoms and other people tell you something else.

(continued)

Continued

They'll be talking about their back aching, but the real problem is that they're having trouble with a child, or maybe they're in trouble with the law. They don't come out and say, "My son just got arrested yesterday." That might come out 20 minutes later.

Q. How do you get people to relax and feel comfortable?

A. When I first start talking to them, especially if I don't know them well, I'm cautious about looking open—not sitting with my arms folded—and just looking approachable. Smiling, eye contact, looking interested, nodding my head that I'm hearing what they're saying, making notes intermittently. I try not to just write and write—that looks less interested, but I try to carefully make notes about what I think is important. As I get to know people, I ask them things about their family, things that might help them feel at ease and get to the bottom of the matter a little quicker. I use what personal knowledge I know about them to sometimes get at the problem. If I think the problem might be stress, I'll say "How's your daughter doing?" And, knowing that she lost her job and has two kids to take care of, I can add, "are you still helping out with them?" I often find out that those types of things are featured into the problem. Those are the tough ones.

Q. Was this something you were trained to do in medical school and your residencies or was this something you brought with yourself as a person?

A. We got some training in interviewing, but it was much more cut and dried—Where does it hurt? How long has it been there? What makes it better? What makes it worse? Those are fine questions, except that they work only half the time. So I think most of this is on-the-job training, seeing people who you think actually do it well and seeing others that you think interview miserably.

Q. On average, patients come to a physician with about three complaints. Typically, a lot of physicians will only respond to the first one. Why do you think that happens?

A. Some physicians are in the mode of "I-just-do-one-problem-a-day" because they're rushed for time. Also, if that first complaint is something serious, you get caught up in it. Your mind may be already looking ahead, thinking, "Oh, I have to get a CAT scan." Then the person mentions that "My sinuses have been bothering me, too," you might tend to dismiss that and just think, "Oh, we'll get to that later." Then you might possibly forget about it because you're sidetracked on something you think is really important. So some of that may be because of a shortage of time, and sometimes it's just forgotten because of the acuity of another problem.

Q. Is it hard to stay in the moment and not think ahead too much?

A. It depends on the problem. Sometimes when I'm seeing a patient, we'll talk about a problem or even get to what we'll do about it. Sometimes you'll hear about all their concerns, check them off, and say "Ok, number one, we're going to do this and that." I try to take care of all their complaints in one visit because I hate for people to come back three times for three things. But sometimes you can't. Some people have 10 things. The average may be 3, but sometimes there are at least 10 and you just can't get to them all.

Q. On the other side of the coin, how should a patient prepare to meet a doctor?

A. I'm someone who doesn't mind lists. Sometimes I get a little depressed when I see the length of the list—if there are something like 12 things on it—but a list is helpful whether it's a mental one or an actual one. It ensures that you've gone over everything. What's sometimes frustrating is when people come in and, toward the end of the visit when you think you're done, they pull out the punch line of why they're really here. That

Continued

can be hard to handle. You're walking out the door, and they'll say, "by the way . . ." and the thing that is really bothering them comes out. I'd much rather have a list than to have that happen. We have more time constraints than the doctors of the past. When the patient has a list of goals they'd like to talk about, and we can work through those, we both feel a little better that we haven't left anything out.

Q. How do you separate the individual and their treatment at that point?

A. You try not to make people feel guilty. Sometimes you need to encourage them to make some lifestyle changes, but you realize that it's often difficult. Guilt may help a few people make that change, but I usually try to use encouragement. Some doctors yell at patients and some berate them and tell them they're stupid. I don't know what works the best, but I don't think it helps to make people feel guilty about it. When you do that, they often don't come back. They don't want to feel guilty again. So I prefer to stay optimistic that we're going to fix the problem and get it under control. It's just not all me or a pill; they've got to work, too. Everybody's got to work on it.

---

relates to the medical topic before them. Planning helps in the identification of the goal for the interview. To make the interview more effective and efficient, Edwards and Brilhart (1982) recommend that medical personnel use preparation time to identify the goal of the interview and then be prepared to reveal it to the other person quickly.

Initiation

The initial contact sets the tone and mood for the interaction that follows, creating a climate for the rest of the interview (Klinzing & Klinzing, 1985). Those first few moments can be important in any health-care interview, but it is absolutely critical in therapeutic situations. In those instances, the interviewer's first goal must be to establish a climate that will foster trust and understanding (Northouse & Northouse, 1985). For this reason, the interviewer cannot rush into some topics. A relationship must be established before the interviewer can ask the patient to disclose uncomfortable information.

For information-oriented interviews, the opening stages of the interview should be used to clarify the purpose of the interview and to establish mutual goals with the patient. A common understanding of those goals is a key to the interview's success. If the patient and the interviewer dance around issues for the remainder of the interview, little will have been accomplished.

In their rush to move from patient to patient, medical personnel may move through this stage too quickly. False agreement easily can be achieved by speaking to the patient in vague terms. The interviewer may move on to the next stage under the mistaken belief that the patient is ready to follow and participate freely in the discussion.

Exploration

The exploration stage is the "working phase" of the interview. It is during this stage that the interviewer helps the patient identify and express his or her problems. In therapeutic interviews, this stage also should be used to help the patient identify and manage his or her feelings through the development of coping skills.

This may sound simple, but the process can be relatively awkward and complex. Benjamin (1981) notes that the working phase of the health-care interview may not necessarily proceed at a smooth and consistent pace. The development of trust between the patient and health-care professional is a developmental process in which levels may be achieved that are adequate for revealing some facts, but not others. The patient may quickly respond to some of the interviewer's questions, while back away from others. The interviewer must constantly monitor the feedback of the patient to seek some indication that not all of the necessary information has been provided.

Not surprisingly, the medical interviewer often tiptoes through a communication minefield during this stage, particularly if the interview is largely therapeutic in nature. Sayre (1978) notes that the health-care professional could easily make a number of crucial mistakes during this stage. One common problem is *prematurely changing subjects*. Patients may incrementally divulge sensitive information, but the information that remains hidden may be important to the medical assessment of the patient's problems; changing the topic too quickly could result in a loss of that information.

Interviewers also must carefully monitor their own communication behaviors. The use of animated facial expressions, smiles, and eye contact encourages the patient to disclose information (Bullis & Horn, 1995; Duggan & Parrott, 2001). Conversely, the patient's reticence will increase if the interviewer fails to give sufficient feedback. Similarly, the patient may be reluctant to speak if the interviewer gives too much feedback, particularly of a stereotypical nature. If the patient gets the impression that the interviewer is merely "going through the motions" of asking questions, the patient will just as quickly go through the motions of answering them.

The worst possible response, though, occurs when the interviewer gives an inappropriate response, particularly inappropriate advice or reassurance. When this occurs, the trust in the relationship is likely to be destroyed, with the patient feeling that the interviewer does not understand or appreciate the severity of the situation. Some doctors, for example, like to joke with their patients; however, jokes are not always appropriate for some patients.

Termination

One sign of a successful health-care interview is that both the patient and the health-care professional reach their goals and both know that it is time to close the interview (Sundeen et al., 1981). Unfortunately, Klinzing and Klinzing (1985) note that patient interviews often are terminated abruptly, with the health-care professional departing without providing a summary of important points or offering the patient an opportunity for a final question or comment. Ideally, the closing of the interview should summarize the key points of the interview and ensure that both parties have had an opportunity to say everything they wanted to say.

The closing is a major factor in therapeutic interviews, one that often requires advance preparation on the part of the interviewer to ensure that it provides closure for the patient (Lego, 1980). Not all therapeutic patients will take such closure easily. Nehren and

Gilliam (1965) note that many patients will suffer from "separation anxiety," a problem that will make them reluctant to seek closure. The prospect of stopping the interview may trigger feelings of sadness, anger, abandonment, guilt, and helplessness in the patient. These feelings can be so strong that some counselors recommend that the interviewer develop an elaborate plan for the final session as a way of ensuring closure (Koehne-Kaplan & Levy, 1978). Such an approach signifies the importance of the termination and allows the patient to express his or her feelings.

Techniques for Medical Interviews

Those medical personnel who become most effective in conducting medical interviews are those who have mastered a variety of interview skills that are appropriate for the medical environment. In broad terms, those skills often are based on knowledge of (1) question sequences, (2) verbal tools, and (3) monitoring skills.

Question Sequences

As noted in Chapter 1, Stewart and Cash (1982) identify three different types of question sequences: (1) the funnel sequence, (2) the inverted funnel, and (3) the tunnel sequence. Each of these may be used by medical personnel. The *funnel sequence* gradually focuses the discussion to a specific topic. Thus, a doctor using the funnel sequence might begin with a broad general question (e.g., "What seems to be the problem?") and gradually focus on a specific symptom (e.g., "Does it hurt when you bend your knee?"). The funnel sequence can be effective in helping the medical worker focus in on the patient's key symptoms.

With the *inverted funnel*, the medical worker begins by asking a series of specific questions (e.g., "Is the pain constant?") and gradually broadens the approach to obtain a sense of the patient's overall response to the problem (e.g., "How does the pain affect you emotionally?"). The inverted funnel is particularly useful in stimulating responses from a reticent patient. Patients who are reluctant to talk tend to fend off broad, open-ended questions, particularly those at the beginning of the interview. But they will respond to short, specific questions, and these can be used as an ice-breaker to get them to talk more freely about all of their symptoms and their emotional responses to their problems.

The *tunnel sequence* uses a series of similar questions of the same format. The tunnel sequence is the one most frequently used by clerical personnel for admission interviews. It works well in that situation because the interviewer needs to cover a number of different topics but in-depth information on those topics is not necessary.

Verbal Tools

The interviewer's ultimate tools for the patient interview are his or her personal set of verbal skills. The adept interviewer will learn a variety of techniques that can be used to elicit information from the patient. These tools include, but are not limited to, the phrasing of questions and the use of silence.

Phrasing of Questions   One key element in the effective medical interview is the way the medical worker phrases questions. At a basic level, the interviewer has the option of phrasing questions from an open-ended approach (e.g., "Tell me about your problem") that allows for a wide range of patient responses or using closed-ended questions (e.g., "Does your jaw hurt?") that have a limited number of possible answers. Interviewers using the funnel sequence, for example, typically start with open-ended questions and switch to closed-ended ones as the interview progresses. Use of the inverted funnel sequence could result in the reversal of that process, with the interviewer starting with closed-ended questions and waiting until he or she feels the reticent patient is comfortable enough to answer open-ended questions.

Another important factor is the word choices used in phrasing the question. The skillful medical interviewer learns to ask questions without using medical jargon. Questions are phrased so that the patient can respond to them in the patient's terms; the medical worker then translates the answer into medical terms for diagnostic purposes.

Care also must be taken not to use words or phrases that will place the patient in a psychologically defensive position. Doctors, in particular, must be careful about this factor. Doctors enter into the relationship with generally high credibility, which makes it particularly easy for them to intimidate patients through their use of language. Benjamin (1969), for example, argues that medical workers should avoid using the word "why" in their questions, because that word could be perceived by the patient as implied criticism or disapproval.

Probing.   Follow-up questions or other continuation techniques allow medical personnel to gather additional information and to seek more specific information. Typically, if the physician does not use some form of probe—either asking a follow-up question or prompting further information from the patient—the topic of the conversation is likely to change (McNeilis, 2002).

Silence.   One underused interview technique is simply saying nothing. Sometimes, by remaining silent, an interviewer can encourage the patient to provide more information. However, Baker (1955) notes that there is a difference between positive silence and negative silence. Negative silence makes the participant feel uncomfortable, particularly when tension is high; positive silence indicates acceptance and satisfied contentment. It can effectively be used, particularly during the exploration stage, to encourage the patient to continue talking. It is highly ineffective, though, in both the initiation and terminations stage. In the initiation stage, silence creates an awkwardness and sense of uncertainty that may make the patient feel uncomfortable. In the termination stage, it may indicate that the interviewer does not know how to close the conversation.

Monitoring

Klinzing and Klinzing (1985) argue that the cornerstone of effective medical interviews is the ability of the interviewer to employ empathic listening skills to monitor what the patient is saying. Patients become frustrated when they think the doctor or nurse is not listening to them. Listening is effective, though, only if the interviewer has an accurate assessment of what the patient is trying to say. The interviewer must occasionally employ one of several techniques to assess the accuracy of the information. The most common techniques for doing this are (1) paraphrasing, (2) requesting clarification, and (3) checking perceptions.

Paraphrasing is simply the restatement of the patient's response using the interviewer's words rather than the patient's. It is an effective way for the interviewer to test his or her understanding of the patient's problem while demonstrating a commitment to understanding the patient. A variation of the paraphrase is the *reflective comment*, a statement that provides a verbal mirror for the patient. Thus, a doctor may use a reflective statement to summarize his or her general impression of several of the patient's comments (e.g., "You seem to be saying that the pain gets progressively worse during the day").

A less frequently used technique is the *request for clarification*. With this technique, the interviewer asks for further explanation as to what the patient means. Clarification requests seek more detail about who, where, and when. A common variation of this approach is to ask the patient for an example. Medical workers are sometimes reluctant to use this technique, because it sometimes requires an admission of confusion. Further, when it is used, it can be misused. If stated in an improper tone and with the wrong words, the patient may interpret the request for clarification as an implicit criticism (Klinzing & Klinzing, 1985).

Perception checking is a technique in which the medical worker gives the patient a chance to correct any of his or her previous statements. With this approach, the doctor or nurse interrupts the interview for a moment to ask the patient about the accuracy of his or her impression. Thus, the doctor might say, "Am I right in thinking that you can see better out of your right eye than your left eye?"

Feedback

Most of these techniques not only increase the listening skills of the interviewer, but also provide feedback to the patient. This feedback is essential in providing the patient with a sense that the medical worker understands and is concerned about his or her problem. Three other feedback techniques can be used to enhance this perception even further: (1) reflection, (2) interpretation, and (3) confirmation. Unlike paraphrasing, which is a restatement of what the patient has said, *reflection* focuses on how something was expressed (e.g., "This whole problem seems to be beating you down"). Such statements can increase the patient's perception that the medical worker understands his or her problem. *Interpretation* is similar to perception checking, but its purpose is different. In this instance, the medical worker offers an explanation to the patient and solicits his or her reaction. Brammer (1973) notes that the goal of this form of feedback is to encourage the patient to provide his or her own interpretation of the situation. Finally, *confirmation remarks* (e.g., "I see what your mean") can be used to acknowledge understanding while encouraging the patient to continue talking.

The Reverse Interview: What the Patient Should Ask the Doctor

The patient bears some responsibility for a successful medical interview (Street & Millay, 2001). However, patients often do not directly ask for information (Beisecker & Beisecker,

1990). Frankel (1990) argues that patients use a *dispreference* process when talking with the doctor by tagging indirect questions to answers that they provide to a doctor's question. Such reticence inhibits patients' ability or willingness to express their real concerns about their medical condition (West & Frankel, 1991).

The prudent patient prepares to get maximum advantage from a visit with a doctor (Post, Cegala, & Miser, 2002). Patients who ask questions are more likely to recall the information offered by the doctor (Socha-McGee & Cegala, 1998). The result of patient involvement also pays off for the doctor. Patients who have been trained in health communication have a higher compliance rate and are more likely to have a successful treatment outcome (Cegala, Marinelli, & Post, 2002) and are more likely to have their needs addressed immediately (Roter et al., 1997). Patients should keep the following in mind during a medical interview:

- The patient should provide a complete medical history and a list of medications currently being taken. The patient should not worry about shocking or embarrassing the doctor. Most physicians have seen it all (or at least most of it) before. Further, by providing this information, the patient shows the doctor that he or she is committed to the treatment process, which encourages the doctor to be more active in the patient's treatment (Walker, Arnold, Miller-Day, & Webb, 2002). A complete medical history is particularly important when dealing with medical problems, because it increases the chances of the doctor effectively solving the problem (Ptacek, Ptacek, & Ellison, 2001).
- The patient should identify the major problem and express it early in the interview. Reticence can compel some patients to withhold discussing their real problem until they absolutely must. Patients should not wait until the doctor is ready to leave the room before telling the doctor the reason for their visit. The physician may become irritated that the patient has wasted so much of his or her time or—even worse—may assume that the problem is minor since the patient waited so long before bringing it up.
- The patient should be specific about his or her symptoms. A person does not need to be a medical expert in order to identify the source of pain or discomfort. Patients should develop a basic understanding of medical terminology in order to be more specific in their descriptions (Du Pre, 2002). Vague complaints can generate multiple interpretations by the doctor, which could potentially lead to an improper diagnosis.
- The patient should ask specific questions. Patients often are tempted to embed a question into a longer statement, a communication tactic often used in informal communication interactions. However, the intent is likely to be lost when this occurs. Research has shown that doctors generally do not respond to embedded questions as questions and thus are not likely to provide the information requested (McNeilis, 2002).
- Patients should ask what they should do when they get home. Discomfort can (and probably will) interfere with the patient's processing of the doctor's instructions. Before leaving the office, the patient should ask for final instructions, paying par-

ticular attention to information related to prescription drugs (Parrott, 1994; Smith, 1998).

The reverse interview should become a focal point of the doctor–patient relationship if surgery is a possibility. When the doctor recommends surgery, the interview roles between the doctor and patient are reversed. It becomes, for practical purposes, a job interview. The doctor seeks a job assignment from the patient, while the patient has to decide (1) whether the job is necessary and (2) if this is the person for that job. When facing surgery, the patient should be prepared to ask several questions of the doctor:

- *Why do I need this surgery?* If the explanation is not adequate, wait before making a final decision.
- *Is this surgery the typical treatment for this problem? What other alternatives are available?* Surgeons are more likely to recommend surgical treatments that represent their expertise. The particular treatment recommended may or may not be the one most frequently advocated for the patient's problem.
- *How many similar surgeries have you done?* One of the author's friends frequently says that he wants his surgeon to have some gray in his hair, because he assumes this means the doctor has more experience. While that oversimplifies the concept, it does represent the idea that the surgeon should be an expert in the particular procedure that is being recommended.
- *What is the success rate? What can go wrong?* The sad fact is that not all surgeries are successful, and some types of surgeries are less successful than others. Side effects from surgery may range from temporary discomfort to death. The patient should know the odds before making a decision.
- *What type of anesthesia will be used?* Despite the routine nature of most surgeries, some danger is involved when anesthesia is used. The doctor should discuss what type of anesthesia will be used and any possible side effects.
- *How long will recovery take?* Different surgeries can keep a person down for different lengths of time. An athlete who has ligament surgery will be sidelined longer than a person who has cataract surgery. Knowing the length of the recovery time can help the patient psychologically adjust for recovery.
- *Is this a procedure that can be done on an outpatient basis?* Modern medical technology has resulted in an increased number of operations that can be conducted on an outpatient basis. Knowing that an extended amount hospital stay is not expected may influence a person's decision of whether to have the surgery. However, some patients should not opt for outpatient procedures. Because of the risk of complications, some patients—particularly the elderly—may want a brief hospital stay for even simple surgeries to ensure that nothing goes wrong.

Assessment

Research in the area of medical interviews is ongoing, but some progress has been made in the development of assessment and measuring instruments (Boon & Stewart, 1998).

Past efforts at developing assessment techniques have encompassed a range of method-ologies, both quantitative and qualitative (Roter & Frankel, 1992). The problem has been one of gathering reliable and valid information when one of the participants (the doctor) is the object of the study (Beckman & Frankel, 1984).

One approach is the Medical Communication Competence Scale developed by Cegala, Coleman, and Turner (1998). This instrument is a simple self-report questionnaire in which people evaluate and rate the competence of themselves and the other participant in the interview. Its weakness is that it is a subjective evaluation from the participants themselves, and it does not directly link competence to any particular set of physician behaviors. However, other research does indicate that such a link exists (Cegala et al., 1995) and that such self-report techniques are consistent with data obtained from inde-pendent observers (Cegala et al., 1996).

The initial analysis of the instrument found that physicians and patients generally contribute an equal number of communication units to the interview. Further, the approach provides a means of looking at sequential patterns of information exchange within the doc-tor–patient relationship. For example, in terms of content, much of the time of the inter-view is devoted to medical history. However, McNeilis (2002) acknowledges that more work is needed before this approach can be used for evaluating the competency levels of the participants.

Summary

In the medical setting, interviews are used to gather information, assess patients' problems, develop doctor–patient relationships, and enhance the doctor's credibility. Successful med-ical interviews do not happen by chance, though; quite the contrary, their effectiveness can be hampered by the patient's inability or reluctance to describe his or her symptoms, by the doctor's insensitivity or premature judgment, the confusion caused by medical jargon, or by situational factors that inhibit communication.

Medical interviews typically have four stages: preparation, initiation, exploration, and termination. Those medical personnel who become most effective in conducting med-ical interviews are those who have mastered a variety of interview skills that are appropri-ate for the medical environment. In broad terms, those skills include an understanding of question sequences, a variety of verbal tools, and highly attuned monitoring skills.

The patient bears some responsibility for a successful medical interview. The patient should be prepared to identify the main complaint and provide the doctor with a thorough medical history. Through the use of reverse interview questions, the patient should gather information from the doctor that will help them make decisions regarding surgery.

FOR FURTHER DISCUSSION

1. Identify someone—yourself or a friend—who has visited a doctor recently. What types of questions were asked by the receptionist? By the nurse? By the physician?

2. Consider your last visit to the doctor. Were you satisfied that the physician understood fully the purpose of your visit? What factors contributed to this evaluation?

3. How could the location of the doctor's office affect the interview style and techniques of a medical interview? Consider, for example, the differences between the nature of interviews that might occur in a physician's office as opposed to those in an emergency room? Between an affluent medical practice and a clinic in a poor neighborhood? Or the differences between an interview by a general practitioner and a specialist such as a plastic surgeon?

CHAPTER
16
Counseling Interviews

Counseling is an integral part of modern American social and organizational life. Most people first encounter professional counselors in school and use their services throughout their academic careers from elementary school (James & Meyer, 1987; Campbell, 1993) through college and career training (Emmett & Harkins, 1997). Many people encounter counselors in the organizations in which they work. Counselors help people make important professional decisions (Watkins & Savickas, 1992). They help individuals with personal problems, such as dealing with illness (Fitzpatrick, 2002), grief (Carter, 1987; Quarmby, 1993), anxiety (Sarason, 1988; Eysenck & Calvo, 1992), obesity (Collins et al., 1983), eating disorders (Vandereycken, DePreitere, & Probst, 1987), alcohol addiction (Miller, 1996; Senft et al., 1997; Borsari & Carey, 2000), and gambling disorders (Hodgins, Currie, & el-Guebaly, 2001; Kuentzel et al., 2003). Counselors also assist people in dealing with family and marital problems (Gil, 1994).

One thing that is common to all counselors, regardless of their purpose or style, is that they must have good interviewing skills. Ivey and Ivey (2003) call interviewing and counseling "interrelated processes" (p. 29), because the foundation of any counseling relationship is the counselor's ability to develop a trusting and open relationship with his or her client (Fong & Cox, 1983). The primary means of doing so is through the exchange of information that occurs during the counseling interview. This chapter will explore the structure of counseling sessions, the various contexts of counseling, the various counseling methods and styles, and interviewing skills and techniques that are employed by counselors.

Structure

Most counseling sessions follow a standardized structure that is aimed at establishing and maintaining a productive relationship between the counselor and the client. Cormier and Hackney (1993) have formalized the structure into a five-stage process. Note that this structure is a general guideline, much as a standardized agenda is for a group meeting; individual sessions may vary. In some way this structure can be viewed as both a microstructure (a structure for a single session) and as a macrostructure (a structuring of multiple sessions).

Stage 1: Relationship Building

As with many forms of interviewing, it is necessary for the counselor and client to establish a trusting and empathetic relationship (Miller, 1989). Because self-disclosure is at the heart of the counseling interaction, the client must feel safe and secure. A significant amount of research has focused on measuring client–counselor rapport (Sharpley & Ridgway, 1992) or the working relationship (Horvath & Symonds, 1991).

One way that a counselor achieves this type of relationship is by creating a climate of acceptance. The counselor must communicate to the client, both verbally and nonverbally, that he or she holds the client in high regard. Martin (1989) claims that this does not mean that the counselor must agree or accept everything that the client does, but rather that the counselor acknowledges the client with positive regard while setting limits on the client's behavior.

Stage 2: Assessment and Diagnosis

Using both standardized and nonstandardized measures, the counselor must formulate a diagnosis (Kottler & Brown, 1996). Such an assessment is not always easy, because some clients—particularly children—may be resistant to the therapeutic process (Gardner, 1990). The counselor must use some technique to stimulate responses that can be used for evaluative purposes (Pedersen, 1994). The counselor then uses feedback to encourage further self-disclosure. Each school of thought has its own methods of assessment, but the counselor of any school must keep fundamental issues of reliability and validity in mind when making an assessment.

Stage 3: Formulation of Goals

The counselor and the client must agree on some sort of goal. For the counseling session(s) to be productive, both parties must see that it is leading to a predetermined point. This goal may be some sort of behavioral, attitudinal, or emotional change on the part of the client. Regardless of the specific goal, Cormier and Hackney (1993) claim that setting goals is critical to the counseling process because they (1) motivate the client to change, (2) are educational to the client in how to proceed, and (3) provide an important feedback mechanism for both the client and counselor to determine the success of ongoing sessions so that adjustments in treatment can be made.

Stage 4: Interventions

Once the goals of the counseling have been determined, specific intervention strategies can be implemented. Certainly the nature and type of strategies will depend on the diagnosis and type of counseling that is practiced by the counselor. The counselor should, however, provide the client with a variety of treatment options and then negotiate with the client as to which treatments will be pursued. Costs and risks of treatments also should be discussed at this time (Cormier & Cormier, 1993). By involving the client in the decision-making process, the counselor will more likely find a treatment that will be more productive to the client and provide a treatment to which the client will be more committed (Cormier & Hackney, 1993).

Stage 5: Termination and Follow-up

To be sure, the goal of counseling should be to make the counselor unnecessary to the client (Nystul, 1999). Quintana and Holahan (1991) state that a successful termination should include a discussion of the end of counseling, a review of the counseling session(s), closure of the counselor–client relationship, and post-counseling plans.

Context

When most people think of therapy and counseling, they conjure an image of a dark office with a large leather couch and a balding gentleman with a gray beard who takes copious notes. The truth is that counseling takes place in a variety of contexts for a variety of reasons. Feltham's (2000) taxonomy of counseling contexts is as follows.

Private Practice   Perhaps the most traditional form of counseling is the counselor in private practice. Many of these counselors practice traditional long-term psychotherapy with clients who come to them with a variety of psychological problems.

Voluntary Agencies   Nonprofit groups support a variety of psychological support services to help people cope with problems such as alcoholism, victim support, rape counseling, and so on. Feltham (2000) notes that counselors in these situations often have duties that go beyond the scope of traditional therapy and counseling (e.g., public awareness raising, governmental advocacy, and so on).

Residential Care   Often combined with physical care, residential care counselors work in a number of settings, including nursing homes and halfway houses. Often these counselors work in conjunction with other heath-care professionals such as nurses or social workers. Often the goal is to work the client back into a private-living circumstance.

Education   Counseling has become an integral part of the educational landscape at all levels. Counselors in educational settings deal with a variety of problems. Almost all students use counseling services for scheduling and career counseling. Educational counselors also spend a great deal of time dealing with problem students who may be involved with drugs or alcohol or who have serious family problems that impact their academic performance.

The Workplace   More and more companies in and outside the United States are providing counseling services to their employees. Like their educational counterparts, workplace counselors provide services to employees suffering from some sort of crisis that is affecting their performance. Organizations often value such counselors in increasing employees' occupational health. These counselors often spend time with employees facing layoffs or job reassignments.

Health Care/Hospital   More and more hospitals are providing residential counseling for nonpsychiatric patients who are suffering psychological trauma because of their condition. These services often are utilized by patients facing surgery.

Interview with Gordon Pugh

Gordon Pugh (MDiv., Mphil., MLAP, ICADC, BCC) is a Chaplin at Children's Hospital in Birmingham, Alabama, and President of Adventure Life Inc., an employee-assistance program offering professional counseling for substance abuse.

Q. Tell me a little more about Adventure Life Inc.

A. Adventure Life is an organization that exists to help employers help their employees who have tested positive on drug screens. If somebody who's in a safety-sensitive role comes up positive on a drug screen or an alcohol test, they are referred to the counselor (me) or the substance abuse professional who evaluates what's going on with them and figures out the best course of action to take so that they can return to their safety-sensitive duty.

Q. How much do you know about the employees when you first see them?

A. Very little—only what the employers have reported. Often I just have the fact of a "confirmed positive" drug screen. I have to gather information from a clinical interview.

Q. How do you gather this information?

A. There are two concerns. First, because the risk of a lawsuit must always be considered, you want everything in writing. But more importantly, you want to set a tone, to make it safe. These are people who are highly defensive. They don't know whether I'm there to punish them or help them. There's a great deal of apprehension, and they want to put their best foot forward. I want some basic information about who they are and how they came to be there. Second, we learn to get a good psychosocial history. We look at their family background. We look at any number of things about how they grew up, how they've lived life. What sort of things are important to them? What are things they avoid talking about?

Q. What tips you off that you need to probe further?

A. It's hard to say, but a clinician will develop a feeling. It really is something that comes from experience. That's why it's so important to do these interviews face-to-face. This way we get the nuance of the conversation: How do their eyes look? What faces do they make? Do they make eye contact? Do they hesitate and pause when they answer? What physical things are they doing? What does their body look like? We look at all the things going on in the background while the conversation goes on.

Q. How do you approach them when you feel you're being deceived?

A. Every counselor has a different style. My primary goal is to build trust, so I can have some sort of relationship and can figure out what's going on with them. I want to let them know that I'm not there to punish them, I'm not there to judge them, and I'm there to assist them. So if they can help me answer some questions—to explain some things to me—then I can help them get back to work.

Q. Do you have any specific techniques?

A. You don't want to ask people why something happened, that automatically puts them on the defensive. I can ask "How come," and even though it means "Why," it doesn't trigger their defenses for some reason. When you ask, "Why did you do so-and-so?" they feel like a third grader. But if I ask, "How come you did this? Help me understand," they

(continued)

Continued

open up. Sometimes I tell them I missed a piece of information, that they need to help me understand better. This gets past some of the filters. Some therapists call this the Colombo technique. If I seem as dumb as I look, then they can help me along. It doesn't always work, but that's one way to get them to relax and open up.

Q. Is a therapeutic interview more to get them to learn something or for you to get information?

A. I actually do only the initial interview, so I focus more on where we are and where we need to go. Then I do a follow-up interview to evaluate their clinical progress. I can work within the context of their circumstances, saying, "It doesn't really matter how we got here, but how do we fix the problem? How do we get you back to work?" This way they don't get the chance to minimize or rationalize about how they got there. That's no longer the issue. My role is to determine what level of intervention and assistance is most helpful. It can range from giving some very basic information to more intense therapies, including detoxification and in-patient rehabilitation treatment. So it's during the interview that I determine what to recommend for the employee to do, so they can resolve the problem that led them to my office. There are guidelines that we follow that are put out by different professional organizations. Ultimately, we need to make a determination, so part of what we're looking for is how much insight do they have, how willing are they to pursue treatment. There are times, quite honestly, where I'll recommend something to somebody knowing that they won't follow through, or only do so nominally. When that happens, they end up choosing to lose their jobs. But that becomes their choice. I can couch it in such a way that it becomes their idea, that they have the insight. It's really better to use a carrot than a stick. A good counselor tries to help them gain some internal motivation. I can talk to them about their family life, get them talking about how it felt to get arrested or when a coworker found them passed out at their desk, or waking up in a hospital room with their arms restrained. I want to get them to understand that I'm not there to hurt them, that I need to understand them and then get them to buy into the treatment plan. I try to make them feel I'm their partner in this and that it's like any other medical treatment, that I'm there to give information and help them make the best-informed decision.

Q. Do you think this team approach is best for all counselors, or is it a style that works for your specific personality?

A. It depends more on the purpose of the counseling. Clearly, if you have a bipolar schizophrenic who is actively hallucinating, it is not really going to do much good to be confrontational. Those are the situations where people get hurt. And it's abusive to the patient. When you have somebody who is very comfortable, they might not tell you that they are stealing drugs from their coworkers, or not tell you that their spouse wants to leave them. Or, if they don't tell you about their legal problems, you might want to use some confrontation. Of course, this assumes the counselor knows of the life problems to begin with. But you have to be judicious, because there are many reasons why they might not want or be able to talk about these things. Sometimes confrontation can get them to open up, but often can also make it worse. You don't want the client thinking you're the enemy, although they still might if they're being very defensive. When we're feeling threatened, our most primal response is fight or flight.

Q. Where do you really learn to be a good counselor?

Continued

    A. There is no better teacher than experience. Many training processes require face-to-face supervision with someone who can walk you through the process. Mentoring is critical. You have to learn to deal with your own problems so that your clients' problems don't paralyze you. Maintaining good professional boundaries is important.

Television Counseling. Dr. Phil made television counseling a popular staple for American audiences, but he was hardly the first. Talk shows such as *Oprah* and *Jerry Springer* became popular by featuring dysfunctional codependents who share their complaints and air their personal weaknesses before an audience of television viewers. Those sessions are, in a way, counseling and/or therapeutic interviews conducted in front of a mass audience. Such interviews have a dual purpose: counseling for the guest and entertainment for the audience.

    Although their primary purpose is to attract an audience, such programs may have a positive impact on the public's mental health. One major study examined the public impact of a British TV program that broadcast real psychological counseling sessions (Burns, 1997). Burns (1997) identified three major benefits for the audience and one major conclusion about audience preferences. First, the program had a positive impact on attitudes toward self-disclosure. Regular viewers of the show became more willing to talk about their own social and psychological problems and were more willing to seek psychological help when it was needed. Second, as viewing increased, the social stigma sometimes attached to psychological counseling decreased. Again, this resulted in an increased willingness of the public to seek counseling assistance when it was needed. Third, also due to the reduced stigma, viewers of the program were found to be more willing to talk about their problems without the screen of anonymity or confidentiality. The individual programs were more popular if the television counselor made a specific suggestion to the patient as to how he or she could overcome problems. Indirect intervention, in which the patient identified his or her own path to improvement, was less successful as an entertainment format. TV audiences, it seems, like episodes with a definite conclusion.

Telephone. Self-help groups sometimes provide telephone counseling for those in need of emergency counseling services. The prototype for such counseling is the typical "suicide hotline" that provides individuals who feel suicidal with a chance to discuss their feelings with someone via a telephone. Such counseling services are easily accessible, but they also represent a complex counseling process in which the success of the intervention is heavily dependent on the skills and experience of the individual telephone counselor and that person's ability to maintain a moderate but effective level of emotional involvement (Bobevski & McLennan, 1998).

    Given the brevity of the interview and the limited amount of interaction between the counselor and the client, the telephone interview has limited applicability. Its primary purposes are (1) to address the immediate crisis and (2) to encourage the caller to seek additional therapeutic treatment for his or her problem (Baird & Bosset, 1994).

Classical Therapy

Modern psychodynamic theories tend to integrate more physiological and psychological data to create a more comprehensive model of psychological development. Erikson (1963) created a system of stages of psychological development that spans an entire lifetime. In Erikson's (1963) view, the human psyche continues to grow and change throughout a person's life, just as the person's body does. Like Freud, Erikson believes that one's failures in psychological development continue into adulthood. Using Erikson's stages, the therapist tries not only to identify the patient's past traumas and problems, but also to identify where the client should be in terms of his or her development. Thus, the counselor, also called an *ego counselor*, helps ordinary normal clients look for maladaptive ego functions relating to the appropriate stage they are in.

Reality and Choice Therapy

Popularized in the 1960s by Dr. William Glasser (1965), the goal of reality theory is to help people understand their fundamental psychological needs and then develop a workable plan toward meeting them. Far from a complete rejection of traditional psychotherapy, reality therapy employs many of the same techniques but provides a more focused approach. Rather than attempting to identify childhood (and other) traumas, reality therapy takes a forward-looking approach, largely ignoring a patient's past.

Glasser (1998) also offers a five-part taxonomy of basic human psychological needs:

- **Survival**—Food, water, safety, etc.
- **Fun**—Activities pursued for enjoyment, such as hobbies, sports, etc.
- **Freedom**—The need for autonomy
- **Love and belonging**—Sexual and familial love as well as friendships
- **Power**—Power over one's achievements; the feeling of winning

Glasser claims that everyone has all of these needs all of the time. What matters is how well they are addressed. Just as it is foolish to argue whether food is more important to survival than water (or vica versa), it is foolish to say which of these needs is the more important. Psychological happiness comes from making sure that all of one's needs are being met.

The first step in reality therapy is to determine the patient's "wants." Most people are very good at expressing what they want; however, many people have difficulty expressing what they need. For example, a person may say "I want more money," "I want more sex," "I want more attention," but does not see the larger pattern of "I need more power" or "I need more fun."

The therapist helps the patient identify common themes in his or her list of wants and leads the patient to understand that he or she really has needs that are not being met. For instance, an alcoholic may say that he drinks to have fun, but by examining his other wants the therapist may show him that he is having plenty of fun, but that his other wants of love or power are what are truly lacking. The patient may come to realize that his quest for fun is harming his other needs. Maybe by finding other, less destructive ways to have fun the patient can improve the other needs.

Counselors who subscribe to reality theory take on an educational role. The counselor focuses on current behaviors and identifies future actions for the client to take. The counselor teaches clients how to make choices that maximize their true happiness. The counselor guides the client through four stages (Glasser & Wubbolding, 1995) identified by the acronym WDEP (Wants, Doing, Evaluation, Plan):

- *W*—The counselor explores the client's wants and needs. Using guided reflection, the counselor will help the client create an inner picture album of his or her wants and needs.
- *D*—The counselor then focuses on the client's current behaviors that are, or are not, helping the client meet his or her needs.
- *E*—The counselor then guides the client into a phase of self-evaluation. At this point, the client is asked to assess the effectiveness of his or her behaviors as they relate to his or her wants and needs.
- *P*—Finally, a formal plan is developed and activated. The plan helps the patient to develop new behaviors that will help the patient meet his or her needs in a more productive way.

Motivational Interviewing

Motivational interviewing is used in some substance-abuse treatment programs (Miller & Rollnick, 1991). The approach has been documented as an effective tool for treating alcohol addiction (Miller, 1996) and pathological gambling disorders (Hodgins, Currie, & el-Guebaly, 2001; Kuentzel et al., 2003). The technique uses directive and patient-centered interviewing to get patients to discuss their problems. The interviewing process is used to elicit patient responses that will help those patients identify and resolve their own barriers to behavioral change.

Advocates of motivational interviewing argue that traditional approaches to treating addiction (i.e., attempting to persuade the patient to change their behavior) usually fail because the nature of the persuasive attempt engenders resistance from the patient. Instead of persuasion, then, interviewing is used as an alternative approach. Through interviews, patients identify their own barriers, thus theoretically enhancing the likelihood that they will engage in those behaviors necessary to break from the addiction (Miller, Benefield, & Tonigan, 1993).

Proponents of motivational interviewing identify five "guiding principles" that are essential to the process. These five principles can be viewed as five progressive stages to the interview (Rollnick & Miller, 1995). First, the therapist *expresses empathy* with the patient. Like most interviews, this stage places a priority on gaining the trust of the interviewee. Second, the therapist *avoids argumentation*. Confrontational remarks or reactions are avoided, and the therapist avoids any behavior that could increase the patient's defensiveness. The goal is to establish an environment in which the patient feels comfortable talking about his or her problem. Because the patient's problem likely is a sensitive one, the therapist will likely encounter patient resistance as the conversation continues. When this occurs, the therapist moves to the third phase and *rolls with the resistance* to reduce the defensiveness of the patient as much as possible. The key concept in this stage is to remember that such resistance is to be expected and must be worked through before additional progress can be made. As the patient works through this resistance, the therapist then uses the interview to *develop discrepancy*. Questions are asked that allow the patient to see the inconsistency between his or her behavior and long-term goals. This is the key stage; when done correctly, the patient identifies these discrepancies—not the therapist. Successful articulation of this discrepancy then sets up the fifth and final stage in which the therapist *supports self-efficacy* by using the conversation to increase the patient's confidence in his or her ability to change the destructive behavior.

The strength of motivational interviewing as an intervention technique is that the process is a "self-help" program that allows for increased participation by the patient in the therapy (Hodgins, Currie, & el-Guebaly, 2001). As a result, it has the potential to produce positive changes in behavior more quickly than some other approaches. Two separate studies have found that motivational interviewing can sometimes be effective after as little as one treatment session (Senft, Polen, Freeborn, & Hollis, 1997; Borsari & Carey, 2000). This approach also is used by some telephone intervention programs in which the therapist may have only one chance to talk to the patient (Hodgins, Currie, & el-Guebaly, 2001). However, most therapists would advise against relying on a single session. Therapists using the motivational approach generally require fewer sessions (4 sessions is common) than traditional intervention programs (12-session series are common). Success from such a small number of intervention sessions is rarely achieved with traditional intervention programs. It works for motivational interviewing, its proponents would say, because the interviewing process elicits more involvement from the patient in the therapy.

The Use of Questions

Counselors use a variety of questions that initially appear similar to those used by other types of interviewers. Counselors, however, use questions to gain specific reactions and spur realizations on the part of the client. Cormier and Cormier (1993) suggest that counselors use questions for very specific purposes. They recommend a variety of interview techniques that help the counselor listen to the client and keep the counselor from weighing in with his or her own opinions too quickly. They present a three-level taxonomy of counseling questions: probes, confrontations, and interpretations.

Probes

Probes are the basic information-gathering questions that counselors use to make an initial diagnosis. Basically, they are questions of inquiry. *Open-ended probes* are open questions that are used to encourage a client to respond in an unstructured fashion. This allows that client to guide the conversation to areas of specific concern. They often are used to open a counseling session or establish the initial counselor–client relationship. For example, the following probes would be helpful in establishing a good counselor–client relationship: "So, what would you like to talk about?" or "What seems to be bothering you?"

One pitfall for many counselors is that they do not allow enough time for the client to respond freely. They pepper clients with closed-ended questions, which often makes them feel like they are being interrogated (Long, Paradise, & Long, 1981). Ivey and Ivey (2003) note that such an approach is often the product of poor listening behavior on the part of the interviewer, noting that some counseling instructors prefer "teaching questioning after the listening skills ... [because] ... some students have difficulty 'going beyond' questions and really listening to clients" (p. xvii). Generally, training for listening emphasizes four dimensions of attending to the client's behavior. These are the "three Vs" plus body language: (1) visual/eye contact, (2) vocal qualities, (3) verbal tracking, and (4) nonverbal behavior (Ivey et al., 1968).

An opening probe is a good way to help the client relax and feel like he or she is still in control. Open-ended probes also are used to encourage a client to elaborate on a particular issue. The most common approach is what Ivey and Ivey (2003) describe as the "what else" question: "*What else* do you know about this situation?" Other examples are:

- *What*—"What were you feeling when this was going on?"
- *How*—"How do you feel about that?"
- *Why*—"Why did you do that?"
- *Could*—"Could you give me an example?"

Such questions allow the counselor to guide the client to a specific topic but still lets the client respond in his or her own words. The counselor also may do this by encouraging the client to provide specific examples about a given situation (e.g., "Can you think of another time when you felt this way?").

Counselors also use *closed-ended probes*, particularly with less-verbal clients. The closed-ended probe is used to focus the client's attentions toward specific issues and only allow the client a short response. For example, the following are all examples of closed-ended probes: "Have you seen a counselor before?" "Where does your son live now?" or, "Did you feel depressed when you woke up today?" One of the dangers of using closed-ended probes is that they do not encourage the client to discuss an issue in any depth. Closed-ended probes are used to gain very specific and often superficial bits of information. If overused, the client often will withdraw and avoid talking about sensitive issues (Cormier & Cormier, 1993).

Counselors can use closed-ended questions to interrupt an overly talkative client, especially one who seems evasive. Using a closed-ended probe is often more productive than just cutting off or admonishing the client. The closed-ended probe allows the counselor to guide the conversation without making the client feel defensive. For example, the following is an example of a closed-ended probe that a counselor could use to refocus a rambling client on his or her maternal relationship: "You mentioned something about your mother earlier, is she still living?"

Confrontations

Clients often give counselors conflicting information. A client may deny having an addiction and then describe the problems he or she is having because of excessive drug use. The client may express a desire to be open with the counselor, but display closed or conflicting nonverbal signals. The client may say that he or she is concerned about a problem, but then keep changing the subject whenever the problem comes up. Patterson and Eisenberg (1983) recommend that counselors use confrontational questions to help clients cope with these conflicts.

Similarly, Ivey and Ivey (2003) recommend *confrontational interviewing*. This type of interviewing involves a three-step process: (1) identifying conflict through mixed messages, discrepancies, and incongruities; (2) pointing out those issues to clients; and (3) evaluating the effectiveness of the intervention on subsequent behavior by the client. The final stage is evaluated through the use of a measuring technique known as the *confrontation impact scale*. The confrontation impact scale records the counselor's evaluation of the client's response on a five-point scale: (1) denial; (2) partial examination (i.e., working on only part of the discrepancy, but failing to consider other dimensions); (3) acceptance and recognition, but no change; (4) generation of a new solution; and (5) development of new patterns of behavior.

Confrontation questions are used to make the client confront the conflicting information, not the counselor (Patterson & Eisenberg, 1983). Such questions are used to focus the client on his or her own areas of internal conflict. For example, a counselor may ask, "You say you're happy that you're getting divorced, but why do you change the subject every time the subject comes up?" In this way, the counselor makes the client confront an issue that is causing internal conflict.

Obviously, confrontational questions must be used sparingly, because they will likely make the client feel uncomfortable. Egan (1990) claims that clients will use a variety of techniques to avoid the issue that is causing the conflict. The client may verbally attack the counselor (e.g., "How could you possibly understand what it's like to be an orphan?"), minimize the subject (e.g., "Why are we bothering with this?"), or discredit the counselor's observation (e.g., "You don't understand what I was trying to say"). It is important that the client trust the counselor before asking confronting questions.

Interpretation

Questions that focus the client on interpreting the meanings and hypotheses of behaviors is at the heart of the counseling process (Brammer et al., 1989). Interpretation provides a verbalization of the implicit and explicit messages that the client has created through the counseling process (Johnson, 1986). Overall, interpretation aims to provide clarity about the seminal issues of the counseling process.

The process of interpretation varies from perspective to perspective. Indeed, classical schools of therapy avoid interpretation altogether (Egan, 1990). In more modern therapies, the counselor uses interpretive questions to help the client see his or her behaviors in light of the model of behavior that the therapist is employing.

Most therapies focus on the issue of locus of control. *Locus of control* refers to how the client sees the forces that are controlling his or her life. Someone with an *internal* locus of control believes that he or she controls the direction of his or her life. For instance, a cigarette smoker with an internal locus of control would believe that she controls her cigarette consumption, that she started the habit, and therefore must take responsibility for ending the habit.

Someone with an *external* locus of control believes that outside forces control his or her life. A cigarette smoker with an external locus of control might believe that he began smoking because of advertising or peer pressure and now believes that he is addicted and powerless to overcome the habit without outside help (Forsyth & Forsyth, 1982).

Although it is clear that people's lives are influenced by both internal and external factors, the notion of locus of control is an overarching philosophy. While some exceptions have been identified in terms of counseling children (Elliott, 1997), the general role of locus of control in adults is widely accepted. The extent to which a person attributes causal explanations to events affects both that person's motivation and behavior (Lee et al., 2002).

The purpose of interpretation in most modern therapies, regardless of philosophy, is to focus the client on the distinction between those issues that can and cannot be controlled. For instance, a person may not be able to control how her boss speaks to her, but she can control her reaction to her boss's behaviors. "What makes you think you can change how your boss behaves?" or "Do you think hiding in your office every time your boss is angry is helping your career?" are examples of interpretive questions that cut to the issue of control.

Additional Techniques

More than 250 theories have been developed to explain and guide counseling interviews (Ivey & Ivey, 2003), resulting in a wide variety of interviewing techniques. Some approaches use innovative techniques to elicit the information necessary to make a diagnosis and to provide recommended treatment. Three such innovative methods are nonverbal techniques, play therapy, video interviewing, and the use of Rorschach inkblots.

Nonverbal Behavior

Nonverbal behavior is important in any interview situation, but it is especially important in counseling situations. Whereas the litany of nonverbal behaviors discussed in Chapter 1 also apply here, at least two specific nonverbal actions—eye contact and the forward lean—have been identified as key behaviors in helping counselors during the relationship-development stage. Sharpley and Sagris (1995a, 1995b) found that the frequency of eye contact varied when the counselor was establishing moderate or high rapport with the client (Sharpley & Sagreis, 1995a). Similarly, an extreme forward lean (of more than 40 degrees forward) was more common during minutes rated as "very high" in rapport. Both studies thus indicate that the nonverbal behavior of the counselor plays an important role in establishing and maintaining a relationship with the client.

Play Therapy

Counselors often use indirect techniques, what some counselors call "creative interventions" (Bradley & Gould, 1993, p. 83), to encourage children to articulate their problems

(Carter & Mason, 1998). One common indirect approach used in such situations is play therapy (Axline, 1947; Irwin, 1991). It is so widely used among small children that one counselor has called it "the fabric of elementary school counseling programs" (Campbell, 1993, p. 10).

The process involves having the child engage in a play activity (e.g., playing with dolls, drawing) that will allow the child to tell what happened during an interaction with another person. A variation is the puppet interview, a technique first advocated by Woltmann (1940). The counselor uses puppets to interact indirectly with the child, with the child talking to the puppet instead of the counselor. The technique has been effectively used in a variety of situations involving children (Carter, 1987; Gil, 1994), including counseling sessions for preschoolers (Kemple, 1994) and those in the elementary grades (James & Meyer, 1987). It can be used to explore topics such as grief (Carter, 1987) and family therapy (Gil, 1994). Proponents of the approach state that it assists children in expressing their feelings, allows them to reenact anxiety-laden events, and encourages them to try new behaviors (Axline, 1947; James & Meyer, 1987; Bradley & Gould, 1993).

Video Interviewing

Video interviewing is a process in which the patient's responses to the counselor's questions are videotaped and subsequently replayed so that the patient can observe his or her behavior from the counselor's perspective. The replay session becomes a stimulus for further interaction (Bailey, Deardorff, & Nay, 1977). Proponents argue that it is particularly useful when dealing with adolescents (Emunah, 1990; Furman, 1990), probably because it reduces the perceived threat of the communication and encourages more participation (Becker & Welch, 1994).

Narrative Theory

Narrative theory emphasizes the role of storytelling in the counseling process (White & Epston, 1990; Monk, Winslade, Crocket, & Epston, 1997; Semmier & Williams, 2000). This approach works under the assumption that the first goal of the counseling interview is to "hear the [clients'] story" and "to find clients' positive strengths to help these individuals generate new stories" (Ivey & Ivey, 2003, p. 221). Such an approach relies heavily on the use of oral history interviews to generate that first set of narratives.

Marriage counselors can learn a great deal about the state of a couple's relationship by getting each partner to provide an oral history of the relationship. Typically, each individual is asked to discuss such topics as how the couple met, what attracted them to the other person, what influenced his or her decision to get married, what marital adjustments had to be made, and what their philosophy of marriage is.

Honeycutt (1999) identified seven themes of marital interaction that may appear during an oral history interview: "we-ness," glorifying the struggle, responsiveness, volatility (arguing among partners), fondness for the partner, disappointment (unmet expectations of marriage), and chaos (the extent to which events were outside of their control). Coding of these themes was not always effective in resolving marital disagreements, but data from such interviews can be highly predictive of the future of the relationship. Buehlman,

Gottman, and Katz (1992) were able to predict the likelihood of divorce on the basis of such interviews. Key signals in interviews involving a failed relationship revolved around the theme of disappointment and nonverbal indicators of contemptuousness on the part of the partners. In particular, the wives' contemptuousness was associated with the partners' level of disappointment and use of "we-ness" when discussing the relationship. Disappointment, in particular, was associated with volatility, with both factors being predictive of divorce (Buehlman, Gottman, & Katz, 1992).

Rorschach Inkblots

In projective interviewing, the therapist encourages the patient to view an object and then interpret it. The therapist hopes to gain insight into the patient's psyche by analyzing the patient's responses. Perhaps the best known projective interviewing technique used by counselors is the Rorschach inkblot test. Over the years, the Rorschach test has evolved into a standardized technique for interviewing those seeking therapeutic treatment (Weiner, 1998; Exner, 2002).

The idea behind the process is that a counselor can gain some insight into a patient's mental state based on how the patient describes a series of inkblots. The patient's responses are noted and coded according to predetermined content categories. The distribution of the responses into these categories is then used to evaluate the respondent's frame of mind. Typically, one point is assigned for each response that falls into any mutually exclusive category (i.e., no single response is categorized into two or more categories). Then, a score for each individual category can be computed by the number of responses in that category divided by the total number of responses. Although it may sound complicated, the specific nature of the categories is sufficient that multiple raters consistently categorize most responses in the same manner (Exner, 2002).

Summary

Interviewing is a critical tool employed by counselors and therapists. In general, counseling can be broken down into a five-stage process that includes (1) relationship building, (2) assessment and diagnosis, (3) formulation of goals, (4) interventions, and (5) termination and follow-up. The give and take between counselors and clients during these stages is key to the diagnosis and treatment of psychological problems.

The specific nature of counseling interviews will vary depending on the context in which they occur. These contexts include private practice, voluntary agencies, residential care, educational settings, the workplace, health-care facilities, television, and over the telephone.

Classical counseling interviews are based on the work of Sigmund Freud, but Freud's approach has fallen out of favor with many psychologists. Instead, many rely on techniques developed from reality and choice theory or from other approaches such as motivational interviewing.

Regardless of the approach, though, counselors often use similar types of questions in their interviews, including the use of probes, confrontation questions, and interpretation

Coding Rorschach Inkblot Tests

Although there are many different classification schemes for coding responses to projective inkblot tests, most schemes have similar characteristics. The Rorschach Oral Dependency (ROD) system (Masling, Rabie, & Blondheim, 1967) divides responses into 14 different categories:

1. Food and drinks
2. Food sources
3. Food objects
4. Food providers
5. Passive food receivers
6. Food organs
7. Supplicants
8. Nurturers
9. Gifts and gift-givers
10. Good luck symbols
11. Oral activity
12. Passivity and helplessness
13. Pregnancy and reproductive anatomy
14. Negations of oral precepts (e.g., a man with no mouth, not pregnant)

Source: Masling, J. M., Rabie, L., & Blondheim, S. H. (1967). Obesity, level of aspiration and Rorschach and TAT measures of oral dependence. *Journal of Counseling Psychology, 31*, 233–239.

questions. Counselors will also use questions that encourage expressions of locus of control, particularly when working with adults. Additional techniques that may be used by counselors include nonverbal behavior, play therapy, video interviewing, and the use of Rorschach inkblots. In each instance, the goal of the question is to lead the discussion in such a manner that the counselor assesses the client's situation and recommends treatment.

FOR FURTHER DISCUSSION

1. Do you control your behaviors or do outside forces control them? Pick a behavior that you engage in that you would like to change (e.g., getting more exercise or eating a healthier diet). Identify those reasons that you believe prevent you from making these lifestyle changes (e.g., "I live in the dorm and they serve fatty foods there"). Which of these things can you change? Which are beyond your control?

2. Should therapists focus on past traumas that the client has experienced or on future behaviors?

3. Classical therapists avoid making interpretations for their clients, whereas interpretations are an integral part of most modern schools of thought. Who do you think should provide interpretation, the client or the counselor? Why?

REFERENCES

Abramowitz, A. I. (1978). The impact of a presidential debate on voter rationality. *American Journal of Political Science, 22,* 680–690.

Abramowitz, A. (2001). The time for change model and the 2000 election. *American Politics Research, 29,* 259–262.

Abramson, L., & Flaste, R. (1997). *The defense is ready: Life in the trenches of criminal law.* New York: Simon & Schuster.

Acuff, F. L. (1997). *How to negotiate anything with anyone, anywhere around the globe.* Chicago: Amacom.

Adams, J. S. (1965). Inequity in social exchange. In L. Berkowitz (Ed.), *Advances in experimental social psychology* (Vol. 2, pp. 267–299). New York: Academic Press.

Adams, T., & Stalder, A. (2002). *Themes and connections from individual member interviews.* Paper presented at the annual meeting of the National Communication Association, New Orleans, LA.

Adkins, A. D., & De Witt, S. (2000). *Nurse–patient relationships: The function of social support and immediacy in a hospice setting.* Paper presented at the annual meeting of the Southern States Communication Association, New Orleans, LA.

Akehurst, L., & Vrij, A. (1999). Creating suspects in police interviews. *Journal of Applied Social Psychology, 29,* 192–210.

Albright, M. D., & Levy, P. E. (1995). The effects of source credibility and performance rating discrepancy on reactions to multiple raters. *Journal of Applied Social Psychology, 25,* 577–600.

Alessandra, A., & Wexler, P. (1985). Breaking tradition: The sales pitch as customer service. *Training & Development Journal, 39(11),* 41–43.

Alfino, L. (2003, May). 10 tips for top-notch interviews. *Writer, 115(5),* 39–41.

Allen, K. R., & Pickett, R. S. (1987). Forgotten streams in the family life course: Utilization of qualitative retrospective interview in the analysis of lifelong single women's family careers. *Journal of Marriage & the Family, 49,* 517–526.

Allison, B. (1999). Witness preparation from the criminal defense perspective. *Texas Tech Law Review, 30,* 1333–1341.

Alsever, J. (2004, April 9). Auto Experts Gives Consumer Tips on Purchasing New Cars. *The Denver Post,* Bus. p. 1.

Anderson, C. B. (1990). The gentle art of conversational English in direct examination. *American Journal of Trial Advocacy, 14(1),* 111–132.

Anderson, R. E. (1984). Did I do it or did I only imagine doing it? *Journal of Experimental Psychology: General, 113,* 594–613.

Ansolabehere, S., Behr, R., & Iyengar, S. (1994). Riding the wave and claiming ownership over issues: The joint effects of advertising and news coverage in campaigns. *Public Opinion Quarterly, 58,* 335–337.

Armstrong, C. (2004). The influence of reporter gender on source selection in newspaper stories. *Journalism & Mass Communication Quarterly, 81,* 139–154.

Arpan, L. M., & Raney, A. A. (2003). An experimental investigation of news source and the hostile media effect. *Journalism & Mass Communication Quarterly, 80,* 265–281.

Arvey, R. D., & Murphy, K. R. (1998). Performance evaluation in work settings. *Annual Review of Psychology, 49*, 141–168.

Atkin, C., Hocking, J., & McDermott, S. (1979). Home state voter response and secondary media coverage: In S. Kraus (Ed.), *The great debates: Carter vs. Ford, 1976* (pp. 429–436). Bloomington: Indiana University Press.

Axline, V. (1947). *Play therapy*. Boston: Houghton Mifflin.

Aziz, S. J., & Bolick, D. C. (2000). The national telemarketing victim call center: Combating telemarketing fraud in the United States. *Journal of Elder Abuse & Neglect, 12(2)*, 93–98.

Bailey, K. G., Deardorff, P., & Nay, W. R. (1977). Students play therapists: Relative effects of role playing, videotape feedback, and modeling in a stimulated interview. *Journal of Consulting and Clinical Psychology, 45*, 257–266.

Bailey, W. S. (1985). The attorney/client relationship: The hidden dimension of advocacy. *Trial Diplomacy Journal, 8(3)*, 17–20.

Bain, V. (2001). Individual performance isn't a solo activity. *Journal for Quality & Participation, 24(3)*, 32–34.

Baird, B. N., & Bosset, S. B. (1994). A new technique for handling sexually abusive calls to telephone crisis lines. *Community Mental Health Journal, 30(1)*, 55–60.

Baker, S. J. (1955). The theory of silences. *Journal of General Psychology, 53*, 145–167.

Balch, R. W., et al. (1976). The socialization of jurors: The voir dire as a rite of passage. *Southern California Law Review, 4*, 271.

Ballard-Reisch, D. S. (1990). A model of participative decision making for physician–patient interaction. *Health Communication, 2*, 91–104.

Ballew, B. (2002). *The pastime in the seventies: Oral histories of 16 major leaguers*. Jefferson, NC: McFarland.

Bandy, J. (2004). Paradoxes of transnational civil societies under neoliberalism: The coalition for justice in the Maquiladoras. *Social Problems, 51*, 410–431.

Banyard, V. L., & Fernald, P. S. (2002). Simulated family therapy: A classroom demonstration. *Teaching of Psychology, 29(3)*, 223–226.

Barkai, J. L. (1984). Active listening: One way to be a better advocate, counselor, and business person. *Trial, 20(8)*, 66–69.

Barney, D., & Coughlin, G. (1996). Cognitive interviewing. *Solicitors Journal, 140(24)*, 608.

Barthold, W. (1975). *Attorney's guide to effective discovery technique*. Englewood Cliffs, NJ: Prentice Hall.

Bartoo, H., & Sias, P.M. (2004). When enough is too much: Communication apprehension and employee information experiences. *Communication Quarterly, 52*, 15–26.

Bates, B., & Harmon, M. (1993). Do "instant polls" hit the spot? Phone-in vs. random sampling of public opinion. *Journalism Quarterly, 70*, 369–380.

Baum, D. B. (1983). *The art of advocacy*. New York: Matthew Bender.

Baum, W. (1987). *Oral history for the local historical society*. Thousand Oaks, CA: Sage.

Baxter, L. A. (2001). Communicatively remembering turning points of relational development in heterosexual romantic relationships. *Communication Reports, 14*, 1–17.

Baxter, L. A., & Bullis, C. (1986). Turning points in developing romantic relationships. *Human Communication Research, 12*, 469–493.

Baxter, L. A., Braithwaite, D. O., & Nicholson, J. (1999). Turning points in the development of blended family relationships. *Journal of Social and Personal Relationships, 16*, 291–313.

Becker, G. A., & Miller, C. E. (2002). Examining contrast effects in performance appraisals: Using appropriate controls and assessing accuracy. *Journal of Psychology, 136*, 667–683.

Becker, K., & Welch, I. D. (1994). Using video interviewing to enhance verbal participation in counseling interviews: A case study. *School Counselor, 42,* 161–166.

Becker, L. B., Sobowale, I. A., Cobbey, R. E., & Eyal, C. H. (1978). Debates' effects on voters' understanding of candidates and issues. In G. F. Bishop, R. G. Meadow, and M. Jackson-Beeck (Eds.). *The presidential debates: Media, electoral, and policy perspectives* (pp. 126–139). New York: Praeger.

Beckman, H. B., & Frankel, R. M. (1984). The effect of physician behavior on the collection of data. *Annals of Internal Medicine, 101,* 692–696.

Beisecker, A. E., & Beisecker, T. D. (1990). Patient information-seeking behaviors when communicating with physicians. *Medical Care, 28,* 19–28.

Belli, M. (1976). *My life on trial: An autobiography.* New York: William Morrow.

Bendremer, E. (2003). *Top telemarketing techniques.* Franklin Lakes, NJ: Career Press.

Benjamin, A. (1981). *The helping interview.* Boston: Houghton Mifflin.

Berelson, B. (1952). *Content analysis in communication research.* New York: Free Press.

Berg, A. S. (1999). *Lindberg.* New York: Putnam.

Berg, A. S. (2003). *Kate remembered.* New York: Putnam.

Berger, A. A. (1998). *Media research techniques* (2nd ed.). Thousand Oaks, CA: Sage.

Berger, C. R., & Calabrese, R. J. (1975). Some explorations in initial interaction and beyond: Toward a theory of interpersonal communication. *Human Communication Research, 1,* 99–112.

Bergman, P. (1979). *Trial advocacy in a nutshell.* St. Paul, MN: West Publishing.

Berkowitz, D., & Limor, Y. (2003). Professional confidence and situational ethics: Assessing the social-professional dialectic in journalistic ethics decisions. *Journalism & Mass Communication Quarterly, 80,* 783–801.

Berkowitz, D., & TerKeurst, J. V. (1999). Community as interpretive community: Rethinking the journalist–source relationship. *Journal of Communication, 49(3),* 125–136.

Bernstein, C., & Woodward, B. (1994). *All the president's men.* New York: Touchstone.

Bernstein, L., & Bernstein, R. (1980). *Interviewing: A guide for health professionals.* New York: Appleton-Century-Croft.

Berry, K. J., & Mielke Jr., P. W. (1997). Measuring the joint agreement between multiple raters. *Educational & Psychological Measurement, 57,* 527–530.

Bertakis, K. D., Azari, R., Callahan, E. J., Robbins, J. A., & Helms, L. J. (1999). Comparison of primary care resident physicians' practice styles during initial and return patient visits. *Journal of General Internal Medicine, 14(8),* 495–498.

Betts, N. M., & Baranowski, T. (1996). Recommendations for planning and reporting focus group research. *Journal of Nutrition Education, 28(5),* 279–281.

Bevan, J. L., Cameron, K. A., & Dillow, M. R. (2003). One more try: Compliance-gaining strategies associated with romantic reconciliation attempts. *Southern Communication Journal, 68,* 121–135.

Biagi, S. (1986). *Interviews that work: A practice guide for journalists.* Belmont, CA: Wadsworth.

Bifulco, A., Brown, G. W., & Harris, T. O. (1994). Childhood experience of care and abuse (CECA): A retrospective interview measure. *Journal of Child Psychology & Psychiatry & Allied Disciplines, 35,* 1419–1435.

Billings, J. A., & Stoeckle, J. D. (1998). *The clinical encounter: A guide to the medical interview* (2nd ed.). St. Louis, MO: Mosby.

Binder, D., Bergman, P., & Price, S. (1990). Lawyers as counselors: A client-centered approach. *New York Law School Law Review, 35(1),* 29–86.

Birdwhistle, R. L. (1970). *Kinesics and context*. Philadelphia: University of Pennsylvania Press.

Bishop, G. F., & Fisher, B. S. (1995). Secret ballots' and self-reports in an exit-poll experiment. *Public Opinion Quarterly, 59*, 568–588.

Black, D., & Reiss, A. (1967). Patterns of behavior in police and citizen transactions. In *Studies in crime and law enforcement in major metropolitan areas* (pp. 1–139). Washington, D.C.: U.S. Government Printing Office.

Blackburn-Brockman, E., & Belanger, K. (2001). One page or two?: A national study of CPA recruiters' preferences for résumé length. *The Journal of Business Communication, 3(1)*, 29–69.

Blanchard, K. H. (1983). *The one-minute manager*. New York: William Morrow & Company.

Blumenkopf, J. S. (1981). Deposition strategy and tactics. *American Journal of Trial Advocacy, 5*, 231–251.

Bly, R. W. (1997). *Secrets of successful telephone selling: How to generate more leads, sales, repeat business, and referrals by ¿hone*. New York: Henry Holt and Co.

Bobevski, I., & McLennan, J. (1998). The telephone counseling interview as a complex, dynamic, decision process: A self-regulation model of counselor effectiveness. *Journal of Psychology, 132*, 47–60.

Bodin, H. (1976). *Civil litigation and trial techniques*. New York: Practicing Law Institute.

Boon, H., & Stewart, M. (1998). Patient–physician communication assessment instruments: 1986–1996 review. *Patient Education and Counseling, 35*, 161–176.

Boose, L. E., & Flowers, B. S. (1989). *Daughters and fathers*. Baltimore: Johns Hopkins University Press.

Borg, V., & Kristensen, T. S. (1999). Psychosocial work environment and mental health among traveling salespeople. *Work & Stress, 13(2)*, 132–143.

Bornstein, R. F. (1996). Construct validity of the Rorschach Oral Dependency Scale, 1967–1995. *Psychological Assessment, 8*, 200–205.

Borsari, B., & Carey, K. B. (2000). Effects of a brief motivational intervention with college student drinkers. *Journal of Consulting and Clinical Psychology, 68*, 728–733.

Bossart, D. R. (1998). Direct examination of fact witnesses. *Trial Lawyer, 21(5)*, 200–204.

Braden, S. W. (2001). *The rhetorical use of the benign political scapegoat: Ronald Reagan attacks the federal government*. Paper presented at the annual meeting of the Southern States Communication Association, Lexington, KY.

Bradford, A. (2003). The résumé, the pitch, the close. *Black Enterprise, 33(7)*, 78–80.

Bradley, L. J., & Gould, L. J. (1993). Individual counseling: Creative interventions. In A. Vernon (Ed.), *Counseling children and adolescents* (pp. 83–117). Denver, CO: Love.

Brady, J. (1976). *The craft of interviewing*. Cincinnati, OH: Writer's Digest Books.

Bragg, R. (1997). *All over but the shoutin'*. New York: Random House.

Bragg, R. (2002). *Ava's man*. New York: Random House.

Brammer, L. M. (1973). *The helping relationship: Process and skills*. Englewood Cliffs, NJ: Prentice Hall.

Brammer, L. M., Shostrum, E. L., & Abrego, P. J. (1989). *Therapeutic psychology: Fundamentals of counseling and psychotherapy* (5th ed.). Englewood Cliff, NJ: Prentice Hall.

Brechbüühl, H. (2004). Best practices for service organizations. *Business Strategy Review, 15(1)*, 68–70.

Brenner, M. (1985). Intensive interviewing. In M. Brenner, J. Brown, & D. V. Canter (Eds.). *The research interview: uses and approaches* (pp. 147–161). London: Academic Press.

Brewer, N., & Hupfeld, R. M. (2004). Effects of testimonial inconsistencies and witness group identity on mock-juror judgments. *Journal of Applied Social Psychology, 34,* 493–513.

Brock, D. (1994). *The real Anita Hill.* New York: Free Press.

Broeder, D. W. (1965). Voir dire examinations: An empirical study. *Southern California Law Review, 38,* 503–528.

Brokaw, L. (1991). The mystery-shopper questionnaire. *Inc., 13(6),* 94–96.

Brown, M. H. (1990). "Reading" an organization's culture: An examination of stories in nursing homes. *Journal of Applied Communication Research, 18,* 64–75.

Brown, P., and Levinson, S. (1987). *Politeness; Some universals in language usage.* Cambridge: Cambridge University Press.

Bruner, J. (1987). Life as narrative. *Social Research, 54,* 11–32.

Bruni, F. (2000, May 8). Bush runs, with a lexicon of his own. *New York Times,* p. A11.

Buchanan, B. (1991). *Electing a president: The Markle Commission research on campaign '88.* Austin: University of Texas Press.

Buckley, W. F., & Bozell, L. B. (1977). *McCarthy and his enemies: The record and its meaning.* New York: Crown.

Bucqueroux, B., & Carter, S. (1999, Dec.). Interviewing victims. *Quill, 87(9),* 19–21.

Buehlman, K., Gottman, J. M., & Katz, L. (1992). How a couple views their past predicts their future: Predicting divorce from an oral history interview. *Journal of Family Psychology, 5,* 295–318.

Buehlman, K., Gottman, J. M., & Katz, L. (1992). How a couple views their past predicts their future: Predicting divorce from an oral history interview. *Journal of Family Psychology, 5,* 295–318.

Buell, J. (2001). Media myopia and the future of democratic politics. *Humanist, 61(1),* 35–36.

Bull, R. (1994). How to interview child witnesses. *Solicitors Journal, 138(13),* 332–333.

Bullis, C., & Horn, C. (1995). Get a little closer: Further examination of nonverbal comforting strategies. *Communication Reports, 8,* 10–17.

Bullock, M., & Jones, J. (1999). Beyond surveys: Using focus groups to evaluate university career services. *Journal of Career Planning & Employment, 59(4),* 38–40.

Burgoon, J. K. (1993). Interpersonal expectations, expectancy violations, and emotional communication. *Journal of Language and Social Psychology, 12,* 30–48.

Burgoon, M., & Miller, G. R. (1985). An expectancy interpretation of language and persuasion. In H. Giles & R. St. Clair (Eds.), *Recent advances in language, communication, and social psychology* (pp. 199–229). London: Lawrence Erlbaum.

Burgoon, M., Bark, T. S., & Hall, J. A. (1991). Compliance and satisfaction with physician–patient communication: An expectancy theory interpretation of gender differences. *Human Communication Research, 18,* 177–208.

Burke, K. (1973). *The Philosophy of Literary Form* (3rd ed.). Berkeley: University of California Press.

Burleson, B. R., & Denton, W. H. (1997). The relationship between communication skill and marital satisfaction: Some moderating effects. *Journal of Marriage and the Family, 59,* 884–902.

Burleson, B. R., & Samter, W. (1996). Similarity in the communication skills of young adults: Foundations of attraction, friendship, and relationship satisfaction. *Communication Reports, 9,* 127–139.

Burns, T. (1997). TV counseling. *Journal of Mental Health, 6,* 381–387.

Busch, R. J., & Lieske, J. A. (1985). Does time of voting affect exit poll results? *Public Opinion Quarterly, 49,* 94–104.

Bush. A.J., & O'Hair, J.F. (1985). An assessment of the mall intercept as a data collection method. *Journal of Marketing Research, 22(May),* 158–167.

Bushman, B. J., & Anderson, C. A. (1998). Methodology in the study of aggression: Integrating experimental and non-experimental findings. In R. G. Geen & E. Donnerstein (Eds.), *Human aggression: Theories, research, and implications for social policy* (pp. 23–48). New York: Academic Press.

Butts, S. J., & Mixon, K. D. (1995). Gender differences in eyewitness testimony. *Perceptual & Motor Skills, 80,* 59–63.

Cady, H. M. (1924). On the psychology of testimony. *American Journal of Psychology, 35,* 110–112.

Campbell, C. (1993). Play: The fabric of elementary school counseling programs. *Elementary School Guidance & Counseling, 28,* 10–16.

Carey, M. A. (1995). Comment: Concerns in the analysis of focus group data. *Qualitative Health Research, 5,* 487–495.

Carey, M. A., & Smith, M. W. (1994). Capturing the group effect in focus groups: A special concern in analysis. *Qualitative Health Research, 4,* 123–127.

Carter, R. B., & Mason, P. S. (1998). The selection and use of puppets in counseling. *Professional School Counseling, 1(5),* 50–53.

Carter, S. R. (1987). Use of puppets to treat traumatic grief. A case study. *Elementary School Guidance & Counseling, 21,* 210–215.

Cegala, D. J. (1997). A study of doctors' and patients' patterns of information exchange and relational communication during a primary medical consultation. *Journal of Health Communication, 2,* 169–194.

Cegala, D. J. (2002). *Physicians' and patients' perceptions of patients' communication competency in a primary care medical interview.* Paper presented at the annual meeting of the National Communication Association, New Orleans, LA.

Cegala, D. J., Coleman, M. T., & Turner, J. W. (1998). The development and partial assessment of the medical communication competence scale. *Health Communication, 10,* 261–288.

Cegala, D. J., Marinelli, T., & Post, D. (2002). The effects of patient communication skills training compliance. *Archives of Family Medicine, 9,* 57–64.

Cegala, D. J., McNeilis, K. S., Socha-McGee, D. S., & Jonas, P. (1995). A study of doctors' and patients' perceptions of information processing and communication competence during the medical interview. *Health Communication, 7,* 179–203.

Cegala, D. J., Socha-McGee, D. S., & McNeilis, K. S. (1996). Components of patients' and doctors' perceptions of communication competence during a primary care medical interview. *Health Communication, 8,* 1–28.

Chaffee, S. H. (1978). Presidential debates: Are they helpful to voters? *Communication Monographs, 45,* 330–346.

Chanen, J. S. (1995). The heart of the matter. *ABA Journal, 81,* 78–80.

Chen, G., & Chen, H. (2002). An examination of People's Republic of China business negotiating behaviors. *Communication Research Reports, 19,* 399–408.

Cheney, J. V. (1968). *Talk your way to success with people.* West Nyack, NY: Parker.

Chong, D. (1993). How people think, reason, and feel about rights and liberties. *American Journal of Political Science, 37,* 867–899.

Chong, D. (1999). Creating common frames of reference on political issues. In D. C. Mutz, P. M. Sniderman, & R. A. Brody (Eds.), *Political persuasion and attitude change* (pp. 195–224). Ann Arbor, MI: University of Michigan Press.

Citrin, J., Schickler, E., & Sides, J. (2003). What if everyone voted? Simulating the impact of increased turnout in Senate elections. *American Journal of Political Science, 47*, 75–90.

Clark, E. C. (1995). *The schoolhouse door: Segregation's last stand at the University of Alabama.* New York: Oxford University Press.

Clark, N. K., & Stephenson, G. M. (1990). Social remembering: Quantitative aspects of individual and collaborative remembering by police officers and students. *British Journal of Psychology, 81(1),* 73–94.

Clark, R. A., Pierce, A. J., Finn, K., Hsu, K., Toosley, A., & Williams, L. (1998). The impact of alternative approaches to comforting, closeness of relationship, and gender on multiple measures of effectiveness. *Communication Studies, 49,* 224–237.

Clayman, S. E., & Heritage, J. (2002). Questioning presidents: Journalistic deference and adversarialness in the press conferences of U.S. Presidents Eisenhower and Reagan. *Journal of Communication, 52,* 749–775.

Clowers, M. (2002). Young women describe the ideal physician. *Adolescence, 37(148),* 695–794.

Cobbin Jr., W. F., Kozar, K. A., & Michaele, S. J. (1989). Establishing telemarketing leadership through information management: Creative concepts at AT&T American Transtech. *MIS Quarterly, 13(3),* 360–372.

Cohen, D. (2001). *The talent edge: A behavioral approach to hiring, developing, and keeping top performers.* New York: Wiley.

Cohen, H. (1980). *You can negotiate anything.* New York: Bantam.

Collins, J., McCabe, M., Jupp, J., & Sutton, J. (1983). Body precept change in obese females after weight reduction counseling. *Journal of Clinical Psychology, 39(4),* 507–511.

Collins, K. (2001, April 8). Mind your manners at lunch-time interviews. *The (Knoxville) News Sentinel,* p. 1J.

Conley, J. M., O'Barr, W. M., & Lind, E. A. (1978). The power of language: Presentational style in the courtroom. *Duke Law Journal, 6,* 1375–1399.

Cope, V. (1989). Interview techniques help jog witnesses' memories. *Trial, 25(3),* 95.

Cordner, G., Greene, J., & Bynum, T. (1983). The sooner the better: Some effects of police response time. In R. Bennett (Ed.), *Police at work: Policy issues and analysis* (pp. 145–164). Beverly Hills, CA: Sage.

Cormier, L. S., & Hackney, H. (1993). *The professional counselor: A process guide to helping.* Englewood Cliffs, NJ: Prentice Hall.

Cormier, W. H., & Cormier L. S. (1993). *Interviewing strategies for helpers* (3rd ed.). Monterey, CA: Brooks-Cole.

Cornett-DeVito, M. M., & McGlone, E. L. (2000). Multicultural communication training for law enforcement officers: A case study. *Criminal Justice Policy Review, 11,* 234–253.

Cotter, P. R., Perry, D. K., & Stovall, J. G. (1994). Active and passive indicators of public opinion: Assessing the call-in poll. *Journalism Quarterly, 71,* 169–175.

Coulson, D. C., & Lacy, S. (2003). Television reporters' perceptions of how television and newspaper competition affects city hall coverage. *Mass Communication & Society, 6,* 161–174.

Craft, S., & Wanta, W. (2004). Women in the newsroom: Influences of female editors and reporters on the news agenda. *Journalism & Mass Communication Quarterly, 81,* 124–138.

Cragan, J., & Shields, D. (1998). *Understanding communication theory: The communicative forces for human action.* Boston: Allyn & Bacon.

Crouse, T. (1974). *The boys on the bus.* New York: Ballantine Books.

Daley, D. M. (1992). Pay for performance, performance appraisal, and total quality management. *Public Productivity and Management Review, 16(3),* 39–51.

Dalton, G., & Standholtz, K. (1990). How am I doing? *Executive Excellence, 7(5),* 6–8.

Del Piccolo, L., Mazzi, M., Saltini, A., & Zimmermann, C. (2002). Inter- and intra-individual variations in physicians' verbal behavior during primary care consultations. *Social Science & Medicine, 55,* 1871–1885.

Delia, J. G. (1980). The initial attorney client consultation: A comment. *Southern Speech Communication Journal, 45,* 408–410.

Delli Carpini, M., Ketter, S., & Webb, S. (1997). The impact of presidential debates. In P. Norris (Ed.), *Politics and the press: The news media and their influence gaps* (pp. 145–164). Boulder, CO: Lynne Rienner.

Delrey, J. E., & Kacmar, K. M. (1998). The influence of applicant and interviewer characteristics on the use of impression management. *Journal of Applied Social Psychology, 28,* 1649–1669.

DeLuca, M. J. (1997). *Best answers to the 201 most frequently asked interview questions.* New York: McGraw-Hill.

DePaulo, B. M., Lindsay, J. J., Malone, B. E., Muhlenbruck, L., Charlten, K., & Cooper, H. (2003). Cues to deception. *Psychological Bulletin, 129,* 74–118.

Devitt, E. G., Jr. (1997). Framing politicians: The transformation of candidate arguments in presidential campaign news coverage, 1980, 1988, 1992, and 1996. *American Behavioral Scientist, 40,* 1139–1160.

Dillingham, C. (1995, May–June). Confessions 101. *Police and Security News, 11(3),* 8–11.

Dillingham, C. (1995, September–October). Confessions 101: Part III—Enhancing interviews with databasing. *Police and Security News, 11(5),* 33–36.

Dipboye, R. L., Gaugler, B. B., Hayes, T. L., & Parker, D. (2001). The validity of unstructured panel interviews: More than meets the eye? *Journal of Business & Psychology, 16(1),* 35–50.

Doll, P. A., & Jacobs, K. W. (1988). The exit interview for graduating seniors. *Teaching of Psychology, 15(4),* 213–214.

Domke, D., Garland, P., Billeaudeaux, A., & Hutcheson, J. (2003). Insights into U.S. racial hierarchy: Racial profiling, news sources, and September II. *Journal of Communication, 53,* 606–623.

Downs, C. W., Smeyak, G. P., & Martin, E. (1980). *Professional interviewing.* New York: Harper & Row.

Drucker, P. (1954). *The practice of management.* New York: Harper and *Brothers.*

Du Pre, A. (2002). Accomplishing the impossible: Talking about body and soul and mind during a medical visit. *Health Communication, 14(1),* 1–21.

Dudley, G. W., Goodson, S. L., & Weissenburger, D. A. (1993). Overcoming fear in salespeople. *Training & Development, 47(12),* 34–38.

Duggan, A. P., & Parrott, R. L. (1997). Physicians' nonverbal rapport building and patients' talk about the subjective component of illness. *Human Communication Research, 27,* 299–316.

Duggleby, W. (2004). Methodological issues in focus group data analysis. *Nursing & Health Sciences, 6(2),* 161.

Dunnette, D. (1966). *Personal selection and placement.* Belmont, CA: Wadsworth.

Earl, A. R. (1993). Conducting the initial interview: Rules and red flags. *Trial, 29(4)*, 58–62.

Edelstein, S. I. (1992). Well begun is half done: Initial client meeting. *Trial, 28(12)*, 28–32.

Edwards, B. J., & Brilhart, J. K. (1981). *Communication in nursing practice.* St. Louis, MO: C. V. Mosby.

Efendioglu, A. M., & Murray, L. W. (2000). Education at a distance: Teaching executives in China. *THE Journal, 27(6)*, 84–89.

Egan, G. (1990). *The skilled helper: Model, skill and methods for effective helping* (4th ed.). Pacific Grove, CA: Brooks-Cole.

Egeth, J. (1967). Selective attention. *Psychological Bulletin, 67*, 41–57.

Eisenberg, J. (2001). *From 33rd Street to Camden Yards: An oral history of the Baltimore Orioles.* New York: McGraw-Hill.

Eklund, M., Rottpeter, J., & Vikstrom, F. (2003). The meaning of psychosocial occupational therapy in a life-story perspective. A long-term follow-up of three cases. *Occupational Therapy International, 10(3)*, 185–205.

Ekman, P., & Friesen, W. V. (1969). The repertoire of nonverbal behavior: Categories, origins, usage, and coding. *Semiotica, 1*, 49–98.

Elliott, J. G. (1997). Locus of control, personal control, and the counselling of children with learning and/or behaviour problems. *British Journal of Guidance & Counselling, 25*, 27–46.

Elson, A. (1994). *They were all young kids.* Maywood, NJ: Chi Chi Press.

Elson, A. (1999). *9 lives: An oral history.* Maywood, NJ: Chi Chi Press.

Elson, A. (2002). *Tanks for the memories.* Maywood, NJ: Chi Chi Press.

Elson, A., & English, S. (1998). *A mile in their shoes: Conversations with veterans.* Maywood, NJ: Chi Chi Press.

Emmett, J. D., & Harkins, A. M. (1997). StoryTech: Exploring the use of a narrative technique for training career counselors. *Counselor Education & Supervision, 37(1)*, 60–73.

Emunah, R. (1990). Expression and expansion in adolescence: The significance of creative arts counseling. *Arts in Psychotherapy, 16(2)*, 101–107.

Enelow, A. J., & Swisher, S. N. (1979). *Interviewing and patient care.* New York: Oxford University Press.

Erbert, L. A. (2000). Conflict and dialectics: Perceptions of dialectical contradictions in marital conflict. *Journal of Social & Personal Relationships, 17*, 638–659.

Erikson, E. H. (1963). *Youth: Change and challenge.* New York: Basic Books.

Eriksson, K., & Sharma, D. D. (2003). Modeling uncertainty in buyer-seller cooperation. *Journal of Business Research, 56*, 961–970.

Exner, J. E., Jr. (2002). *The Rorschach: A comprehensive system. Volume 1: Basic foundations* (4th ed.). New York: Wiley.

Eysenck, M. W., & Calvo, M. G. (1992). Anxiety and performance: The processing efficiency theory. *Cognition and Emotion, 6*, 409–434.

Fahrenz, F. D., & Preiser, M. L. (1980). The initial client interview: A critical prelude to every criminal case. *Trial, 16(10)*, 26–29.

Fedler, F. (1989). *Reporting for the print media* (4th ed.). San Diego: Harcourt Brace.

Felder, F. (2001). *Reporting for the media* (7th ed.). Stamford, CT: Thomson Publishing.

Fellows, C., & Mawhinney, T. C. (1997). Improving telemarketers' performance in the short-run using operant concepts. *Journal of Business & Psychology, 11*, 411–425.

Feltham, C. (2000). What are counseling and psychotherapy? In Feltham, C. & Horton, J. (Eds.), *Handbook of counseling and psychotherapy.* Thousand Oaks, CA: Sage.

Feltovich, N., & Papageogiou, C. (2004). An experimental study of statistical discrimination by employers. *Southern Economic Journal, 70(4)*, 837–849.

Festinger, L. (1957). *A theory of cognitive dissonance*. Stanford: Stanford University Press.

Fink, M. (2002). *Never forget: An oral history of September 11, 2001*. New York: Regan Books.

Fisher, R. P., & Gieselman, R. E. (1992). *Memory enhancing techniques for investigative interviewing: The cognitive interview*. Springfield, IL: Thomas.

Fisher, R. P., & Gieselman, R. E. (1986). Client memory enhancement with the cognitive interview. *Florida Bar Journal, 7(8)*, 27–31.

Fisher, R. P., Gieselman, R. E., Raymond, D. S., Jurkevich, L. M., & Warhagtig, M. L. (1987). Enhancing eyewitness memory: Refining the cognitive interview. *Journal of Police Science and Administration, 15*, 291–297.

Fisher, W. R. (1984). Narration as a human communication paradigm: The case of public moral argument. *Communication Monographs, 51*, 1–18.

Fisher, W. R. (1989). Clarifying the narrative paradigm. *Communication Monographs, 56*, 55–58.

Fitzpatrick, M. A. (2002). Some reflections on meaning and identity in illness. *Journal of Language & Social Psychology, 21*, 68–71.

Fitzwater, F. M. M., & Gilgun, J. (2001). Relational control in physician–patient encounters. *Health Communication, 13(1)*, 75–87.

Fletcher, C. (2001). Performance appraisal and management: The developing research agenda. *Journal of Occupational & Organizational Psychology, 74*, 473–487.

Foege, A. (2004). The return of the dumb blonde. *Brandweek, 45(9)*, 22.

Fong, M. L., & Cox, B. G. (1983). Trust as an underlying dynamic in the counseling process: How clients test trust. *Personnel and Guidance Journal, 62*, 163–166.

Forsyth, N. L., & Forsyth, D. R. (1982). Internality, controllability, and the effectiveness of attributional interpretations in counseling. *Journal of Counseling Psychology, 29*, 140–150.

Frank, J. (1973). *Courts on trial*. Princeton, NJ: Princeton University Press.

Frankel, M. R., & Frankel, L. R. (1987). Fifty years of survey sampling in the United States. *Public Opinion Quarterly, 51*, S127–S138.

Frankel, R. M. (1984). From sentence to sequence: Understanding the medical encounter from microinteractional analysis. *Discourse Processes, 7*, 135–170.

Frankel, R. M. (1990). Talking in interviews: A dispreference for patient-initiated questions in physician–patient encounters. In G. Psathas (Ed.), *Interaction competence* (pp. 231–262). Washington, D.C.: University Press of America.

Frankel, R. M., & Beckman, H. B. (1989). Evaluating the patient's primary problem(s). In M. Stewart & D. Roter (Eds.), *Communicating with medical patients* (pp. 86–98). Newbury Park, CA: Sage.

Franzinger, K. (2001). Covering the cover letter. *Machine Design, 73(1)*, 164.

Fraser, N., & Gordon, L. (1994). A genealogy of dependency. *Signs, 19*, 309–336.

Freeman, H. A., & Weihofen, H. (1972). *Clinical law training: Interviewing and counseling*. St. Paul, MN: West.

Freud, S. (1935). *A general introduction to psychoanalysis*. New York: Liverright.

Fried, A. (1997). *McCarthyism: The great American red scare*. New York: Oxford University Press.

Fry, R. (2000). *101 great answers to the toughest interview questions* (4th Ed.). Franklin Lakes, NJ: Career Press.

Fuller, G. T. (1991). *The negotiation handbook*. Upper Saddle River, NJ: Prentice Hall.

Furman, L. (1990). Video counseling: An alternative for the treatment of adolescents. *Arts in Psychotherapy, 17(2)*, 165–169.

Gaines, L.K., Kappeler, V.E., & Vaughn, J.B. (1997). *Policing in America* (2nd ed). Cincinnati, OH: Anderson Publishing Company.

Gamson, W. A. (1996). Media discourse as a framing resource. In A. N. Crigler (Ed.), *The psychology of political communication* (pp. 111–131). Ann Arbor: University of Michigan Press.

Gant, C., & Dimmick, J. (2000). Making local news: A holistic analysis of sources, selection criteria, and topics. *Journalism & Mass Communication Quarterly, 77*, 628–638.

Gantz, W. (1983). The diffusion of news about the attempted Reagan assassination. *Journal of Communication, 33*, 56–66.

Gardner, R. A. (1990). *Psychotherapeutic approaches to the resistant child* (3rd ed.). Dunmore, PA: Aronson.

Gardner, W. L., & Martinko, M. J. (1988). Impression management in organizations. *Journal of Management, 14*, 321–340.

Garfinkel, H. (1967). *Studies in ethnomethodology*. Englewood Cliffs, NJ: Prentice Hall.

Garment, L. (2001). *In search of Deep Throat: The greatest political mystery of our time*. New York: Basic Books.

Gates, R., & Solomon, P.J. (1982). Research using the mall intercept: State of the art. *Journal of Advertising Research, 22*, 43–50.

Geddes, D., & Baron, R. A. (1997). Workplace aggression as a consequence of negative performance feedback. *Management Communication Quarterly, 10*, 433–454.

Gerber, S. D. (2002). *First principles: The jurisprudence of Clarence Thomas*. New York: New York University Press.

Gerhard, M. E. (1990). A newspaper's 900 telephone poll: Its perceived credibility and accuracy. *Journalism Quarterly, 67*, 508–513.

Giacalone, R. A., & Duhon, D. (1991). Assessing intended employee behavior in exit interviews. *Journal of Psychology, 125(1)*, 83–90.

Giacalone, R. A., & Knouse, S. B. (1997). Motivation for and prevention of honest responding in exit interviews and surveys. *Journal of Psychology, 131*, 438–448.

Gieselman, R. E., Fisher, R. P., MacKinnon, D. P., & Holland, H. L. (1985). Eyewitness memory enhancement in the police interview: Cognitive retrieval mnemonics versus hypnosis. *Journal of Applied Psychology, 70*, 401–412.

Gieselman, R. E., Fisher, R. P., MacKinnon, D. P., & Holland, H. L. (1986). Eyewitness memory enhancement in the cognitive interview. *American Journal of Psychology, 99*, 385–401.

Gieselman, R. E., & Padilla, J. (1988). Cognitive interviewing with child witnesses. *Journal of Police Science and Administration, 16(4)*, 236–242.

Gil, E. (1994). *Play in family therapy*. New York: The Guildford Press.

Giles, W. F., Findley, H. M., & Field, H. S. (1997). Procedural fairness in performance appraisal: Beyond the review session. *Journal of Business & Psychology, 11*, 493–506.

Gill, A. M., & Lewis, S. M. (1996). *Help wanted*. Prospects Heights, IL: Waveland.

Gilmore, D. C., & Ferris, G. R. (1989). The effects of applicant impression management tactics on interviewer judgments. *Journal of Management, 15*, 557–564.

Gitlin, T. (1965). *The whole world is watching*. Berkeley: University of California Press.

Glasser, W. (1965). *Reality theory: A new approach to psychiatry*. New York: Harper & Row.

Glasser, W. (1986). *Control theory in the classroom*. New York: Harper and Row.

Glasser, W. (1998). *Choice theory: A new psychology of personal freedom*. New York: Harper Collins.

Glasser, W., & Wuubbolding, R. E. (1995). Reality therapy. In Corsini, R. J., & Wedding, D. (Eds.), *Current psychotherapies* (5th ed.). Itasca, IL: F. E. Peacock.

Glenn, R. (2001). *Debating the debates: Assessing the value of televised presidential debates in producing an informed electorate*. Paper presented at the annual meeting of the Southern States Communication Association, Lexington, KY.

Glick, J. A. (1999). Focus groups in political campaigns. In D. D. Perlmutter (Ed.), *The Manship School guide to political communication* (pp. 114–121). Baton Rouge, LA: Louisiana State University Press.

Goldner, P. S. (1995). *Red-hot cold call selling: Prospecting techniques that pay off*. New York: AMACOM.

Goldsmith, J. D. (1980). The initial attorney/client relationship: A case history. *Southern Speech Communication Journal, 45*, 394–407.

Goldstein, B. H. (1992). Professional responsibility and the introductory interview. *The Practical Real Estate Lawyer, 8(2)*, 11–12.

Golenbock, P. (2000a). *Bums: An oral history of the Brooklyn Dodgers*. New York: McGraw-Hill.

Golenbock, P. (2000b). *The spirit of St. Louis: A history of the St. Louis Cardinals and Browns*. New York: Avon.

Golish, T. D. (2000). Changes in closeness between adult children and their parents: A turning point analysis. *Communication Reports, 13*, 79–97.

Goodman, E. (2002). Important questions happen before reporting beings. *Nieman Reports, 56(2)*, 86–91.

Goodman, G. S., & Michelli, J. A. (1981, Nov.). Would you believe a child witness? *Psychology Today*, 83.

Goodman, G. S., Aman, C., & Hirschman, J. (1987). Child sexual and physical abuse: Children's testimony. In S. J. Ceci, M. P. Toglia, & D. F. Ross (Eds.), *Children's eyewitness memory* (pp. 1–23). New York: Springer-Verlag.

Goodman, M., & Gring, M. (1999). *The visual byte: Bill Clinton and the polysemic town hall meeting*. Paper presented at the annual meeting of the Southern Speech Communication Association, St. Louis, MO.

Goodpaster, G. S. (1975). The human arts of lawyering: Interviewing and counseling. *Journal of Legal Education, 27*, 24.

Gordon, A. D., & Kittross, J. M. (1999). *Controversies in media ethics*. New York: Longman.

Gottesman, D., & Mauro, B. (1999). *The interview rehearsal book: 7 steps to job-winning interviews using acting skills you never knew you had*. New York: Berkley.

Grabe, M. E., & Zhou, S. (1999). Sourcing and reporting in news magazine programs: *60 Minutes* versus *Hard Copy*. *Journalism & Mass Communication Quarterly, 76*, 293–311.

Grabe, M. E., & Zhou, S. (2003). News as Aristotelian drama: The case of 60 Minutes. *Mass Communication & Society, 6*, 313–336.

Graber, D. A. (1987). Framing election news broadcasts: News context and its impact on the 1984 election. *Social Science Quarterly, 68*, 552–568.

Graetz, K. A., Boyle, E. S., Kimble, C. E., Thompson, P., & Carloch, J. L. (1998). Information sharing in face-to-face, teleconferencing, and electronic chat groups. *Small Group Research, 29*, 714–743.

Graham, E. E. (1997). Turning points and commitment in post-divorce relationships. *Communication Monographs, 64*, 350–367.

Gray, G. (2002). Performance appraisals don't work. *IIE Solutions, 34(5)*, 15–17.

Greco, S. (1994). Keeping tabs on rivals. *Inc., 16* (9), 118.

Greenberg, B., Elliot, C., Kraft, L., & Procter, H. (1975). *Felony investigation decision model: An analysis of investigative elements of information*. Washington, D.C.: U.S. Department of Justice.

Greenberg, B. S. (1964). Diffusion of news of the Kennedy assassination. *Public Opinion Quarterly, 28*, 225–232.

Greene, S. A. (1999). *I'd rather have a root canal than do cold calling*. Success Works Publishing.

Greenwood, D. (1986). The first interview. *Family Law, 16*, 143.

Greenwood, P., Chaiken, J., & Petersilia, J. (1977). *The investigative process*. Lexington, MA: Lexington Books.

Grossman, L. K. (2000). Exit polls, academy awards, and presidential elections. *Columbia Journalism Review, 39(1)*, 70–71.

Grossman, M. B., & Kumar, M. J. (1981). *Portraying the president: the white house and the news media*. Baltimore: Johns Hopkins Press.

Grow, B., & Sager, I. (2004). Rising tide of edociones espanolas. *Business Week, 3894*, 135.

Gutgold, N. (2003). *Interviewing 'Ramrod and Rainbow' (Bob and Elizabeth Dole)*. Paper presented at the annual convention of the Eastern Communication Association, Washington, D.C.

Gutheil, T. G. (2003). Reflections on coaching by attorneys. *Journal of the American Academy of Psychiatry and the Law, 31(3)*, 6–9.

Hale, J. L., Tighe, M. R., & Mongeau, P. A. (1997). Effects of event type and sex on comforting messages. *Communication Research Reports, 14*, 214–220.

Hall, E. T. (1959). *The silent language*. Greenwich, CT: Fawcett.

Hall, E. T. (1969). *The hidden dimension*. Garden City, NY: Anchor Books.

Hall, R. (2004). Welcome to Resumania. Retrieved January 23, 2005 from *http://www.resumania .com/roberthalfindex.html*.

Halperin, K. (2004). Training the next wave of Spanish speaking reporters. *Criticas, 4(3)*, 2.

Hamilton, B., & Beattie, D. (1999). Modern campaign polling. In D. D. Perlmutter (Ed.), *The Manship School guide to political communication* (pp. 95–106). Baton Rouge, LA: Louisiana State University Press.

Hamilton, C., & Parker, C., (1990). *Communicating for results*. Belmont, CA: Wadsworth.

Hamlin, S. (1985a). *What makes juries listen*. New York: Harcourt Brace Jovanovich.

Hamlin, S. (1985b). Preparing a witness to testify. *ABA Journal, 71*, 80–84.

Hansen, A., Cottle, S., Negrine, R. E., & Newbold, C. (1998). *Mass communication research methods*. Washington Square, NY: New York University Press.

Hansen, J. C., Rossberg, R. H., & Cramer, S. H. (1994). *Counseling: Theory and process* (5th ed.). Boston: Allyn and Bacon.

Hanson, G. (2002). Learning journalism ethics: The classroom versus the real world. *Journal of Mass Media Ethics, 17*, 235–246.

Harley, R. G. (1995). Calling witnesses to the stand. *New York Law Journal, 213(29)*, S1.

Harrigan, K. L. (1986). Deposing the plaintiff's expert witness. *For the Defense, 28(5)*, 12–18.

Harris, A. K. (1985). Introduction. In R. J. Grele (Ed.), *Envelopes of sound: The art of oral history*. Chicago: Precedent Publishing.

Haskins, W. A. (1985). Interviewing clients in a legal setting: A dialogic approach. *Trial Diplomacy Journal, 8(2)*, 27–30.

Hassenplug, C. A., & Harnish, D. (1998). The nature and importance of interaction in distance education credit classes at technical institutes. *Community College Journal of Research & Practice, 22(6)*, 591–605.

Haug, M. R. (1996). Elements in physician/patient interactions in late life. *Research on Aging, 18*, 32–51.

Havice, M. J. (1990). Measuring nonresponse and refusals to an electronic telephone survey. *Journalism Quarterly, 67*, 521–530.

Hawes, J. M., & Baker, T. L. (1993). Building exchange relationships: Perceptions of sales representatives' performance. *Psychological Reports, 72*, 607–614.

Heller, R. (1999). *Selling successfully*. New York: DK Publishing.

Helliker, K. (1994, November 30). Smile: That cranky shopper may be a store spy. *Wall Street Journal, 224(106)*, p. B1.

Hellweg, S. A., Pfau, M., & Brydon, S. R. (1992). *Televised presidential debates: Advocacy in America*. New York: Praeger.

Herman, A. (2000). *Joseph McCarthy: Re-examining the life and legacy of America's most hated senator*. New York: Free Press.

Herman, R. M. (1995). Stop . . . look . . . listen: Interviewing and choosing clients. *Trial, 31(6)*, 48–56.

Hess, S. (1988). *The presidential campaign*. Washington, D.C.: The Brookings Institution.

Hicke, C. (1997). *One-minute guide to oral histories*. Berkeley: University of California Berkeley Library.

Hickman, H., & Scanlon, T. M. (1963). *Preparation for trial*. Philadelphia: ALI and ABA Joint Committee on Continuing Legal Education.

Hickson, M. L., & Stacks, D. W. (1992). *NVC: Nonverbal communication studies and applications* (3rd ed.). Dubuque, IA: Brown & Benchmark.

Hickson, M., Hill, S. R., & Powell, L. (1978). Smoking artifacts: Factors of source evaluation. *Perceptual and Motor Skills, 47*, 933–934.

Hickson, M., III (1974). Participant–observation technique in organizational research. *Journal of Business Communication, 11*, 37–42, 54.

Hickson, M., III (1977). Communication in natural settings: Research tool for undergraduates. *Communication Quarterly, 25*, 23–28.

Hill, A. (1997). *Speaking truth to power*. New York: Doubleday.

Hinck, E. A., & Hinck, S. S. (1998). *Audience reactions to Clinton and Dole: Some evidence for explaining audience assessments in terms of political strategies*. Paper presented at the annual meeting of the National Communication Association, New York, NY.

Hinck, E. A., & Hinck, S. S. (2000). Politeness theory and political debates. In D. Bystrom, D. B. Carlin, L. L. Kaid, M. Kern, & M. S. McKinney (Eds.), *Communicating politics: Engaging the public in Campaign 2000 and beyond* (pp. 124–130). Washington, D.C.: National Communication Association Summer Conference.

Hindle, T. (1998). *Negotiating skills*. New York: DK Publishing.

Hines, S. C., Moss, A. H., & Badzek, L. (1997). Being involved or just being informed: Communication preferences of seriously ill, older adults. *Communication Quarterly, 45*, 268–281.

Hingstman, D. B. (1983). Legal interviewing and counseling: Communication as process. In R. J. Matlon and R. J. Crawford (Eds.), *Communication strategies in the practice of lawyering* (pp. 56–57). Annandale, VA: Speech Communication Association.

Hirschmann, K. M. (2002). *Risk and pleasure: How physicians narrate sex differently for females and males.* Paper presented at the annual meeting of the National Communication Association, New Orleans, LA.

Hobbs, P. (2003). 'You must say it for him': Reformulating a witness' testimony on cross-examination at trial. *Text, 23*, 477–511.

Hodgins, D. C., Currie, S. R., & el-Guebaly, N. (2001). Motivational enhancement and self-help treatments for problem gambling. *Journal of Consulting and Clinical Psychology, 69*, 50–57.

Hofstetter, C. R., Donovan, M. C., Klauber, M. R., Cole, A., Huie, A. J., & Yuasa, T. (1994). Political talk radio: A stereotype reconsidered. *Political Research Quarterly, 47*, 467–479.

Holdway, R. M. (1968). Voir dire: A neglected tool of the art of advocacy. *Military Law Review, 40*, 1–6.

Holmberg, U. (2004). Crime victims' experiences of police interviews and their inclination to provide or omit information. *International Journal of Police Science & Management, 6(3)*, 155–170.

Honeycutt, J. M. (1999). Typological differences in predicting marital happiness from oral history behaviors and imagined interactions. *Communication Monographs, 66*, 276–291.

Hoopes, R. (Ed.) (2002). *Americans remember the home front: An oral narrative of the World War II years in America.* New York: Berkley.

Hopkins, E. (1931). *Our lawless police.* New York: Viking.

Hornik, J., & Ellis, S. (1988). Strategies to secure compliance for a mall intercept interview. *Public Opinion Quarterly, 52*, 539–551.

Horvath, A. O., & Symonds, B. D. (1991). Relation between working alliance and outcome in psychotherapy: A meta analysis. *Journal of Counseling Psychology, 38*, 139–149.

Horvitz, T., & Pratkanis, A. R. (2002). Laboratory demonstration of the fraudulent telemarketers' 1-in-5 prize tactic. *Journal of Applied Social Psychology, 32*, 310–317.

Hu, W. (2000, January 20). Interviewer gets personal with First Lady. *New York Times*, p. C37.

Hudson, S., Snaith, T., Miller, G. A., & Hudson, P. (2001). Distribution channels in the travel industry: Using mystery shoppers to understand the influence of travel agency recommendations. *Journal of Travel Research, 40(2)*, 148–154.

Hunter, P. (2000, August). Using focus groups in campaigns: A caution. *Campaigns & Elections, 21(7)*, 38–40.

Hurmence, B. (1989). *Before freedom, when I just can remember: Twenty-seven oral histories for former South Carolina slaves.* Winston-Salem, NC: John F. Blair Publishing.

Hurowitz, N. (1985). *Support practice handbook.* New York: Kluwer.

Huston, T. L., Surra, C. A., Fitzgerald, N. M., & Cate, R. M. (1981). From courtship to marriage: Mate selection as an interpersonal process. In S. Duck & R. Gilmore (Eds.), *Personal relationships 2: Developing personal relationships* (pp. 53–90). New York: Academic Press.

Hybels, S., & Weaver, R. L., II (2001). *Communicating effectively* (6th ed.). Boston: McGraw-Hill.

Hyde, P. (1999). Whatever you do, don't be nervous! (And other tricks of the pundit trade). *Masthead, 51(4)*, 26–27.

Imwinkelried, E. J. (1985). Demeanor impeachment: Law and tactics. *American Journal of Trial Advocacy, 9(2)*, 183–235.

Inbau, F. E. (1999). Police interrogation—A practical necessity. *Journal of Criminal Law & Criminology, 89*, 1403–1412.

Infante, D. A., Rancer, A. S., & Womack, D. F. (1997). *Building Communication Theory* (3rd ed.). Prospect Height, IL: Waveland Press, Inc.

Iroio, S. H., & Huxman, S. S. (1996). Media coverage of political issues and the framing of personal concerns. *Journal of Communication, 46*, 97–115.

Irwin, E. C. (1991). The use of a puppet interview to understand children. In C. E. Schaefer, K. Girlin, & A. Sangrund (Eds.), *Play diagnosis and assessment* (pp. 617–642). New York: John Wiley & Sons.

Ishikawa, H., Takayama, T., Yamazaki, Y., Seki, Y., & Katsumata, N. (2002). Physician–patient communication and patient satisfaction in Japanese cancer consultations. *Social Science & Medicine, 55*, 301–311.

Ives, E. D. (1980). *The tape-recorded interview: A manual for field workers in folklore and oral history.* Knoxville, TN: University of Tennessee Press.

Ives, E. D. (1995). *The tape-recorded interview: A manual for field workers in folklore and oral history.* Knoxville: University of Tennessee Press.

Ivey, A. E., & Ivey, M. B. (2003). *Intentional interviewing and counseling: Facilitating client development in a multicultural society.* Pacific Grove, CA: Thomson.

Ivey, A., Normington, N., Miller, D., Morrill, E., & Haase, R. (1968). Microcounseling and attending behavior: An approach to pre-practicum counselor training. *Journal of Counseling Psychology, 15*, 1–12.

Iyengar, S. (1996). Framing responsibility for political issues. *Annals of the American Academy of Political and Social Science, 456*, 59–70.

Iyengar, S., & Kinder, D. R. (1987). *News that matters.* Chicago: University of Chicago Press.

Jackson, J. L., & Kroenke, K. (1999). Difficult patient encounters in the ambulatory clinic. *Archives of Internal Medicine, 159*, 1069–1075.

Jacobs, L. R., & Shapiro, R. Y. (1994). Issues, candidate image, and priming: The use of private polls in Kennedy's 1960 presidential campaign. *American Political Science Review, 88*, 527–540.

Jacobs, R., Kafry, D., & Zedeck, S. (1980). Expectations of behaviorally anchored rating scales. *Personal Psychology, 33(3)*, 595–640.

Jacoby, J., Troutman, T. R., & Whittler, T. E. (1986). Viewer miscomprehension of the 1980 presidential debate: A research note. *Political Psychology, 7*, 297–308.

James, C. (1999, December 19). We're ready for our close-ups now. *New York Times*, p. Y30.

James, R. K., & Meyer, R. (1987). Puppets: The elementary school counselor's right or left arm. *Elementary School Guidance & Counseling, 21*, 292–299.

Jamieson, K. H., & Birdsell, D. S. (1988). *Presidential debates: The challenge of creating an informed electorate.* New York: Oxford University Press.

Janesick, V. J. (1998). *"Stretching" exercises for qualitative researchers.* Thousand Oaks, CA: Sage.

Jenkins, T. (1990). The overlooked communication skill. *Law Practice Management, 16(7)*, 34–37.

Johnson, A. (1996). 'It's good to talk': The focus group and the sociological imagination. *Sociological Review, 44*, 517–538.

Johnson, D. W. (1986). *Reaching out: Interpersonal effectiveness and self-actualization* (3rd ed.). Englewood Cliff, NJ: Prentice Hall.

Johnson, G. (2004). Forced ranking: the good, the bad, and the alternative. *Training, 41(5)*, 24–31.

Johnson, M. K. (1988). Reality monitoring: An experimental phenomenological approach. *Journal of Experimental Psychology: General, 117*, 390–394.

Johnson, M. K., & Raye, C. L. (1981). Reality monitoring. *Psychological Review, 88*, 67–85.

Johnson, M. K., Foley, M. A., Suengas, A. G., & Raye, C. L. (1988). Phenomenal characteristics of memories for perceived and imagined autobiographical events. *Journal of Experimental Psychology: General, 117*, 371–376.

Jolson, M. A. (1986). Prospecting by telephone pre-notification: An application of the foot-in-the-door technique. *Journal of Personal Selling & Sales Management, 6(2)*, 39–42.

Jones, C. (1988). *How to speak TV*. Tallahassee, FL: Video Consultants.

Jones, C. M. (2001). Missing assessments: Lay and professional orientations in medical interviews. *Text, 21*, 113–150.

Joseph, N. (1983). *Uniforms and nonuniforms*. New York: Greenwood.

Jud, B. (1999). The seven C's of effective media interviews. *Creative Nursing, 5(4)*, 11–12.

Jud, B. (2003, March 5). How to do radio and TV interviews that actually sell your book. *1st News from 1st Books*, 2.

Juncaj, T. (2002). Do performance appraisals work? *Quality Progress, 35(11)*, 45–49.

Kabanoff, B. (1991). Equity, equality, power and conflict. *Academy of Management Review, 16*, 416–441.

Kacmar, K. M., Delrey, J. E., & Ferris, G. R. (1992). Differential effectiveness of applicant impression management tactics on employment interview decisions. *Journal of Applied Social Psychology, 22*, 1250–1272.

Kalechstein, A., & Nowicki Jr., S. (1994). Social learning theory and the prediction of achievement in telemarketers. *Journal of Social Psychology, 134*, 547–548.

Kassin, S. M. (1998). More on the psychology of false confessions. *American Psychologist, 53(3)*, 320–321.

Katz, D., & Kahn, R. L. (1966). *The social psychology of organizations*. New York: John Wiley and Sons.

Kearney, W. J. (1979). Behaviorally anchored rating scales: MBO's missing ingredient. *Personnel Journal, 58(1)*, 75–83.

Keeton, R. (1973). *Trial tactics and methods*. Boston: Little, Brown.

Keeva, S. (1999). Beyond words: Understanding what your client is really saying makes for successful lawyering. *ABA Journal, 85(1)*, 60–63.

Kelly, S., Jr. (1983). *Interpreting elections*. Princeton, NJ: Princeton University Press.

Kemple, K. M. (1994). *Understanding and facilitating preschool children's peer acceptance*. Washington, D.C.: United States Department of Education, Office of Educational Research and Improvement.

Kennedy, M.M. (1980). *Office politics*. New York: Warner.

Keyton, J. (2001). *Communication research: Asking questions, finding answers*. Mountain View, CA: Mayfield.

Kinder, D. R., & Sanders, L. M. (1990). Mimicking political debate with survey questions: The case of white opinion on affirmative action for blacks. *Social Cognition, 8*, 73–103.

Kinsley, M. (1999, March 15). The trouble with scoops. *Time, 153(10)*, 104.

Kinsman, M. (2001, May 13). Exit interviews help both parties understand why employees leave. *Birmingham News*, 1G–2G.

Kinsman, M. (2001, Sept. 2). Asking questions important means of making connections. *Birmingham News*, pp. 1G–2G.

Kitchens, J. T., & Powell, L. (1975). Discriminant analysis as an instrument for political analysis. *Southern Speech Communication Journal, 40*, 313–320.

Kitzinger, J. (1994). The methodology of focus groups: The importance of interaction between research participants. *Sociology of Health & Illness, 16*, 103–121.

Klinzing, D., & Klinzing, D. (1985). *Communication for allied health care professionals.* Dubuque, IA: William C. Brown.

Knippen, J. T., & Green, T. B. (1995). Responding to an unfair performance appraisal. *Management Development Review, 8(5)*, 29–31.

Knouse, S. B., & Beard, J. W. (1996). Willingness to discuss exit interview topics: The impact of attitudes toward supervisor and authority. *Journal of Psychology, 130*, 249–261.

Koehne-Kaplan, N. S., & Levy, K. E. (1978). An approach for facilitating the passage through termination. *Journal of Psychiatric Nursing and Mental Health Services, 16(6)*, 11–14.

Koppel, T. (2000). *Off camera: Private thoughts made public.* New York: Alfred A. Knopf.

Kornblum, G. O. (1971, May). The oral deposition: Preparation and examination of witnesses. *The Practical Lawyer, 27(3)*, 15–26.

Kottler, J. A., & Brown, R. W. (1996). *Introduction to therapeutic counseling* (3rd ed.). Monterey, CA: Brooks-Cole.

Kraus, S. (1962). *The great debates.* Bloomington: Indiana University Press.

Kraus, S. (2000). *Televised presidential debates and public policy* (2nd ed.). Hillsdale, NJ: Lawrence Earlbaum.

Kraus, S., Davis, D., Lang, G. E., & Lang, K. (1976). Critical events analysis. In S. H. Chaffee (Ed.), *Political communication: Issues and strategies for research* (pp. 195–216). Beverly Hills, CA: Sage.

Krosnick, J. A., & Kinder, D. R. (1990). Altering the foundations of support for the president through priming. *American Political Science Review, 84*, 497–512.

Krueger, R. A. (1998). *Analyzing and reporting focus group results.* Thousand Oaks, CA: Sage.

Kuentzel, J. G., Henderson, M. J., Zambo, J. J., Stine, S. M., & Schuster, C. R. (2003). Motivational interviewing and fluoxetine for pathological gambling disorder: A single case study. *North American Journal of Psychology, 5*, 229–248.

Ladd, M. (1966–67). Some observations on credibility: Impeachment of witnesses. *Cornell Law Quarterly, 52*, 241.

Lamude, K. G., Scudder, J., & Simmons, D. (2003). The influence of applicant characteristics on use of verbal impression management tactics in the employment selection interview. *Communication Research Reports, 20*, 299–307.

Lange, J. E. T., & DeWitt, K. (1993). *Chappaquiddick: The real story.* New York: St. Martin's Press.

Langille, D. B., Kaufman, D. M., Laidlaw, T. A., Sargeant, J., & MacLeod, H. (2001). Faculty attitudes towards medical communication and their perceptions of students' communication skills training at Dalhousie University. *Medical Education, 35*, 548–554.

Langworthy, R. H., & Travis, L. F., III. (1994). *Policing in America: A balance of forces.* New York: Macmillan.

Lannutti, P. J., & Cameron, K. A. (2003). Beyond the breakup: Heterosexual and homosexual post-dissolutional relationships. *Communication Quarterly, 50*, 153–170.

LaVine, J. M. (2000). How to land a job using the Web. *R&D Magazine, 42(4)*, 25–26.

Lawrence, J. (2000, Oct. 3). Candidates look to previous debates to sharpen strategies. *USA Today*, 14A.

Ledbetter, J. (2000). Should voter data be released? New media, old media disagree. *Columbia Journalism Review, 39(1)*, 71–72.

Lee, D. Y., Kim, S. Y., Park, S. H., & Uhlemann, M. R. (2002). Clients' attributions of recalled important or helpful events in a counseling interview. *Psychological Reports, 91*, 10–16.

Lee, E., Whalen, T., Sakalauskas, J., Baigent, G., Bisesar, C., McCarthy, A., Reid, G., & Wotton, C. (2004). Suspect identification by facial features. *Ergonomics, 47*, 719–747.

Lee, S. L. (2004). Lying to tell the truth: Journalists and the social context of deception. *Mass Communication & Society, 7*, 97–120.

Lefkowitz, J. (2000). The role of interpersonal affective regard in supervisory performance ratings: A literature review and proposed causal model. *Journal of Occupational & Organizational Psychology, 73*, 67–85.

Lego, S. (1980). The one-to-one nurse–patient relationship. *Perspectives in Psychiatric Care, 18(2)*, 67–89.

Lehrman, F. L. (1995). Strategies for interviewing domestic violence clients. *Trial, 31(2)*, 38–42.

Leo, R. A. (1996a). Inside the interrogation room. *Journal of Criminal Law & Criminology, 86(2)*, 266–303.

Leo, R. A. (1996b). Miranda's revenge: Police interrogation as a confidence game. *Law & Society Review, 30(2)*, 259–288.

Leo, R. A. (2001). Questioning the relevance of Miranda in the twenty-first century. *Michigan Law Review, 81(4)*, 1091–1120.

Leo, R. A., & Ofshe, R. J. (1998). The consequences of false confessions: Deprivations of liberty and miscarriages of justice in the age of psychological interrogation. *Journal of Criminal Law and Criminology, 88*, 429.

Lester, D. (1972). *Ted Kennedy triumphs and tragedies.* New York: Putnam.

Lester, D. (1993). *Good Ted, bad Ted: The two faces of Edward M. Kennedy.* New York: Birch Lane Press.

Levine, J. M., & Murphy, G. (1943). The learning and forgetting of controversial statements. *Journal of Abnormal and Social Psychology, 38*, 507–517.

Levinson, W., Roter, D.L., Mulloolly, J.P., Dull, U.T., & Frankel, R.M. (1997). Physician–patient communication: The relationship with malpractice claims among primary care physicians and surgeons. *JAMA, 277*, 553–559.

Levy, P.E., Cawley, B.D., & Foti, R.J. (1998). Reactions to appraisal discrepancies: Performance ratings and attributions. *Journal of Business & Psychology, 12*, 437–456.

Lezin, V. (1987). Can we talk? The first interview with potential clients can make or break your practice. *California Lawyer, 7(8)*, 27–31.

Lidman, R. C. (1998). The power of narrative: Listening to the initial client interview. *Seattle University Law Review, 22(1)*, 17–29.

Lieberman, T. (2004). Answer the &%$#* question! *Columbia Journalism Review, 42(5)*, 40–44.

Lindell, M.K. (2001). Assessing and testing interrater agreement on a single target using multi-item rating scales. *Applied Psychological Measurement, 25*(1).

Lindlof, T. R. (1995). *Qualitative communication research methods.* Thousand Oaks, CA: Sage.

Lindsley, S. L. (1999). Communication and "the Mexican way": Stability and trust as core symbols in maquiladoras. *Western Journal of Communication, 63*, 1–31.

Lipke, D. J. (2000). Mystery shoppers. *American Demographics, 22(12)*, 41–43.

Lippman, T. (1976). *Senator Ted Kennedy.* New York: W.W. Norton.

Litvin, S.W., & Kar, G.H. (2001). E-surveying for tourism research: Legitimate tool or a researcher's fantasy. *Journal of Travel Research, 39*, 308–314.

Loewenthal, K. M., MacLeod, A. K., Lee, M., Cook, S., & Goldblatt, V. (2002). Tolerance for depression: are there cultural and gender differences? *Journal of Psychiatric & Mental Health Nursing, 9,* 681–688.

Loftus, E. F., Goodman, J., & Nagatkin, C. (1983). Examining witnesses: Good advice and bad. In R. J. Matlon & R. J. Crawford (Eds.), *Communication strategies in the practice of lawyering* (pp. 299–302). Annadale, VA: Speech Communication Association.

Long, L., Paradise, L., & Long, T. (1981). *Questioning skills for the helping process.* Pacific Grove, CA: Brooks-Cole.

Lousig-Nont, G. M. (2003). Seven deadly hiring mistakes. *Supervision, 64(4),* 18–19.

Lubet, S. (1993). Expert testimony. *American Journal of Trial Advocacy, 17(2),* 399–442.

MacDougall, C., & Baum, F. (1997). The devil's advocate: A strategy to avoid groupthink and stimulate discussion in focus groups. *Qualitative Health Research, 7,* 532–540.

Maggiano, M. (1998). Evidence with impact. *Trial Lawyer, 21(5),* 300–308.

Magid, L. (2001). Deceptive police interrogation practices: How far is too far? *Michigan Law Review, 99(5),* 1168–1210.

Makoul, G. (2002). *Empathic communication in the physician–patient encounter.* Paper presented at the annual meeting of the National Communication Association, New Orleans, LA.

Malandro, L. A., & Barker, L. (1983). *Nonverbal communication.* New York: Random House.

Malone, D. M. (1988). Direct examination of experts. *Trial, 24(4),* 42–49.

Malpass, R. S., & Kravitz, J. (1969). Recognition for faces of own and other race. *Journal of Personality and Social Psychology, 13,* 330–334.

Manning, P., & Ray, G. B. (2002). Setting the agenda: An analysis of negotiation strategies in clinical talk. *Health Communication, 14,* 451–473.

Manshor, A. T., & Kamalanabhan, T. J. (2000). An examination of raters' and ratees' preferences in process and feedback in performance appraisal. *Psychological Reports, 86,* 203–314.

Marlow, D. R. (1997). *Textbook of pediatric nursing.* Philadelphia: W. B. Saunders.

Marshall, S., & Cooper, R. K. (2000). *How to grow a backbone: 10 strategies for gaining power and influence at work.* New York: McGraw-Hill.

Martel, M. (1983). *Political campaign debates: Images, strategies, and tactics.* New York: Longman.

Martin, D. G. (1989). *Counseling and therapy skills.* Prospect Heights, IL: Therapy Press.

Marvel, M.K., & Doherty, W. J. (1998). Medical interviewing by exemplary family physicians. *Journal of Family Practice, 47,* 343–348.

Marvel, M.K., Epstein, R.M., Flowers, K., & Beckman, H.B. (1999). Soliciting the patient's agenda: Have we improved?, *Journal of the American Medical Association, 281,* 283–287.

Masling, J.M. (1986). Orality, pathology, and interpersonal behavior. In J.M. Masling (Ed.), *Empirical studies of psychoanalytic theories* (Vol. 2, pp. 73–106). Hillsdale, NJ: Erlbaum.

Masling, J.M., Rabie, L., & Blondheim, S.H. (1967). Obesity, level of aspiration and Rorschach and TAT measures of oral dependence. *Journal of Counseling Psychology, 31,* 233–239.

Matlon, R. J. (1988). *Communication in the legal process.* New York: Holt, Rinehart and Winston.

Matthews, C. (2001). *Now, let me tell you what I really think.* New York: Simon & Schuster.

Mauet, Thomas A. (1988). *Fundamentals of trial techniques* (2nd ed.). Boston: Little, Brown.

Mayer, J., & Abramson, J. (1994). *Strange justice: The selling of Clarence Thomas*. Boston: Houghton Mifflin.

McCall, R. (1972). Smiling and vocalization in infants as indices of perceptual-cognitive processes. *Merrill-Palmer Quarterly, 18*, 341–348.

McCann, J. T. (1998). Broadening the typology of false confessions. *American Psychologist, 53(3)*, 319–320.

McCarron, A. L., Ridgway, S., & Williams, A. (2004). The truth and lie story: Developing a tool for assessing child witnesses' ability to differentiate between truth and lies. *Child Abuse Review, 13*, 42–50.

McCombs, M. E., & Shaw, D. L. (1993). The evolution of agenda-setting research: Twenty-five years in the marketplace of ideas. *Public Opinion Quarterly, 36*, 176–185.

McCormack, M. H. (1988). *What they don't teach you at Harvard Business School*. New York: Bantam.

McCracken, G. (1988). *The long interview*. Newbury Park, CA: Sage.

McCullum, C., & Achterberg, C. L. (1997). Food shopping and label use behavior among high-school-aged adolescents. *Adolescence, 32(125)*, 181–197.

McDonough, M. (2004). A sneak peak. *ABA Journal, 90(5)*, 72.

McElaney, J. E. (1981). *Trial notebook*. Chicago: American Bar Association.

McElhaney, J. E. (1988). Pressure points: Tactics for taking a witness by surprise. *ABA Journal, 74(8)*, 101–102.

McElhaney, J. W. (1989). Leading questions. *ABA Journal, 75(10)*, 104–106.

McElhaney, J. W. (1993a). Helping the witness: Techniques for keeping witnesses out of trouble. *ABA Journal, 79(8)*, 85–86.

McElhaney, J. W. (1993b). Rehabilitation: Different ways to climb out of a hole. *ABA Journal, 79(8)*, 92–93.

McElhaney, J. W. (1997). Exposing fatal flaws: Deposition is the time to find weaknesses in witnesses. *ABA Journal, 83(4)*, 78–79.

McElhaney, J. W. (2000). The cross-exam minefield. *ABA Journal, 86(12)*, 68–69.

McElhaney, J. W. (2003). Take a good look at direct. *ABA Journal, 89(10)*, 38–39.

McFigg, R., McCullough, R. C., & Underwood, J. L. (1974). *Civil trial manual*. Los Angeles: Joint Committee on Legal Education of the American Law Institute and the American Bar Association.

McGinnis, D., & Roberts, P. (1996). Qualitative characteristics of vivid memories attributed to real and imagined experiences. *American Journal of Psychology, 109*, 59–77.

McKinley, M. A., & Jensen, L. O. (2003). In our own voices: Reproductive health radio programming in the Peruvian Amazon. *Critical Studies in Media Communication, 20*, 180–203.

McLeod, J. M., & Detenber, B. H. (1999). Framing effects of television news coverage of social protest. *Journal of Communication, 49*, 3–23.

McMahan, E. M. (1987). Speech and counter speech: Language-in-use in oral history fieldwork. *Oral History Review, 15*, 185–208.

McMahan, E. M. (1989). *Elite oral history discourse: A study of cooperation and coherence*. Tuscaloosa: University of Alabama Press.

McMahan, E. M., & Rogers, K. L. (eds.) (1994). *Interactive oral history interviewing*. Mahwah, NJ: Lawrence Erlbaum.

McNeilis, K. S. (2002). Assessing communication competence in the primary care medical interview. *Communication Studies, 53*, 400–428.

McNellis, K. S. (2001). Analyzing communication competence in medical consultations. *Health Communication, 13*, 5–18.

McPeek, R. W., & Edwards, J. D. (1975). Expectancy disconformation and attitude change. *Journal of Social Psychology, 96*, 193–208.

McVeigh, J. A., Norris, S. A., & de Wet, T. (2004). The relationship between socio-economic status and physical activity patterns in South African children. *Acta Paediatrica, 93*, 982–988.

McWhorter, D. (2001). *Carry me home: Birmingham, Alabama: The climactic battle of the civil rights movement.* New York: Simon & Schuster.

Mehrabian, A. (1981). *Silent messages: Implicit communication of emotions and attitudes.* Belmont, CA: Wadsworth.

Meissner, C. A., & Brigham, S. C. (2001). Thirty years of investigating the own-race bias in memory for faces: A meta-analytic review. *Psychology, Public Policy, and Law, 7*, 3–35.

Memon, A., & Wark, L. (1997). Isolating the effects of the cognitive interview technique. *British Journal of Psychology, 88(2)*, 179–197.

Memon, A., Bartlett, J., Rose, R., & Gray, C. (2003). The aging eyewitness: Effects of age on face, delay, and source-memory ability. *Journals of Gerontology Series B: Psychological Sciences & Social Sciences, 58B(6)*, 338–344.

Mendelsohn, H. (1964). Broadcast versus personal sources of information in emergent public crises: The presidential assassination. *Journal of Broadcasting, 8*, 147–156.

Meredith, L. L., Stewart, M., & Brown, J. B. (2001). Patient-centered communication scoring method on nine coded interviews. *Health Communication, 13(1)*, 19–31.

Mero, N. P., Motowidlo, S. J., & Alexandra, L. A. (2003). Effects of accountability on rating behavior and rater accuracy. *Journal of Applied Social Psychology, 33*, 3493–3514.

Merron, J. (2002, April 4). Reel life: Bull Durham. *ESPN Magazine*, 2.

Merton, R. K., Lowenthal, M. F., & Kedall, P. L. (1956). *The focused interview: A manual of problems and procedures.* Glencoe, IL: Free Press.

Metzler, K. (1977). *Creative interviewing.* New York: Prentice Hall.

Meyerowitz, S. A. (1996). The 'first contact': When the client phones. *New York Law Journal, 216(126)*, 5.

Milavsky, R. (1985). Early calls of election results and exit polls: Pros, cons, and constitutional considerations. *Public Opinion Quarterly, 49*, 1–18.

Miller, A. H., & MacKuen, M. (1979). Informing the electorate: A national study. In S. Kraus (Ed.), *The Great Debates: Carter vs. Ford, 1976.* Bloomington: Indiana University Press.

Miller, G. A. (1956). The magic number seven, plus or minus two: Some limits on our capacity for processing information. *The Psychological Review, 63*, 81–97.

Miller, H. B., & Biggerstaff, R. R. (2000). Application of the Telephone Consumer Protection Act to intrastate telemarketing calls and faxes. *Federal Communications Law Journal, 52(3)*, 667–686.

Miller, J. J. (1999). *The campaign theme and an election's controlling frame.* Paper presented at the annual meeting of the Southern Communication Association, St. Louis, MO.

Miller, M. J. (1989). A few thoughts on the relationship between counseling techniques and empathy. *Journal of Counseling & Development, 67*, 350–351.

Miller, W. E., & Shanks, J. M. (1996). *The new American voter.* Cambridge, MA: Harvard University Press.

Miller, W. W. (1996). Motivational interviewing: Research, practice, and puzzles. *Addictive Behaviors, 21*, 835–842.

Miller, W. W., & Rollnick, S. (1991). *Motivational interviewing: Preparing people to change addictive behaviors*. New York: Guilford.

Miller, W. W., Benefield, R. G., & Tonigan, J. S. (1993). Enhancing motivation for change in problem drinking: A controlled comparison of two therapists styles. *Journal of Consulting and Clinical Psychology, 61*, 455–461.

Mitchell, A. (1999, Dec. 12). Underdog McCain develops anti-campaign style. *New York Times, 149(517334)*, 42.

Molloy, J. T. (1996). *New women's dress for success*. New York: Warner.

Monk, G., Winslade, J., Crocket, K., & Epston, D. (1997). *Narrative theory in practice: The archaeology of hope*. San Francisco: Jossey-Bass.

Monroe, C., Brarzi, M.G., & DiSalvo, V.S. (1989). Conflict behaviors of difficult employees. *Southern Communication Journal, 54*, 311–329.

Moore, S. D., O'Hair, D., & Ledlow, G. R. (2002). The effects of health delivery systems and self-efficacy on patient compliance and satisfaction. *Communication Research Reports, 19*, 362–371.

Moore, T. (2003). Promoting change through the African American church and social activism. *Journal of Psychology & Christianity, 22*, 357–362.

Morgan, D. L. (1995). Why things (sometimes) go wrong in focus groups. *Qualitative Health Research, 5*, 516–523.

Morgan, D. L. (1997). *Focus groups as qualitative research* (2nd ed.). Thousand Oaks, CA: Sage.

Morgan, D. L., & Krueger, R. A. (1993). When to use focus groups and why. In D. L. Morgan (Ed.), *Successful focus groups: Advancing the state of the art* (pp. 3–19). Newbury Park, CA: Sage.

Morrill, A. E. (1972). *Trial diplomacy*. Chicago: Court Practice Institute.

Morrison, D. E. (1986). *Invisible citizens: British public opinion and the future of broadcasting*. London: John Libbey.

Mudd, K., & Govern, J. M. (2004). Conformity to misinformation and time delay negatively affect eyewitness confidence and accuracy. *North American Journal of Psychology, 6*, 227–238.

Mullen, L. (2003). *Communication and community in Las Vegas: Interviews with political leaders past and present*. Paper presented at the annual convention of the Eastern Communication Association, Washington, D.C.

Munday, R. (1989, Dec.). Calling a hostile witness. *Criminal Law Review*, 866–876.

Murdaugh, C., Russell, R. B., & Sowell, R. (2000). Using focus groups to develop a culturally sensitive videotape intervention for HIV-positive women. *Journal of Advanced Nursing, 32*, 1507–1513.

Murray, J. (2004, June 11). Don't let them leave in silence. *Times Educational Supplement, 4587*, 32.

Murray, P. J. (1997). Using virtual focus groups in qualitative research. *Qualitative Health Research, 7*, 542–549.

Myers, G. (2000). Entitlement and sincerity in broadcast interviews about Princess Diana. *Media, Culture & Society, 22(2)*, 167–185.

Natarajan, R. (2003). Racialized memory and reliability: Due process applied to cross-racial eyewitness identification. *New York University Law Review, 78*, 1821–1858.

Nayyar, S. (2003, March). A window into what consumers think and feel. *American Demographics, 25(2)*, 6.

Nehren, J., & Gilliam, N. R. (1965). Separation anxiety. *American Journal of Nursing, 65(1)*, 109–112.

Nelson, W. D. (1998). *Who speaks for the President? The White House press secretary from Cleveland to Clinton.* Syracuse: Syracuse University Press.

Nicholson, J. (1999). *Dressing smart in the new millennium.* Manassas Park, VA: Impact Publications.

Noller, P. (1995). Parent–adolescent relationships. In M. A. Fitzpatrick & A. L. Vangelisti (Eds.), *Explaining family interactions* (pp. 77–111). Thousand Oaks, CA: Sage.

Noonan, P. (1998). *On speaking well.* New York: Regan Books.

Norby, C. J. (2002). Investigating teacher–student interactions that foster self-regulated learning. *Educational Psychologist, 37(1)*, 5–15.

Norris, P., Curtice, J., Sanders, D., Scammell, M., & Semetko, H. A. (1999). *On message: Communicating the campaign.* London: Sage.

Northouse, P. G., & Northouse, L. L. (1985). *Health communication: A handbook for health professionals.* Englewood Cliffs, NJ: Prentice Hall.

Novotny, P. (2000). From polis to agora: The marketing of political consultants. *Harvard International Journal of Press/Politics, 5(3)*, 12–26.

Nunnally, J. C. (1967). *Psychometric theory.* New York: McGraw-Hill.

Nylund, M. (2003). Quoting in front-page journalism: Illustrating, evaluating and confirming the news. *Media, Culture & Society, 25*, 844–851.

Nystul, M. S. (1999). *Introduction to counseling: An art and science perspective.* Boston: Allyn and Bacon.

O'Barr, W. O., & Conley, J. M. (1976, Summer). Language use in the courtroom: Vehicle or obstacle. *Barrister*, 1–9.

Ogawa, T., Taguchi, N., & Sasahara, H. (2003). Assessing communication skills for medical interviews in a postgraduate clinical training course at Hiroshima University Dental School. *European Journal of Dental Education, 7(2)*, 60–65.

O'Hair, D. (1989). Dimensions of relational communication and control during physician–patient interactions. *Health Communication, 1*, 97–15.

O'Hair, D., & Friedrich, G. W. (1992). *Strategic communication in business and the professions.* Boston: Houghton Mifflin.

O'Keefe, D. J. (1990). *Persuasion theory and research.* Newbury Park, CA. Sage.

O'Keefe, M., Roberton, D., & Sawyer, M. (2001). Medical student interviewing skills and mother-reported satisfaction and recall. *Medical Education, 35*, 637–644.

Olsen, D. (2003). *Interviewing National Endowment of the Arts players.* Paper presented at the annual convention of the Eastern Communication Association, Washington, D.C.

O'Reilly, B. (2000). *The O'Reilly Factor.* New York: Broadway.

Osen, D. (Ed.) (2002). *The book that changed my life: Interviews with National Book Award winners and finalists.* New York: Modern Library.

Owen, S. (2001). The practical, methodological and ethical dilemmas of conducting focus groups with vulnerable clients. *Journal of Advanced Nursing, 36*, 652–658.

Packel, L. (1982, Jan. 15). How to prepare and conduct a direct examination of witness. *Practical Lawyer, 38(1)*, 70.

Paine, D. G. (2000). The ten commandments of direct examination. *Tennessee Bar Journal, 36(3)*, 20–23.

Park, H. S., Levine, T. R., McCornack, S. A., Morrison, K., & Ferrara, M. (2002). How people really detect lies. *Communication Monographs, 69*, 144–157.

Parker, D. B., Mills, W. K., & Patel, J. (2001). Expert grilling. *Los Angeles Lawyer, 24(8)*, 41–46.

Parrott, R. (1994). Exploring family practitioners' and patients' information exchange about prescribed medication: Implications for practitioners' interviewing and patients' understanding. *Health Communication, 6(4)*, 267–280.

Parry-Giles, T., & Parry-Giles, S. J. (1996). Political socpophilia, presidential campaigning and the intimacy of American politics. *Communication Studies, 47*, 191–205.

Patterson, L. E., & Eisenberg, S. (1983). *The counseling process* (3rd ed.). Boston: Houghton Mifflin.

Patterson, R. (1999). *Bill Bennett and 'common culture' politics: Moral and economic fusion in the Reagan presidency.* Paper presented at the annual meeting of the Eastern Communication Association, Charleston, WV.

Pedersen, P. (1994). Simulating the client's internal dialogue as a counselor training technique. *Simulation & Gaming, 25(1)*, 40–50.

Pepinsky, H. (1970). A theory of police reaction to *Miranda v. Arizona. Crime and Delinquency, 17(2)*, 379–392.

Perina, A. (2003). "I confess": Why would an innocent person profess guilt? *Psychology Today, 36(2)*, 11–12.

Perkins, J. H. (1981). How to prepare for the first interview with a client, and what it should cover. *Estate Planning, 8(2)*, 92–99.

Perlman, A. M. (1998). *Writing great speeches.* Boston: Allyn & Bacon.

Perloff, R. M. (1998). *Political communication: Politics, press, and the public in America.* Mahwah, NJ: Lawrence Erlbaum.

Peterson, T. R., Witte, K., Enkerlin-Hoeflich, E., Expericueta, L., Flora, J. T., Florey, N., Loughran, T., & Stuart, R. (1994). Using informant directed interviews to discover risk orientation: How formative evaluations based in interpretive analysis can improve persuasive safety campaigns. *Journal of Applied Communication Research, 22*, 199–213.

Pfau, M., Haigh, M., Gettle, M., Donnelly, M., Scott, G., Warr, D., & Wittenberg, E. (2004). Embedding journalists in military combat units: Impact on newspaper story frames and tone. *Journalism & Mass Communication Quarterly, 81*, 74–88.

Phillipsen, G. (1975). Speaking "like a man" in Teamsterville: Culture patterns of role enactment in an urban neighborhood. *Quarterly Journal of Speech, 61*, 13–22.

Piliavin, I. (1973). *Police–community alienation: Its structural roots and a proposed remedy.* Andover, MA: Warner Modular Publications.

Pincus, M. (1999). *Interview strategies that lead to job offers.* Hauppauge, NY: Barrons.

Pogrebin, M. R., & Poole, E. D. (1995). Emotional management: A study of police response to tragic events. *Social Perspectives on Emotion, 3*, 149–168.

Pollock, T. (2003). How to command the prospect's attention. *American Salesman, 48(8)*, 22–26.

Post, D. M., Cegala, D. J., & Miser, W. F. (2002). The other half of the whole: Teaching patients to communicate with physicians. *Family Medicine, 34*, 344–352.

Poundstone, W. (2003). Beware the interview inquisition. High-stress, brain-teasing job interviews are all the rage. But what do they really reveal? *Harvard Business Review, 81(5)*, 2.

Powell, G. R. (1991). Take control: The right question gets the right answer. *Barrister, 21(1)*, 17–20.

Powell, J. L., Belcher, D. V., Kitchens, J. T., & Emerson, L. C. (1975). The influence of selected variables on the employment interview situation. *Journal of Applied Communication Research, 3*, 33–53.

Powell, L. (1994). Country's quiet phenomenon. *Orlando Sentinel: Calendar*, pp. 6, 8.

Powell, L., & Cowart, J. (2003). *Political campaign communication: Inside and out.* Boston: Allyn & Bacon.

Powell, L., & Hickson, M. (1977–78). The influence of macrospace and job status on organizational communication. *Georgia Speech Communication Journal, 9*, 39–41.

Powell, L., & Kitchens, J. T. (1975). Elements of participant satisfaction in dyads. *Southern Speech Communication Journal, 41*, 59–68.

Powell, L., & Shelby, A. N. (1981). The strategy of assumed incumbency: A case study. *Southern Speech Communication Journal, 46*, 105–123.

Power of Polling (1999, November 24). *Louisiana Political Fax Weekly*, p. 2.

Prochnau, W. (2002). 'How did I do this before Google?' *American Journalism Review, 24(9)*, 24–29.

Ptacek, J. T., Ptacek, J. J., & Ellison, N. M. (2001). "I'm sorry to tell you . . ." Physicians' reports of breaking bad news. *Journal of Behavioral Medicine, 24(2)*, 205–217.

Quarmby, D. (1993). Peer group counselling with bereaved adolescents. *British Journal of Guidance & Counselling, 21*, 196–210.

Quintana, S. M., & Holahan, W. (1991) Termination in short-term counseling: Comparison of successful cases. *Journal of Counseling Psychology, 39(3)*, 299–305.

Rahn, W.M., Krosnik, J.A., & Brenning, M. (1994). Rationalization and derivations processes in survey studies of political candidate evaluation. *American Journal of Politics Science, 32*, 582–600.

Raines, H. (1983). *My soul is rested: Movement days in the deep South remembered.* New York: Viking Press.

Ramirez, A., Jr. (2002). The role of overall communication quality in the association between partner's perceived decision-making style and relational satisfaction in heterosexual same-sex and cross-sex friendships. *Communication Research Reports, 19*, 107–117.

Rasch, L. (2004). Employee performance appraisal and the 95/5 rule. *Community College Journal of Research & Practice, 28*, 407–414.

Raugust, K. (1994, Dec.). Using quotes in nonfiction. *Writer, 107(12)*, 23–24.

Ravaja, N. (2004). Effects of image motion on a small screen on emotion, attention, and memory: Moving-face versus static-face newscaster. *Journal of Broadcasting & Electronic Media, 48*, 108–133.

Ray, Darryal (2003, July 27). Living history: Pell City project captures residents' fading memories of past. *Birmingham News*, p. 20A.

Raymark, P. H., Balzer, W. K., & Delatorre, F. (1999). A preliminary investigation of the sources of information used by raters when appraising performance. *Journal of Business & Psychology, 14*, 319–339.

Re, E. D. (1987). *Cases and materials on remedies.* Mineola, NY: Foundation.

Redmond, J., Shook, F., & Lattimore, D. (2001). *The broadcast news process* (6th ed.). Englewood, CO: Morton.

Reed, J., & Roskell, V. (1997). Focus groups: Issues of analysis and interpretation. *Journal of Advanced Nursing, 26*, 765–771.

Reeves, T. C. (1997). *The life and times of Joe McCarthy: A biography.* New York: Madison Books.

Reiboldt, W., & Vogel, R. E. (2001). Critical analysis of telemarketing fraud in a gated senior community. *Journal of Elder Abuse & Neglect, 13(4)*, 21–38.

Reuben, D. H. (1987). Getting the truth from the client. *Litigation, 14(1)*, 11–13.

Reynolds, A., & Barnett, B. (2003). This just in . . . How national TV news handled the breaking "live" coverage of September 11. *Journalism & Mass Communication Quarterly, 80*, 689–703.

Richmond, V. P., Smith, R. S., Heisel, A. D., & McCroskey, J. C. (2001). Nonverbal immediacy in the physician/patient relationship. *Communication Research Reports, 18*, 211–216.

Richmond, V. P., Smith, R. S., Heisel, A. D., & McCroskey, J. C. (2002). The association of physician socio-communicative style with physician credibility and patient satisfaction. *Communication Research Reports, 19*, 207–215.

Rimal, R. N. (2001). Analyzing the physician–patient interaction: An overview of six methods and future research directions. *Health Communication, 13*, 89–99.

Ritchie, D. A. (1995). *Doing oral history*. New York: Twayne Publishers.

Rivers, W. L. (1992). *Freelancer and staff writer*. Belmont, CA: Wadsworth.

Roberts, C. (2003, November 6). Harvest the words of those who walk out. *BRW, 25(43)*, 66.

Roberts, K. J. (2002). Physician–patient relationships, patient satisfaction, and antiretroviral medication adherence among HIV-infected adults attending a public health clinic. *AIDS Patient Card & STDs, 16*, 43–50.

Robinson, J. D. (2003). An interactional structure of medical activities during acute visits and its implications for patients' participation. *Health Communication, 15(1)*, 27–57.

Robinson, P. (2002). *The CNN effect: The myth of news, foreign policy and intervention*. New York: Routledge.

Robinson, R., Smith, C., Murray, H., & Ennis, J. (2002). Promotion of sustainably produced foods: Customer response in Minnesota grocery stores. *American Journal of Alternative Agriculture, 17(2)*, 96–104.

Rodgers, K. (2002, April 2). Grade: Forced ranking strategies and techniques. *Personnel Today*, 21–22.

Roebuck, J. B., & Hickson, M., III (1982). *The southern redneck: A phenomenological case study*. New York: Praeger.

Rollnick, S., & Miller, W. W. (1995). What is motivational interviewing? *Behavioral and Cognitive Psychotherapy, 89*, 1369–1376.

Roloff, M. E. (1980). Self-awareness and he persuasion process: Do we really know what we're doing? In Rolof, M. E. & Miller, G. R. (Eds.), *Persuasion new directions in theory and research*. Beverly Hills, CA. Sage.

Roloff, M. E., & Johnson, D. I. (2001). Reintroducing taboo topics: Antecedents and consequences of putting topics back on the table. *Communication Studies, 52*, 37–50.

Ross, L., Amabile, T. M., & Steinmetz, J. L. (1977). Social roles, social control, and biases in social-perception processes. *Journal of Personality and Social Psychology, 35*, 485–494.

Roter, D. L., Hall, J. A., & Katz, N. R. (1988). Patient–physician communication: A descriptive summary of the literature. *Patient Education and Counseling, 12*, 99–119.

Roter, D., & Frankel, R. (1992). Quantitative and qualitative approaches to the evaluation of the medical dialogue. *Social Science and Medicine, 34*, 1097–1103.

Roter, D., Stewart, M., Putnam, S. M., Lipkin, M. F., Stiles, W., & Inui, T. S. (1997). Communication patterns of primary care physicians. *JAMA, 277*, 350–357.

Rothstein, D. (2002). Questions help to hold people in power accountable. *Nieman Reports, 56(2)*, 93.

Rowan, K. E., Sparks, L., Pecchioni, L., & Villagran, M. M. (2003). The CAUSE model: A research-supported aid for physicians communicating with patients about cancer risk. *Health Communication, 15*, 235–248.

Rowley, J. (2003). Free media relations: The state of the fourth estate. In L. Powell & J. Cowart, *Political Campaign Communication:* Inside and out. Boston: Allyn and Bacon.

Rubinowitz, B., & Torgan, E. (2002). Direct examination: The basics. *New York Law Journal, 228(3)*, 3.

Rugg, W. D. (1971–1972). Interviewer opinion on the 'salesman as interviewer' problem. *Public Opinion Quarterly, 35(4)*, 625–626.

Ruvoldt, H. (2001, December 3). Key to perfect cross lies in deposition. *New York Law Journal, 226*, L6.

Ryan, C. (1959). *The longest day: June 6, 1944.* New York: Simon & Schuster.

Ryan, C. (1961). *The last battle.* New York: Simon & Schuster.

Ryan, C. (1974). *A bridge too far.* New York: Simon & Schuster.

Ryan, J., & Wentworth, W. M. (1999). *Media and society: The production of culture in the mass media.* Boston: Allyn & Bacon.

Samp, J. A. (2002). Dependence power, severity appraisals, and communicative decisions about problematic events in dating relationships. *Communication Studies, 52*, 17–36.

Sandberg, J. (2004, March 31). Departure tales: When farewells fare poorly, goodbyes aren't good. *Wall Street Journal* (Eastern Edition), *243(63)*, B1.

Saner, H., Klein, S., Bell, R., & Comfort, K. B. (1994). The utility of multiple raters and tasks in science performance assessments. *Educational Assessment, 2*, 257–272.

Sannito, T. (1982). How to discredit eyewitness testimony. *Trial Diplomacy Journal, 4(4)*, 5–12.

Sannito, T., & McGovern, P. (1999). Jury selection: The winning edge. *Trial Lawyer, 22(5)*, 341–352.

Sarason, I. G. (1988). Anxiety, self-preoccupation and attention. *Anxiety Research, 1*, 3–7.

Sargent, J. (2002). Topic avoidance: Is this the way to a more satisfying relationship? *Communication Research Report, 19*, 175–182.

Sayre, J. (1978). Common errors in communication made by students in psychiatric nursing. *Perspectives in Psychiatric Care, 16(4)*, 175–183.

Schiffman, S. (2003). *Cold calling techniques (that really work!).* Avon, MA: Adams Media.

Schilling, L. M., Scatena, L., Steiner, J. F., Albertson, G. A., Lin, C. T., Cyran, L., Ware, L., & Anderson, R. J. (2002). The third person in the room: Frequency role and influence of companions during primary care medical encounters. *Journal of Family Practice, 51*, 685–690.

Schneider, S. J., Kerwin, J., Frechtling, J., & Vivari, B. A. (2002). Characteristics of the discussion in online and face-to-face focus groups. *Social Science Computer Review, 20(1)*, 31–42.

Schram, M. (1976). *Running for president: A journal of the Carter campaign.* New York: Pocket Books.

Schrecker, E. (1998). *Many are the times: McCarthyism in America.* New York: Little, Brown.

Schudson, M. (1994, Oct.). Inventing the interview. *American Heritage, 45(6)*, 46–48.

Schulhofer, S. J. (2001). Miranda, Dickerson, and the puzzling persistence of Fifth Amendment exceptionalism. *Michigan Law Review, 99(5)*, 941–957.

Schum, D. A. (2001). *The evidential foundations of probabilistic reasoning.* Chicago: Northwestern University Press.

Schweingruber, D., & Berns, N. (2003). Doing money work in a door-to-door sales organization. *Symbolic Interaction, 26*, 447–471.

Seamans, I. (2001). Viewer dissatisfaction understates the anger at local TV news. *Nieman Reports, 55(3)*, 97–98.

Sears, D., & McDermott, D. (2003). The rise and fall of rank and yank. *Information Strategy: The Executive's Journal, 19*, 3, 6–12.

Seiter, J. S., & Sandry, A. (2003). Pierced for success?: The effects of ear and nose piercing on perceptions of job candidates' credibility, attractiveness, and hirability. *Communication Research Reports, 20*, 287–298.

Semmier, P., & Williams, C. (2000). Narrative therapy: A storied context for multicultural counseling. *Journal of Multicultural Counseling and Development, 28*, 51–62.

Senft, R. A., Polen, M. R., Freeborn, D. K., & Hollis, J. F. (1997). Brief intervention in a primary care setting for hazardous drinkers. *American Journal of Preventive Medicine, 13*, 464–470.

Shaikh, A., Knobloch, L. M., & Stiles, W. B. (2001). The use of verbal response mode coding system in determining patient and physician roles in medical interviews. *Health Communication, 13*, 49–60.

Sharpley, C. F., & Ridgway, I. R. (1992). Development and field-testing of a procedure for coached clients to assess rapport during trainees' counselling interviews. *Counselling Psychology Quarterly, 5*, 149–160.

Sharpley, C. F., & Sagris, A. (1995a). Does eye contact increase counselor–client rapport? *Counselling Psychology Quarterly, 8*, 145–155.

Sharpley, C. F., & Sagris, A. (1995b). When does counselor forward lean influence client-perceived rapport? *British Journal of Guidance & Counselling, 23*, 387–394.

Shepard, A. C. (2001). How they blew it. *American Journalism Review, 23(1)*, 20–27.

Sherif, C. W., Sherif, M., & Nebergall, R. W. (1965). *Attitude and attitude change: The social judgment approach.* Philadelphia: Saunders.

Shoaf, E. C. (2003). Using a professional moderator in library focus group research. *College & Research Libraries, 64(2)*, 124–132.

Shook, Frederick (1982). *The process of electronic news gathering.* Englewood, CA: Morton.

Shore, T. H., & Tashchian, A. (2002). Accountability forces in performance appraisal: Effects on self-appraisal information, normative information, and task performance. *Journal of Business & Psychology, 17*, 261–274.

Silver, C. (1999). Preliminary thoughts on the economics of witness preparation. *Texas Tech Law Review, 30(4)*, 1383–1407.

Silverblatt, A. (1995). *Media literacy: Keys to interpreting media messages.* Westport, CT: Praeger.

Silvester, J., Patterson, F., & Ferguson, E. (2003). Comparing two attributional models of job performance in retail sales: A field study. *Journal of Occupational & Organizational Psychology, 76(1)*, 115–132.

Sim, J. (1998). Collecting and analyzing qualitative data: Issues raised by the focus group. *Journal of Advanced Nursing, 28*, 345–352.

Simbasku, J. (January, 2002). Secrets of finding good employees. *USA Today, 30(2680)*, 33–34.

Simon, P. (1992). *Advice and consent: Clarence Thomas, Robert Bork, and the intriguing history of the Supreme Court nomination battles.* Washington, D.C.: National Press Books.

Simon, R. (1987, March 14). Those Sunday interview shows: They're tougher now, but are they better? *TV Guide, 35(11)*, 4–7.

Skolnick, J. H., & Leo, R. A. (1992). The ethics of deceptive interrogation. *Criminal Justice Ethics, 11(1)*, 3–12.

Small, J., Gutman, G., Makela, S., & Hillhouse, B. (2003). Effectiveness of communication strategies used by caregivers of persons with Alzheimer's disease during activities of daily life. *Journal of Speech, Language & Hearing Research, 45(8)*, 353–367.

Smith, A. P. (1991). Noise and aspects of attention. *British Journal of Psychology, 82*, 313–324.

Smith, D. H. (1998). Interviews with elderly patients about side effects. *Health Communication, 10(3)*, 199–209.

Smith, L., Schwarzkopf, H. N., & Adams, E. (2003). *Beyond glory: Medal of Honor heroes in their own voices*. New York: W. W. Norton.

Smith, M. K. (2000). Recovery from a severe psychiatric disability: Findings of a qualitative study. *Psychiatric Rehabilitation Journal, 24(2)*, 149–158.

Smith, P. H., Moracco, K. E., & Butts, J. D. (1998). Partner homicide in context. *Homicide Studies, 2(4)*, 400–421.

Socha-McGee, D., & Cegala, D. L. (1998). Patient communication skills training for improved communication competence in the primary medical care interview. *Journal of Applied Communication Research, 26*, 412–430.

Solomon, R. J., & Hoffman, R. C. (1991). Evaluating the teaching of business administration: A comparison of two methods. *Journal of Education for Business, 66(6)*, 360–365.

Spadley, J. P. (1980). *Participant observation*. New York: Holt, Rinehart and Winston.

Spence, L. (1997). *Legacy: A step-by-step guide to writing personal history*. Athens, OH: Swallow Press/Ohio University Press.

Sroufe, L., & Waters, W. (1976). The ontogenesis of smiling and laughter: A perspective on the organization of development in infancy. *Psychological Review, 83*, 173–189.

Stacks, D. W., & Hocking, J. E. (1999). *Communication research* (2nd ed.). New York: Longman.

Stahl, L. (1999). *Reporting live*. Boston: Simon & Schuster.

Stanley, T. L. (2004). The best management ideas are timeless. *Supervision, 65(6)*, 9–12.

Stano, M. (1992). The performance interview: Guidelines for academic program chairs. In M. Hickson, III & D. W. Stacks (eds.). *Effective communication for academic chairs*. Albany: State University of New York Press.

Stein, M. L. (2002). Good questions emerge out of good information. *Nieman Reports, 56*, 94–95.

Steinfatt, T. M., Gantz, W., Siebold, D. R., & Miller, L. D. (1973). News diffusion of the Wallace shooting: The apparent lack of interpersonal communication as an artifact of delayed measurement. *Quarterly Journal of Speech, 59*, 401–412.

Steinhauer, J. (1998, February 4). The undercover shoppers. *New York Times, 147(51058)*, p. D1.

Stephen, L. D., Allen, B. P., Chan, J. C. K., & Dahl, L. C. (2004). Eyewitness suggestibility and source similarity: Intrusions of details from one event into memory reports of another event. *Journal of Memory & Language, 50*, 96–111.

Stephens, M., & Lanson, G. (1986). *Writing and reporting the news*. New York: Holt, Rinehart, & Winston.

Stepp, L. S. (2000). *Our last best shot: Guiding our children through early adolescence*. New York: Riverhead Books.

Stern, W. (1939). The psychology of testimony. *Journal of Abnormal and Social Psychology, 34*, 3–20.

Stevens, C. K., & Kristof, A. L. (1995). Making the right impression: A field study of applicant impression management during job interviews. *Journal of Applied Psychology, 80*, 587–606.

Stevenson, R. W. (2004, July 4). Presidential interviews follow a script (but not always). *New York Times, 153(52900)*, 3.

Stewart, C. J., & Cash, W. B. (1982). *Interviewing principles and practices*. Dubuque, IA: William C. Brown.

Stewart, D. W., & Shamdasani, P. N. (1990). *Focus groups: Theory and practice*. Applied social Research Methods Series, Vol. 20. Newbury Park, CA: Sage Publications.

Stiles, W. B., Putnam, S. M., James, S. A., & Wolf, M. D. (1979). Dimensions of patient and physician roles in medical screening interviews. *Social Science and Medicine, 13A*, 335–341.

Stockdale, M. S. (2002). Analyzing focus group data with spreadsheets. *American Journal of Health Studies, 18(1)*, 55–69.

Strauss, J. P., Barrick, M. R., & Connerley, M. L. (2001). An investigation of personality similarity effects (relational and perceived) on peer and supervisor ratings and the role of familiarity and liking. *Journal of Occupational & Organizational Psychology, 74*, 637–657.

Street, R. L., Jr., & Millay, B. (2001). Analyzing patient participation in medical encounters. *Health Communication, 10(3)*, 199–209.

Stuart, P. B. (1999). The basics of direct and cross-examination of a fact witness. *Trial, 35(1)*, 74.

Suchman, A. L., Markakis, K., Beckman, H., & Frankel, R. (1997). A model of empathic communication in the medical interview. *JAMA, 277*, 678–682.

Sudman, S. (1980). Improving the quality of shopping center sampling. *Journal of Marketing Research, 17*, 423–431.

Sudman, S. (1986). Do exit polls influence voting behavior? *Public Opinion Quarterly, 50*, 331–339.

Sugarman, N., & Yarashus, V. A. (1995). Case selection: Resolving the threshold question. *Trial, 31(4)*, 66–69.

Sundeen, S. J., Stuart, G. W., Rankin, E. D., & Cohen, A. A. (1981). *Nurse-client interaction: Implementing the nursing process*. St. Louis: C. V. Mosby Company.

Swanson, L. L., & Swanson, D. L. (1978). The agenda-setting function of the first Ford–Carter debate. *Communication Monographs, 45*, 347–353.

Swenson, J. D., & Griswold, W. F. (1992). Focus groups. *Small Group Research, 23*, 459–474.

Szalai, J. P. (1993). The statistics of agreement on a single item or object by multiple raters. *Perceptual & Motor Skills, 77*, 377–378.

Szilagyi, A., & Wallace, M. (1990). *Organizational behavior and performance*. Glenview, IL: Scott, Foresman/Little, Brown.

Tannen, D. (2000, Jan. 20). Bush's sweet talk. *New York Times, 149(512730)*, p. A19.

Taylor, K.P., Buchanan, R.W., & Strawn, D.U. (1984). *Communication strategies for trial attorneys*. Glenview, IL: Scott, Foresman & Co.

Taylor, P. (1990). *See how they run: Electing the president in an age of mediaocracy*. New York: Alfred A. Knopf.

Tedrow, T. L., Tedrow, R. L., & Tedrow, T. (1980). *Death at Chappaquiddick*. Gretna, LA: Pelican Publishing.

Terkel, S. (1997). *The good war: An oral history of World War Two*. New York: New Press.

Terkel, S. (1997). *Working: People talk about what they do all day and how they feel about what they do*. New York: New Press.

Terkel, S. (2000). *Hard times: An oral history of the Great Depression*. New York: New Press.

Terry, W. (1989). *Bloods: An oral history of the Vietnam War by black veterans*. New York: Ballantine.

Thomas, A. P. (2001). *Clarence Thomas: A biography*. San Francisco: Encounter Books.

Thomas, G. C. (2000). The end of the road for Miranda v. Arizona. *American Criminal Law Review, 37(1)*, 12.

Thomas, G. C. (2003). Miranda's illusion: Telling stories in the police interrogation room. *Texas Law Review, 81*, 1091–1120.

Thompson, D. F. (2004). Election time: Normative implications of temporal properties of the electoral process in the United States. *American Political Science Review, 98*, 51–64.

Thompson, W. N., & Insalata, S. J. (1964). Communication from attorney to client. *Journal of Communication, 14*, 22–33.

Thorndike, E. L. (1920). A constant error on psychological rating. *Journal of Applied Psychology, 4*, 25–29.

Tiberius, R. (2001, September). Making sense and making use of feedback from focus groups. *New Directions for Teaching & Learning, 87*, 63–75.

Timmreck, T. C. (1999). Words for behavioral description in performance appraisals. *Psychological Reports, 84*, 201–295.

Toler, R. R. (1994). Times and people change . . . basic sales techniques don't. *Journal of the American Society of CLU & CHFC, 48(2)*, 11–13.

Torres, M. G., Rao, N., Lee, S., Pant, S., Beckett, C. S., & Rupert, D. (2002). *Disclosure, truths, and half-truths in physician–patient communication: An exploration and comparison among Argentina, Brazil, India, and the U.S.* Paper presented at the annual meeting of the National Communication Association, New Orleans, LA.

Tracy, S. J. (2002). When questioning turns to face threat: An interactional sensitivity in 911 call-taking. *Western Journal of Communication, 66*, 129–157.

Traugott, M. W., & Price, V. (1992). The polls—a review: Exit polls in the 1989 Virginia gubernatorial race: Where did they go wrong? *Public Opinion Quarterly, 56*, 245–253.

Traulsen, J. M., Almarsdottir, A. B., & Bjornsdottir, I. (2004). Interviewing the moderator: An ancillary method to focus groups. *Qualitative Health Research, 14*, 514–525.

Truesdale, B. (1999). *Oral history techniques: How to organize and conduct oral history interviews*. Bloomington, IN: Indiana University.

Tubbs, C., & Sloan, J. J., III. (2002, May 12). Media perpetuate myths of criminal justice scenarios. *Birmingham News*, p. 6C.

Tuggle, C. A., & Huffman, S. (1999). Live news reporting: Professional judgment or technological pressure? *Journal of Broadcasting & Electronic Media, 43*, 492–505.

TV newsman can be sued for telling youngsters about a murder (1995, March 25). *Editor & Publisher, 128(12)*, 34–35.

Tziner, A. (1999). The relationship between distal and proximal factors and the use of political considerations in performance appraisal. *Journal of Business & Psychology, 14*, 217–231.

Tziner, A., & Murphy, K. R. (1999). Additional evidence of attitudinal influences in performance appraisal. *Journal of Business & Psychology, 13*, 407–419.

Tziner, A., Murphy, K. R., Cleveland, J. N., Beaudin, G., & Marchand, S. (1998). Impact of rater beliefs regarding performance appraisal and its organizational context on appraisal quality. *Journal of Business & Psychology, 12*, 457–467.

Ury, W. (1993). *Getting past no: Negotiating your way from confrontation to cooperation*. New York: Bantam.

Use exit interviews to improve teacher retention (1999). *Curriculum Review, 39(2)*, 6–7.

Valdespino, J. M. (2004). Cross-examination: The rules of the game. *American Journal of Family Law, 18(2)*, 87–92.

Van Natta, Jr., D. (2000, February 15). Years ago, a Bush adviser helped draft a push poll against a Texas official. *New York Times 149(51299)*, p. A20.

Vancil, D. L., & Pendell, S. D. (1984). Winning presidential debates. *Western Journal of Speech Communication, 48*, 62–74.

Vandereycken, W., Depreitere, L., & Probst, M. (1987). Body-oriented counseling for anorexia nervosa patients. *American Journal of Psychocounseling, 41(2)*, 252–259.

Vessenes, P. M. (2001). Are they right for the job? *Journal of Financial Planning, 14(4)*, 52–54.

Vetter, G. (1977). *Successful civil litigation.* Englewood Cliffs, NJ: Prentice Hall.

Viser, M. (2003). Attempted objectivity: An analysis of the New York Times and Ha'aretz and their portrayals of the Palestinian–Israeli Conflict. *Harvard International Journal of Press/Politics, 8(4)*, 114–120.

Waitzkin, H. (1985). Information giving in medical care. *Journal of Health and Social Behavior, 26*, 81–101.

Walker, K. L., Arnold, C. L., Miller-Day, M., & Webb, L. M. (2001). Investigating the physcian–patient relationship: Examining emerging themes. *Health Communication, 14(1)*, 45–68.

Walster, E., Walster, G., & Berscheid, E. (1978). *Equity theory and research.* Boston: Allyn and Bacon.

Wanzer, M. B., Gruber, K., & Booth-Butterfield, M. (2002). *Parent perceptions of health-care providers' communication practices: The relationship between patient-centered communication and satisfaction with communication and care.* Paper presented at the annual meeting of the National Communication Association, New Orleans, LA.

Wasserman, D. P. (1999). The local contours of campaign coverage. *Communication Research, 26*, 701–725.

Watkins Jr., C. E., & Savickas, M. L. (1992). Studying the vocational counseling process: A preliminary examination. *Counselling Psychology Quarterly, 5*, 17–23.

Watson, A. S. (1976). *The lawyer in the interviewing and counseling process.* Indianapolis: Bobbs-Merrill.

Weaver, R. R. (2003). Informatics tools and medical communication: Patient perspectives of 'knowledge coupling' in primary care. *Health Communication, 15(1)*, 59–78.

Weaver-Lariscy, R. A., Sweeney, B., & Steinfatt, T. (1984). Communication during assassination attempts: Diffusion of information in attacks on President Reagan and the Pope. *Southern Speech Communication Journal, 49*, 258–276.

Weinberger, M., Ferguson, J. A., Westmoreland, G., Mamlin, L. A., Segar, D. S., Eckert, G. J., Greene, J. Y., Martin, D. K., & Tierney, W. M. (1998). Can raters consistently evaluate the content of focus groups? *Social Science & Medicine, 46*, 929–933.

Weiner, I. B. (1998). *Principles of Rorschach interpretation.* Mahwah, NJ: Erlbaum.

Welch, J. F. (2000). Letter to shareholders. *GE 2000 annual report,* 1.

Wellner, A. S. (2003, March). The new science of focus groups. *American Demographics, 25(2)*, 29–33.

Wells, G. L., Lindsay, R. C. L., & Ferguson, T. J. (1979). Accuracy, confidence and juror perceptions in eyewitness identification. *Journal of Applied Psychology, 64*, 440–448.

Wendleton, K., & Dauten, D. (2000, Nov. 5). Networking works best with higher-ups. *Birmingham News,* 1G, 2G.

Wendelton, K., & Dauten, D. (2002, Aug. 4). Small raise, overtime make: squeaky wheel. *Birmingham News* 1G–2G.

Wertheimer, M. M. (2000). *Barbara Bush's refashioning of the White House.* Paper presented at the annual meeting of the Eastern Communication Association, Pittsburgh, PA.

West, C., & Frankel, R. (1991). Miscommunication in medicine. In N. Coupland, H. Giles, & J. Wiemann (Eds.), *Miscommunication and problematic talk* (pp. 166–194). Newbury, CA: Sage.

Westley, W. (1970). *Violence and the police*. Cambridge, MA: MIT Press.

Westling, W. T., & Waye, V. (1998). Videotaping police interrogations: Lessons from Australia. *American Journal of Criminal Law, 25*, 493–543.

Weston, W., & Brown, J. (1989). The importance of patients' beliefs. In M. Stewart & D. Roter (Eds.), *Communicating with medical patients* (pp. 73–86). Newbury Park, CA: Sage.

Whalen, M. R., Whalen, J., & Zimmerman, D. H. (1990). Describing trouble: Practical epistemology in citizen calls to the police. *Language in Society, 19*, 465–492.

White, M., & Epston, D. (1990). *Narrative means to therapeutic ends*. New York: Norton.

White, W. S. (2001a). *Miranda's waning protections*. Ann Arbor: University of Michigan Press.

White, W. S. (2001b). Miranda's failure to restrain pernicious interrogation tactics. *Michigan Law Review, 99(5)*, 1211–1247.

Wigley, C. J., III (1999). Verbal aggressiveness and communicator style characteristics of summoned jurors as predictors of actual jury selection. *Communication Monographs, 66*, 266–275.

Wilcox, D. L., & Nolte, L. W. (1997). *Public relations writing and media techniques*. New York: Longman.

Wilkerson, I. (2002). Interviewing sources. *Nieman Reports, 56(1)*, 16–17.

Williams, A. (2004, August 22). The alchemy of a political slogan. *New York Times, 153(52949)*, 9:1.

Williams, J. R., & Levy, P. E. (2000). Investigating some neglected criteria: The influence of organizational level and perceived system knowledge on appraisal reactions. *Journal of Business & Psychology, 14*, 501–514.

Willing, R. (2004, August 5). 'CSI effect' has juries wanting more evidence. *USA Today*, 1A, 2A.

Wimmer, R. D., & Dominick, J. R. (1994). *Mass media research*. Belmont, CA: Wadsworth.

Wineberg, H. (1994). Marital reconciliation in the United States: Which couples are successful? *Journal of Marriage and the Family, 56*, 80–88.

Woltmann, A. G. (1940). The use of puppets in understanding children. *Mental Hygiene, 24*, 445–458.

Wood, A. (2003). Direct examination. *CBA Record, 17(2)*, 48.

Worman, D. (1992). *Motivating with sales contests: The complete guide to motivating your telephone professionals with contests that produce record-breaking results*. Omaha, NE: Business by Phone.

Xiong, N. (2002, January 29). Words of remembrance: Families capture past on tape with oral histories. *Birmingham Post Herald*, p. C4.

Yalof, D. A. (2001). *Pursuit of justices*. Chicago: University of Chicago Press.

Yardley, J. (2000, February 14). Calls to voters at center stage of G.O.P. race. *New York Times, 149(51298)*, pp. A1, A16.

Yate, M. (1994). *Hiring the best: A manager's guide to effective interviewing*. Holbrook, MA: Adams Media.

Yeager, N., & Hough, L. (1998). *Power interviews: Job-winning tactics from Fortune 500 recruiters*. New York: John Wiley and Sons.

Young, A., & Flower, I. (2001). Patients as partners, patients as problem-solvers. *Health Communication, 14(1)*, 69–97.

Yow, V. R. (1994). *Recording oral history: A practical guide for social scientists.* Thousand Oaks, CA: Sage.

Yu, J., & Cooper, H. (1983). A quantitative review of research design effects on response rates to questionnaires. *Journal of Marketing Research, 20*, 36–44.

Zaller, J. (1990). Political awareness, elite opinion leadership, and the mass survey response. *Social Cognition, 8*, 125–153.

Zaller, J. R. (1992). *The nature and origin of mass opinion.* Cambridge: Cambridge University Press.

Zaller, J., & Feldman, S. (1992). A simple theory of the survey response: Answering questions versus revealing preferences. *American Journal of Political Science, 36*, 579–616.

Zelazo, P. (1971). Smiling to social stimuli: Eliciting and conditioning effects. *Developmental Psychology, 4*, 32–42.

Zelazo, P. (1972). Smiling and vocalizing: A cognitive emphasis. *Merrill-Palmer Quarterly, 18*, 349–365.

Zelazo, P., & Komer, M. (1971). Infant smiling to nonsocial stimuli and the recognition hypothesis. *Child Development, 42*, 1327–1339.

Zimmerman, D. H. (1984). Talk and its occasion: The case of calling the police. In D. Schiffrin (Ed.), *Meaning, form, and use in context* (pp. 210–228). Washington, D.C.: Georgetown University Press.

Zimmerman, D. H. (1992). Achieving context: Openings in emergency calls. In G. Watson & R. M. Seiler (Eds.), *Text in context: Contributions to ethnomethodology* (pp. 35–51). Newbury Park, CA: Sage.

Zimmerman, W. (1992). *Instant oral biographies: How to interview people & tape the stories of their lives.* New York: Guarionex Press.

Zoch, L. M., & Turk, J. V. (1998). Women making news: Gender as a variable in source selection and use. *Journalism & Mass Communication Quarterly, 75*, 762–775.

INDEX

DATE DUE